KELLOGG ON MARKETING

KELLOGG ON MARKETING

Second Edition

Edited by
Alice M. Tybout
Bobby J. Calder

WILEY
John Wiley & Sons, Inc.

Published by John Wiley & Sons, Inc., Hoboken, New Jersey.
Published simultaneously in Canada.

For general information on our other products and services or for technical support, please contact our Customer Care Department within the United States at (800) 762-2974, outside the United States at (317) 572-3993 or fax (317) 572-4002.

Wiley also publishes its books in a variety of electronic formats. Some content that appears in print may not be available in electronic books. For more information about Wiley products, visit our web site at www.wiley.com.

Library of Congress Cataloging-in-Publication Data:

Kellogg on marketing / [edited by] Alice M. Tybout, Bobby J. Calder. – 2nd ed.
    p. cm.
  Includes bibliographical references and index.
  ISBN 978-0-470-58014-1 (hardback);   ISBN 978-0-470-87762-3 (ebk);
ISBN 978-0-470-87738-8 (ebk);   ISBN 978-0-470-87763-0 (ebk)
  1. Marketing. I. Tybout, Alice M. II. Calder, Bobby J. III. J.L. Kellogg Graduate School of Management.
  HF5415.K4443 2010
  658.8–dc22

                                         2010010869

Printed in the United States of America.

V10011464_062019

CONTENTS

Section Three
PERSPECTIVES ON CONTEMPORARY ISSUES IN MARKETING

FOREWORD
THINKING ABOUT MARKETING

In introducing the first edition of this largely revised and expanded book, *Kellogg on Marketing,* I pointed out that a book that seriously examined marketing thinking was greatly needed because *markets* were changing faster than *marketing*. Markets are changing so fast that they hardly resemble those of the 1990s, let alone the 1950s. Yet many of the ideas and frameworks that marketers use have not kept pace.

No matter what features of markets you look at, the pace of change has increased. Advertising has exploded beyond the former mainstay of the television commercial to appear on almost anything that can serve as a medium: blogs, web sites, YouTube, Second Life, electronic billboards, even shopping bags and napkins. Distribution is not confined to one or two physical channels but increasingly takes myriad forms, including the proliferating digital channels. Pricing becomes ever more complex with the pressures of recession and international competition. Brands continue to be vital, but they are more and more difficult to establish and keep relevant to consumers.

On top of all this, the economy is awash in hypercompetition. With so many companies chasing the same markets, the role of innovation and finding new consumers has become necessary for survival. This is a time when everyone in a company, not just the marketers and salespeople, need to think about marketing and collaborate in carrying it out.

The purpose of this new book is to help managers think about marketing in ways that correspond to what is happening in markets around the world. It revisits the fundamental concepts that continue to guide sound marketing practice, updating these concepts to reflect the current market conditions. In addition, the authors discuss the many emerging opportunities and challenges for marketers, drawing on scholarly research as well as their years of experience working with leading companies around the globe. They offer important insights on topics such as marketing to consumers at the bottom of the economic pyramid, the effect of social media on branding, and strategies for effective innovation. They also discuss the connection between marketing and other functional areas, such as sales and operations, and provide strategies promoting cooperation and coordination between these areas.

Kellogg on Marketing, Second Edition, is unique. Textbooks are written by academic scholars with the goal of presenting students of marketing with a comprehensive overview of the topic. Popular business books on marketing are written by managers, consultants, and the occasional academic, typically with the goal of addressing a topical issue and offering a solution based on the authors' practical experiences. This book does both and more. It covers the basics and provides a point of view on current topics. But most important, it raises key questions and challenges readers to think about them in new ways. If you are new to marketing, this book is as good a place to begin as you will find. If you think you know all you need to know about branding, marketing research, advertising, pricing, distribution, innovation, and so on, you still must read this book. You'll likely be surprised at what you'll learn.

As markets become ever more complex, we all need to think and learn more about marketing. I have always said that "marketing takes a few weeks to learn but a lifetime to master."

Philip Kotler

Evanston, Illinois
July 2010

PREFACE

When *Kellogg on Marketing* was published in 2001, the goal was to share the unique perspective of the Kellogg marketing faculty with colleagues, students, alumni, and the larger business community. The initial volume was well-received and led to subsequent books in the series that address specific marketing topics in depth: *Kellogg on Integrated Marketing* (2003), *Kellogg on Branding* (2005), and *Kellogg on Advertising & Media* (2008).

A decade later, the principles of sound marketing strategy addressed in *Kellogg on Marketing* remain the same, but new challenges and opportunities exist. To illustrate with a few of the many such issues discussed in this volume:

- Savvy companies recognize that their success depends on adopting a customer focus. But exactly what does that mean in terms of specific activities for frontline employees, salespeople, those in operations, and so forth?
- Marketers contend with ever-shorter product life cycles and increased pressure to innovate in order to sustain a competitive advantage. How can firms innovate more successfully?
- Consumers "surf," "text," "tweet," and watch YouTube, allowing information to spread virally, sometimes to the benefit and sometimes to the detriment of a brand. What are the implications of these new media on managing a brand? Who's really in charge of the brand, anyway?
- There are billions of potential customers to be won in underdeveloped and developing markets. How can companies adapt their offerings and channels to accommodate these consumers' generally low incomes and the limited distribution systems that characterize these markets?

With an eye to topical issues like these, we have created *Kellogg on Marketing, Second Edition*. This new edition contains significantly revised and updated chapters that address core concepts needed for the development and implementation of sound marketing strategy. In addition, we present eight entirely new chapters that offer the perspective of Kellogg faculty on emerging issues that are important for the future of marketing.

As with this book, a decade later the Kellogg marketing faculty is both similar in some ways and different in others. Many of the faculty members who authored chapters in the original edition of *Kellogg on Marketing* are still active members of the department. They have been joined by new faculty, who bring with them fresh perspectives.

OVERVIEW OF THE BOOK

The book is divided into three sections. Chapters in Section One, entitled "Developing a Marketing Strategy," cover foundational concepts and tools for building a marketing strategy. In Chapter 1, "Creating Customers and Shaping the Competitive Game," Gregory S. Carpenter sets the stage by reminding the reader of Peter Drucker's assertion that the fundamental purpose of business is to create a customer. The challenge is how to do so in the face of customers who don't always know what they want and competitors who are quick to imitate any differentiation. The answer, Carpenter argues, lies in understanding that, "Rather than a race to meet some prespecified consumer objective, competition becomes a struggle to influence what buyers know and, as a result, how they behave." He introduces the "Market Paradigm," a concept that captures the knowledge consumers acquire and the social consensus that emerges from it as a means of defining the competitive landscape. He then discusses competitive strategies, such as market pioneering, fast following, differentiation, and refining markets, that can be used to create value in the Market Paradigm.

In Chapter 2, "Identifying Market Segments and Selecting Targets," Alice M. Tybout and Kent Grayson begin with the premise that any firm's offerings are unlikely to appeal to everyone. Therefore, creating customers requires segmenting markets and selecting the most attractive targets. They recommend that companies begin by segmenting customers on the basis of their current behavior or usage patterns, then describe the resulting subgroups in terms of their distinctive demographic and psychographic characteristics, as well as their profit potential. Targets are finally prioritized on the basis of a "path-of-least-resistance" strategy, where targets that are likely to generate the highest return per marketing dollar invested receive first priority.

Once a firm has identified a target group of consumers, it then should seek insight into the motivations underlying their behavior. Because a company and its customers have inherently different perspectives, market research is employed to bridge the gap between them. In Chapter 3, "Marketing

Research and Understanding Consumers," Bobby J. Calder offers a provocative perspective on how to make effective use of marketing research. He encourages the marketer to focus less on the technique employed or the amount of data collected and more on achieving an understanding of customers and a plausible explanation for their behavior.

A deep understanding of targeted customers' beliefs and motivations serves as the foundation for developing the brand's positioning. A brand's positioning is the specific, intended meaning of the brand in the mind of targeted customers. As such, it is a guidepost for making decisions about all of the elements of the brand that consumers experience. Brand positioning is so central to an effective marketing strategy that we devote two chapters to this topic. In Chapter 4, "Developing a Compelling Brand Positioning," Alice M. Tybout and Brian Sternthal offer two complementary perspectives that can be used to build a strong position. Their competition-based approach emphasizes how a brand is similar to competitors' offerings on some dimensions and superior to these offerings on other dimensions. Their customer-based approach focuses on how the distinguishing features of a brand create abstract benefits that are related to customers' goals. In Chapter 5, "Writing a Brand Positioning Statement and Translating It into Brand Design," Bobby J. Calder then digs into the task of arriving at a single statement that succinctly summarizes the brand positioning. He discusses how a brand's positioning may evolve over time as brand meanings deepen, then recommends that positioning statements be developed in the context of designing the verbal and visual brand elements that will convey the positioning to consumers.

Section One concludes with Chapter 6, "Creating and Managing Brands." In this chapter, Alice M. Tybout and Gregory S. Carpenter discuss the process of building a brand and describe three types of brands that companies build: functional, image, and experiential brands. They then explore the unique challenges associated with managing each type of brand.

Chapters in Section Two, entitled "Implementing the Strategy," address the translation of a brand's positioning into all the things that targeted customers experience: the level of service they receive when they call the company's 800 number; the actual features of the product or service offering; the price; the representation of the product in communications such as advertising and sales force presentations; and the purchase experience. In Chapter 7, "Making the Brand Come Alive within Your Organization," Lisa Fortini-Campbell addresses the link between the intended meaning of the brand (brand positioning) and what happens inside the firm. She argues that an organization's culture *is* its brand. If people within the organization are not aware of and fully committed to the brand's position, be it one of superior product performance, hassle-free customer service, quick, reliable delivery or lowest cost, customers' experiences will fall short and the brand position will exist only in the mind of the marketing manager who developed it. To ensure that the company's culture supports the brand positioning, Fortini-Campbell recommends paying close attention to four key dimensions of the internal organization: hiring, cultural storytelling, job design, rewards and incentives, and leadership.

In Chapter 8, "The Sandwich Strategy: Managing New Products and Services for Value Creation and Value Capture," Dipak C. Jain presents a framework for launching new products and services that are a "triple win"—those that create and capture value for the company, its partners, and its customers. He argues that when a company is attacked by price competition, it should respond by creating at least two new offerings that effectively "sandwich" the competition by attacking it from opposite ends of the value chain: below and above. More generally, he offers guidelines for managing a product line horizontally (i.e., the level of variety at a particular price point) and vertically (i.e., the range of price points offered), with the goal of moving the firm's customers up the value chain.

The issue of price competition, as well as other considerations in setting price, is discussed further in Chapter 9, "Pricing for Profit." Here, Lakshman Krishnamurthi offers a strategic approach to making pricing decisions, which begins with a determination of whether gaining market share or increasing profits is the firm's top priority. Then, five key determinants of price—cost, customer value, competition, the distribution channel, and regulation—are discussed in detail. The overarching theme of the chapter is that indeed price must be set to cover the firm's costs, allow channel partners to make a profit, and comply with regulations. But ultimately the price that a firm can charge is determined by the value of the firm's offering (based on functional, economic, and emotional benefits), as perceived by targeted customers and in comparison to the competitive offerings under consideration.

In Chapter 10, "Advertising Strategy," Derek D. Rucker and Brian Sternthal address the issue of communicating a brand's position through media. First, they discuss the role of advertising and when it is appropriate to use advertising rather than other methods such as personal selling to communicate the brand message. Next, they describe the ways consumers use advertising to make decisions and outline strategies for increasing consumers' engagement with advertising through creative and media strategies. They then present alternative strategies for presenting the brand message and evaluating its effectiveness. A key insight is that mere recall of an advertising message is insufficient to gauge its effectiveness.

No matter how appealing a product or service may be, customers cannot buy it if it isn't made available through some channel of distribution. In Chapter 11, "Marketing Channel Design and Management," Anne T. Coughlan provides a framework for designing and managing channels of distribution. She argues that channel design must begin with an understanding of end-users' demands for the service outputs of the channel (i.e., their need for quick delivery, assortment and variety, bulk breaking, and the like), which typically vary by the type of customer and use occasion. This knowledge is then used to create the optimal channel structure for meeting these demands. Channel management, in turn, requires an understanding of each channel member's sources of power and dependence in order to manage any conflict among these channel members so that the goal of coordination is achieved. The framework presented is illustrated with brief case studies, including one that describes how a company developed an innovative channel to distribute its products to low-income consumers in Mexico.

In many situations (especially business-to-business), salespeople play a critical role in promoting and distributing a company's products and services. Indeed, as Andris A. Zoltners, Prabhakant Sinha, and Sally E. Lorimer note in Chapter 12, "Building a Winning Sales Force," for some such customers, the salesperson *is* the company. Yet salespeople often enjoy autonomy that makes them difficult to control, direct, and manage. The authors begin by identifying the conditions under which a company will benefit from personal selling and discuss when the sales function should be outsourced versus managed internally. They then address the challenge of motivating and managing a sales force. Five key drivers of sales force effectiveness are identified, and best practices for managing these drivers are discussed.

Chapters in Section Three, "Perspectives on Contemporary Issues in Marketing," focus on key challenges and opportunities for marketers in the current environment. The section begins with Chapter 13 by Bobby J. Calder, Richard Kolsky, and Maria Flores Letelier ("Marketing to Consumers at the Bottom of the Pyramid"), in which the authors share lessons they learned about marketing to the poor from their extensive experience with CEMEX's Patrimonio Hoy program in Mexico. This case study, which is an ongoing exercise in experimentation and learning, leads to important insights about how companies must adapt their traditional approach in order to succeed in marketing to consumers at the bottom of the pyramid.

At the other end of the income spectrum, marketers grapple with the benefits and liabilities of new social media, such as blogs, Facebook, Twitter, YouTube, web forums, and more. In Chapter 14, "The New Influence of Social Media," Lakshman Krishnamurthi and Shyam Gopinath note that such media can serve as powerful tools to gain customer feedback but can also weaken the marketer's control over the brand message. They argue that social media engagement is not for all companies and offer a list of questions for firms deciding whether to commit resources to social networking sites. In addition, they review emerging academic research that documents the impact of online word-of-mouth and online customer ratings.

Effective innovation has been a long-standing challenge for marketers. Its importance has only increased as product lifecycles have shortened. Two chapters offer perspectives on how a company can innovate effectively. In Chapter 15, "From the Wheel to Twitter: Where Do Innovations Come From?" David Gal draws on lessons from history regarding the source of successful innovations. His analysis yields three key insights: (1) The focus of innovation should be on novel applications of existing inventions rather than on creating new inventions; (2) the key to successful innovation in a marketing context is the identification of unarticulated customer needs and the envisioning of creative applications to fulfill those needs; and (3) the best sources of ideas for innovation are found by looking outside the company and the industry in which it competes. In Chapter 16, "Brand-Led Innovation," Bobby J. Calder and Edward S. Calder extend the discussion of innovation by noting that there are many paths to successful innovation. Traditionally, companies have relied on customer insight, technological advances, or some combination of these factors as the source of innovations. More recently, innovations have emerged from insights about ways to improve a business model or product design. The authors propose an additional approach to innovation: brand-led innovation. This approach uses a brand's positioning and abstract meanings in the minds of consumers as a springboard for launching new offerings in a category that might otherwise be difficult to penetrate without fresh insight or a technological advance.

Companies' efforts to address the variation in customers' needs often leads to a large assortment of options in a product category. Intuitively, it might seem that this benefits consumers by increasing the odds that they will find an option that is just right for them. However, as Ryan Hamilton and Alexander Chernev document in Chapter 17, "Managing Product Assortments: Insights from Consumer Psychology," there is a downside to offering a large assortment. Too many options can create "choice overload" for consumers, leading some to opt out of choosing altogether. The authors draw on insights from their own research as well as research of other scholars to offer strategies for addressing choice overload and making the product assortment "just right."

As noted earlier in discussing Chapter 3, "Marketing Research and Understanding Consumers," marketing research is an important tool for bridging the divide between a company's perspective and that of targeted customers. However, when times are tough and budgets must be trimmed, marketing research expenditures may be difficult to justify (and should be) if the research isn't driven by a clearly defined goal. In Chapter 18 ("Goal-Driven Marketing Research: The Answer to a Shrinking Budget"), Angela Y. Lee outlines an approach to conducting marketing research that helps ensure the research expenditure will yield answers that truly matter in making marketing decisions. This goal-driven approach to conducting research is illustrated with a case example.

In the final chapters, attention turns to the relationship between marketing and other functional areas. It might seem obvious that sales and marketing need to work together in creating and sustaining customer relationships. However, all too often the failure to delineate the responsibilities of each area results in conflicts that undermine the company's goal of serving its customers. In Chapter 19, "Aligning Sales and Marketing to Enhance Customer Value and Company Results," Andris A. Zoltners, Prabhakant Sinha, and Sally E. Lorimer discuss ways to divide responsibilities between sales and marketing and identify four factors that facilitate successful sales-marketing alignment within an organization. In Chapter 20, "Creating Superior Value by Managing the Marketing–Operations Management Interface," Anne T. Coughlan and Jeffrey D. Shulman tackle the issue of the interface between marketing and operations. All too often, operational factors, incentives, and costs are overlooked or given insufficient weight in marketing decisions and vice-versa. Using case examples, the authors make a persuasive argument that aligning these two functional areas is essential if a firm to deliver on its brand promise and differentiate from competitors.

USING THE BOOK

This book was written with a broad audience in mind. Each chapter is self-contained, allowing readers to use the book in a variety of ways.

An academic might assign the book for a marketing management course at either the MBA or executive level. In such a situation, the chapters in Section One and Section Two might be used as weekly reading assignments, and chapters in Section Three could supplement these readings based on the instructors' and students' interests. For example, the chapter on marketing to consumers at the bottom of the pyramid (Chapter 13) might be used in combination with the chapter on segmentation and targeting (Chapter 2) or the chapter on channels of distribution (Chapter 11). The chapter on social media (Chapter 14) might be assigned along with the chapter on advertising strategy (Chapter 10). The chapters on innovation (Chapters 15 and 16) and on product assortment (Chapter 17) combine well with the chapter on new products and services (Chapter 8). The strategy of goal-driven market research (Chapter 18) complements the overview of market research (Chapter 3). And the chapters on how marketing links with other functional areas (Chapters 19 and 20) extend the discussion of marketing channels (Chapter 11) and managing a sales force (Chapter 12).

Students of marketing not enrolled in a formal course may wish to use this book in much the same manner as an academic would assign it. They might begin by reading chapters in the first two sections to build their basic understanding of core marketing concepts, and then use chapters in the final section to deepen their insight into contemporary issues in marketing as their interest dictates.

Alumni and other more seasoned marketers may wish to skim the chapters in Sections One and Two, treating them as a review of the principles of marketing (which are easy to lose sight of in the context of day-to-day business operations), before diving into the chapters on the contemporary challenges discussed in Section Three.

However you use this book, we hope you find it informative and provocative. We found that writing the book and reading the chapters of our colleagues enriched and helped to clarify our own understanding of marketing in the twenty-first century.

Alice M. Tybout
Bobby J. Calder

ACKNOWLEDGMENTS

Many people contributed to this book directly and indirectly. We are indebted to those who collaborated with us for sharing their wisdom. More generally, we owe thanks to all of our colleagues in the Kellogg Marketing Department over the years. The book is a tribute to their inspiration and intellectual stimulation. We are also grateful for the support provided by the dean's office of the Kellogg School of Management and by Northwestern University.

Several people warrant special mention for the key roles that they played in completing the book. Patty Dowd Schmitz was invaluable as our copy editor. She provided insightful feedback and helpful suggestions that improved both the content and structure of the book. We also could not have completed this book without the support of the marketing department administrative assistants, James Ward and Sabin Gurung. James and Sabin worked tirelessly and with their typical good humor to ensure that the final manuscript was completed on time and in the proper format.

Finally, we thank our editor at John Wiley & Sons, Richard Narramore, for encouraging us to undertake this project and for supporting us throughout the process. Above all, we thank our families for their constant patience, support, and encouragement.

Alice M. Tybout
Bobby J. Calder

SECTION ONE

DEVELOPING A MARKETING STRATEGY

CHAPTER 1

CREATING CUSTOMERS AND SHAPING THE COMPETITIVE GAME

GREGORY S. CARPENTER

INTRODUCTION

In his landmark, *Management*, Peter Drucker wrote about the purpose of business—not *a* business, but *business*. Contrary to the commonly held view that the only meaningful purpose of business is profit, Drucker articulated what we recognize today as the marketing concept: "There is only one valid definition of business purpose: *to create a customer.* . . . The customer is the foundation of a business."[1] According to this view, products, technology, or brands do not, per se, produce profits. Products, technology, and brands are all devices through which an organization creates value for its customers. Profit and success are *outcomes* of creating customers and of successfully managing that process, which is not simply the responsibility of a marketing function. "Marketing is so basic that it cannot be considered a separate function," Drucker continues. . . . "It is the whole business seen from the point of view of its final result, that is, from the customer's point of view. Concern and responsibility for marketing must, therefore, permeate all areas of the enterprise."[2] In Drucker's view, only marketing and innovation generate revenue; all other activities are simply costs.

The concept Drucker advanced has become *the* central concept of marketing and, as originally envisioned, it has moved beyond its functional limits to become increasingly important as a central concept of management.[3] The diffusion of the marketing concept has been fueled by mounting evidence of its value. Leading scholars and consultants have written for years about how a market orientation is central to organizational success.[4] But much of

Figure 1.1
Customer Satisfaction and Return on Investment

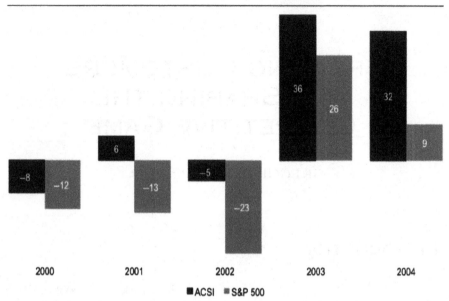

the evidence they cited was anecdotal. More recently, however, empirical evidence is demonstrating what others suspected but were unable to state with more conviction. Some of that evidence appears in Figure 1.1, which shows the return on investment of the S&P 500 over five years compared to the return on investment of the top 25 percent of firms with respect to customer satisfaction, as measured by the American Customer Satisfaction Index. The data show that firms with more satisfied customers have higher returns—beating market averages over five years—with lower variability over time.[5] Mounting evidence suggests that creating satisfied customers appears associated with higher return on investment and reduced risk.[6]

As the power of the marketing concept has been recognized, a growing number of organizations have begun to transform their businesses to become more market-oriented. Procter & Gamble, Unilever, and others that have long embraced the marketing concept have worked to continually transform their organizations to remain at the forefront. But other firms in industries where marketing has played a less central role—usually as a distinct function rather than as a guiding principle—have begun to embrace the concept more fully. These firms can be found in every corner of the economy, from rapidly growing, high-technology companies to mature, established industrial businesses.

For example, in the mid-2000s, Intel's CEO announced plans to transform the company so that "every idea and technical solution should be focused on meeting customers' need from the outset."[7]

Although the concept of marketing appears straightforward—focus the organization on creating a customer—two challenges are central to implementing it. First, customers are complex, fascinating, and not always easy to understand. Customers often seek value they can articulate, but they are unaware of what they don't know, and they are largely blind to their subconscious desires. Therefore, understanding customers *holistically* is necessary to be an excellent marketing organization. Second, creating competitive advantage by creating customers requires a deep understanding of the role of consumers in the process of competition. The traditional view is that marketing is essentially about responding to buyer needs, and doing so will create competitive advantage. Mounting evidence, however, suggests that marketing does much more. It educates buyers and significantly shapes the nature of competition. Successful competitive strategy helps define and redefine the competitive game. Understanding that role is important to understand more fully the role of marketing strategy in creating competitive advantage.

DEVELOPING MARKETING STRATEGY TO CREATE CUSTOMERS

The process of developing marketing strategy to create customers is shown in Figure 1.2. It shows that, based on an understanding of the markets (customers and competitors), organizations establish objectives. These are the outcomes they hope to achieve through the application of resources and typically include market outcomes (e.g., sales), financial metrics (return on investments), and

Figure 1.2
Developing Marketing Strategy

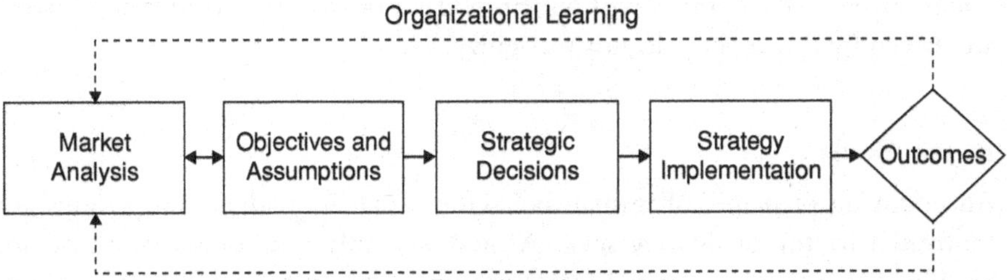

measures of customer knowledge (e.g., brand awareness or perception). Based on these objectives, organizations make key strategic decisions, implement strategy, and observe results. Buyers learn as a result of their experience in the market, and organizations learn about how to produce the outcomes they desire. And so it continues. Here, we focus on the overall process, with emphasis on market analysis and the process of creating customer value.

Market Analysis

The foundation of a successful competitive marketing strategy is a deep and holistic understanding of buyers, their motivation, what they value, and how they choose. Many times, individuals and organizations lack sufficient knowledge about buyers to create a solid foundation for a competitive marketing strategy. Lacking that information, they substitute plausible assumptions. Those assumptions are often widely shared views about buyers and individuals more generally. We often assume, for instance, that buyers know what they want, that they are rational about seeking it, that offering more options is preferable to fewer, that a lower price is preferred to a higher price, and that more information improves choice. In some cases, these assumptions are accurate summaries of buyer behavior. In other cases, as mounting research shows, they are seriously misleading, despite their intuitive appeal. Buyers are much more complex than we might imagine; they are much more sophisticated in some ways and much simpler in others.

For example, we do not always know what we want, nor do we choose rationally. Knowing what we want in any product category—motor oil, a family physician, or life insurance—requires data, time, expertise, and experience. We often lack one or more of these in making choices. Moreover, humans are emotional beings, driven by forces that we do not always understand or even recognize. As a result, we are unable or unwilling to articulate the full range of our needs or wants. Crafting a solid foundation for competitive strategy requires deeper understanding of buyers to capture the essence of behavior when buyers make choices without time, data, or expertise, and when buyers are driven by forces they do not recognize.

Buyer Goals

An enduring principle of human behavior is that individuals and groups are motivated by the goals they seek. A goal is simply a desired state of being. Simple as that sounds, desired human states of being can be complex. Goals reflect the full richness of the future we desire—our aspirations, our dreams,

Figure 1.3
Buyer Goal Hierarchy

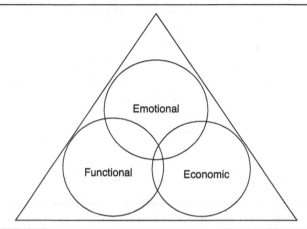

our hopes, and our economic ambitions. Simply put, goals are our hopes and dreams. Individuals seek a vast range of goals—to be good parents, to be successful professionally, to be at peace, to make a positive contribution to the world, and to have fun. The range and number of goals an individual seeks over a lifetime is virtually unlimited and evolves over time.

The existence of such a vast number and range of goals, each with multiple dimensions, creates a fundamental dilemma for individuals. Time is too limited to pursue them all, so we must prioritize. One buyer's goal hierarchy, shown in Figure 1.3, suggests that as buyers we seek value on at least three dimensions: emotional, functional, and economic. Emotional goals are higher-order goals such as self-image, power, control, and affiliation. We pursue these over a long period of time; they are complex and important to us. These goals change slowly, are limited in number, and are pursued consciously but also subconsciously—the concept of our self-image, for instance, in a multidimensional goal. Lower in the hierarchy are functional and economic goals. These do not exist independently of higher-order goals. Selecting a vehicle with four-wheel drive and rugged features serves obvious functional goals but also conveys a particular image to others. Functional and economic goals tend to be less complex than emotional goals, are pursued over a shorter time horizon, and are less important than emotional goals.[8]

The full range of goals—emotional, functional, and economic—are sought in both business-to-consumer and business-to-business settings, although the mix of goals can differ. For consumers, self-image and affiliation can be important in the categories such as beer, athletic shoes, or automobiles. In business settings, buyers are thought to be more "rational," focusing on functional and economic to the exclusion of emotion. Humans are, however, fundamentally emotional beings. Our emotions are a part of a system of reasoning—our subconscious—produced over thousands of years of evolution. Our emotional systems are impossible to switch off, even for the most expert buyer. When American Airlines buys aircraft engines, when Google goes public, or when a university invests its endowment, these organizations bring much expertise to bear on the decisions, but the risk associated with each is high, making sure that emotions are central to each decision.

Creating Value, Focusing Resources, and Competitive Positioning

Goals create a problem for an individual or organization to solve. How can we achieve greater social status? How can we have more financial security? How can we have a relaxing and exciting vacation? Each of these is a problem reflecting an important individual goal. Organizations have goals as well. Corporations seek faster growth, recognition among peers, and, of course, financial success. Each of these goals creates a *problem* for the organization to solve. Individuals and organizations create value by solving such problems.

The value we attach to the solutions varies greatly by the importance of the problem being solved. Although many factors influence a goal's importance, the position in the hierarchy is the single most important factor. Higher-order, emotional goals are difficult to achieve, are sought over a long time period, are complex and multidimensional, and require considerable personal or organizational commitment. Achieving a higher-order goal requires a greater personal commitment, making it more important than a more easily achieved goal. Emotional goals are often pursued subconsciously. Instead, buyers focus on a more concrete or *focal* goal, such as *losing weight* versus the more abstract *live a healthier life*. Although buyers are more aware of focal goals, they are less important than higher-order goals because they fall in the middle of the goal hierarchy. Subgoals in each of these categories are specific and considered over a short time period. These lower-order goals are subordinate to the focal goals they serve and ultimately to the smaller number of higher-order goals.

Competitive marketing strategies propose solutions to buyer problems—they propose means for buyers to achieve their goals. Successful marketing strategies, however, must do more than simply create value for buyers. Successful strategies create *unique* solutions for *the most important problems* buyers confront. Doing so requires focusing resources. Although all buyers have goals, different buyers seek solutions to different problems. These differences create market segments, which create a fundamental challenge for competitive strategy. With limited resources, a firm simply cannot solve all customers' problems, and it certainly cannot create unique solutions for the full range of customer problems. Choices must be made. All strategies reflect decisions about where resources will be deployed and, therefore, where they will not. By focusing resources, the firm magnifies their impact. This concept, derived from the military roots of strategy, can be traced back to Roman military commanders who grouped legions of troops to overwhelm their opponents' smaller numbers. Focus is the essence of guerilla warfare. One of the most effective guerilla strategists, Mao Zedong, wrote, "Although I fight one against 10, I engage 10 against one." Concentration of resources multiplies the impact of limited resources for advantage.

Once a firm has decided where it will focus its resources to solve a consumer problem, the next key decision is selecting the competitive positioning. The positioning is simply a statement of the unique value the firm will offer to selected customers. From the buyers' perspectives, the competitive positioning is a *value proposition*, an articulation of the unique solution the firm will offer to solve the target buyers' problems. As such, it describes the value the firm offers and what it will not offer. Crafting a value proposition requires identifying the various alternatives that buyers consider as solutions to their problems. Each of these solutions shares aspects in common, called *points of parity*, and they offer unique aspects of value, called *points of difference*. For example, if the goal is an indulgent treat, all may be high in calories but only some may include chocolate. The goal of positioning is to craft a unique, compelling solution to customers' problems that takes into account the competitive options available and the strengths and weaknesses of the organization. Some classic value propositions appear in Table 1.1.[9]

Implementation

From within the firm, the competitive positioning provides a focus for aligning organizational resources and incentives to deliver the solution buyers anticipate. Thus, beyond focusing resources on particular segments in particular markets, competitive marketing strategy further focuses the firm's activities on those that uniquely create value for buyers. By focusing resources, firms multiply the impact of those resources. Focus, however, creates internal conflict. Each function has its own view of important tasks that need to be accomplished. Competitive positioning provides a means to align functions and reduce functional conflict. As such, the value proposition acts like a score for a symphony, focusing the efforts of the firm to the selected markets, target segments, and a unique competitive position.

Table 1.1
Classic Value Propositions

Superior satisfaction of a common goal. A powerful point of difference arises when a brand delivers superior satisfaction on the core functional benefit of the product category. Although appealing to buyers and logical to firms, such a position often invites competitive imitation and escalation, which can render such a position less valuable.

Uniquely satisfy a neglected goal. A potentially more enduring advantage is created by a brand distinguishing itself from rivals based on satisfying a neglected buyer goal. The changing lives of buyers have made this rich territory. The time pressure many buyers face means that individuals pursue some urgent goals such as financial security, social responsibility, and social acceptance, at the expense of more internal (perhaps more important) self-oriented goals.

Satisfy a unique combination of common goals. Even without the ability to deliver superior value on any one goal, a compelling point of difference is possible by satisfying a unique combination of goals. By delivering value on a unique combination of dimensions, firms can create a competitively distinct value proposition and make simple comparisons difficult for buyers.

Resolve goal conflict. Many times goals conflict. Being a better parent, gaining greater professional acceptance, and devoting more time to community service are wonderful goals but fundamentally in conflict. Associating a brand with a unique and effective resolution to this dilemma can produce a powerful point of difference.

Consumer Learning and Competition

Once strategies are developed and implemented, firms compete to create customers. Buyers in the target segment are confronted with a range of value propositions, each proposing a solution to a certain problem. Based on the options, buyers act. They either choose or not, and their objectives are realized or not. In the process, organizations and customers learn from the experience.

The Evolution of Buyer Learning

To understand competition, it's important to understand how buyers *learn*. Buyers learn over time in a systematic way; their problem solving evolves. Early in the life of a market, buyers are inexpert. Buying a new home robot is difficult because we know so little. In such *extensive problem solving*, buyers actively seek and process such information, constructing the basic knowledge necessary to be a buyer. As buyers become more experienced, making a choice in the category is no longer an entirely novel task. It is familiar but not routine. Buyers have basic awareness of options, perceptions of the alternatives, preferences for the perceived differences and similarities, and logic for choosing among them. Information is processed less actively, and buyers use less complicated strategies for brand choice. Buyer behavior in such a situation can be described as *limited problem solving*. Finally, buyers become very experienced. They become aware of the relevant brands and competitors and knowledgeable about differences between alternatives. They have clear preferences for those differences and established strategies for choosing among options. Buying becomes more practiced—it becomes *routine problem solving*.[10] Learning slows and a period of stability emerges that depends fundamentally on the knowledge that buyers have acquired. Based on that learning a social consensus emerges that defines the competitive game.

Market Stability: Types of Buyer Knowledge

Competition during the period of stability is defined as what buyers have learned through this process of evolution. Buyer learning, however, is an imprecise process. We learn as buyers differently than as students learning calculus or art history. As buyers, we learn casually, sometimes without conscious recognition and sometimes by fleeting observation or more careful consideration. We have limited experiences and observations, and we devote finite attention to interpreting what we experience or observe. Nevertheless, we draw conclusions that guide our actions as buyers. Those actions are based on at least four types of knowledge we acquire through the learning process: *categories, perceptions, preferences,* and *choice*.

Categories A fundamental element of our routines is the set of potential solutions we discover. For those seeking a college education, the United States offers more than 3,000 choices; many grocery stores have 20,000 different items for sale; Apple offers more than 100,000 applications for the iPhone. Knowing all these alternatives is impossible. Customers simplify the number of alternatives to make a decision. To do so, they construct a set of alternatives based on the alternatives of which they are aware and, from that set, a smaller set to consider more carefully. Consumers typically consider three to five alternatives. For example, buyers consider on average three brands of antacids, eight brands of automobiles, and four brands of shampoo in making purchases in these categories.[11] Therefore, a primary task of buying is to learn how to eliminate most alternatives from further consideration.

Buyers construct small consideration sets for a number of reasons. The process of learning about brands is costly in terms of time and effort. Searching, whether electronically or physically, requires the individual to incur certain so-called *search* costs. If the cost of learning about another brand remains constant but the benefit declines with the number of brands considered, buyers will search over some optimal number of brands. Other brands will simply remain unknown to the buyer. Moreover, cognitive capacity is limited, so individuals are willing to allocate only so much memory to various brands of shampoo, for example. Buyers add or drop brands from consideration based on the perceived cost and benefit of doing so, all the while maintaining a set of better-known, frequently considered brands.

Perceptions Buyers learn perceptions of the alternatives in the consideration set. Perceptions are the thoughts, feelings, and images we attach to otherwise complex entities. Buyer perceptions are useful simplifications of reality. Even for a small set of alternatives, making full and complete comparisons across all meaningful attributes and features would be a daunting, burdensome, and complex task for most consumers. Buying a first computer is a difficult task, in part because our perceptions are not yet well formed. We do not know how to process the massive amount of information we confront. With experience, we structure those thoughts using perceptions. We simplify alternatives on a set of common and unique dimensions, highlighting similarities and differences, making comparisons easier. In that process, we discard much relevant information that is simply too costly or too difficult to process or organize. As such, perceptions are sufficiently complete, but always incomplete.

Preferences Based on perceptions, buyers form judgments about the value of perceived similarities and differences among alternatives. Those judgments are based on experience. Buyers have no preferences prior to their first experience. With the exception of some foods, for which humans have an innate taste preference (such as sweetness), it is impossible to have preferences for something about which consumers have no knowledge. Without knowledge of the product, buyers have no means to create perceptions of it, and without perceptions they are forced to value the individual attributes of the product. Even if buyers have objective information on brand attributes, the value of an individual attribute of the superiority of one attribute combination over another may not be obvious. Through trial and experience, consumers develop a naive theory relating perceptions to value or outcomes.[12] For example, we learn that we prefer blue shirts over white, white wine over red, and warm-climate vacations over cold. With a small number of exceptions, the preferences we have are learned.

Choice Finally, buyers develop logic for choosing among the alternatives they consider based on their goals, the perceptions of the alternatives, and their preferences. We construct a logic for choosing. Although we sometimes choose carefully, thoughtfully, and deliberately, more often than not (even for important decisions) we devise a shortcut to minimize the effort of making a choice. Simplification is necessary for mundane and important choices. Entering a grocery store with 20,000 items requires a repertoire of shortcuts. If we send a friend or neighbor to the store, we may unknowingly reveal our shortcut when providing such hints as "look at these two brands and choose the cheaper," or "buy only one brand." Even in the most important decisions, we create simplifications. When choosing a personal physician, rather than doing an exhaustive search, comparing patient outcomes, and weighing the risks and benefits, we often simply ask a friend or colleague for a recommendation. Some of the shortcuts consumers use are shown in Table 1.2.

Table 1.2
Strategies for Decision Making

Compensatory. In a compensatory strategy, consumers weigh all the perceived characteristics of all the alternatives and reach an overall judgment about choice. A strength on one perceived dimension can offset, or compensate for, a weakness on another.

Lexicographic. Buyers using a lexicographic choice rule identify the most important goal and then select the alternative that delivers most on that one goal, ignoring all other goals. A lexicographic strategy has the benefit of being very simple, easy to apply, and thus not very demanding of cognitive resources. In deriving such economy, however, the buyer ignores considerable information.

Satisficing. A buyer using this strategy develops a set of minimum levels on each perceived dimension and then considers each alternative sequentially. Looking at each dimension of the first brand, the buyer decides if it meets a preset minimum level. If it fails on any one dimension, it is rejected, and the next alternative is considered. The buyer selects the first option that meets all the minimum requirements. If no alternative meets the established standards, then the cut-off levels are revised and the process is repeated.

Elimination by aspect. In the first stage of this multi-stage choice rule, the buyer selects the most important dimension, determines a cut-off, and eliminates all alternatives that do not meet the cut-off on that dimension. With a reduced set of alternatives, the buyer then identifies the second most important dimension, sets a cut-off level for that dimension, and eliminates the alternatives that fail to satisfy the second cut-off. This process continues until only one alternative remains.

Phased decision rules. In some cases, buyers combine strategies in a sequence throughout the process. Early in the process, buyers use one process to screen alternatives and reduce the set; in the next stage, they rely on a more elaborate strategy to choose among the screened alternatives.

The Market Paradigm: The Rules of the Competitive Game

The knowledge that consumers acquire, and the social consensus that emerges from it, defines a *market paradigm*. This is a well-developed understanding on the part of buyers about how to achieve their goals and includes the set of brands buyers consider, the dimensions on which they are judged, the value they attach to perceived similarities and differences, and the logics they develop for choosing among them given their goals. This knowledge, incomplete as it may be, creates the *rules of the competitive game*. For example, if your goal is to send a package overnight, a small set of alternatives pop to mind (including possibly FedEx, UPS, and the U.S. Postal Service); all share certain similarities and differ on established dimensions (reliability, image, price, convenience). You may have already assigned weights to those perceived differences, establishing your willingness to pay for each, and you may have constructed a logic for choosing among the alternatives depending on the urgency and importance of your shipment.

This paradigm rests on buyers' mutual experiences and observations, as well as the consensus that has emerged from that experience. It does not, however, rest on exhaustive knowledge on the part of buyers. Buyers develop the knowledge that forms the basis for the paradigm through casual learning. Buyers learn just enough to solve the problem at hand and then have no incentive to learn more. Although the paradigm is effective, it is based on a limited (although sufficiently correct) view of reality from the perspective of buyers. For example, although we may not know much about shipping packages overnight, we know enough to get our packages where they need to be, and we have no desire to learn much more.

UNDERSTANDING COMPETITIVE DYNAMICS

Once established, a paradigm can remain stable for many years. Eventually, however, all market paradigms are redefined as the social consensus on which the market rests changes. Three forces operate to undermine any established social consensus and establish a new consensus and a new competitive paradigm: *technological innovation, strategic innovation,* and *buyer change.*

Technological Innovation

Changes in technology create the opportunity for existing players or new entrants to redefine the competitive game through a new approach to solving buyer problems. The implicit foundation of the paradigm is a technology that defines the economics of the industry, which has a powerful if implicit effect on the paradigm that emerges. Innovation can occur at any level in one of three ways.[13] *Incremental innovation* is perhaps the most common. It is the further refinement of existing technologies in an established direction of improvement. The microprocessor gets faster and uses less electricity, just as the mobile phone becomes more sophisticated and smaller. Incremental innovations are usually not disruptive. *Architectural innovations* are rare and have a greater impact. These are innovations in a subsystem or some mechanism linking subsystems.[14] Architectural innovations alter the way in which subsystems relate to one another, creating fundamental change. Canon's introduction of smaller printers is an example of one such innovation. *Discontinuous innovation*, perhaps what we most often associate with the term innovation, is a fundamental change in a crucial subsystem of the technology. The invention of digital imaging is a discontinuous innovation. Architectural and discontinuous innovations create the opportunity to redefine the competitive game through the creation of new solutions to existing buyer problems.

Strategic Innovation

The inequities of an established game create incentives for those who are disadvantaged (or entirely excluded from the game) to redefine it, even without the benefit of new technology. Although strategic innovation is conceptually possible by crafting a new strategy that is unorthodox on any dimension of the received paradigm, in practice many innovative strategies begin with either a novel scope of the market or the competitive strategy. A novel *scope of the market* enables an innovative firm to address ignored buyers or to focus on a specific, overlooked, or underserved niche of buyers. Southwest Airlines, one of the most profitable airlines in the United States, has achieved a powerful position in its market by drawing new customers to air travel through extremely low fares. Southwest has been able to create a low-cost model that has been emulated and refined by others such as Ryan Air in Ireland and JetBlue. India's Tata Nano, an inexpensive car offered at about $2,500, offers a similar example. The target is the massive number of Indian consumers who currently own no car. The concept of basic, low-cost transportation, though hardly new, is innovative given the strategies currently being pursued in the global auto business.

One powerful source of strategic innovation is devising an entirely new set of activities to achieve the same or even superior organizational outcomes. Such an innovation redefines the *scope of competitive strategy*. Over time, in any competitive game, organizations learn what actions produce desired results.

Experience, of course, is limited. Organizations cannot experiment with every possible combination of actions. Based on this limited experience, organizations develop an imperfect but useful understanding of how actions product outcomes. More experience reinforces that other sets of strategic decisions are not viable by the absence of evidence demonstrating their viability. Strategic innovation that goes beyond the limits of currently pursued strategies remains a viable option in virtually all markets. The popular Blue Ocean Strategy concept, as exemplified by Cirque de Soleil, demonstrates the potential power of strategic innovation.[15] Toyota's entry into the luxury car market with Lexus and Apple's launch of the iPod both represent classic examples of strategic innovation. Neither depends on fundamentally new technology. Indeed, in the case of the iPod, a central aspect of the innovation is in the novel distribution of music through iTunes. Lexus distinguished itself from Mercedes-Benz and other luxury carmakers through excellent service that was made possible through product changes.

Buyer Change

Absent technological or strategic innovation, change remains inevitable. Existing buyers, both individuals and organizations, evolve. As buyers evolve, their goals change. Our goals at age 15 are certainly different from our goals at age 55. These changes are created by aging and the different challenges it brings (first job, new home, changing careers, etc.) but also by external pressures (social change, economic opportunities and concerns, etc.). Change is one constant in our lives. Beyond that, new buyers are entering established markets every day. These new buyers may have different goals than existing buyers, different perceptions, and fundamentally different preferences compared to existing buyers. Over time, of course, existing buyers will slowly exit the market. This slow but inevitable process of buyer entry and exit creates the opportunity to create a new game with new buyers. These changes in buyers are so important because buyer changes threaten the social consensus on which every market rests.[16]

Sequential Paradigms

Through the development of marketing strategy, competition produces a series of competitive paradigms. Initially, firms develop strategies to solve buyer problems, then buyers learn based on the observations and experiences those strategies create. As buyers learn, a consensus emerges and the game evolves, reaching a relative stability. The resulting paradigm benefits some firms and

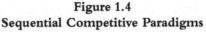

Figure 1.4
Sequential Competitive Paradigms

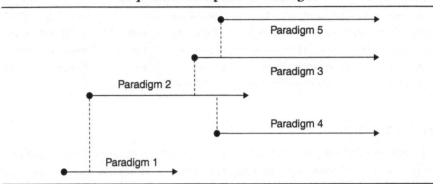

disadvantages others. Technology may change, those who are disadvantaged will seek a more advantageous order, and buyers will evolve. Eventually the established paradigm fades away as buyers evolve or collapses as a result of innovation. From that change a new paradigm arises, and the process continues, as illustrated in Figure 1.4.

This process of competition is well illustrated by the automobile industry. Invented by Karl Benz, the first automobiles were individually manufactured luxuries. Henry Ford created the low-cost, no-variety concept that brought the car to the masses. Shortly after his success, Alfred P. Sloan created the mass-variety idea with the founding of General Motors, imitated by Ford, Chrysler, and others. Toyota developed the current dominant concept associated with limited variety, high quality, and low price. This, too, has been imitated by others. In each paradigm, the competitive game differed significantly from the previous paradigm. Some changes were enabled by technological innovation, such as mass production, while others were the result of strategic innovation, such as General Motors. Each paradigm clearly produced competitive advantage for some and competitive disadvantage for others. For example, Ford dominated the low-cost concept, but General Motors clearly dominated Ford by using the mass-variety paradigm.

UNDERSTANDING COMPETITIVE ADVANTAGE

The goal of competitive strategy is to create competitive advantage. Traditional concepts of competitive advantage have focused on industry analysis, unique resources, and customer focus. Some industries are surely more attractive than others due to economic structure that limits entry, reduces competition, and increases profits. Furthermore, within an industry, some firms possess unique, valuable skills that improve their performance. Some firms more effectively meet customers' needs, creating value that translates directly into higher profits. Beyond these sources, the competitive process illustrated in Figure 1.4 reveals new avenues for creating competitive advantage. Gaining those insights requires a deeper understanding of the competitive process it reflects.

Social Rivalry

The process of competition in Figure 1.4 is a *social* process. Social processes differ in at least four fundamental ways from a biological process (survival of the fittest) that is typically associated with competition: First, the rules of the game are created by consensus among buyers and sellers. In other words, those who play the game define the rules. Second, changing the rules of the game requires only achieving a new consensus. Third, the paradigm creates winners and losers among competitors. Those disadvantaged have an incentive to replace the paradigm with a new one; those advantaged by the paradigm have the incentive to preserve it, creating a tension between winners and losers. Fourth, elimination from the game—death in the biological world—is not inevitable, unambiguous, or permanent in social rivalry. Unlike living beings, corporations are social creations and have the possibility of infinite life. Bankruptcy may signal the end of one form of a corporation but it is by no means *the end*. So long as investors have confidence in an organization it can rise from death, unlike mere mortals.

The social view suggests that competition may be viewed as a series of card games, rather than a process of natural selection. Each player starts with certain resources, and all players are subject to the natural laws of probability. The cards fall as they may. The rules of the game, however, are not left to natural selection. The rules are established by agreement among all players. For example, all players must agree on the number of cards, the process for drawing cards, the way they are played (face up, face down), and the ordering of the resulting hands. Without such an agreement, there simply is no game. Subject to agreed-upon rules, players will use different strategies; some will win and others will lose. Some players may be forced from the game if their funds are depleted; they are free to compete again, and possibly win, if they can secure additional funds. Eventually, one player will emerge as winner. Winning in such a context is much more than skill or good fortune. Winning depends on designing the game wisely so that it exploits your advantages and opponents' weaknesses, and then exercising those advantages (and hopefully receiving some good fortune along the way). Having confident investors never hurts, of course.

In markets, competition is much more complex than a simple game of cards, and the stakes can be much greater. But there are important similarities. In all markets, the nature of the game, at least initially, is completely undefined. Buyers lack the knowledge to create a meaningful game. It awaits definition. Before Motorola created the technology to make cellular phones, buyers did not have enough understanding of the impact of cellular technology on their lives to make meaningful judgments about it. Similarly, at any point in a market, the future is undefined. It awaits definition. Once defined, the game begins.

Defining the Game: Market Pioneering

The battle to define the future (and set the rules of the game) begins with the definition of the market. Wrigley's chewing gum, Coca-Cola drinks, Levi's blue jeans, Gerber baby food, and Kleenex tissues all created the markets that they continue to lead. Although pioneers such as these are indeed overtaken by later entrants, many pioneers continue to outsell their rivals for years, sometimes decades. In some cases, the length of time in which these brands have led their markets is nothing short of remarkable. Levi Strauss & Company, founded in 1853, remains the best-selling blue jean company in the world more than 150 years later, as does Coca-Cola, which was founded in 1886.

Pioneering a market produces many significant competitive advantages. Pioneers are often better known, more easily recalled, and, therefore, chosen more frequently, even if they are perceived as identical to others in all important respects. Human memory is not at all like a computer memory, where all encoded information is recalled with equal ease and precision. A pioneer is more easily recalled and, therefore, considered more frequently. The pioneer can set the standard for later entrants, becoming strongly associated and even synonymous with the category (think of Kleenex or Coca-Cola). As the standard, the pioneer can influence the perceptions that buyers develop and the value buyers attach to perceived similarities and differences among brands. Coca-Cola or Levi's have had a huge, enduring impact on how buyers think about colas and jeans. Experience with the pioneer affects consumers' choice strategy. Being better known the pioneer is lower risk, which affects consumers' price sensitivity. Combined, these differences in awareness, perception, preferences, and choices create a significant competitive advantage.[17]

The empirical evidence on the benefits associated with pioneering are substantial. Figure 1.5 shows a study of market share relative to the pioneer, adjusted for differences in marketing strategy based on brands' orders of entry

Figure 1.5
Relative Market Share Based on Order of Entry

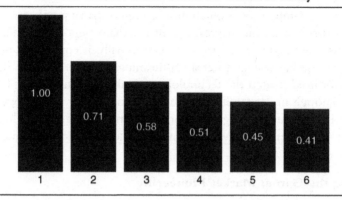

into the market.[18] Across all brands and all categories, Figure 1.5 suggests that the second entrant typically earns about 70 percent of the market share of the pioneer, the third entrant earns 60 percent, and so on until the sixth entrant earns less than half the market share of the pioneer. This contradicts expectations. It is reasonable to suspect that if two brands pursue the same marketing strategy, both should achieve the same results, dividing the market. Figure 1.5 shows that expectation is contradicted. To achieve the same sales, later entrants need to spend more on advertising, select a lower price, and offer a superior product. This creates a burden that the pioneer does not share. This effect, dubbed *pioneering advantage*, has been reported in a wide range of markets.

Fast Following

Observation suggests that some firms have achieved success not through pioneering but through fast following. Fast followers typically enter the market soon after its emergence, on a large scale, but without dramatic innovation. Such imitation has proven to be a successful strategy in many markets. For example, Yahoo pioneered Internet search engines only to be overtaken by Google; the de Havilland Comet created the commercial aircraft market that Boeing soon led; Raytheon was overtaken in microwave ovens; and IBM eclipsed Sperry-Univac in mainframe computers.[19]

What advantages arise from fast following? One study offers some potential insight. The study examines the impact of marketing activity, order of entry, sales diffusion, and the timing of entry (pioneer, growth-stage, or late-stage entry) on the sales of 29 pharmaceutical brands in six markets. In these markets, fast followers grow faster than the pioneers because buyers are more responsive to their product quality, and fast followers are less vulnerable to the success of competitors.[20] These findings suggest that entry at the right moment in the evolution of a market can facilitate growth and provide significant insulation from competitors. By entering soon after the emergence of a market, the fast follower can become the brand with which many consumers first gain experience. As a result, fast followers can be seen as lower risk, better known, and distinctively positioned. They can establish the standard in a market and enjoy many of the advantages associated with pioneering. Fast following, however, requires scale, resources, and nimbleness, characteristics that are not found in all organizations.

Differentiation

Differentiation is a classic competitive strategy. The goal of differentiation is to create a meaningful difference between one alternative and its rivals within an established paradigm, in order to shape rather than redefine the competitive game. Any aspect of buyer knowledge can be the basis for differentiation. A brand can be distinguished by a unique image, thus providing an advantage of being recalled more easily and more often. For example, for years Morton Salt has been strongly associated with an advertising campaign claiming that "When it rains it pours." Salt is sodium chloride and has no meaningful product differentiation, but as a result of more effective advertising, it is better known and chosen more often. Similarly, Perrier is more sophisticated than La Croix water and Volvos are safe (if unexciting) compared to BMWs.

Some brands are distinguished by offering more value than competitors on a common dimension of value. Toyotas may be more dependable than their rival cars, for example. Brands can be differentiated by being easier to choose; they are a powerful device for helping consumers make choices among many otherwise similar alternatives. Brands can even be differentiated through the use of an irrelevant but distinguishing attribute to simplify brand choice.[21] These differences become meaningful if they become part of the social consensus. Volvo need not be the safest car, but it needs to be strongly associated with safety in the minds of buyers. Important differences are, therefore, *created* rather than *discovered*.

Differentiation has many advantages. With a strong brand, a company's products are more easily recognized, more easily recalled, more competitively distinct. That uniqueness is the basis for competitive advantage and the value of the brand itself. If a brand loses its uniqueness, it loses its effectiveness as a brand. As such, brands are intangible assets. The value of brands in the minds of consumers translates into value for the owners of those brands. Changes in key intangible factors, such as brand assets, have a significant effect on the stock market valuation of the firm. This link between brand and market value has been documented across a wide variety of markets and environments. These analyses show a significant positive link between changes in brand strength and stock return, suggesting that a brand is an asset with the ability to generate a stream of future cash flows.[22]

Redefining Markets

Another avenue for creating competitive advantage is redefining an established market. This amounts to defining the next-generation paradigm. As discussed earlier, technological innovation, strategic innovation, and capitalizing on buyer change are effective at creating a new paradigm within an established market. In personal computing, IBM pioneered the market, Microsoft overtook IBM with a shift in value from hardware to software, and Google appears poised to take the lead from Microsoft as the technology shifts to cloud-based computing. Each new generation of technology brings the opportunity to redefine the market. Even without technological change, strategic innovation can create new paradigms, as illustrated by the automobile industry. As new buyers enter a market without established concepts, brands can use that point of entry to redefine the market, as Pepsi has done in its rivalry with Coca-Cola or as Toyota has done following its entry into the United States.

Research suggests that these innovative late movers enjoy enduring competitive advantage through the same mechanisms that produce pioneering advantage. In one study of two prescription drug markets, researchers examined the success of the pioneers, innovative late entrants, and imitative later entrants. Analyzing brand sales over time as a function of marketing activities, the success of competitors, and other factors, the study shows that pioneers enjoy clear advantages: Buyers are less responsive to the marketing spending of imitators compared to pioneers, while imitators grow more slowly, have lower potential sales and lower rates of repeat purchase, and have no effect on pioneers' sales as a result of their marketing activities. Innovative late movers, however, enjoy important competitive advantages relative to the pioneer. Innovative later entrants create larger potential markets, grow faster, and have higher rates of repeat purchase. As innovative late entrants become more successful, their sales momentum slows the growth of the pioneer and reduces the effectiveness of the pioneer's marketing efforts. The success of an innovative late mover, in other words, creates a clear *disadvantage* for the pioneer. To achieve the same level of sales, the pioneer now must spend more, price lower, or offer a more appealing product. Innovation thus produces a late-mover *advantage*, which is ironically based on the same processes that create pioneering advantage.[23]

SUMMARY

Drucker's call to create customers leads marketers down an interesting path. By creating customers—segmenting markets, selecting target markets, developing value propositions, and delivering value to solve problems—buyers learn, and as buyers learn, markets become established. Marketing strategy simultaneously creates value for buyers and creates markets and the competitive game. Rather than a race to meet some prespecified consumer objective, competition becomes a struggle to influence what buyers know and, as a result, how they behave. This ultimately influences the rules of the game. Organizations compete over every aspect of buyer knowledge: how to define the category, how brands within that category are perceived, how valuable differences should be, and how consumers should choose among the alternatives in the category. Defining the game, even if for a brief interval, can create enormous benefits. Those who are disadvantaged will eventually create a new paradigm, or the prevailing one will fall victim to changes in buyers. This creative destruction produces another period of strategic turmoil, from which a new stability will emerge, and so the process continues. Rather than being a race to make the better mouse trap, or to identify the optimal competitive strategy, competition produces a sequence of paradigms. Each produces winners and losers, victors and victims, and each falls victim to change. Competition becomes a battle to define the future of the market, to create tomorrow's customers. In such a world, competitive advantage is, as Drucker might agree, the fruit of marketing and innovation.

Gregory S. Carpenter is the James Farley/Booz Allen Hamilton Professor of Marketing Strategy and a former chair of the Marketing Department at the Kellogg School of Management, Northwestern University. He is also director of the Kellogg School's Center for Market Leadership, a research center focused on understanding competitive strategy and competitive advantage. He received his BA from Ohio Wesleyan University, and MBA, MPhil, and PhD degrees from Columbia University.

NOTES

1. Drucker, Peter (1973), *Management: Tasks, Responsibilities, Practices*, New York: Harper & Row, 61.

2. Drucker, Peter (1973), *Management: Tasks, Responsibilities, Practices*, New York: Harper & Row, 63.

3. For the importance of the marketing concept in the field of marketing, see P. Kotler, and K. Keller (2003), *Marketing Management*, Englewood Cliffs, NJ: Prentice Hall. For a discussion of the role of the marketing concept in strategic management, see Besanko, Dranove, and Shanley (2009), *Economics of Strategy*, New York: John Wiley & Sons.

4. For example, see Peters, Thomas J., and Robert H. Waterman, Jr. (1982), *In Search of Excellence: Lessons from America's Best Run Companies*, New York: Harper & Row, and P. Barwise, and S. Meehan (2004), *Simply Better: Winning and Keeping Customers by Delivering What Matters Most*, Boston: Harvard Business School Press.

5. Fornell, C., S. Mithas, F. Morgeson, and M. Krishnan (2006), "Customer Satisfaction and Stock Prices: High Returns, Low Risk," *Journal of Marketing*, January, 15–33.

6. Aksoy, L., B. Cooil, C. Groening, T. Keiningham, and A. Yalcinet (2008), "The Long Term Stock Market Valuation of Customer Satisfaction," *Journal of Marketing*, January, 105–122. Kapil, T. R., and S. Bharadwaj (2009), "Customer Satisfaction and Stock Returns Risk," *Journal of Marketing*, 73 (November), 184–197.

7. Edwards, Cliff (2005), "Shaking Up Intel's Inside," *BusinessWeek*, January 31, 35.

8. Bagozzi, R., and U. Dholokia (1999), "Goal Setting and Goal Striving in Consumer Behavior," *Journal of Marketing*, 63, 19–32.

9. Tybout, A. M., and G. S. Carpenter (1998), "Meeting the Challenge of the Post-Modern Consumer," *Financial Times, Mastering Marketing* supplement, October 5, 1–2.

10. Professor John A. Howard's pioneering research describes how buyer decision making evolves over the product lifecycle. See Howard, John A. (1989), *Consumer Behavior in Marketing Strategy*, Upper Saddle River, NJ: Prentice Hall.

11. Hauser, J. R., and Birger Wernerfelt (1990), "An Evaluation Cost Model of Consideration Sets," *Journal of Consumer Research*, March 16, 393–408.

12. Carpenter, G. S., and K. Nakamoto (1989), "Consumer Preference Formation and Pioneering Advantage," *Journal of Marketing Research*, 285–298.

13. Tushman, M., and W. Smith (2002), "Organizational Technology," in J. Baum (Ed.), *The Blackwell Companion to Organizations*. United Kingdom: Blackwell Publishers, 386–414.

14. Henderson, R., and K. Clark (1990), "Architectural Innovation: The Reconfiguration of Existing Product Technologies and the Failure of Established Firms," *Administrative Science Quarterly*, 35, 9–30.

15. Chan, W. K., and R. Mauborgne (2004), "Blue Ocean Strategy," *Harvard Business Review*, October, 76–84.

16. For an excellent analysis of the impact of social change on markets, see H. Rao (2009), *Market Rebels: How Activists Make or Break Radical Innovations*, Princeton, NJ: Princeton University Press.

17. Lieberman, M., and D. B. Montgomery (1998), "First-Mover (Dis)Advantages: Retrospective and Link with the Resource-Based View," *Strategic Management Journal*, 19, 1111–1122.

18. Urban, G. L., T. Carter, S. Gaskin, and Z. Mucha (1986), "Market Share Rewards to Pioneering Brands: An Empirical Analysis and Strategic Implications," *Management Science*, 32, 645–659.

19. Schnaars, S. P. (1994), *Managing Imitation Strategies: How Later Entrants Seize Markets from Pioneers*, New York: The Free Press.

20. Shankar, V., G. S. Carpenter, and L. Krishnamurthi (1999), "The Advantages of Entry in the Growth Stage of the Product Lifecycle: An Empirical Analysis," *Journal of Marketing Research*, 36, 2 (May), 269–276.

21. Brown, C., and G. S. Carpenter (2000), "Why is the Trivial Important? A Reasons-Based Account for the Effects of Trivial Attributes on Choice," *Journal of Consumer Research*, 26 (4), 372–385.

22. See, for example, Aaker, D. A., and R. Jacobson (1994), "The Financial Information Content of Perceived Quality," *Journal of Marketing Research*, May, 191–201, and Barth, M. E., M. Clement, G. Foster, and R. Kasznik (1998) "Brand Values and Capital Market Valuation," *Review of Accounting Studies*, 3, 41–68.

23. Shankar, V., G. S. Carpenter, and Lakshman Krishnamurthi (1998), "Late Mover Advantage: How Innovative Late Entrants Outsell Pioneers," *Journal of Marketing Research,* 35, 54–70.

CHAPTER 2

Identifying Market Segments and Selecting Targets

ALICE M. TYBOUT and KENT GRAYSON

Introduction

The Hyatt hotel chain offers a variety of brands in order to serve different types of travelers and use occasions. Park Hyatt properties are designed for affluent, individual business travelers who desire elegant, contemporary luxury and attentive, personalized service. These properties, which are found in major cities around the world, feature high-end art collections in the public spaces and award-winning chefs in the kitchens of the restaurants. Hyatt Regency properties cater to a somewhat less elite traveler and, accordingly, offer more modest furnishings and food. A subset of Park Hyatt and Hyatt Regency properties are sub-branded as "resorts," conveying that these properties are tailored to travelers who seek a full-fledged vacation rather than a short-term stay for business or leisure. Hyatt Summerfield Suites were developed to address the needs of business travelers on extended assignments. These suites resemble furnished condominiums, providing everything the traveler might need to prepare meals, relax, and socialize.

Hyatt recently launched yet another brand, Hyatt Place. These properties were developed in response to market research that identified an emerging segment of travelers who live a 24/7 technology-enhanced lifestyle that blurs the distinction between work and leisure. They work at home while listening to music or keeping one eye on the television, and they view their time on the road as an opportunity for both work and personal growth and relaxation.

Hyatt Place addresses the needs of these travelers by offering a casual hospitality similar to what travelers might experience at home. Rooms include a living area with a sofa-sleeper, a 42-inch flat panel, high-definition television with access to a wide range of channels, a plug panel that enables guests to connect their own entertainment media to the high-definition TV, and free Wi-Fi access. Common areas, such as the wine café, bakery, and TV den, allow guests to socialize, while the StayFit@Hyatt gym enables guests to maintain their fitness regimen.

However, despite its many brands, Hyatt does not attempt to address the needs of all travelers and use occasions. There are no Hyatt properties for the traveler who merely wants a basic room at a bargain-basement price.

Hyatt's strategy illustrates two key elements of marketing planning: *Segmentation* and *targeting*. Segmentation involves dividing the market of potential customers into homogeneous subgroups. These subgroups may be distinguished in terms of behavior patterns, attitudes, demographic characteristics, psychographic profile, and the like. Targeting then involves selecting those subgroups whose needs the firm has the capability of addressing and designing offerings in accord with those needs. Although it is relatively easy to identify examples of successful segmentation and targeting, such as that done by Hyatt, many managers find undertaking these tasks for their own products and services daunting. One reason is that the list of potential ways to segment a market is seemingly endless, making it difficult to decide where to begin. Further, once the segmentation analysis is complete, many or even all of the subgroups may appear to be attractive targets, making it difficult to set priorities for allocating resources.

The goal of this chapter is to address the challenges of segmentation and targeting by offering a *strategic* approach that begins with a focus on patterns of usage. This approach may be particularly valuable to companies that are just beginning to embrace segmentation and targeting. It also may be helpful to companies that are experienced at these tasks and are seeking a fresh approach. Customers are grouped according to category use, brand use, and perhaps also the frequency, occasion, and purpose of use of either the category or brand. The resulting subgroups are then characterized in terms of other factors, such as demographics, geographic location, attitudes, and lifestyle—factors that both distinguish between the groups and that are relevant to marketing decisions. Once segmentation is complete, targets are selected by prioritizing the subgroup(s) whose needs can be better served by the company versus its competitors. Before turning to the details of how to segment and target, we briefly consider the question of whether segmentation is necessary at all.

WHY SEGMENT?

For marketers, segmentation is usually considered to be the strategy of last resort. Managers would rather attract a single, large universe of potential buyers than partition the market into subgroups and target one or several of these subgroups. Occasionally, if consumer preferences are sufficiently homogeneous, it is possible to appeal to nearly everyone in a particular market (see later discussion of "mass marketing"). For example, Arm & Hammer has been able to pursue all potential baking soda users due to a lack of competition as well as a lack of variation in customer preferences.

When a new product or service category is created, customers may have little choice but to accept a "one-size-fits-all" offering from the category pioneer. However, if the market offers attractive margins as well as low barriers to entry, competitors are likely to enter and differentiate from the pioneer by providing offerings that are more closely aligned with the preferences of some subgroup of customers. For example, Apple's entry into the personal computer market with an operating system that was more user-friendly and intuitive than IBM's effectively segmented a universal market into two types of customers: those who preferred Macs that were easy to use versus those who preferred PCs that were "safe" because they were the industry standard. Likewise, the introduction of personal digital assistants (PDAs) based on Microsoft's operating system segmented the market previously dominated by Palm's PalmPilot. The market segmented to include customers who wanted a PDA that integrated seamlessly with enterprise PC software and those who were drawn to the elegant simplicity and ease of use of the PalmPilot.

Although it may seem counterintuitive, segmenting the market and tailoring the marketing strategy to a subgroup of potential customers may prove to be more profitable than attracting a broader customer base. The experience of Yorkie candy bar in the United Kingdom is a case in point. The Yorkie bar is a calorie-heavy "meal replacement" that features blue-collar men in its advertising. Nevertheless, historically 40 percent of Yorkie's sales were to women who were also interested in meal replacement. When research revealed that women were becoming more concerned about calories, and Yorkie's main competitor showed signs of targeting women, Yorkie chose to sharpen its focus on men, positioning the product in its advertising as "not for girls." Although the campaign may have alienated some female customers, it energized the targeted male customers and resulted in a net sales increase.

As implied by the Yorkie example, segmentation and targeting go hand-in-hand with positioning, the topic of Chapter 4, "Developing a Compelling Brand Positioning." A successful segmentation strategy is one that yields a target(s) for which the firm can develop a compelling positioning and meet its growth goals. If the strategy for a product involves trying to attract two distinct customer segments with two different needs, efforts to appeal to both segments with a single positioning are likely to fail because they will not be optimal for either segment. Sometimes this problem can be solved by adopting different positioning strategies to different segments. However, when the positioning is conveyed by using media seen by both segments, this may create confusion or alienate core customers.

Consider Eastern Mountain Sports (EMS), an outdoor apparel and equipment retailer in the northeastern United States. EMS discovered that its products appealed not only to its intended target—people who are passionate about the outdoors and who purchase clothing and gear to help them live their passion—but also to people who simply liked outdoorsy clothing. However, when the company adjusted its product line and advertising in an effort to embrace both segments, it ran into trouble. The outdoor enthusiasts interpreted the move as a reduced commitment to serving their needs. Rather than risk alienating its profitable core customer base, EMS quickly reverted to focusing on serving the needs of the outdoor enthusiast.

Because customer preferences for products and services in most categories are heterogeneous, firms often find it difficult to attract everyone with a single marketing program. This is where segmenting becomes important, allowing a company to tailor marketing efforts toward subgroups of consumers who are likely to be most responsive to their offerings, resulting in maximized profits.

THE EVOLUTION OF APPROACHES TO SEGMENTATION

Firms have not always focused on market segmentation and targeting. In the United States immediately following World War II, conditions enabled companies to adopt what is sometimes called a "mass marketing" approach, emphasizing what people had in common rather than how they differed. Men returned from war, married, and began families, creating the Baby Boom. Many took advantage of the GI Bill to attend college, which they combined with new skills learned during the war to fuel upward mobility and create a large middle class. The U.S. government's investment in infrastructure projects such as highways enabled these middle-class households to live in suburban communities, where they shared experiences not only in their personal lives but also in the lives they experienced vicariously through the newly affordable radios and televisions (which offered a limited range of programming). These factors resulted in a large market of customers whose needs and preferences were relatively homogeneous and who could be efficiently reached through network programming. In the 1960s an advertiser could reach 80 percent of U.S. women with a spot aired simultaneously on CBS, NBC, and ABC.

At that time, companies' capabilities were well-matched to serving the needs of such a market. Recent innovations in manufacturing enabled firms to produce large quantities of the same product cost-effectively; commercials inserted in radio and network television programming provided an efficient way to reach consumers and tout the benefits of these products. New, large-scale retailers emerged to serve the needs of suburban communities and provided an efficient means for producers to distribute their goods. Thus, U.S. companies enjoyed the luxury of appealing to most consumers by focusing on what they had in common rather than how they differed.

Since that time, many developed markets have become more differentiated and fragmented. Some marketing managers still focus on important similarities among these fragments in an effort to identify a target segment that is large and inclusive. Walmart focuses on low prices and good value—a benefit that is attractive to downscale and upscale consumers alike, and one that encourages more than a third of U.S. consumers to shop at the store each week. The 100 million weekly Walmart shoppers are often further segmented on dimensions such as life stage and attitudes. However, by defining its target segment primarily in terms of need for value, Walmart is able to focus on a large cross-section of consumers because, despite their differences, these consumers share an important need.

In practice, few companies are able to segment the market in a way that defines such a large set of target consumers. Managers in recent decades have therefore placed a greater emphasis on market niches that reflect different preferences attributable to differences in demographics, lifestyle, life stage, or values and attitudes. The 32-year-old woman with a young child may or may not be married, may or may not be in the workforce, and may or may not think that shopping "green" is important. All of these factors are likely to color her view of alternative brands of detergent and the type of car she buys. Furthermore, although a broad cross section of consumers shop at Walmart, the company's customer base has an income that is lower than average, political beliefs that are more conservative than average, and a lower-than-average likelihood of holding a bank account when compared to customers of Costco. Thus, even Walmart's broad appeal resonates more with some and less with others.

The insight that consumers differ in their preferences and will be more responsive to marketing efforts tailored to their needs is not new. However, advances in technology enable marketers to address the needs of ever-narrower targets more profitably than they could in the past. The Internet and smart phone technology, as well as a proliferation of vehicles in traditional media (cable channels, specialized magazines, etc.), make it possible to reach smaller segments of consumers in a cost-effective manner. Further, mass customization techniques allow producers to quickly and efficiently tailor their offerings to customers' tastes. Want M&Ms to match your office decor and sport the company logo? No problem, just order online. Are you a chocolate lover seeking a Caribbean escape vacation? A quick search online will turn up several options, including a stay at the Cotton Tree Lodge in Belize, where guests harvest cacao pods, make their own chocolate, and learn about fair-trade issues from members of the Toledo Cacao Grower's Association.

In his book *The Long Tail,* Chris Anderson argues that innovations in technology make marketing narrowly targeted goods and services as economically attractive as marketing more mainstream fare.[1] Consider products such as movies, games, books, or software. Historically, the high production, distribution, and promotion costs meant that only a few well-funded players could afford to compete, and they required a focus on blockbusters. However, advances in technology such as digital video cameras, desktop music and editing software, or desktop publishing enable any creatively minded individual to record a song or movie, publish a book, or design a new game. Further, digital versions of products can be stored digitally and distributed online for almost no cost, in contrast to the high inventory carrying costs a manufacturer or retailer incurs when these products are distributed in hard copy format. Finally, instead of the producer investing in an extensive mass-media advertising campaign in hopes of reaching prospective customers, search engines, blogs, and other filtering devices allow customers to efficiently search a near-infinite array of offerings to find the ones that suit their idiosyncratic tastes. Although Anderson's view has generated some debate, there can be no doubt that technology has made it economically viable to reach smaller segments with more targeted offerings.[2] As a result, new ventures such as TCHO, an artisanal chocolate company offering "fair trade" chocolate, are able to reach the niche of customers who care about the origins of their chocolate bar. Similarly, established players such as Amazon are able to strengthen their hold on the book market by serving customers in search of the latest blockbuster and customers looking for one-of-a-kind books.

How segments are defined has also evolved over time. In the early days of market segmentation, focus centered on identifying subgroups based on descriptive characteristics such as demographics and geography. The logic was that men and women, young and old, rich and poor, northerners and southerners would differ in their preferences and, therefore, require different marketing programs. Although this holds true in some situations, often there is significant variation among individuals who share the same demographic profile. Accordingly, segmentation schemes based on attitudes, values, opinions, and lifestyle were developed. This so-called "psychographic" approach identifies subgroups of "Thinkers," "Experiencers," and the like, each of whom shares a set of psychological and attitudinal characteristics. Segments defined by psychographics have proven to be especially helpful when designing marketing communications. However, psychographics are often poor predictors of specific behaviors related to a category and brand. As a result, in an effort to segment in ways that help managers set strategic priorities, there has been a recent emphasis on partitioning the market based on usage patterns and related behaviors.[3] Brand users may be distinguished from competitors' users and nonusers of the category. Further segmentation may identify subgroups based on when and how often usage occurs and whether the user is actively loyal to the brand, endorsing it to others.

Our view is that an insightful and actionable approach to segmentation requires not choosing among the different approaches to segmentation but rather combining them. It is important to understand who (demographics and geography) is engaging in what behavior (usage) and why (psychographics and specific motivations). At the same time, the insight provided by different bases for segmentation will vary as a function of the decision being made.

Consider Vosges, a company that makes exotic "East meets West" chocolates, such as the Black Pearl Bar, which combines ginger, wasabi, black sesame seeds, and dark chocolate. If Vosges were to segment the market based on *who* is most likely to purchase its products, it might divide the market based on gender (women versus men), age (25 to 35 versus 35 to 45), or geography (urban versus rural). Or if the company segmented the market based on *what* behaviors customers exhibit in relation to the product category, it might divide the market based on those who do or don't purchase high-end chocolate, those who buy frequently versus infrequently, or those who buy from a particular competitor. Another alternative is focusing on *why* consumers buy the product, in which case Vosges might divide the market based on people who are buying for a gift versus themselves, or people who buy because they love chocolate in particular versus those who like all kinds of artisan food products.

As the Vosges example illustrates, all of the dimensions (who, what, and why) contribute to a rich understanding of segments in the marketplace and the attractiveness of targeting these segments. Nevertheless, different dimensions of a targeted segment will be more or less relevant depending on the decision at hand. For example, if Vosges were making decisions related to selecting new retail outlets, information about where targeted customers live and shop would be critical; whereas if the company were designing communications, information about the motives for purchase as well as general values, aspirations, and attitudes would be more informative.

USAGE-BASED SEGMENTATION

We recommend that companies begin the segment definition process by creating subgroups based on *patterns of usage*. In general, current usage is most likely to predict (albeit imperfectly) future usage. Therefore, understanding current usage patterns helps marketers prioritize targets and design marketing strategies to achieve the firm's goals by altering current usage patterns.

The usage-based segmentation approach begins by dividing the market into subgroups on the basis of current behavior patterns. Nonusers of the category are separated from users, and users are grouped according to the brand that they use. Users of a brand may be further segmented based on their frequency, occasion, and motivation for use.

Next, the usage segments are analyzed and understood in terms of the demographic, geographic, psychographic, and motivational characteristics that distinguish them from each other. These characteristics help the marketer estimate the current size and growth potential of a segment from population data, select media that reaches a particular segment in a cost-effective manner, and tailor communications to the general lifestyle, values, and attitudes of the segment.

Finally, the current and potential profit associated with a segment is estimated. Some segments may be well-defined in terms of their usage and descriptive characteristics, but they may be unattractive targets because their long-term value is low and/or there are too few members in the segment to justify a unique marketing effort.

Segmenting Steps

The first step in usage-based segmentation is to divide the market into users and nonusers of the product category. This categorization is valuable because users and nonusers pose different challenges for the marketer. Nonusers may be unaware of the category and its benefits or believe that the category does not fit their needs. They also may be ineligible to use the product (i.e., 16-year-olds are not legally permitted to consume beer). Marketers must overcome these barriers when targeting nonusers. For example, to attract nonusers, a vacation cruise company will need to spend resources describing the experience of taking a cruise, dispelling potential misconceptions about cruises, and explaining how a cruise is different from (and better than) other categories of vacation experiences, such as visiting a resort.

Category users are familiar with and (presumably) find some value in consuming within the category. Thus, the task is to sustain and perhaps expand their usage. Usually marketers further segment users on the basis of brand—do they use your brand or a competitor's brand? Consumers generally choose a particular brand because they believe that it provides a benefit that is different from (and presumably better than) other brands. Thus, current customers are likely to be more receptive to the firm's marketing efforts. Further, a firm typically can obtain more detailed data on its customers versus competitors' customers. This data may allow more efficient, customized marketing activities directed at current customers. These advantages become challenges when a firm attempts to attract the customers of a competing brand.

Marketplaces often include consumers who are not loyal to any single brand. For example, some consumers are variety seekers who habitually consume a handful of brands, rather than just one. Others are price-conscious consumers who gravitate to whatever brand offers the lowest price or the best perceived value. These additional usage segments (and the associated challenges) are important to consider when developing a usage-based segmentation plan.

The basic segmentation of customers into nonusers, brand users, and competitor-brand users is often further refined by considering the level and occasion of use. These variables help identify customers who differ in their value to the firm. Frequently, a small number of customers or use occasions account for a disproportionate amount of brand usage. Indeed, brand usage is often said to follow the "80/20 rule," where 80 percent of consumption is done by 20 percent of the users. This statistic holds true for most major beer brands, as well as fast-food franchises such as McDonald's. Further, use occasion and brand loyalty may be associated with the level of use; heavy users may use the brand across multiple occasions and may be highly loyal. For example, a heavy drinker of Bud Light may drink the brand nightly at home as well as in a bar on the weekend, and he may endorse the brand to friends. By contrast, a light drinker might drink the brand only occasionally in a bar and also drink other brands of beer. Similarly, frequent customers of Hyatt hotels are business travelers who stay on weeknights and are vested in the company's frequent stay program, whereas light users are leisure travelers who stay on weekends.

The purchase motivation or purpose of a product or service should also be considered. Purchasing may be motivated by features of the product, such as its price, performance, or convenience, or by how the product makes the purchaser feel or appear to others when using it. Knowledge of the primary motivation for purchasing is useful when deciding how to position a product. For example, a $1,299 ecologically friendly washing machine might be presented as "saving the consumer $90 per year on water bills" or as being "good for the environment," depending on whether the target is more likely to be motivated by functional versus emotional considerations (see Chapter 4, "Developing a Compelling Brand Positioning," and Chapter 6, "Creating and Managing Brands").

One factor that influences the motivation for purchase is the role that the targeted individual plays in the purchase process, which is sometimes called the "buying center." Buying center roles include the influencer, decider, purchaser, and user. In categories such as toys or presweetened cereals, parents typically play the roles of deciders and purchasing agents while children are influencers and users. Parents are likely to weigh heavily functional considerations such as the nutritional value and safety of products. In contrast, children are more likely to focus on the experience of using the product (i.e., taste, fun).

In business-to-business settings, buying center roles might be filled by engineers (influencer), VPs of marketing or finance (decider), purchasing agents (purchaser), and operatives (user). These individuals are often rewarded differently, leading to different motivations. For example, the compensation of a CFO might be tied to the overall profitability of the firm, the compensation of a purchasing agent might be based on extracting price concessions from suppliers, and the compensation of a plant foreman (who actually uses the products) might be tied to measures of production efficiency.

The astute marketer understands that the motivations of those playing different roles in the decision process vary and thus focuses the marketing effort on the person in a household or company whose motives are best served by the firm's brand. Such was the case when Philips sought to make inroads into General Electric's (GE) dominant position in the lighting industry. GE focused on corporate purchasers, who seek lower purchase prices and longer bulb life. GE's strong share position gave the company economies of scale that allowed them to market traditional fluorescent bulbs for as little as 80 cents, a price that competitors could not match. However, such bulbs have a hidden cost due to their high content of toxic mercury. Replacing a traditional fluorescent bulb can cost $1 due to restrictions in collection and disposal and due to the need for legal protections against damage in dumping sites. Although purchasing agents are not sensitive to these replacement costs, corporate financial officers are. Philips developed Alto, a low-mercury bulb that can be disposed in the regular trash, and they marketed it to corporate financial officers. The bulb gained favorable press coverage and political support due to its environment-friendly status. More importantly, thanks to Philips's decision to target a different role

Figure 2.1
Usage-Based Segmentation Tree for Hotels

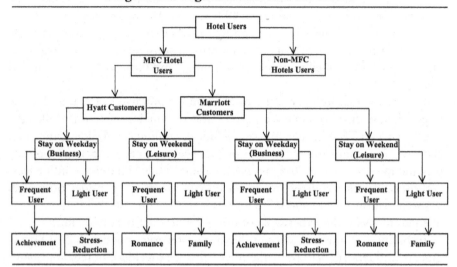

in the buying center, the company was able to win some new customers and deliver high margins, despite GE's historical stronghold on the lighting business.

An example of a usage-based segmentation tree for customers in the "mass first class (MFC)" hotel industry appears in Figure 2.1. For simplicity, only two hotel chains that compete in this category, Hyatt and Marriott, are shown. Although the tree could be expanded to include additional players such as Westin, Sheraton, and Renaissance, often a company focuses on its most direct competitors when segmenting a market based on usage.

Profile Characteristics

Having initially defined segments based on behaviors and motivations for behaviors, the firm can turn to questions about who exhibits these behaviors. Such information is critical to assessing the attractiveness of targeting different usage segments and to designing and implementing marketing programs aimed at changing their behavior. Variables that are commonly employed at this stage in the segmentation process are discussed next.

Demographics In consumer markets, usage segments are typically described in terms of demographics such as gender, age, marital status, life stage, education, occupation, and income. Accordingly, those who frequently purchase Corona beer might be described as unmarried, college-educated men ages 20 to 25 who work in white-collar professions and have a household income between $30,000 and $40,000.

Identifying customers in terms of demographics serves several purposes. First, the profile can be applied to census data to arrive at a rough estimate of how many people share the demographic profile of the current customers. This enables the company to assess its success in penetrating the segment and the potential for further growth by attracting customers similar to current ones. Second, demographic characteristics may be helpful in making product design and pricing decisions, because market research reports often include data on the behaviors and consumption patterns of people with certain demographic characteristics. For example, if people who share the demographic profile of Hyatt Place customers have been found to be more concerned about fitness than the population at large, adding a state-of-the-art gym to each of these properties might strengthen customer loyalty. However, if people who share the demographic profile of Hyatt Place customers are typically "couch potatoes," the same dollars might be better spent on larger flat-screen televisions for the guest rooms.

Demographic characteristics also have implications for the placement and content of marketing communications. Demographics are correlated with media habits, and market research companies such as Nielsen frequently use demographic characteristics to categorize those who use different kinds of media. Young children watch different television programs than teens, teens visit different web sites and read different magazines than their parents, men attend more sporting events than women (and thus have greater exposure to venue-based advertising). If a company has a clear demographic profile for a targeted segment, it can then select media that cost-effectively reaches targeted individuals while avoiding nontargeted people.

Further, knowledge of the demographic characteristics of a target is helpful when designing communication content. If the message includes visual elements, such as a product user or spokesperson, that person can be chosen to be similar to the target customer in age, gender, and social class, reinforcing the perception that the product is for people like them. However, caution should be used here, as evidence suggests that customers' self-perceptions and aspirations may be different from reality. For example, older adults often perceive themselves as looking 10 to 15 years younger than their chronological age, so an advertisement targeted to 65-year-olds would do better featuring adults closer to age 50. Conversely, teens often aspire to appear older than their years and are likely to respond more favorably to images of people in their twenties rather than teens. Further, consumption in categories such as beauty and fashion is motivated more by aspirations than by the target's current self-perception.

In addition, demographics inform message presentation because certain demographic characteristics have been linked to differences in processing information. For example, adults 45 and older are somewhat slower than younger adults to master tasks that require skills that they did not learn earlier in life. As a result, self-paced media (such as print) are likely to be more effective than externally paced media (such as television or radio) when targeting older adults and conveying new, complex information.

Gender is also associated with different processing styles. Women tend to be communal, considering both themselves and others in decision making. In the context of marketing communications, this orientation leads women to consider disparate bits of information, such as multiple product benefits, when forming judgments. By contrast, men are more agentic, focusing more narrowly on self-expression, goal-directedness, and critical decision-making information. Accordingly, in forming their judgments, men are likely to focus on a single product benefit as well as exhibit greater reliance on prior knowledge and other cognitive shortcuts.

Finally, individuals' cultural backgrounds affect their general orientation and judgments. For example, evidence shows that people from Asian cultures tend to be more interdependent, whereas people from western cultures tend to be more independent. Like gender, this difference in orientation may influence the willingness to consider multiple benefits and perspectives when processing marketing communications and forming judgments. It suggests that Asians may be more likely to consider multiple benefits and perspectives than Westerners.

This approach is equally applicable to business-to-business markets. In these situations, potential customers can be initially divided into groups based on the usage characteristics we outlined previously (e.g., user/nonuser, user of Brand X versus Brand Y). As with consumer usage segments, business-to-business usage segments may then be further characterized in terms of distinctive descriptive characteristics, which are sometimes termed "firmographics." The most commonly used descriptive characteristics are industry/SIC code and firm size because information on the number of companies in these categories is publicly available, allowing a firm to estimate how effectively it has penetrated a segment, as well as the growth potential associated with targeting a particular segment. These characteristics are useful not only because they are easily available, but also because product and service needs often vary by industry and firm size. The electronic test equipment needs of a large telecommunications company are likely to be quite different from the needs of a small general industrial company. Industry and firm size also may be helpful in designing marketing communications. Most industries have their own publications and conferences, enabling firms in particular industries to reach these communities efficiently. Finally, the buying process may vary as a function of industry and firm size. For example, the decision process is likely to be more complex and formal when selling to the government versus private industry and when selling to a large versus a small firm.

Geography   It can be useful to describe both consumer and business segments in terms of their locations, because where customers live and work may influence their preferences and behaviors. For example, geography is often correlated with economic status. In developing countries, consumers may aspire to purchase global brands offered by companies such as Cadbury, Procter & Gamble, and Unilever, but they lack the purchasing power to afford such products in the large package sizes used in more developed countries. In response, companies introduce smaller package sizes (i.e., a single razor blade) at lower prices in these areas of the world.

Further, consumers in a particular geographic area may share a cultural orientation. For instance, individuals raised in the Japanese culture prefer different compartments for different things. This insight led Panasonic to introduce refrigerators with four to six doors in Japan, a feature unlikely to appeal to the U.S. consumer, who does not have this preference. Different geographic areas are also governed by different laws and regulations. In the alcoholic beverage market, some European countries have relatively few regulations about where liquor can be distributed and to whom it can be sold. At the other extreme, some Middle Eastern countries have tight restrictions—or even outright prohibitions—regarding the sale of alcohol. Accordingly, Diageo focuses more on marketing nonalcoholic beer in some countries than in others.

The geographic location of a segment is also important because it has implications for a variety of marketing decisions beyond product design. For example, in regions where customers are widely dispersed (rather than heavily concentrated), the sales territories are likely to be larger. Therefore, media such as outdoor advertising may not be effective, because billboards are not seen by enough customers to justify the expense.

Geographic information about customers can also provide insight about demographic characteristics. Additech, a company that markets and distributes fuel additives at the gas pumps of retailers such as Murphy U.S.A., has detailed usage data for each customer transaction (i.e., time of day, method of payment, amount and type of gas pumped, pump location), but it does not have a demographic profile of its customers. It uses transaction data to identify geographic areas with a high concentration of Additech customers and then profiles these areas demographically and psychographically using services such as Nielsen's PRIZM, which defines household types of geographic areas on 66 demographic and behavioral dimensions (http://en-us.nielsen.com/tab/product_families/nielsen_claritas/prizm).

At the same time, it is important to recognize that, just as is the case for demographic characteristics, preference will not always vary with geography. Procter & Gamble has found that teenage girls around the world have similar concerns regarding puberty. In response, the company created a global web site for products and information related to this life stage. The Phonak group, which sells hearing aids, has found that both European and American baby boomers have similar needs for enhanced hearing, as well as similar qualms about using hearing aids. These observations reinforce the importance of defining segments based on characteristics that are not merely differences, but rather differences that impact how, why, and whether the product or service is used. In the preceding P&G and Phonak examples, age segmentation is meaningful, but geographic segmentation fails to capture important differences in consumption.

Psychographics   It is also useful to characterize segments in terms of general psychological or personality traits and lifestyle. SRI Consulting Business Intelligence offers a tool for psychographic classification known as VALS. This framework classifies consumers into one of eight groups (see Figure 2.2) that vary along two dimensions—motivation and resources—on the basis of their responses to a survey. The survey asks respondents to indicate their levels of agreement/disagreement with 35 attitudinal statements such as, "I like to try new things," "I consider myself an intellectual," "I like to make things with my hands," and "The federal government should encourage prayer in public schools." The respondents also report their gender, age, education, and income.

Each of the groups is profiled in terms general motivation and decision making. For example, *thinkers* are described as:

> mature, satisfied, comfortable, and reflective people who value order, knowledge, and responsibility. They tend to be well-educated and actively seek out information in the decision-making process. They are well-informed about the world and national events and are alert to opportunities to broaden their knowledge. Thinkers have moderate respect for the status quo institutions of authority and social decorum, but are open to consider new ideas. Although their incomes allow them

Figure 2.2
VALS™ Framework

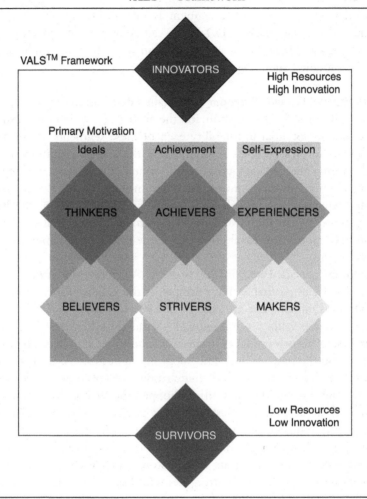

many choices, Thinkers are conservative, practical consumers; they look for durability, functionality, and value in the products they buy. (www.sric-bi.com/VALS/thinkers.shtml)

A psychographic profile of a targeted segment may be particularly helpful in designing marketing communications that resonate with those customers' general values and orientations. For example, logical arguments and data, as well as endorsements by well-regarded authorities, are likely to enhance the persuasiveness of a message with thinkers. If direct information regarding the psychographic profile of a segment is unavailable, but the segment is concentrated geographically, GEO-VALS can be used to obtain some general insight. GEO-VALS estimates the proportion of each of the eight segments across all residential zip codes and block groups.

Profitability and Growth Potential　A detailed description of the usage-based segments provides the foundation for the next step, which is assessing the current and/or potential profitability each of these segments might provide. When a firm has an established customer base, this analysis begins by scrutinizing the revenue and costs associated with serving current customer segments. Typically, data reveals that some segments are more profitable than others. For example, many airlines find that it is more profitable to serve the business traveler segment than the leisure traveler segment because business travelers typically take more trips, exhibit lower price sensitivity, and generate a higher per-trip margin.

Sometimes a detailed examination of current customers identifies subgroups that are actually unprofitable. For example, at the height of the Internet bubble, CDnow Online spent an average of $40 to acquire a customer whose estimated lifetime value was a mere $25.[4] Similarly, when Best Buy analyzed the purchasing histories of its customers, it found that 20 percent had a negative impact on the bottom line. This subgroup of customers, termed "devils," primarily purchased "loss leader" merchandise (deeply discounted products that are featured to build store traffic), shopped the Web to find rock-bottom price quotes, demanded that Best Buy make good on its lowest-price pledge, and frequently returned products, forcing their resale at a lower "open-box" discount price. Armed with this knowledge, Best Buy took measures to discourage the devils from shopping at their stores, such as charging customers a 15 percent restocking fee and cutting ties with FatWallet.com, a web site that had collected referral fees for delivering bargain-hunting consumers to Best Buy's web site.

However, in many instances, customers who might seem unprofitable in the short term become more attractive if the value of a relationship over time is considered. Gillette may lose money when it sends free razors to young men who are just beginning to shave, but the firm ultimately makes a tidy profit because a subset of these men become customers and purchase high-margin replacement blades year after year. Similarly, car dealers may make a modest profit from the sale of a car, but this is supplemented by profits from maintenance and repairs and future sales to the customers that they acquire.

Therefore, when examining the profitability of a segment, it is important to begin by calculating Customer Lifetime Value (CLV), as shown below.[5]

$$CLV = \sum_{a=1}^{N} (M_a - c_a)_r^{(a-1)} \big/ (1+i)^a - AC$$

where:

N = the number of years over which the relationship is calculated

M_a = the margin (i.e., the revenue-cost) the customer generates in year a

c_a = the cost of marketing communications or promotions targeted to the customer in year a

r = the retention rate ($r^{(n-1)}$ is the survival rate for year a)

i = the interest rate (also called discount rate, which represents the time value of money; a dollar today is worth less than a dollar next year)

AC = the initial cost to acquire a customer

An estimate of the potential profits associated with the segment can be made by multiplying the CLV by the number of customers thought to belong to the segment. In addition, the CLV formula can serve as a framework for assessing growth strategies targeted at a particular segment. For example, a manager might calculate the increase or decrease in CLV that would result if a 10 percent increase in spending on marketing communications (c_a) resulted in an increase in retention rate (r) of 2 percent.

In sum, usage patterns serve as a useful starting point for segmentation because they identify groups that pose different demand stimulation tasks for the marketing manager: Nonusers must be persuaded to use the category, users of competing brands must be persuaded to switch, and users of the firm's brand must be persuaded to remain loyal and expand their usage. Profiling usage segments in terms of their distinguishing demographic and psychographic characteristics, as well as estimating their profitability and growth potential, lays the foundation for the next step: setting targeting priorities.

SETTING TARGETING PRIORITIES

The selection of target segments should be based on the firm's current position in the market as well as its goals and resources. We begin by discussing targeting priorities for established brands and then consider how to modify this approach when the launch of a new product requires that the firm identify a target for the first time.

Established Brands in Existing Categories

When a brand is established in a product category, there are three options for growth. Growth may be achieved by (1) targeting current customers and convincing them to increase their spending on the brand, (2) targeting competitors' customers and persuading them to switch their purchasing to the firm's brand, and (3) convincing noncategory users both to consume in the category and to choose the firm's brand when so doing. We consider each of these strategies in turn.

Targeting Current Customers   Established brands, by definition, have an existing base of customers. Accordingly, a natural first step in targeting is to consider the growth potential afforded by investing resources in this segment. There are several reasons to make current customers the first priority. Current customers are aware of the brand and presumably have a more favorable disposition toward it than those who have chosen other brands or are nonusers of the category. Further, a firm is likely to have data about past purchases as well as contact information for current customers. This information allows it to deliver customized products and services, as well as messages, to current customers in a cost-effective manner. Finally, the high cost of acquiring customers means that return on investment is often greater for customer retention than customer acquisition. Specifically, one study reports that a 10 percent improvement in customer retention increases overall value of the customer base by 30 percent, whereas a 10 percent reduction in acquisition costs improves the overall value of the customer base by only 1 percent.[6] Another study reveals that increasing customer retention by as little as 5 percent can result in a corresponding 100 percent increase in profits. For example, in the case of regional banks, a 20-year customer is worth 85 percent more in profit than a 10-year customer. As the years pass, older loyal customers take out loans for cars, homes, and so on, without incurring the costs that are attendant to acquiring new clients.

The process of focusing on existing customers begins by assessing customer loyalty. Two related questions are useful in this regard. First, what percentage of customers are retained from one year (or buying period) to the next? The more customers that are retained, the more loyal the customer base is. The average customer retention in the United States is estimated to be around 80 percent, suggesting that there is room for improvement at many firms. Second, what proportion of customers' category spending does the firm capture? If the firm captures only a small percentage of a customer's category spending, this suggests opportunities for growth.

If retention is low or customers spread their category spending across multiple brands, the firm should implement strategies designed to increase loyalty. The company might implement loyalty programs, such as the frequent stay or frequent flyer rewards programs used by hotels and airlines. Or, for suppliers of frequently used products such as toiletries or pet food, customers might be encouraged to sign up for an automatic replenishment program. If the reason for defection is that customers are facing tough economic times and are trading down to store brands to save money, increasing retention may require introducing a more affordable version of the brand. Accordingly, during the 2008-09 recession, Procter & Gamble introduced Tide Basic, a product that lacks the full cleaning power of the base brand but offers good performance at a price that is competitive with store brands.

If retention is high and the firm captures the majority of a customer's current category spending, then growth might be achieved by identifying new use occasions for the product or by persuading loyal consumers that their needs would be better served by a more expensive, higher-margin version of the product. A classic example of this approach to growth has been Arm & Hammer's identification of new uses for its basic baking soda product. Building from baking soda's original cooking uses, Arm & Hammer has encouraged consumers to use the product for everything from deodorizing drains, refrigerators and carpets to whitening teeth. In a similar vein, Starbucks coffee has expanded its product line in an effort to increase the amount consumers spend each time they visit a store. Sandwiches, newspapers, coffee-making equipment, and even music on DVDs are available for sale in addition to the firm's trademark coffee. Brands such as Gillette regularly introduce improved versions of their shavers to encourage consumers to trade up to better-performing and higher-margin products.

Targeting Competitors' Customers Although it is critical to target current customers for retention and growth, the long-term success of a firm requires that it also acquire new users of the brand. One approach is to target customers of competitors' brands who are similar to the firm's current customers or who have aspirations to be like the firm's customers. These people are already users of the category, and their similarity to current customers increases the likelihood that they might be persuaded to switch to the firm's brand. Thus, Apple, whose users are considered to be young and hip, targets PC users who are (or aspire to be) seen as young and hip. Similarly, the Dove brand, which has aligned itself with women who accept the body changes that come with aging, targets users of competing brands, such as Olay, who may be attracted to this attitude.

However, a word of caution is in order. Efforts to steal competitors' customers sometimes provoke a counterattack, especially if the competitors' core business is threatened. For example, Burger King spent $100 million to promote the superiority of its new fries over those offered by McDonald's. This campaign involved advertising that reported more favorable consumer reactions to Burger King's fries than McDonald's fries, as well as offering free samples to customers at Burger King. McDonald's responded by increasing advertising spending on its fries and by conducting its own taste test, which not surprisingly favored its fries. The result was that while Burger King experienced an increase in the sales of its fries, its share of the fast-food business dropped in relation to McDonald's. By contrast, efforts to steal noncore customers from competitors may be more successful. ThoughtWorks, a medium-sized IT consultancy known for highly sophisticated, custom applications, has been able to attract some specialized projects from competitors without attracting a strong response. Because these specialized projects are not central or critical to ThoughtWorks's competitors, these competitors do not spend resources trying to win such business back and sometimes even recommend ThoughtWorks as an option.

Targeting Noncategory Users   When opportunities are limited to increase category consumption through an existing customer base, firms should turn attention to attracting nonusers of the category. Two strategies are point-of-entry (targeting first-time users) and building out the category.

Point of Entry (Attracting First-Time Users)   In many product categories there are nonusers who are likely to enter the category coincident with some life stage or life event. The goal of a point-of-entry strategy is: (1) to identify who will enter the category; (2) to determine when entry is likely; and (3) to direct their consumption to the firm's brand. A point-of-entry strategy is analogous to a first-mover strategy, because both strategies involve a focus on being the first product in the category that the consumer buys. However, with a point-of-entry strategy, the user is new to the category rather than the product being new to the market.

Targeting customers at the "point-of-entry" to the category is appealing because these individuals have reached a point in their lives when they are particularly receptive to the category. Also, because these consumers do not yet purchase in the category, companies can avoid the switching costs normally associated with targeting users of a competitive brand. In addition, acquiring a customer at the moment they are ready to start using a product category maximizes the time period over which the product will be used, increasing the CLV.

As an example, PNC Financial Services focuses on attracting members of Generation Y with its online product "Virtual Wallet." Virtual Wallet is three linked accounts called "Spend," "Reserve," and "Growth." Customers can drag money from account to account on one screen, get bank balances via text message, and view balances on a calendar that displays estimated future cash flow based on when they are paid, when they pay bills, and when they tend to spend. These point-of-entry customers are attractive because they hold higher-than-average balances and are inexpensive to serve because they rarely call customer service or visit branches. And, they also accept an interest rate that is lower than the national average in exchange for the convenience of the online product. PNC knows that these customers will be at the point-of-entry for other services, such as home loans and brokerage accounts, in the not-so-distant future.

Similarly, Procter & Gamble and Kimberly Clark aggressively compete to win the disposable diaper business from couples expecting their first child. AARP markets long-term care insurance to individuals who have recently passed an age milestone such as 65. And Budweiser pursues young men who are coming of legal age to drink alcoholic beverages.

Building the Category An alternative approach to attracting nonusers involves building the category. Category-build strategies are appropriate when managers believe that demand for the category is unsaturated and might be stimulated through marketing. Unlike point-of-entry strategies, where entry into the category is a matter of timing, category-build strategies focus on individuals who have no intention of using products from a category. They might also target customers who do use such products but not for the purpose the firm has in mind.

There are a number of reasons why a category might be unsaturated. When a category is relatively new, as was the case with digital video recorders (DVRs) in the early 2000s, prospective customers may be unaware of the category and its benefits. In such instances, diffusion of information about the category may increase consumption. Alternatively, the lack of saturation may be attributable to consumers' failure to recognize the problem for which the category is a remedy. This situation arises frequently in the pharmaceutical arena, where consumers are often unaware of their depression, low thyroid condition, or high blood pressure and thus do not prompt their physicians to prescribe the products available to treat these conditions. At other times, consumers may desire to consume products from the category but perceive barriers to their consumption. For example, low-income households may not purchase a computer because they believe they lack the means to do so.

Sales for seasonal categories may also be viewed as being unsaturated during seasons when sales are traditionally low. For example, a significant proportion of sales for Bailey's Irish Cream occur during the winter holiday months of October, November, and December. Over the years, the brand's managers have committed resources toward encouraging consumers to use Bailey's during other times of the year, such as by advertising consuming the beverage over ice as a summer drink.

It is often difficult to know whether a category is unsaturated in the absence of data regarding the reasons for nonuse. Electric razors are purchased by about 30 percent of the U.S. population. Is this category saturated or not? Most shavers are aware of the option of using an electric razor and have chosen to use a wet shaving system, presumably because they perceive it is a superior shaving solution. If this choice is based on accurate information, such as personal experience with an electric shaver, demand may be saturated. However, if the choice of a wet shaving system was based on incomplete or out-of-date information about electric shavers or if shaving needs change over time (which they do, as skin gets drier with age), then demand may be unsaturated. Thus, market research to gather insight into the reasons for category nonuse may be required to assess whether a category-build strategy is appropriate.

In general, a category-build strategy is more likely to be effective when nonuse is attributable to lack of awareness, rather than to a negative disposition toward the category. Thus, the observation that 13 million Americans are unaware of (and undiagnosed for) thyroid conditions, suggests a substantial opportunity to grow demand for thyroid medications.

Before investing in category-build strategies, the firm should assess the likelihood that it will be the primary beneficiary of any category expansion. A useful starting assumption is that firms will capture new category sales in proportion to their current market share. Thus, only firms holding a strong share position may find it worthwhile to undertake category-build efforts on their own. When no single firm dominates in a market but category-build activities are needed, companies might band together through a trade association and contribute funds that are used to build the category. A familiar example is the "Got Milk?" campaign, which was funded by dairy farmers' contributions to the Milk Processor Education Program. In addition, there are a variety of devices that can be used to ensure that a firm's brand benefits from any efforts it makes to build the category. Firms with strong sales forces may use advertising to build the category and then employ their sales force to direct the increased demand to the firm's brand.

On occasion, it is possible to succeed in pursuing both point-of-entry and category build targeting. Consider the category of small, lightweight, inexpensive ($200 to $500), network-enabled laptop computers known as "netbooks." When netbooks were introduced in 2007, the vision was to target first-time buyers in emerging and developing markets who were unable to afford computers with greater functionality and computing power. However, netbooks have also appealed to owners of one or even two PCs, who view them as secondary machines or as durable options for younger children.

In summary, we recommend that companies with current customers follow what we term is the "path of least resistance" in targeting. They should begin by exploring the opportunity to grow by increasing the revenue from current customers through increased loyalty or expanded purchasing. The next step is to attract new customers who are similar to current customers, perhaps by stealing them from competitors. If these approaches prove to be inadequate to meet growth goals, then targeting nonusers either at the point of entry or by attracting new users to the category should be considered.

Targeting When Launching a New Product

Achieving growth over the long term often leads a firm to introduce a new product. When the firm has a current customer base in one category, research that uncovers unmet needs of existing customers in other, related categories may prompt entry into the new category. In such situations, targeting proceeds in much the same manner as when the firm has an existing customer base in a category. Focus centers on current customers, but the emphasis is on persuading them to consume the firm's brand in a new category. For example, research on Mr. Clean customers revealed that some customers were unable to protect their hands while doing heavy cleaning because they were allergic to latex, which is used to make most household gloves. Thus, Procter & Gamble developed a nonlatex glove, Mr. Clean Nyplex Reusable Gloves, to serve the needs of these customers.

In other instances, entry into a new category is motivated more by the opportunity to leverage the firm's competencies and resources to attract new customers than by a desire to serve existing customers. For example, BIC grew by launching pens, then lighters, and then razors. All of these products leveraged the company's expertise in manufacturing inexpensive, molded plastic products and distributing these products through mass-merchandising outlets. However, the targeted customers were not necessarily the same; smokers were targeted for lighter sales, but pens and razors appealed to smokers and nonsmokers. What unifies customers across the product categories is the type of value they seek: all three products appeal to consumers who want basic, functional products, conveniently available at a low price.

In the case of "really new" or "new to the world" products, the firm not only launches a new product, but it also pioneers a new category. TiVo created a new category of digital video recorders (DVRs), Swiffer Sweeper created a new category of sweeper mops, and the launch of Kindle created a new category of wireless electronic reading devices. In such situations, all prospective customers are nonusers, and the firm must build the brand and category simultaneously. Addressing this targeting challenge requires insight into both the goals that the new product helps the customer achieve and how those goals are being served currently.

For example, TiVo empowers TV watchers by enabling them to easily control what they watch and when they watch. Prior to the introduction of TiVo, VCRs were used to achieve this goal in a more limited fashion. Accordingly, the DVR category and the TiVo brand were built by targeting VCR users who sought greater control over their viewing experience and who had the means and willingness to embrace new technology. The Swiffer Sweeper provides a simple, efficient way to clean floors. Before Swiffer, floor cleaning typically was a two-step process that involved first sweeping the floor with a broom to remove particles and then mopping to shine the surface. Procter & Gamble built the sweeper mop category and the Swiffer brand by targeting homemakers who sought a more convenient way to clean floors. Kindle gives avid readers easy, digital access to a vast library of books and other printed material wherever they happen to be. Before Kindle, books could only be obtained by visiting a bookstore or ordering them online for later delivery. Thus, when launching a new product in a new category, a firm must target nonusers who are achieving the goal served by the new product with products from a different category that serves the same goal.

When entering a new category, the firm should begin by reflecting on its distinctive competencies and the way it creates value. Such an approach may seem counter to the common marketing advice that companies should focus less on what they make and more on the customer's needs. However, when identifying new market opportunities, a firm that begins with consumers' needs may identify opportunities that it is ill-suited to serve. By understanding what it does well, the firm can then examine the market to determine the likelihood that there are segments of customers whose needs it can meet better than existing competitors.

In their book, *The Discipline of Market Leaders,* Michael Treacy and Fred Wiersema describe three broad approaches or disciplines that a firm may adopt to create value: operational excellence, product leadership, or customer intimacy.[7]

Operational Excellence   Walmart and McDonald's are prime examples of firms that have risen to the top in their categories via operational excellence. Operationally excellent firms create value by providing middle-of-the-market products at great prices and with minimal inconvenience. In order to create such offerings, these firms have core business processes that sharpen distribution systems and provide no-hassle service; a management structure with a strong, central authority and a finite level of empowerment; management systems that maintain standard operating procedures; and a culture that acts predictably and believes one size fits all.

The offerings of an operationally excellent firm are likely to appeal to customers who prefer habitual consumption experiences and don't like surprises or significant variation from one purchase to the next. They seek functional products and base their choice of brands on logic rather than emotion. When entering a new category, the operationally excellent firm typically seeks a large target segment in order to leverage its ability to produce large quantities at a low cost and distribute broadly. This may lead it to target customers of the existing market share leader with the promise of a low price or greater convenience.

Product Leadership   Intel, Apple, and Nike employ a product leadership approach to creating value. Firms that pursue this approach focus on developing new and better products. In so doing, they often make prior generations of their own products obsolete. Firms embracing the product leadership discipline have core business processes that nurture ideas, translate them into products, and market them skillfully. They have a structure that acts in an organic way, management systems that reward individuals' innovative capacity, and new product success and a culture that rewards experimentation and "out-of-the-box" thinking.

The offerings of firms practicing product leadership appeal to consumers who become easily bored with product or service experiences and who therefore are instinctively attracted to new ways of consuming. However, mere newness is often not enough to satisfy these consumers—they are often highly knowledgeable about the products and services they purchase and need to be convinced that a new offering will provide better and/or different value relative to the old one. Thus, these consumers tend to be existing category users who seek the very best and are willing to pay for it. Such users are likely to be customers of the competitor that currently offers the most advanced technology or best product. These consumers are likely to view themselves as capable and sophisticated buyers of products in the category and will be skeptical of empty claims of superiority.

Customer Intimacy   Ritz–Carlton, Nordstrom's, and Intuit are companies that create value through customer intimacy. Firms that select customer intimacy as the primary means of delivering value to customers focus on building strong customer relationships through solutions that are tailored to their unique needs. Such firms have organizations that are relatively flat and management structures that empower front-line employees. The culture is flexible and customer-driven, with employees' rewards being tied to customer satisfaction and loyalty measures. The offerings of customer-intimate firms appeal to customers who are emotionally involved with and seek self-expression through their purchases in the category. They desire an approach tailored to their needs and lots of personal attention. When surprises occur and when their needs change, these customers expect companies to be both responsive and adaptive. Firms that are customer intimate may be best able to attract a subset of the market leader's customers who are dissatisfied and open to switching to an option that is more tailored to their needs.

It is difficult for a firm to excel at more than one value discipline because the different disciplines are served by distinct processes, management systems and structure, and culture. However, successful firms must perform in accordance with the industry standard on the remaining two disciplines at which they do not excel. Thus, Apple, which has adopted a product leadership approach with its computers, must not only offer new, cutting-edge computers that replace the company's older models, it must also have operations that enable it to produce and distribute computers with reasonable efficiency and a product line that accommodates variation in customer needs for attributes like memory capacity.

TARGETING DYNAMICS

Our analysis of segmentation and targeting suggests that there are a variety of approaches to growing and sustaining a firm's position in the market. In this section, we examine issues that arise over time.

For established firms in a product category, targeting begins by focusing on current customers and then moves to targeting competitors' customers and nonusers who are similar to current customers. However, if current customers and others like them represent a shrinking or stagnant segment, this approach may limit growth.

Consider the case of Old Spice, a line of men's toiletries. The brand was purchased by Procter & Gamble in 1990 so that the company could build sales in the high-margin men's deodorant business. Aside from its high margins, the deodorant business was attractive to P&G because consumers tend to be relatively loyal to their deodorant brand, which increases the average CLV in this category. However, at the time Old Spice was purchased, the average user was in his early- to mid-fifties. Since men of that age already had loyalty to a particular deodorant brand, stealing share was difficult, and Old Spice sales were stagnant. What is an appropriate strategy when faced with a loyal but stagnant or shrinking customer base? Should the firm focus on current customers or shift its attention to high-growth segments? The answer depends both on the reason for the stagnant or declining growth and on the relationship between current customers and higher-growth segments of the population.

Several years ago Entenmann's baked goods observed that its current customer base liked its product but was consuming less due to concerns about middle-aged "spread." The company considered expanding its customer base to include younger, less weight-conscious customers for its existing products. It also considered developing new, lower-calorie products for its aging current customers. Entenmann's chose to serve the needs of its current customer base with a low-fat line extension. In the process, they found that the low-fat products attracted younger customers who were concerned with health and fitness. Apparently, the new line of products served an unmet goal and thus stimulated category build while also sustaining current user consumption.

Old Spice, on the other hand, found success by shifting its focus from existing consumers to young consumers—new category users whose loyalty to a deodorant brand has not yet been established. The danger in shifting focus from one segment to another is that the new target consumers may be unconvinced by the product's new positioning, and they may continue to believe that the product is better suited for a different consumer. Although the Old Spice brand did face challenges overcoming its image as the product used by grandfathers, it was able to avoid many of these problems by "skipping a generation"—focusing on consumers who were less aware of who the brand's core customer had been. By 2004, Old Spice had become the top-selling deodorant for teen males.

As the Old Spice example suggests, distinct segments often do not wish to be affiliated with the same brand, so success with one segment undermines the appeal to another segment. Such was the case when Porsche introduced the Cayenne SUV. Prior to the introduction of Cayenne, 85 percent of Porsche cars were bought by men. Although Cayenne expanded Porsche's customer base by attracting female drivers, it also created backlash with male customers who felt the Cayenne and the drivers it attracted diluted the sports-car purity and "chick-magnet" status of the Porsche brand. Such problems can be avoided if, as in the Old Spice example, consumers in one segment are unaware of how the product is marketed to the other segment. For example, clinical-strength deodorants, such as Secret Clinical Strength, are designed for consumers with above-average perspiration problems. As a treatment for problem perspiration, these products are often recommended by doctors and other health professionals. However, these products are also advertised to consumers without such problems but who are about to face "cannot fail" situations where sweating must be avoided at all costs (i.e., outdoor summer weddings, job interviews). These consumers might be hesitant to purchase a clinical deodorant if they associated it with having "problem perspiration." However, because the problem perspiration use is primarily marketed to physicians, most consumers are unaware of this use.

SUMMARY

This chapter presents a usage-based approach to segmentation and targeting. We prefer this approach to alternative approaches for two reasons. First, the segments that are identified using this approach require distinct marketing *strategies*, not simply different marketing tactics. When current customers are targeted, the goal is to retain these customers and, if possible, expand their usage. When competitors' customers are targeted, the goal is to offer a proposition that is sufficiently attractive to overcome switching costs. And, when nonusers are targeted, the reasons for abstaining from category consumption must be addressed. Second, the usage-based approach focuses on the costs and potential return associated with pursuing alternative targets. Current customers are easiest to reach and are most profitable to focus on in the short run. Attracting nonusers can be costly, but they may be important to sustaining the brand over the long run.

Alice M. Tybout is the Harold T. Martin Professor of Marketing and a former chairperson of the Marketing Department at the Kellogg School of Management. She is also co-director of the Kellogg on Branding *Program and director of the Kellogg on Consumer Marketing Strategy Program at the James L. Allen Center. She is co-editor of* Kellogg on Branding *(John Wiley & Sons, 2005). She received her BS and MA from Ohio State University and her PhD from Northwestern University.*

Kent Grayson is the Bernice and Leonard Lavin Professor of Marketing at the Kellogg School of Management. Before joining Kellogg in 2002, he served on the faculty at London Business School for eight years, where he also directed the LBS Centre for Marketing for two years. He has written several published cases on segmentation and has worked on segmentation issues with a number of Fortune 500 companies. He received his BA and MA from the University of Michigan and his PhD from Northwestern University.

NOTES

1. Anderson, Chris (2008), The Long Tail, New York: Hyperion.
2. Elberse, Anita (2008), "Should You Invest in the Long Tail?" *Harvard Business Review*, July–August, 88–96, for a critique of *The Long Tail*.
3. Yankelovich, Daniel, and David Meer (2006), "Rediscovering Market Segmentation," Harvard Business Review, February.
4. Gupta, Sunil, and Donald R. Lehmann (2002), "What Are Your Customers Worth?" Online newsletter. http://www.simon.rochester.edu/fac/demers/What%20are%20your%20customers%20worth%20-%20optimize%202002.pdf.
5. Ofeck, Elie (2002), "Customer Profitability and Lifetime Value," Harvard Business School Publishing, #9-503-019.
6. Gupta, and Lehmann op cit.
7. Treacy, Michael, and Fred Wiersema (1995), *The Discipline of Market Leaders* Reading, MA: Addison-Wesley.

CHAPTER 3

MARKETING RESEARCH AND UNDERSTANDING CONSUMERS

BOBBY J. CALDER

INTRODUCTION

The goal of understanding consumers brings to mind a favorite joke about a bartender. One day a dog walks into a bar. The dog jumps up on a barstool.

Dog:	I'll have a draft beer.
Bartender (pouring):	That'll be $14.
Bartender (pausing):	Gee, I have to ask ... we don't get many talking dogs in here?
Dog:	At these prices, I'm not surprised.

As only humor can do, the joke jolts us with a truth that ordinarily is too uncomfortable to admit. The truth here is how different one point of view can be from another—and how our point of view can make us oblivious to another's.

To many companies, consumers (or customers) seem as strange as the talking dog above. Seller and buyer have inherently different points of view. The difference may be more or less, but the gap is always there.

Yet successful marketing requires bridging this gap. It could even be said that successful marketing *is* the bridging of this gap. To market successfully, a company must transcend its own internal point of view to understand what the product means, and could mean, to consumers. The goal of understanding consumers is fundamental.

But how do you achieve this goal? For many the answer is simple: marketing research. Surveys, focus groups, internal and syndicated databases, and the like provide the understanding necessary to make marketing decisions. Marketers only have to "do a study" or "get the data." However, the real answer is not so simple. The truth is that using marketing research to understand consumers requires a sophisticated understanding of complex issues—not technical, analytical issues (though these do exist), but rather more fundamental issues regarding how to think about the research process.

In this chapter we address these fundamental issues. In so doing, we emphasize the importance of being explanation-driven in marketing research as well as data-driven. By this we mean being explanation-driven in the sense of focusing on understanding the consumer. All too often, marketing research is an exercise in collecting data in as extensive a way as financially feasible, of getting the largest sample, of using the latest statistical techniques, or of producing the biggest report. Managers need consumer understanding; what they often get is information. A report stuffed with data, put before managers who themselves have thought little about consumers, simply becomes another decoration for someone's office, another file that no one remembers in a few months.

WHAT IS YOUR PHILOSOPHY OF MARKETING RESEARCH?

It is easy to get caught up in the technicalities of marketing research (and, again, this is not to say there are not real issues around these). However, success in achieving consumer understanding through marketing research has far less to do with the pros and cons of sundry research techniques than with the philosophy that guides the entire research endeavor. For this reason, it's important for a marketer to have thought through his or her philosophy and to apply it in using research. Unfortunately, many marketers too readily accept bad conventional wisdom about research and do not really think through some important issues. And this is the root cause of a lack of consumer understanding in the end.

A philosophy of marketing research involves having considered opinions about at least three critical issues: *Proof versus conjecture; precision versus vagueness; data versus explanation.*

Proof versus Conjecture

In your marketing research process, which is to be valued more—certainty or creativity? Does research ideally yield findings that can be regarded as statements of fact that are proven to be true? Or should research be thought of as consisting of conjectures that have been held up to contradiction by data?

Precision versus Vagueness

Which is to be valued more—specificity or flexibility? Are more precise research findings the most valuable? Or are vague findings not only acceptable but also desirable?

Data versus Explanation

Is it better to be data-driven or explanation-driven? The issue here is not about the importance of data—in fact, the whole idea of research is to make use of data. The question is rather about the role of data. Should research findings only be about the data—about what is observed or recorded (number of recorded or reported doctor visits, for example)? Or should research observations be linked to more abstract, unobservable concepts (classifying people as "Health Seekers," for example)?

The Conventional Wisdom

Most marketers seem to embrace approaching marketing research as a quest for precise, proven, data-driven conclusions. This is usually the conventional wisdom about research. Although these marketers might suspect some value in conjecture and explanation, but probably not in vagueness, they would be most comfortable with conclusions tied to data, proof, and precision.

Just because this is the conventional wisdom does not make this approach right, however. Orthodoxies are sometimes just that, beliefs that people have not really reflected on. Later we examine each of the three choices above in the context of a typical marketing research scenario. Not only do we see that attaining precise data-driven proof is difficult, but that it is also a Sisyphean challenge, equivalent to trying to push the rock up the hill again and again, only to have it roll back down. Viewing research as a search for precise, data-driven proof actually gets in the way of understanding consumers.

A TYPICAL CASE OF MARKETING RESEARCH

Suppose that we wanted to market a new cooking appliance. The appliance is designed to substitute for a conventional oven. Among other things, it cooks meats twice as fast as an oven. How might we go about understanding consumer response to this product? The following marketing research approach would be typical.

We might begin by examining available data about consumer behavior from syndicated panel surveys and the like. We might first check data on how often consumers are eating at home versus eating out (the trend is toward home). We might look into how often consumers are using their ovens (frequency is down) or how much time they are spending preparing dinner (less time). We might also examine how the sales of other specialty cooking appliances are doing (sales are up).

We would likely also want primary research information specific to our product. First, we might do a series of focus groups to explore reactions to cooking with a new appliance. Hearing consumers talk about meal preparation would give us a feel for what questions to ask and the language used by the consumer. But, as our director of marketing research reminds us, it is important not to make any decisions based on this information. Focus groups are qualitative; responses are not precise. Reports only cover the general things people had to say, with perhaps a few idiosyncratic quotes. Moreover, the sample size, which may be only 40 people or so, is too small. And everyone knows that one or two people tend to dominate a focus group discussion while the other participants go along with what is being said. So the focus groups may be useful "directionally," but we would not want to rely on them.

Ideally, we want to do a consumer survey to obtain a quantitatively valid understanding of consumers. The answers to questions would be quantified and the sample size large enough to generalize. By surveying hundreds of consumers we would be assured of statistical validity.

Our quantitative survey research might well take the form of asking consumers to rate the importance of various attributes of our appliance on a 1 to 10 scale, with 10 being very important. Key results might be:

Speed of cooking	8.2
Quality of food	7.1
Ease of cleaning	6.5
Counter space	4.8

We could even do analyses to explore the relationship of these attributes to responses to questions about things such as price sensitivity. We might find that price sensitivity goes down with increases in the importance of speed of cooking. In any case, the results of the survey would provide the understanding required to make decisions. Our appliance would become the Speed Cooker and be marketed accordingly.

The thinking underlying this case scenario illustrates the main threads of the conventional wisdom about marketing research discussed earlier. The hallmark of this approach is that data is primary and quantitatively precise, and the ability to generalize from data comes from large samples. Its mantra is: How big is the sample size?

In our example, we have precise proven data that people are eating at home more, spending less time on cooking, and valuing speed as the most important thing about cooking by precisely 1.1 scale units.

The Problem with Proof: Understanding Is Conjectural

There is nothing wrong with this conventional thinking about understanding consumers. Quantification is powerful; more data and larger samples are desirable. The problem is that *there is more at stake in understanding consumers than this*.

Conventional wisdom falls into the trap of simply assuming that understanding increases with the amount of data available. Conventional wisdom fixates on achieving understanding through accumulating data; that is, more data gathered from more people equals greater validity of the research results and a better understanding. Managers under the sway of conventional wisdom care most about the question, "How big is the sample size?" regardless of their involvement or sophistication with research. Assured on this score, research results tend to be accepted as equal to understanding.

This fixation on the amount of data in general and sample size in particular is, unfortunately, misplaced. Say we were to do our survey asking about the importance of various attributes of our cooking appliance by including the questions in a syndicated national probability sample survey of 2,000 people. With this size sample, our results (such as the 8.2 rating for the speed of cooking attribute), will be wildly statistically valid. We would get the same results if we had surveyed the entire population. Suppose further that we repeat the questions in the next quarterly wave of the survey and get the same results. Surely we have proven that speed of cooking is the most important attribute of the product.

The problem is that proof is a very difficult thing, even an impossible thing. We must understand that we are attempting inductive proof—we asked not just a few people, but 2,000 people. Based on this we induce (not deduce) that the next 100 or 10,000,000 would show the same pattern, and the mean would stay about 8.2. And maybe it would. But if we did the survey the next quarter, we might get a mean of 7.2. How is this possible? If we used different question wording, or changed the order of the questions in the survey, we might get a different mean. If the weather turned much colder, we might get a different mean. The point is that there is no logical basis for assuming that the truth is 8.2 just because we have a large sample and multiple surveys.

Induction simply does not work as a logical principle. The sun has always come up every morning, so the thinking is that it will come up tomorrow. But there is no proof here—an asteroid could hit, and no sunrise tomorrow. It does not help to say the sun will *probably* come up. As long as we are talking about the future or open-ended possibilities, it is not possible to talk about probabilities. Probabilities require finite sets of possibilities. You could say that *practically* speaking we are justified in saying the sun will come up, because after all it always has, but we are using induction to justify this belief.

The inescapable conclusion is that induction is not proof, and no amount of data or replication of data can in itself confer proof. We have not, and cannot, prove that consumers will rate speed of cooking to be 8.2 beyond the confines of the surveys we have done, no matter how large the samples we have used or how many surveys we do. Sampling statistics help us to generalize survey data to a larger population that could have been surveyed but was not. They do not prove that the result will hold in the future or in other situations.

So where does this leave us? It leaves us with the realization that research is always conjectural. The 8.2 rating for speed of cooking has led us to conjecture, or hypothesize, that speed is the most important thing to consumers. This is no less a conjecture if it comes from a survey of 10 consumers than if it comes from a survey of 10,000. The larger sample is nice because we can be confident that we would get exactly this number if we asked more people, but it is not a proven fact. In the end we are still left with a conjecture.

But someone could say that at least the 8.2 rating from the 10,000-person survey is precise, right? So let's turn to the concept of precision.

The Problem with Precision: Our Concepts Are Inherently Vague

When we as marketers state that, on average, consumers rate speed of cooking 8.2 (or that 78.6 percent rate speed an 8), we use exact quantification that has about it the aura and prestige of science. We should look more closely at this, however. What does a rating of "8" really mean? We may say it means that consumers find speed "very important." But how do we know this? It is either our categorization—or perhaps the consumer's in the case of a labeled scale—where "very important" might equal an 8 or higher. However, the category name "very important" loses some of the aura of the precise number 8.2. The point is that eventually we must describe numerical data in some way, usually by using verbal concepts like "very important." These labels are obviously less precise than the quantification made it seem.

Moreover, a concept such as "very important" is inherently vague in the following way. If 8.2 means "very important," then what about an average rating of 7.9, which is very close to 8.2? And what about 7.8, 6.8, and so on?

There is a paradox here that was originally described by the ancient Greeks—the Sorites paradox. Sorites is Greek for "heap." The paradox is this: If we have a heap of sand and take away one grain, we will still have a heap. But if we keep applying this principle, eventually we will have a heap of two grains, or one, or even zero grains. It would be paradoxical to conclude that two grains is a heap of sand, however. We can get around this by refusing to say that a heap minus one grain is still a heap. But, if this were so, there must then be one point where taking away a grain leaves us with something other than a heap. The paradox becomes, how could this single grain make such a difference?[1]

Sorites paradoxes arise with all the concepts that we naturally use to think about things. Take height, for instance. When is a woman tall? Let's say a woman who is 6'1" is tall. And a woman 6'0" is tall, as is a woman 5'11", 5'10", and so on. At some point we paradoxically have a tall woman who is 5'2". If we deny this—that 5'2" is tall—how could the one inch, from 5'3" to 5'2", have made the difference between being tall versus not tall?

We can try to get around this inherent vagueness by trying to clarify what we mean through definitions: Tall is any woman over 5'9". Not only is this arbitrary, but it also does not solve the problem. How do we determine if a woman is 5'9"? Do we measure from the scalp or the top of her hair? What time of day do we measure? What should the posture of the woman be? The concepts involved in these questions are vague in the same way that the concept of "tall" is vague and hence do not solve the problem of achieving precision in our research.

What the Sorites paradox points up is that our concepts are inherently vague. We really don't know when a person is tall. Classifying a person as tall or bald or anything else is a judgment that we make. We are always imprecise. Vagueness is not a detriment, however. It is actually an advantage. It allows us to talk about things that we cannot know about in a precise way. It allows us to cope with the world. Thus, a quantitative finding of 8.2 looks precise, but it is not. We will necessarily be obliged to think about what this means by relying on our ability to think in vague terms.

Even if proof and precision are chimerical, someone can say that at least we can otherwise be data-driven. We can at least directly base our decisions on actual factual information. So now let's turn to being data-driven.

The Problem with Being Data-Driven: Explanations Are Never in the Data

We should certainly try to be objective in avoiding biases that might distort our research findings, as in wording a question in such a way that consumers respond the way we think they should. Often marketers approach objectivity as more than this, however. Value is placed on reaching conclusions that are directly tied to data. As in, "The data show that speed of cooking is most important to consumers."

The problem is that understanding is not just a matter of data. It is first and foremost a matter of explanation. To understand something is to explain how it happens. Part of this process is to make a prediction about what will happen. But explanation is more than prediction. An explanation is about why something will happen or how it will come about. In the case of our new appliance, what we are looking for is an explanation for why consumers might like the appliance and how they might use it. In looking for explanations, the important thing to realize is that *explanations are never in the data*. Explanation is always separate from the data.

Let's take a close look at this point. Consider the following little parable (adapted from Bertrand Russell). Suppose we are in the food-service business, and we do a survey of a certain demographic group. We find that 85 percent of the consumers in this group have eaten chicken at least four times in the week surveyed. Our survey sample of 400 consumers seems like a lot, but it is not statistically representative. We do a second survey and get the same results, for a probability sample of 2,000 people. We conclude that our understanding is quantitatively precise and statistically valid. These consumers are chicken eaters!

This may seem about as simple and straightforward a case of consumer understanding as we could possibly hope for. Certainly it would seem this way from the perspective of conventional wisdom. Here is the problem: Where is the explanation? We could predict that these consumers would keep eating chicken (and therefore it should be a bigger part of our menu). But this is a prediction, not an explanation. We could say that the explanation is simply the extrapolation: If this many people eat chicken now, many will probably eat chicken in the future. But how do we know we can extrapolate in this way? As already discussed, this cannot simply be taken as a proven conclusion. A survey may indicate that people are eating (or say they are eating) chicken, but extrapolating this behavior into the future because such extrapolation sometimes works is an act of faith, not logic.

Things are even more complicated than this, however. Explanation really precedes data; you must have an explanation before you can extrapolate from data. One simple explanation for why our consumers are eating so much chicken is that they like the taste of chicken. This explanation would lead to the prediction that they will eat chicken in the future. Note that it is the explanation that generates the prediction. Our consumers will eat chicken in the future because they like its taste and will want more. The prediction is not mere extrapolation of the data.

But now consider that other explanations are possible. Perhaps our consumers are concerned about their weight and are eating chicken to diet. Or maybe they are eating it to save money. With an explanation along either of these two lines, one could predict that, after accomplishing (or tiring of) their goal, consumers will no longer eat as much chicken. Thus, our data suggesting that people eat a lot of chicken could lead to either prediction: that people will keep eating chicken or that they will stop. The same data can fit either of the two opposite predictions. Thus, the prediction depends only on the explanation, not the data. The explanation is not in the data, and therefore the prediction is not in the extrapolation of the data. The point here is that explanations are primary and are separate from data. The only way to predict is to have an explanation; predicting from data alone is not logically justified.

This conclusion is not as obtuse as it may seem. The salient point is that marketers should not simply take market research data, check the sample size, and then extrapolate the data. Sample size and sampling statistics have nothing to say about whether people will eat chicken in the future.

If explanation is primary, it follows that data is not really useful without explanation. You must approach the data with an explanation in mind. Data does not tell you what to think; you must do the thinking first. But the role of data is important: It allows you to be more confident in the explanation you hold (though proof is not the objective). More important, it may also lead you to give up that explanation and look for a better one. Data is the most powerful way of critiquing an explanation.

So where do explanations come from? Logically, they cannot come from data, because they are not in data to begin with. But, if not from data, where do they come from? Explanations come from creativity. Explanation is the creative act of figuring out what is going on with consumers. Such creativity may be inspired by looking at patterns of data to get an idea about what is going on. Or it may follow from other creative impulses, including experience and intuition.

The crucial thing is to *have* an explanation—to start the process with an explanation in mind. Once an explanation occurs to you, regardless of where it comes from, it is primary. You think about explanation first and data second. The problem with the conventional wisdom is that it holds that research is only about data, or about data with explanation assumed somehow to be in the data. However, *savvy marketers should aim to be explanation-driven, rather than data-driven.*

The Value of Vague Conjectural Explanation

Return to the case of the new cooking appliance. Discarding conventional wisdom, we realize that our sample of 2,000 consumers is impressive, but we need to approach consumer understanding more broadly. First, we need to focus on explanation. If we have data, it can be an inspiration for explanation, but one way or another we need to start with an explanation to interpret our data about the importance of speed in cooking. In this case, one explanation might be that people simply value speed more than quality. People are more and more rushed in their meal preparation and therefore willing to sacrifice quality just to get food on the table.

We can now use data to critique our explanation. For starters, does the consumer survey data we have in hand fit the explanation? It turns out that it does. Speed of cooking is rated as more important than the quality of the food. This finding makes us more comfortable with the explanation but in no way proves it.

Despite the large sample size, the survey should not make us too confident. The reason is that the survey is also consistent with many other explanations that would imply higher ratings for speed of cooking. Consumers might, for example, be thinking that speed is something that companies can easily accomplish with technology, whereas quality is more difficult. The explanation then revolves around consumers' expectations about what is technically possible and therefore should realistically be important to them.

One can see that a stronger test of the first explanation is in order. Can we obtain data that would challenge the sacrifice-quality explanation relative to the technology-expectation explanation. A simple test would be this: Tell consumers to assume that there are no technological limits on either speed or quality and ask them to rate importance based on this assumption. If we obtained the same importance ratings, this would support the sacrifice-quality explanation. People are after speed more than quality. But, if ratings of the importance of quality increased relative to speed, this would refute the sacrifice-quality explanation and support the technological-expectations explanation.

There are two principles at work here. The first is that the severity with which data tests an explanation is important. The amount of data, including the size of the sample, is not irrelevant, but it is the overall degree to which the data poses a challenge to the explanation (the severity of the test) that matters most. It is the survival of an explanation by the challenge of data that increases our confidence in the explanation.

The second (even more important) principle is that we learn even more when data causes us to reject an explanation. The rationale? If the data are consistent with an explanation, our confidence in it may increase. But it is still possible that other data from another, more severe test that we have not yet done (or even thought of) would reject the explanation. Thus we cannot know for sure that an explanation is right. We can never prove an explanation. We can only have preferred explanations that we accept and use at a point in time.

Now, if data cause us to reject an explanation, we have learned something new. We know that the explanation we have is not acceptable and that we need a new one. Thus we can use rejection to evolve better explanations. We never have *the* explanation. (The precise, factual certitude of conventional wisdom is illusory.) The explanation that forms our understanding of consumers is accepted based on existing data and it is provisional subject to new data.

It cannot be emphasized enough that data by itself is meaningless. There is no explanation inherent in data. Data can only help in finding an acceptable explanation.

The consequences of this logic have significant practical implications. Many managers approach consumer understanding with the idea that they must begin by looking at data. Only by looking at data will they know what to think about consumers. The truth is that data can be inspirational, but so can general experience and intuition. In any event, you have to think something. And this cannot be so simple as making hypotheses about the data, if this means mere prediction, with no explanation. You have to think through what might be going on, you have to have an explanation in mind, before data can help.

UNDERSTANDING EXPLANATION

Conventional wisdom could easily have led to marketing the appliance in this case as the Speed Cooker. After all, consumers rated speed of cooking as most important—precisely 8.2—thereby "proving" that they would prefer a product marketed as the Speed Cooker. As the ad agency would have tagged it "*Cooking at the speed of light.*"

Fortunately the marketing team was able to break through the conventional wisdom. The team had considerable experience in marketing microwave ovens. It was well known that consumers, especially in the United States, considered cooking in a microwave to be oxymoronic. They felt that anything "cooked" in a microwave tastes bad and looks worse. Microwaves are good for warming things up or making popcorn, but anything cooked in one is "nuked." Even defrosting is problematic for many consumers. Previous surveys and focus groups routinely pointed to this. The team conjectured that these beliefs would apply to the new oven as well. It would be easier for consumers to believe that new technology could be faster than it was to believe it might produce better quality.

This insight about microwaves led the team to question whether the current survey in fact proved that speed of cooking was most important for consumers. It also led them to conjecture another explanation. Perhaps consumers were thinking that they were already preparing and eating meals very quickly. The average length of meal preparation has been going down for years. Perhaps consumers had reached the point where shaving a few minutes off of a 30-minute dinner has diminishing returns. They were already eating fast. Speed was most important, but not in the sense that people were looking for something to take them down to the 15-minute dinner range.

So what might a consumer in this situation value? Speed is indeed important, but consumers were already cooking fast. What might they really value going forward? Possibly they might value having dishes that they don't currently have time to prepare but would enjoy if they could prepare them within the time available. With this explanation we understand that quality is important, and quality means being able to prepare dishes associated with eating better in the time available. That is, "*Cooking at the speed of life.*"

With this possible explanation in mind, the next step would be to ask consumers how important it would be to be able to cook dishes that they cannot now prepare in the time available. It would be nice if their responses were consistent with our explanation. But we should realize that there is no proof here, not even if the average rating was 8.8. Even if it were 6.6, this might only mean that they do not really believe that the dishes would be the equivalent of oven-prepared food.

A strong test of the explanation could be as follows: Give two groups of consumers a dish that they ordinarily could not make in the time available and let them try it. Inform them that the dish normally takes 35 minutes in the oven but in this new oven it would take 16 minutes. Show them a picture of the oven as well. In one case the oven pictured looks like a microwave, in the other it has controls designed to resemble those of a classic oven.

The latter group likes the dish much more. What does this say about our explanation?

We still have not proven anything—precision is largely elusive, and the explanation is not in the data itself. But by adopting the philosophy of accepting vagueness and conjecture around explanations that are more than the data itself, we have reached a better level of understanding.

Types of Explanation

All explanations are not created the same. They are always created through conjecture, and inspired by data, experience, or intuition. But there are two types of explanations: *everyday explanations* and *theoretical constructs*. The distinction between them can be important.

An everyday explanation is stated in lay terms from the perspective of the consumers involved and their potential experiences with the product. The explanation may be the one that consumers themselves would give for their behavior (termed a naive explanation). Or it may be one that a marketer can formulate in terms that would be familiar to consumers but that they could not articulate themselves. The explanations created for our appliance are everyday explanations couched in terms of peoples' own experiences.

Everyday explanations contrast with a more theoretical explanation because the latter employs concepts and terms that consumers themselves would not use. A theoretical explanation is formulated in its own terms, which are invented for the purposes of explanation. These terms are sometimes referred to as *theoretical constructs*. A theoretical construct does not depend on anyone's everyday understanding. (Just as general relativity does not depend on anyone thinking about space-time distortions when they drop something.)

Theory has a bad connotation in some business circles. To many managers, it suggests "not proven" and "abstract." The rub is that no explanation is proven, and any explanation is necessarily abstract relative to data. However, theory can add constructs to our explanations that consumers might not use. Thus, consumers might think that something that they have thought about in the past but that is not currently on their mind would not affect them. But the construct of "attitude" as developed in the academic literature allows for just this. Likewise, consumers would not typically think of their behavior as being affected by things they are not conscious of in a situation, but in fact behavior can be primed or directed by many things consumers are not consciously aware of.

A smart philosophy of marketing research should at least be open to the use of theoretical constructs. The academic literature has much to offer in this regard.[2]

RESEARCH METHODS

Now we come to one of the great divides in how marketers think about research. The divide is over the primacy of quantitative methods over more qualitative methods, epitomized by the focus group interview. Many see quantitative methods such as consumer surveys as the ideal. Consistent with conventional wisdom, quantitative methods supply precise data that can be generalized because of sample size. Such surveys can be extremely useful, but viewed through the philosophy of marketing research advocated in this chapter, marketers should not infer that qualitative data and smaller samples are inherently inferior and should be regarded with suspicion.[3]

There are many kinds of qualitative methods. Focus groups and one-on-one, in-depth interviews are the most common. All necessarily involve small samples for reasons of cost and time. Given more resources, one would normally prefer bigger samples for qualitative methods. This is all a matter of practicality.

But there is more at issue here than practical limitations. If we break through the mindset of conventional wisdom, the most important thing is that we try to create explanations and to pit them against data to find the one that is most acceptable. It is crucial to keep this in mind in evaluating qualitative methods.

Consider the focus group. It is possible to use focus groups in an exploratory way in keeping with conventional wisdom.[4] It is also possible to use focus groups as a phenomenological method. This means "a method that has one overriding objective: to allow the researcher to share, participatively, the experience of a group of people."[5] The focus group is used as an instrument for describing what it is like to be a person in a particular setting.

The very name "focus group" reflects this phenomenological purpose. Originally called the "focused interview" in the 1940s by Robert Merton and Paul Lazersfeld, the explicit goal was to focus people, individually or in groups, on a specific stimulus so that their comments would reflect their experience of the stimulus. It could be argued that this method wound up as our "focus group" because of the natural focusing properties of a group discussion. Even without a stimulus (though one is often used), people in a group must focus on a topic if they are going to interact with each other. Their comments are, therefore, more rooted in the actual experience (the phenomenon) of what they are discussing, thereby making this experience easier to describe. Groups have the advantage of focusing people on common experience; one-on-one interviews are preferable when more control is desired over what people focus on.

As we have discussed, for any type of data (whether produced by a "qualitative" or a "quantitative" method) we need to have an explanation in mind that the data can support or reject. Often these are everyday explanations. Given that an everyday explanation is by definition couched in terms of everyday experience, it makes eminent sense to use qualitative research to test such explanations. In practice, both focus groups and one-on-one interviews lend themselves to confronting everyday explanations with data. It is often easier to examine everyday explanations with qualitative research because the two employ the same language. Also, the conventional wisdom of marketing research does not get in the way as much.

My experience suggests that in as few as 10 one-on-one interviews, it is possible to see that an everyday explanation does or does not fit the data (and that in the latter case a better explanation is suggested). Many marketers would ask how this could be possible with just 10 interviews. Would not 100 or 1,000 have been better? Yes, in a sampling sense. Remember the broader issues, however—we need to go beyond conventional wisdom. Even 10 interviews can make us question an explanation and entertain a new one. Of course, it could be argued that a different mix of people would have produced different results. But this is not fundamentally a matter of sampling. If the explanation *should* have applied to the 10 people, then it should be accepted if it does and refuted if it does not. If we find that the explanation fits some people and not others, this just means that we need to revise the explanation to account for differences in people and that we need to test the revised explanation. A larger sample might be useful in detecting that the explanation does not fit some people, but without some conjecture as to who these people might be and why they are different, this is a fishing expedition more than a sampling issue.

Again, sample size is an issue, but the big issue is getting data that constitute a severe test and then changing explanations if required by the data. This explanation, and any other, can only be provisionally accepted and should ideally be exposed to further testing itself. Merely adding sample size is not in itself the best use of resources for further testing. Increasing the severity of the test is more powerful.

The traditional tension between quantitative versus qualitative methods in marketing research is a red herring that has long stood in the way of consumer understanding. Some marketers dislike statements from qualitative research such as, "Most consumers do not like the taste of food prepared in a microwave oven" (though it is hard to deny that such findings are useful, as in the case of our oven). Nonetheless, many find such statements vague and imprecise. These marketers love knowing that the average rating of food quality from a microwave is 3.2, with a confidence interval of plus or minus .3, on a 10-point scale ranging from "very bad tasting" to "very good tasting." In fact, both statements can be only vaguely right and are only as useful as the explanation they test.

SUMMARY

We need to broaden our thinking about understanding consumers beyond the perspective of conventional wisdom about marketing research. Understanding is an active process; it is not a matter of static information.

Trying to understand and explain why people do what they do is difficult. Moreover, it is difficult to explain the behavior of people we know well and who are like us. It is even more challenging to explain consumers who may seem as different as "talking dogs."

To meet this challenge, marketers must keep these points in mind in approaching marketing research:

- Understanding consumers is not about the superiority of one method over another, and certainly not the superiority of qualitative over quantitative methods.
- The amount of data we collect, or the number of interviews we conduct, is not the critical success factor.
- Understanding consumers is about creating explanations that can be inspired by data but ultimately come from experience and intuition.
- Vagueness and conjecture are indispensable for understanding.
- The critical success factor is the ability and willingness to confront explanations with data so that the data poses a severe test of the explanation.
- If an explanation survives testing, it is accepted, but not proven.
- If an explanation fails, we must create a better explanation and test it so that explanations can evolve over time.
- This process should produce not marketing research reports, but knowledge.

In the past we may have been able to avoid the complexities of marketing research. The future, however, is the knowledge economy and the learning organization. Consumer (customer) knowledge is one of the most important kinds of knowledge a company can have. It is crucial that companies question the conventional wisdom about marketing research and learn how to get better at understanding consumers.

Bobby J. Calder is the Kellstadt Professor of Marketing and currently the chair of the Marketing Department at the Kellogg School of Management. He is also a professor of journalism in the Medill School of Journalism and a professor of psychology in the Weinberg College of Arts and Sciences at Northwestern University. He has been a consultant to many companies and to government and not-for-profit organizations. His most recent books are Kellogg on Integrated Marketing (John Wiley & Sons, 2003) and Kellogg on Advertising and Media (John Wiley & Sons, 2008). He received his BA, MA and PhD degrees from the University of North Carolina at Chapel Hill.

NOTES

1. Williamson, Timothy (2002), *Vagueness*, Surrey, UK: Ashgate Publishing.
2. For discussion of this and related issues, see the following: Bobby J. Calder and Alice M. Tybout, "What Consumer Research Is," *Journal of Consumer Research*, vol. 14 (1987): 136–140; Bobby J. Calder and Alice M. Tybout, "A Vision of Theory, Research, and the Future of Business Schools," *Journal of the Academy of Marketing Science*, vol. 27 (1999): 359–366; Bobby J. Calder, Lynn Phillips, and Alice M. Tybout, "Designing Research for Application," *Journal of Consumer Research*, vol. 8 (1981): 197–207; Bobby J. Calder, Lynn Phillips, and Alice M. Tybout, "The Concept of External Validity," *Journal of Consumer Research*, vol. 9 (1982): 240–244; Bobby J. Calder, Lynn Phillips, and Alice M. Tybout, "Beyond External Validity," *Journal of Consumer Research*, vol. 10 (1983): 112–114; John Lynch Jr., "On the External Validity of Experiments in Consumer Research," *Journal of Consumer Research,* vol. 9 (1982): 225–239; John Lynch Jr., "The Role of External Validity in Theoretical Research," *Journal of Consumer Research*, vol. 10 (1983): 109–111; Brian Sternthal, Alice M. Tybout, and Bobby J. Calder, "Experimental Design: Generalization and Theoretical Explanation," in *Principles of Marketing Research*, Ed. Richard P. Bagozzi (Cambridge, MA: Blackwell Publishers. 1994): 195–223; Russell S. Weiner, "Experimentation in the Twenty-First Century: The Importance of External Validity," *Journal of the Academy of Marketing Science*, vol. 27 (1999): 340–358; and William D. Wells, "Discovery-Oriented Consumer Research," *Journal of Consumer Research*, vol. 19 (1993): 489–504.
3. Calder, Bobby J. (1994), "Qualitative Marketing Research," in *Principles of Marketing Research*, Ed. Richard P. Bagozzi, Cambridge, MA: Blackwell Publishers, 50–72; Bobby J. Calder (1986), "Exploratory, Clinical, and Interaction Centered Focus Groups," *Journal of Data Collection*, vol. 26, 24–27; and Bobby J. Calder (1977), "Focus Groups and the Nature of Qualitative Marketing Research," *Journal of Marketing Research,* vol. 11, 353–364.
4. See note 3.
5. See note 3, Calder (1994), 54.

CHAPTER 4

DEVELOPING A COMPELLING BRAND POSITIONING

ALICE M. TYBOUT and BRIAN STERNTHAL

INTRODUCTION

Brand positioning refers to the specific, intended meaning of the brand in the mind of targeted customers. A brand is positioned by relating it to competitive offerings and to customers' goals and lives. Consider the positioning of Zipcar, a car-sharing service that was founded in 2000 by Robin Chase, an MBA from MIT, and Antje Danielson, a Harvard geochemist with an interest in reducing carbon emissions. For a $50 annual fee, the 325,000 Zipcar members pay an hourly or daily rate (which varies by city, make of car, and day of the week) to use a vehicle that is parked in their neighborhood. The rates include insurance and gas, though the tank must be left no less than one-quarter full. Reservations can be made online or by using an iPhone app. Almost a decade after its founding, in 2009, Zipcar revenues were $130 million and growing at 30 percent a year.

When Zipcar was launched, the company focused on attracting customers who were college-educated, higher-income, environmentally conscious, and techno-savvy. It positioned the service as superior to private car ownership for short-term transportation needs in urban areas on the grounds that it was less expensive for the user and better for the environment. This positioning was supported by evidence that Zipcar users saved as much as $500 a month and drove 44 percent fewer miles than those who owned their cars. Thus, each shared vehicle was estimated to take an estimated 20 cars off the road and cut CO_2 emissions by 50 percent per user. This positioning not only appealed to the original target, it also attracted additional segments, such as empty-nesters moving back to the city who did not need a car on a daily basis, and businesses and universities where parking is limited and employees or students require only occasional use of a car.[1]

Nearly a decade after the launch of Zipcar, the competitive landscape had changed. Traditional rental car companies such as Hertz, whose airport-based hubs and emphasis on daily or weekly rental initially made it ill-equipped to serve the market for convenient, short-term, within-city rentals, launched services similar to Zipcar. Hertz's offering, called Connect, enjoys economies in purchasing and maintaining cars due to its traditional rental operation. More important, Connect can make the same claims as Zipcar regarding the benefits of its service in comparison to car ownership. This new competition forces Zipcar to rethink its positioning. Who should Zipcar target and how should it differentiate in the face of well-funded direct competitors?

Many companies face similar issues in developing a position at the time they launch a brand and adapting that position as competition changes and consumers' knowledge of the brand choices evolves. In this chapter, we examine the development of a brand positioning strategy from two perspectives. The first approach emphasizes how a brand is similar to competitors' offerings on some dimensions and superior on other dimensions. This *competition-based* approach to positioning is particularly important when a new brand is being introduced to the market and consumers strive to relate it to brands and product categories that are familiar. The second approach focuses on how the distinguishing features of the brand create abstract benefits that can be linked to targeted customers' goals. This *customer-based* approach is used to enrich and deepen a brand's position by situating it in the customers' lives. The two perspectives are complementary rather than competing. As we demonstrate, both play a role in developing and sustaining a strong brand positioning. We conclude the chapter by illustrating how the perspectives are captured in a brand positioning statement. The topic of writing a positioning statement is then addressed at length in Chapter 5, "Writing a Brand Positioning Statement and Translating It into Brand Design."

THE COMPETITION-BASED PERSPECTIVE

Competition-based positioning entails choosing a *category* and a *point of difference*. The category provides a frame of reference by identifying other brands that might be used to achieve the same goal as the focal brand. The point of difference then specifies the way in which the brand is superior to other brands within that frame.

Suppose that you are unfamiliar with a brand called "Two Hands." If you were told that Two Hands is a wine, you would quickly understand what the brand is and when it might be appropriate to consume it. You might further refine your feelings about whether to purchase Two Hands wine if you also were told that it is a Shiraz from Australia that sells for about $30. For Two Hands, the category would be wine or, more narrowly, an Australian Shiraz. The *point of difference* from another Australian Shiraz, such as Yangarra, might be the longer finish and the silky mouth feeling provided by the concentrated blackberry, pepper, and spice flavors.

The competition-based approach to positioning has its origins in the hierarchical, taxonomic organization of memory. People organize their knowledge about the world by grouping objects that share features and separating them into objects that have different features. This organizational structure begins with highly abstract, inclusive categories and becomes more specific. Moving down the hierarchy, similarities within a category increase and the differences between categories decrease. In the context of the wine example, this organization might be represented as depicted in Figure 4.1. The broad category of "alcoholic beverages" is heterogeneous; wines, beers, and hard liquors all belong, but they share few features beyond their alcohol content, which distinguishes them from nonalcoholic beverages such as milk, juice, and soft drinks. At the level of an Australian Shiraz, category members have a great deal in common—the grape varietal, the country of origin, the fullness and body— and brands may only differ in relatively subtle ways, such as the finish and mouth feel.

Often an intermediate-level category, such as wine or beer, is used in the competition-based approach positioning. Categories at this level are well understood and frequently used by consumers when framing a consumption decision. For example, a consumer may first decide that wine (rather than beer, hard liquor, or a nonalcoholic beverage) fits a particular occasion and then select among the brands of wine available by comparing their distinguishing

Figure 4.1
Positioning and the Organization of Information in Memory

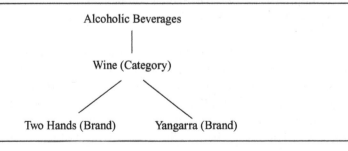

features (i.e., points of difference). However, there are occasions when a more specific or a more abstract categorization may be used. For example, if Two Hands were targeted to wine connoisseurs, using the more specific categorization of an "Australian Shiraz" rather than a "wine" might be appropriate, because consumers with greater expertise naturally tend to think in terms of more specific categories. Alternatively, a brand may be categorized at a broad level in hopes of attracting customers from a variety of products that have little in common. Thus, Two Hands might represent its brand as an alcoholic beverage appropriate for situations where one wishes to appear sophisticated and demonstrate good taste, making it an alternative to champagne and cocktails. In general, the categorization that highlights a brand's strongest point of difference is preferred.

Establishing Category Membership

Categories serve as the foundation for the competition-based approach to positioning because they imply the goal that a consumer achieves by using a brand. Informing consumers that a brand has membership in the wine category tells them its purpose: it enhances the enjoyment of an elegant meal, and it promotes social relations. If consumers know the category, linking the brand to it quickly brings to mind the goal that is achieved by brand use; in other words, asking someone to have a glass of wine is an invitation to visit and to socialize.

In some instances, people may be unfamiliar with the category in which a brand holds membership. To address this issue, the *points of parity* associated with the category, rather than the category label, can be used to convey the goal served by the brand. If people did not know the goals achieved by drinking wine, a frame of reference could be created by describing a brand as a beverage that contains alcohol, goes well with food, and is enjoyed in formal and casual social interactions. Points of parity can also serve to clarify the goal served by the brand when category membership alone is insufficient to do so. Indicating that Two Hands is an accompaniment to an elegant meal or is appreciated at special occasions informs people that it is a high-end brand, not an everyday one.

Alternatively, marketers may employ *exemplars* of a product category rather than the category label to signal the goal served by a brand. Exemplars are brands that are widely known for a particular benefit. In the men's designer clothing category, Adam Kimmel or Patrik Ervell may be unknown. But when they are placed in a context of famous American designers of men's clothing such as Calvin Klein, Perry Ellis, and Tommy Hilfiger, consumers are likely to make the connection that the Kimmel or Ervell brand serves the goal of wearing clothing with cutting-edge design.

When a new brand is introduced, consumers attempt to categorize it in a manner that helps them understand at least one goal that can be achieved by using it. This is easily done when the brand fits neatly into a familiar category, as would be the case for a new brand of wine or beer. Selecting a category becomes more challenging for innovative products. By definition, such brands do not neatly align with the points of parity associated with specific, existing categories. In response to this problem, it may be tempting to employ an abstract category and associated goal. However, this approach can be risky.

Consider TiVo, which pioneered the digital video recorder category. TiVo's initial advertising merely told consumers that the brand empowered users to "watch what they want when they want." Although this proposition was appealing (who wouldn't want such freedom), in the absence of more specific product categorization, consumers had difficulty grasping exactly what TiVo was and, therefore, how they might use it. A better strategy would have been to begin by relating TiVo to a familiar category such as VCRs, explaining that like a VCR, TiVo enabled the TV viewer to record shows for viewing at a later time. Against this backdrop, consumers could appreciate what made TiVo unique (i.e., the point of difference), such as easier searching and recording due to the on-screen TV guide listings. Once such a basic understanding of TiVo (and DVRs in general) was established, the more abstract goal of controlling one's entertainment could have been meaningfully introduced.

Whatever the means of representing the category, marketers must help consumers understand the goal in using a brand *before* or *concurrent with* the presentation of information about why it is superior to alternatives with the same frame of reference. For example, when Apple introduced iPhone, it informed consumers that the brand was a communication device *before* it informed consumers about why it was superior to other brands. This category was evoked not only by the brand name, but also by comparing the iPhone to traditional phones in initial advertisements. Once people understood iPhone's primary communication function, additional functions such as ease of Internet search and e-mailing were introduced to highlight its points of difference in relation to other phones.

In other situations, it is important to present both the category and point of difference concurrently. For example, when consumers use a search engine such as Google to find a product, they are likely to be making an on-the-spot decision about which site to click on. Thus, a clear representation of the brand's category membership and point of difference in the Google listing will help consumers make this choice. Along these lines, FTD Flowers' listing states "send flowers, roses, gifts, gift baskets, and more with convenient local delivery." This identifies the specific categories in which the brand competes (flowers, gifts, baskets) as well as the point of difference (local delivery), and thus provides a basis for discriminating among the available alternatives. In contrast, when consumers land on Fogdog.com's listing, they are only informed about its category membership (football, golf, apparel, exercise equipment) and not its point of difference, which invites them to consider also Dick's Sporting Goods or Sports Authority, or some other online sporting goods vendor.

The importance of choosing a competitive frame by identifying a category is illustrated by the recent launch of the Nano economy vehicle by Tata Motors of India. Nano was introduced at a base price of 100,000 rupees (U.S. $2,500), making it substantially cheaper than Maruit Udyog, which was priced at about $5,000 and had 50 percent share of the economy market. With a population of 1.1 billion and low penetration of the car category in India (12 car owners per thousand in the population versus 765 in the United States), there were at least two ways to frame the competition for Nano.[2] One possibility was as a safe alternative to the motorbike (a ubiquitous mode of transportation in India). This categorization was likely to attract those who were at point of entry in the car market, such as college students.

Alternatively, Nano might be positioned as an economy car that provides superior customer value. Nano was inexpensive to purchase, and it was relatively fuel efficient, promising 52 mpg in the city and 61 mpg on the highway. It was also stylish and offered more seating room than the larger economy car and main competitor, the Maruti 800. Such an approach might appeal to families that already had cars but would be attracted to a vehicle that offered superior value. Thus, the choice of the motorbike category versus the economy car category as the competitive frame affects both the target customer and the brand's point of difference.

Selecting a Point(s) of Difference

The selection of a brand's points of difference begins with its competitive strengths and insight about consumers' motivations for using the category and/or brand. The goal is to find a feature or benefit that distinguishes the brand from competitors in the same category and that is valued by consumers. When the point of difference is a benefit (rather than a product feature), the claim is strengthened by providing reasons to believe the benefit claim.

Fast-food chain Subway offers healthier meals than other quick-serve restaurants because its sandwiches have fewer grams of fat. Here, the healthier benefit is supported by an attribute "reason to believe": fewer grams of fat. Although attributes can offer a compelling way to support a benefit point of difference, in many cases they are readily imitable. For this reason, brand positions often rely on *image* to provide a rationale for a benefit point of difference—the type of person who uses the brand and the type of uses it has. Nike, for example, has used professional athletes to support the brand's claim of superior performance in athletic shoes rather than relying on attributes such as unique technology in product design. Image is also used when a category's attributes are not relevant to consumers. The endorsement of celebrities such as Mariah Carey, Kim Kardashian, or Paris Hilton provides consumers with a reason to believe that a particular brand of fragrance will enhance their personal appeal. Image brand positions are sustained by marketing support that links the image with the brand.

Leading brands typically adopt the benefit that motivates category use as their point of difference, whereas "follower" brands choose a niche. Tide, the leading detergent, is simply superior at cleaning clothes. Follower brands make narrower claims: Cheer cleans clothes in cold water and Wisk is strong against stains.

In choosing a point of difference, marketers usually prefer benefits that reflect an existing consumers' belief. For example, Honey Nut Cheerios developed a strong brand franchise by capitalizing on consumers' beliefs that honey is more nutritious than sugar (it is not) and that Cheerios is among the most nutritious brands of cereal. If, however, a brand is distinguished on a benefit or belief that consumers have not yet accepted, efforts can be made to change consumers' opinions. Prompting such change is generally more costly than adopting accepted consumer beliefs about benefits, but it is possible. Along these lines, Listerine mouthwash was successful in overcoming consumers' negative perceptions of its taste by convincing consumers that the unpleasant taste indicated that it was working to kill bacteria and combat bad breath.

For most brands, a single benefit serves as the point of difference. This enables the marketer to convince the consumer more simply and easily of the benefit's importance when making a brand choice. However, there are several circumstances in which a position is based on multiple benefits. When competitors are each focusing on a particular benefit, a brand might compete by claiming to do it all. In the soap category, Ivory is positioned as offering superior cleaning, Dove as providing better moisturizing, and Zest as ensuring greater deodorizing. When Lever 2000 was launched, it was positioned as the bar soap that does it all. This placed Lever 2000 in its own category as the one that offered all the benefits, with the other brands being lumped together as incomplete. As a result, Lever 2000 enjoyed rapid growth in the bar soap market.

Multiple features are also used to position a brand on the basis of its value. A value position may be represented by the following equation:

$$\text{Value} = \frac{\text{Functional Benefits} + \text{Psychic Benefits}}{\text{Monetary Costs} + \text{Time Costs}}$$

This equation is conceptual, with the benefits of a brand presented in the numerator and the costs in the denominator. Value is enhanced by increasing the benefits and reducing the costs.

To illustrate the value equation, consider UPS's positioning. UPS is the leading ground parcel firm in the United States and second in air freight deliveries. UPS offers value by ensuring that packages and letters get to their destination on time. They do this by offering early-morning delivery (8:30 A.M.) and by routing their trucks to make as many right-hand turns as possible so as not to be slowed by oncoming traffic. One benefit of these services is psychic—customers are confident that packages will get to their destination on time. UPS saves companies money because its reliable delivery allows firms to produce product on demand, and thus limit the inventory required. And UPS's wireless tracking of shipments saves managers time by enabling them to monitor the progress of the packages while engaging in other activities. Thus, UPS enhances value by increasing the functional and emotional benefits and by reducing the monetary and time costs.

When selecting multiple benefits, it is important to assess their fit with each other. Specifically, brands possessing potentially opposing benefits can undermine consumer confidence in the brand's position. For example, when the value proposition is that a brand has high quality, a low price might undermine this belief. Similarly, when a food brand offers superior nutrition, consumers might be skeptical of a superior taste claim. And if a car is positioned as safe, consumers may doubt the claim that it also offers exceptional acceleration.

Finally, marketers should use caution in selecting benefits to convey a brand's point of difference on the basis of what consumers say. Consumers profess an interest in some benefits not because of the benefit's importance to their brand choice, but because they feel peer pressure to do so. Thus, consumers often indicate high interest in a car's safety and fuel efficiency even though there is not a correlation between these reports and actual brand choice.

The Competition-Focused Positioning Triangle

A useful tool for understanding the competition-based approach to positioning is a triangle that depicts hierarchical memory organization (see Figure 4.2).

Figure 4.2
The Competition-Based Positioning Triangle

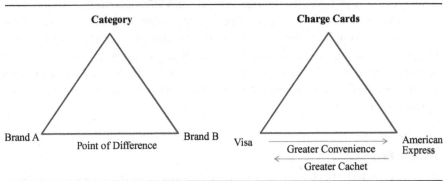

The triangle provides a visual representation of the two key elements of a brand position: the *category* and the *point of difference*. The relationship between each brand and the category is communicated either by a *category label*, by *points of parity that define the category*, or by an *exemplar(s) of the category*. The relationship between the brands is their point(s) of difference. Both product category membership and the points of difference gain integrity in the eyes of consumers when they are supported by concrete reasons to believe these claims. These reasons to believe can take the form of attributes or image. Marketers must ensure that the benefits, attributes, and image are positively correlated with each other and that the benefits selected are not normative. Although it is typical to focus on a single point of difference, when the brand position is vaguely defined as "does it all" or "best value," multiple benefits are necessary to support the claim.

The charge card category provides an illustration of the positioning triangle. Visa and American Express both claim membership in the charge card category. The fact that Visa is the most widely available card provides a reason to believe its convenience point of difference. American Express, on the other hand, has built its equity by highlighting the cachet associated with using its card. One way these brands compete is to make the competitor's points of difference into a point of parity. Along these lines, Visa offers a platinum card to enhance its prestige and thus blunt American Express's point of difference. American Express promotes its growing acceptance at retail as a means of reducing Visa's convenience advantage. The danger in these strategies is that in attempting to render the competitor's point of difference a point of parity, the brands dilute the clarity of their own point of difference.

CUSTOMER-BASED PERSPECTIVE

The competition-based perspective emphasizes distinguishing a brand from competing brands on benefits important to customers. By contrast, the customer-based perspective focuses on how consumption of the brand and the category is relevant to customers' lives. Adopting a customer-based approach requires uncovering the abstract meanings associated with consumption of a particular brand or the general category. We refer to these as *brand essence* and *category essence,* respectively.

Brand Essence

A process called "laddering" is often used to uncover the essence of a brand (Figure 4.3). Laddering is based on the notion that brand meaning can be deepened by examining progressively more abstract implications of a brand's features. The bottom rung of the ladder represents the starting point, which is usually an attribute. The implication of this attribute is a functional benefit, which is the second rung on the ladder. And the implication of a functional benefit is an emotional benefit, which is the third rung on the ladder. Finally, the emotional benefit implies the brand's essence. As the ladder is ascended, the focus is less on the attributes of the brand and more on the role that the brand plays in consumers' lives.

Figure 4.3
The Laddering Process

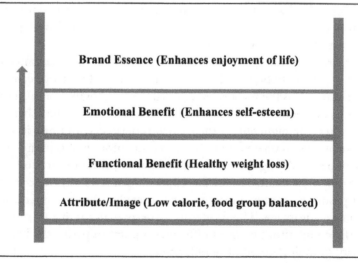

Brand Essence (Enhances enjoyment of life)

Emotional Benefit (Enhances self-esteem)

Functional Benefit (Healthy weight loss)

Attribute/Image (Low calorie, food group balanced)

Figure 4.4
McDonald's Brand Essence

To illustrate the laddering process, consider how the weight-loss brand Jenny Craig might use laddering to market its weight-control meals. Jenny Craig delivers low-calorie meals that provide the needed balance of protein, fat, and carbohydrates. The implication of these attributes is that they will facilitate healthy weight loss. Losing weight will enhance physical appearance and thus self-esteem, as reflected in greater satisfaction with life. Thus, Jenny Craig's essence is enhancing the enjoyment of life, which is the consumer's goal in using the brand.

Brand essence can also be developed by associating a brand with brands in other categories that share a common goal (Figure 4.4). In a McDonald's ad depicting a blind date, a young man named Larry calls on his date. He immediately attempts to manage her expectations by clarifying who he is and who he is not. He points out that he is not a doctor, lawyer, banker, or CPA. He is a store clerk. He tells his date that they will not be dining at a bistro, casa, or maison, nor will they be attending the opera, the symphony, or the ballet. Instead he proposes that they drive in his ordinary car to McDonald's and then go to a movie. The factors common to Larry's job, car, and choice of restaurant and entertainment imply McDonald's brand's essence, an unpretentious place to get a good meal.

The association of a brand with products in disparate categories often results in the anthropomorphizing of the brand. Thus, brands might be viewed as having a gender, age, social class, as well as personality characteristics. Apple is approachable, Burger King is masculine, and Old Navy is family-oriented.

Cartier watches are upscale and Timex is for everybody. Thus, in developing a brand's position, it is important to recognize that the benefits selected reflect the brand's personality, which is as much a part of the brand as its category membership and point of difference. Indeed, when Levi's positioned its brand to attract upscale consumers, it dropped its line of coveralls, which implied that it was a blue-collar brand.

Category Essence

Consumer goals related to the category can also be used to develop a brand's position. Similar to brand essence, the development of category essence entails the association of the brand to other objects that collectively represent a consumer goal. However, for category essence, the connection is among objects that imply the goal in using the *category* rather than the brand. To illustrate category essence, consider the following statement describing the essence of the beer category for 18- to 34-year-old men:

> *These individuals may feel threatened by the complexities and conflicts of everyday life. They are confused and perhaps depressed about how to achieve harmony between their desire to discharge their primal passions and the constraints imposed by society. They desire intimate relations without the attendant commitment. They are searching for the opportunity to give expression to their talents without being encumbered by the demands imposed by formal organizations. Beer allows these individuals to indulge themselves and perhaps to make less salient the conflict between their aspiration and the limitations imposed on their behaviors by society.*

Category essence uses insight about how the category fits with consumers' goals as a brand's point of difference. The assumption is that if consumers perceive that a brand is positioned in a manner that is sensitive to their concerns, the brand is viewed as the solution to those concerns. For example, Lee jeans showed the difficulties women encountered when trying to get into a pair of jeans. Consumers were urged to buy Lee jeans to remedy this problem, though no rationale for this choice was provided.

Category essence bases a brand position on insight about the category. Presumably most brands have access to this insight. This makes category essence a strategy of last resort; it is used when a brand does not have equity that can be used to differentiate it. If it did, a product-based or a brand-essence approach would be used. As brands in more and more categories become commodities, the use of category essence has increased. The result is that many companies use the brand positioning approach of associating their brands with a problem not solved by other brands, which makes it difficult for consumers to link brands to their positions. A better strategy is to use consumer insight to identify consumer motivations that might be uniquely satisfied by a brand.

USING THE PERSPECTIVES TO WRITE A POSITIONING STATEMENT

Once a firm has made decisions related to a brand's category membership and point of difference, it is useful to summarize these decisions in a positioning statement. This statement is an internal document that may be shared with the sales force, the advertising agency, and more generally with anyone who needs to understand who the brand's target market is and when and why this target should choose the company's brand. A positioning statement is *not* ad copy. Rather, it is a general summary of the key aspects of the marketing strategy, and as such it serves as the foundation for decisions about marketing tactics, such as how the product will be packaged, where it will be distributed, the level of service that will be provided, how it will be priced, and what will be said in marketing communications.

Establishing the Position

Our analysis of positioning is summarized in Figure 4.5. Establishing the brand's category membership, and thereby the competitive frame of reference, is the first priority. This can be achieved by using a category label, listing points of parity with other brands that achieve the same goal, or referencing an exemplar that highlights what goal a brand accomplishes. The latter two approaches are particularly useful when the target customer is unfamiliar with the category or there is a need to be precise about what is accomplished by brand consumption.

If consumers are familiar with a brand's category membership, focus centers on establishing a point of difference. This involves finding a product attribute that is important to consumers and that distinguishes the brand from alternative offerings. Brand leaders should consider the benefit that motivates category consumption and out-shout competition on this benefit. Brand followers should use the category-defining benefit to establish membership in the category and focus on some niche benefit where they have a barrier to competitive entry. Points of difference that are congenial with consumers' beliefs are preferred over those that require consumers to change their beliefs. The

Figure 4.5
Summary of Brand Positioning

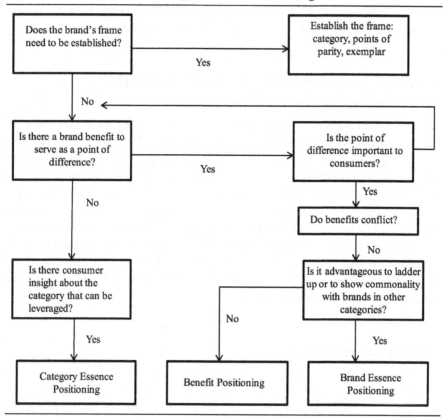

proposed position is then assessed for conflicting benefits. If there are none, the frame and point of difference benefit can be presented as the brand's position.

Alternatively, the marketer may use the laddering technique to present the brand's essence over time, where the brand's emotional benefits and fit in consumers' lives are highlighted. If there is no apparent point of difference on a functional benefit, the viability of using consumer insight as the point of difference can be examined. This entails using the fact that the brand understands consumers' goals and the impediments to reaching those goals as the brand's point of difference. This is a strategy of last resort, because competitors are also likely to have access to such consumer insight as a basis for brand positioning.

Key Questions the Positioning Statement Must Answer

The specific format used when writing a positioning statement may vary from company to company. However, in one way or another, a positioning statement should answer the following four questions.

1. *Who is the target for brand use?*

    Brand positioning begins with a clear understanding of the targeted customers. It is useful to describe these customers in terms of their current usage patterns, demographic characteristics, and general goals (see Chapter 2, "Identifying Market Segments and Selecting Targets"). Insight into the target's goals is especially important because purchase decisions are rarely motivated by a desire for a brand per se. Rather, there is a belief that having the brand will facilitate achieving some more fundamental goal that is important to the target.

2. *Why should the brand be considered (i.e., to what category does the brand belong and what goal does it allow the target to achieve)?*

    As noted earlier, this question is often answered by invoking membership in a particular category. Such an approach is particularly appropriate when launching a new product, because it links the new product to familiar products and thereby facilitates understanding. As customers' knowledge of the brand grows, the competitive frame may evolve to span several product categories and be defined by usage occasions or users. For example, Ariel, a nonalcoholic wine, might define its competitive set in terms of products that are consumed when both sociability and clear thinking are requisite. Competition might include bottled water and soft drinks, as well as other nonalcoholic wines. Similarly, Waterman pens might be positioned as heirlooms that can be passed on to the next generation, thereby competing with antique furniture and jewelry.

3. *Why should the brand be chosen over other alternatives in the competitive set?*

    A brand must offer a compelling point of difference in relation to other options in the marketplace. Moreover, the firm must make the claimed point of difference believable to the consumer. The simplest approach is to promote a unique product attribute. Thus, Visa may claim that it is the most widely accepted card and reference the number of places that it is accepted around the world as support for that claim.

    When the point of difference is more abstract or image-based, support for the claim may reside in more general associations to the company that have been developed over time. Thus, Chanel No. 5 perfume may claim to be the quintessential elegant, French perfume and support this claim by noting the long association between Chanel and haute couture.

Typically, brands focus on a single point of difference, though this point of difference may be an abstraction based on multiple features of the product. For example, BIC might claim that its disposable razors offer greater convenience than other disposable razors. The brand's broad distribution, in-store placement near checkout counters, and low price might all be used to support this claim.

It is important that the point of difference be specific and meaningful. Claims such as "highest quality" or "best value" are vague. What defines high quality or value for one target may mean only moderate quality or value to another. Quality or value should be defined in terms that are meaningful to the target.

When a brand's benefits are at parity with those of the competition, the point of difference might be the depth of insight into consumers' goals in using the product. Consumers often make the inference that if a brand presents an intimate understanding of consumers' goals in using the product, it must also offer a superior way to achieve those goals.

4. *How will choosing the brand help the target members accomplish their goal(s)?*

The final element of a positioning statement links the brand's point of difference to the target's goal(s), drawing on an understanding of brand essence and category essence. Visa is accepted at more places than any other credit card. This means that Visa customers can shop and travel with the confidence that their card will be accepted. The low price and convenient availability of BIC disposable razors may enable busy people to focus on matters that mean more to them than their razor.

It is important to recognize that the elements of a positioning statement are interrelated. A particular feature or benefit may distinguish the brand when considered against one set of competitors but not another. Further, a point of difference may help accomplish the goals of one target but not another target. Thus, each target requires a distinct positioning; if the same category membership and point of difference are relevant to two targets, these targets should be combined. Moreover, because both competitors and the goals of targeted customers evolve over time, a brand's positioning requires periodic review and updating. To illustrate these ideas, we return to the Zipcar example introduced at the outset of the chapter.

Sample Positioning Statement: Zipcar

When Zipcar was introduced to the market, a competition-based perspective was adopted. The positioning emphasized the superiority of the service in relation to the competitive alternative of owning one's own car. This approach is captured in the following positioning statement:

> To urban-dwelling, educated techno-savvy consumers [target], when you use Zipcar car-sharing service instead of owning a car [competitive frame], you save money while reducing your carbon footprint [points of difference].

Once Zipcar was established as an alternative to owning a car, greater emphasis could be given to how Zipcar helped the targeted customer achieve his or her goals. This might have been done by laddering up from the points of difference to a brand essence of being a "responsible choice" for transportation and linking to the target's goal of demonstrating a commitment to protecting the environment. This more customer-based approach is illustrated below:

> To urban-dwelling, educated, techno-savvy consumers who worry about the environment that future generations will inherit [target and insight], when you use Zipcar car-sharing service you make a responsible choice [brand essence] and demonstrate your commitment to protecting the environment [target's goal].

The positioning of a new brand often evolves from a competition-based approach to one that places greater emphasis on customers' goals as knowledge of the brand increases. Once a brand is well-established, a single statement, such as the one below, may serve to capture elements of both competition-focused and customer-focused positioning:

> To urban-dwelling, educated, techno-savvy consumers who worry about the environment that future generations will inherit [target and insight], Zipcar is the car-sharing service [competitive frame] that lets you save money and reduce your carbon footprint [points of difference], making you feel you've made a smart, responsible choice that demonstrates your commitment to protecting the environment [target's goal].

The job of positioning a brand is never done. As new competitors enter the market, a brand's positioning must be modified. The entry of other car-sharing services, such as Connect by Hertz, force Zipcar to explain why targeted customers should prefer it to services that offer similar attributes. A focus on brand essence may be helpful in this regard. Zipcar may do well to target younger consumers, emphasizing its pioneering role in the car-sharing category and positioning the brand as one that demonstrates a commitment to protecting the environment. By contrast, Connect may concentrate on serving Hertz' existing customer base (older business travelers) on a new occasion (short-term city rentals) and leverage its number-one status and reputation of quality service.

Troubleshooting Your Positioning Statement

Judging the adequacy of a positioning statement is necessarily a subjective exercise. However, common problems can be avoided if your positioning statement passes the following tests:

- Is the statement as compelling if you substitute a competitors' brand for your brand? Leading brands may succeed in adopting positions that might also be credibly claimed by followers, but the resources of the leader allow it to sustain the position. Follower brands should reconsider the competitive set or the claimed point of difference if the claim is not unique to the brand.
- Does reading the statement provide a clear understanding of who should buy the brand, when that person is likely to buy it, and what would motivate purchase? If not, the aspect of the statement that is vague should be made more specific.
- Is it clear why the target should consider the brand to be a compelling way to achieve some important goal? If not, the linkage between the brand's point of difference and the target's goals requires modification.

SUMMARY

We have argued that competition-based and customer-based insights are necessary to develop a clear and compelling brand positioning. The competition-based perspective identifies the category to which the brand belongs and its point of difference from other members of that category. The customer-based perspective, in turn, highlights how the brand fits into the lives of those who consume it. These perspectives may be expressed separately or drawn together in a brand positioning statement, which serves as the guidepost for all the decisions that bring the brand to life in the minds of consumers. The brand positioning statement identifies a targeted group of customers and explains when they should consider the brand, why the brand should be chosen over competing brands, and how the brand fits into their lives and helps them achieve important goals.

Alice M. Tybout is the Harold T. Martin Professor of Marketing and a former chairperson of the Marketing Department at the Kellogg School of Management. She is also co-director of the Kellogg on Branding Program and director of the Kellogg on Consumer Marketing Strategy Program at the James L. Allen Center. She is co-editor of Kellogg on Branding (John Wiley & Sons, 2005). She received her BS and MA from Ohio State University and her PhD from Northwestern University.

Brian Sternthal is the Kraft Professor of Marketing and a past chairperson of the Marketing Department at the Kellogg School of Management. He is also a past editor of the Journal of Consumer Research, an Association for Consumer Research Fellow in Consumer Behavior, and the co-author of Advertising Strategy (Copley). He received his BS from McGill University and his PhD from Ohio State University.

NOTES

1. Keegan, Paul (2009), "The Best New Idea in Business," *Fortune*, September 14, 42–52.
2. Lemley, Amy (2009), "The Tata Nano: The People's Car," Darden Business Publishing, Case # UVA-M-0768.
   Krishnan, Janaki (2009), "The Nano, World's Cheapest Car, to Hit Indian Roads," Reuters Online, March 23. www.reuters.com/article/technologyNews/idUSTRE52M2PA20090323

CHAPTER 5

WRITING A BRAND POSITIONING STATEMENT AND TRANSLATING IT INTO BRAND DESIGN

BOBBY J. CALDER

INTRODUCTION

Meaning is the stuff of brands. All good marketers know this. No matter how tangible, technical, or mundane a product is, the product is not the brand. Products are branded by giving them *meaning*. Through marketing, a product is made more meaningful to the consumer than it would be of its own accord.

Here is an example. Let's assume we're selling hamburgers. We could simply sell hamburgers, just as they are. Our product is a hamburger, and a hamburger is a hamburger. Of course, if we're ambitious, we could make sure our hamburgers are not the same as anyone else's hamburgers. We can offer a special version of the hamburger, a better burger—one with a special sauce, for instance. Alternatively, we can sell an ordinary hamburger but extend the offer to include other things with it, such as free french fries, delivery, or Internet access while you eat. In the end, consumers might find what we do meaningful enough to purchase our hamburgers. But the meaning is left to them to find; we are simply selling a product.

A brand, on the other hand, provides this meaning directly to the consumer. So how do we brand our hamburger? We must go beyond selling the product itself, no matter how superior we believe it is. We must transcend the idea of the product as a physical or objective entity. We must create and convey the meaning of the product so that the consumer's idea of the product is the idea that *we* want them to have.

Thus, we must make a leap from the world of things to the world of ideas. Unfortunately, most discussions of branding in business books seems to make this process more difficult for marketers than it should be. The core issue of meaning is often obfuscated by catchy terms that imply that there is some magic, or even a proprietary secret, at stake. Brands become the unique selling proposition, the big idea, the value proposition, the commitment, or the promise. Even helpful terms, such as benefit and positioning, are often used more as buzzwords. Such discussions often obscure the fact that *branding is the difficult (but actually very straightforward) process of making a product meaningful*. To do this, we must express the brand meaning in words. This chapter shows how to write a *brand positioning statement* to give your brand meaning.

How to Express a Brand in Words

Perhaps the most common way of expressing the meaning of a brand is to write a brand positioning statement. The brand positioning statement is a short, one-sentence description of the meaning of the brand using a simple three-part format. The sentence is written for (but not meant to be read by) targeted consumers.

> To   <target consumer>   our brand is the   <category>   that   <point-of-difference>.

Thus, the brand positioning for a cola-type soft drink might be stated this way:

> To younger or less affluent consumers, this cola brand is the traditional cola known for its refreshing taste; it is part of a stubbornly positive approach to life that is perfect for the pursuit of happy time—the times when only this cola will do.

In formulating a brand positioning in a sentence like the one above, the goal is to articulate a concept that is the idea of the brand: its meaning. It is the *idea or concept* that consumers will have based on their experience of the product. If this experience is rich enough, the concept will be highly meaningful. It will represent in the consumer's mind what the experience has meant. However, because it is our job as marketers to *direct* the experience for our target consumer, we need to anticipate in advance what that concept should be, then articulate it in words—this becomes the *brand positioning statement.*

Thus, our cola brand is the one that customers think of choosing when they are actively seeking happy times. This concept anticipates an experience that consumers could have. The drink is about seeking out tried and true ways to be happy even during the rush of a busy life and difficult times.

The concept is expressed as a single sentence to ensure clarity and focus. The sentence also makes a statement; it is a declaration. Of course, we could add more useful discussion to the statement—even a 50-slide PowerPoint deck—but not at the expense of clarity and focus. The sentence format forces discipline because we should be able to reduce any unitary, coherent idea to a single sentence. It ensures that we cannot talk around the concept. We cannot bury the idea. We cannot equivocate. When creating a brand position, it is important to capture the concept in this elemental form and to make it the center of attention, no matter how much additional information we add to the brand brief. Ultimately this ensures that the implications of the concept for the marketing effort are as clear as possible. It might even be said that the defining litmus test of branding is a product for which a strong positioning statement has been articulated before the marketing effort begins.

Many alternative brand positioning statements are possible, however. In our cola example, another successful concept might be:

> To families who drink cola with meals, this brand of cola tastes as good as the leading brands to everyone in the family but does not break the food budget.

As this example illustrates, ordinarily there are many possibilities in creating a brand positioning statement. But no matter how the brand is positioned, the statement should reflect experiences that will lead consumers to think about the product in a meaningful way.

In coming up with the positioning statement for our brand, we should thus explore the space of alternative positioning statements. Even if we have a direction, such as one of the two cola statements above, it will be possible to explore different wordings. Language matters with brand positioning statements. One way language matters is that we are trying to do the best job possible in expressing exactly what the concept is. So finding the right words is important. Wordsmithing, moreover, can point up nuances between subtly different concepts. As with:

> To families who drink cola with meals, this brand of cola is the family favorite because using it lets you afford to buy other treats for the family.

The concept here is similar to the previous brand statement, but the wording matters. Each statement taps into a somewhat different experience and is meaningful in a slightly different way.

It's also possible to write a weak brand concept statement. Often a sign of this is using vague language or meaningless words, such as "high quality," "reliable," or "great service." For example:

> To consumers who sometimes drink cola, this brand of cola tastes good and is available in several convenient sizes.

This positioning statement uses generic words and phrases ("tastes good," "convenient sizes") that fail to make clear what the meaningful experience for the consumer is.

In the end, then, the test of a positioning statement is that it must point to a *real experience that consumers will find personally meaningful.*

THE THREE PARTS OF THE BRAND POSITIONING STATEMENT

As we described earlier, there are three distinct components of a brand concept as expressed by a brand positioning statement: the *target,* the *category*, and the *point of difference.* Let's take a look at each component.

The Target

The *target* is a description of who the consumer is. Think of it as "to whom" the statement is addressed. Keep in mind, however, that the targeted consumer will not ever read the positioning statement directly; it is simply a tool to help the marketer direct his or her efforts to that particular consumer. To anchor the concept in the consumer's experience, we must be clear about who the consumer is. Not everyone will experience a product in the same way, and only some consumers will experience it in the way we want. We need to be clear about who those consumers are.

Consider the statement below for a hybrid gas-electric automobile about to be relaunched in the Chinese market. The product has a luxury price-point. It is has not been successful in the past because it is considered expensive while lacking features comparable to other luxury automobiles.

> To wealthy individuals and business leaders who can afford an expensive automobile but have a sense of responsibility to others, this brand is a luxury automobile that shows you care about society in a way that others will respect.

The *target* is wealthy people who are characterized as individuals and business leaders who stand out from the crowd and who have prospered with the rise of the Chinese economy. Further, these are people who can show off their wealth but also want to show that they care about others, not just themselves. They want to show respect for the larger society. They may have gotten rich first, but they do not want to seem apart from others. In this case, the target "to whom" that the brand is directed is clear; we can see why this product would appeal to these people and not others.

Of course, much more information about the target is desirable. In a marketing plan, questions of audience size and market attractiveness would arise, as would questions about how to reach the target through which types of media. But we do not need to burden the brand positioning statement with this information. Instead, we are trying to characterize the target with a thumbnail sketch that indicates the target's role in the narrative of the brand experience. Think of this as describing a movie to someone: "This movie is about a young boy coming of age in a small town." The thumbnail sketch captures the essence of the role in the movie just as a positioning statement should capture who the target consumer is.

The target component usually works best if the target is characterized not only demographically but also with some psychological insight. In the example above, this insight is represented with the phrase, "having a sense of responsibility to others." The more we can draw out the psychological insight, the better. Hence, for the Chinese consumer we could ask, "Is this sense of responsibility real or is it only seemingly real, aimed at appearing responsible to others?" Additional insight helps marketers to focus more clearly on the target.

The Category

The *category* is the core component of the concept, and it is central to the brand positioning statement. The category provides a frame of reference that consumers can use to position the product in their minds; they do this by comparing it to other similar products in the same category. To understand anything, we must be able to relate it to other things we already know. Thus, we assign things to categories that are familiar. For example, to help someone understand where Chicago is located, we might say that it is in the midwestern section of the United States and in northeastern Illinois. Here, Chicago is placed in the category "Midwest" and further categorized as "northeastern Illinois." This helps people position the city in their minds by comparing it to other places they (hopefully) already know.

In the case of the hybrid automobile example, consumers understand the brand position by first understanding its basic category, "luxury cars." The brand is further categorized in this example as "things that show a person cares about society." This is a category because the consumer is familiar with things (e.g., wearing a mask if you have a cold) that go together to form a category. Thus, categorization can be literal (a luxury car) but can go beyond this to be much more creative and evocative (things that show caring about society). This creativity is important to the art of the brand positioning statement.

The Point of Difference

The final component of a brand concept is the *point of difference*. This component is necessary to complete a fully realized concept. Once we know what a product is similar to (category), then we need to understand what it is different from (point of difference). How does the product differ from other things categorized the same way? Chicago and Detroit are both Midwestern cities, so in order to understand Chicago we would need to understand how it is different from other cities in its category (the Midwest). In our hybrid automobile example, a point of difference is required to differentiate this product from others. In our statement, this automobile is different because it shows that you care about society "in a way that others will respect." The implication is that there are other ways that would not garner respect (living modestly, perhaps). Again, note the nuance, the importance of choosing words carefully, and the need for consumer insight.

Having a strong point of difference not only makes a concept complete and clear, it makes it harder to copy. Any concept can be copied, but if the brand is successful, a strong point of difference makes it obvious that any product trying to be different in the same way is simply a copy.

The Relationship among the Components

When crafting brand positioning statements, all three components (target, category, and point of difference) should be considered simultaneously. The sentence format of the brand positioning statement is necessarily linear, but this should not be taken to imply that we should think about the components in a linear way—first the target characterization, then the categorization, then the point of difference at the end, and then we're done. It is important to go back and forth between the components. For instance, the target often comes into focus more sharply when thinking about the point of difference. In the cola example, we might have characterized our target as "younger or less-affluent consumers." But in thinking about the point of difference as "perfect for the pursuit of happy times," we might be led to a more insightful characterization of the target, perhaps as people "who live in a world where everyday ordinary pleasures have to take on more importance."

CREATING A STRONG POSITIONING STATEMENT

Even a weak concept can be useful in branding a product if the concept is clearly articulated. Obviously, stronger brand concepts are much more effective at attracting consumers. So what makes a concept stronger? The answer lies in a term much bandied about, but often superficially understood, in marketing circles: engagement.[1]

Using Engagement

In terms of a brand position, engagement is the extent to which consumers see the product as relevant to a larger, more encompassing experience, possibly even encompassing their lives as a whole. In our luxury car example, the Chinese consumer would not view the automobile as just about the experience of driving a car—the car defines who they are in terms of their place in society. Their place in society is profoundly meaningful to them in terms of their whole life. This quality of engagement is the hallmark of strong brand positioning statements. Making concepts more engaging entails moving beyond a basic level of categorization (luxury cars, cola) and toward a more psychological experience of the product and even toward a more encompassing life experience (defining a consumer's place in society).

Let's look at relative levels of engagement of a well-known brand, Tiffany, as it has evolved over time.[2] Originally the brand could be described as:

> To urban rich people, Tiffany is the brand of luxury retail store offering great craftsmanship.

The brand's core category, "luxury retail store," is basic; it refers—in a literal and product-oriented way—to where the store belongs in the set of similar stores (e.g., Gucci and the like). The point of difference (great craftsmanship) adds meaning by distinguishing the store by pointing to a focus on how the product is made rather than showiness. It hints at taste but settles for quality.

As the Tiffany brand matured, the core categorization became more abstract. The key attribute or image (luxury) was "laddered up" (see Chapter 4, "Developing a Compelling Brand Positioning") to a more consumer-oriented benefit that spoke to the *meaning* of luxury for particular consumers. Why does luxury appeal to the consumer? This may seem self-evident, but it is not. Luxury could appeal for many reasons, not least of which is showing off. As always, consumer insight is required. One insight is that luxury could appeal in terms of things that are unique. The consumer appreciates things that not everyone has, that are more valuable because they are not common, and that might gain value over time by virtue of their rarity. The brand positioning statement could read:

> To wealthy elites, Tiffany is the brand of luxury retail store where you can find unique gifts for the rich with "museum-quality" class.

Notice that in extending the core categorization to the benefit of uniqueness, which carries the emotion of pride with it, we have added another insight. When would a person especially appreciate something that is unique? Quite possibly when giving a gift to someone. Now it may seem that we have overly narrowed the brand concept by categorizing it in gift-giving terms. But the gift category is not limited to gifts to someone else; it can include giving a gift to yourself as well. So the purchasing decision is not about buying something expensive that you can afford. It is about giving something to someone else or to yourself that can be appreciated by virtue of its thoughtfulness as a unique gift.

The mature Tiffany brand is more like this:

To those purchasing something for a special, elite occasion, the Tiffany brand of luxury stores is where you can find pride and joy in choosing a timeless gift that is of impeccable taste.

Many people have occasions that they wish to celebrate as if they were among the elite, such as a special anniversary. Thus, it makes sense to mark the occasion with a gift that is timeless, once in a lifetime. Uniqueness becomes expressed at the even higher level of timeless—it is a gift so special it can be passed down to children in the same box that it comes in. (Note how in this scenario, a high price becomes meaningful for people who would otherwise find it an extravagance.) There is not only pride and status here, but joy as well. And even if you are uncomfortable selecting something this expensive (possibly you don't trust your taste since you rarely would buy something so expensive), Tiffany's brand positioning statement reassures you that this purchase will be different because Tiffany is itself "of impeccable taste."

This positioning takes the Tiffany brand to an even higher level of engagement: The brand is relevant to the broader experience of celebrating and commemorating important moments in life. It's not simply about liking the ring or the watch itself—with a Tiffany purchase, there is a much broader engagement with the consumer's life.

When positioning Tiffany, we could even take it one step further. It's one thing to celebrate moments, but a Tiffany purchase could tap into an even larger life goal. Why do we celebrate things like anniversaries? Because celebrations are social rituals aimed at cementing—perhaps even improving—close relationships. We could seek to use this larger life goal to make the brand even more engaging:

To anyone hoping to maintain or improve a close relationship, the Tiffany brand of luxury stores lets you create occasions to celebrate ties that endure over time with the gift of impeccable taste.

As brands mature, they should become more engaging in this way. But it's important to note that strengthening brands through engagement does not necessarily narrow them. At first glance the above statement might seem much narrower than the ones we began with. It is not. The Tiffany brand can move beyond special occasions to *creating* occasions. More engaging brand positioning statements open the door to marketing opportunity.

Using Support and Personality

Brand positioning statements are often associated with two other collateral statements. Often a *support statement* that gives a reason to believe in the concept accompanies the brand positioning statement. A classic example would be a concept for a beer positioned as "Tastes great but less filling." The support statement for this beer is "Great guys say so." While not logically necessary, such support statements can round out the brand positioning statement by making the concept clearer than it might be from the wording of the categorization and point of difference.

More important, support statements sometimes include information about brand character. The notion is that people can more clearly understand anything if it is personified, and brands are no different. So we attempt to describe what type of personality the brand would have as a character. Usually we specify a list of several personality adjectives, such as "rugged" or "creative." Sometimes these traits are embodied in an actual or fictional person. Thus, the brand personality of Tiffany might include the descriptor "elegant" and be embodied in the actress Audrey Hepburn.

Brand personality and character can be a useful adjunct to the brand positioning statement, but it cannot replace the need for a strong concept articulated in terms of categorization and point of difference. The consumer might get that an insurance company is "trustworthy," but this cannot take the place of the larger meaning of the product. Without this, insurance is still just insurance; it has no meaning unless we give it one.

Using Brand Stories

As much as the single-sentence brand positioning statement format is critical, it is also true that a sentence, no matter how well crafted, cannot entirely do justice to a brand. The reason is not a lack of information, or too few words. The reason is that branding is an effort to make products more meaningful to consumers. The place to look for even deeper sources of meaning, as our examples have indicated, is in the lives of consumers.

To do this, we look to their daily experiences and seek out narrative threads. We express these in a "brand story" format: When using the brand, something happens, which then causes something else to happen, and then ultimately the story has an ending. You can think of this sequence as a story, a play, or a movie. In each scene, things unfold and the narrative plays out.

In any story with a narrative thread, there is a certain amount of dramatic tension. Things could turn out for better or worse in the end. Therefore, when we look at the consumer's life for stories, there are three possibilities: Stories where things are already turning out well; stories where things are unresolved; and stories where things are turning out poorly. The latter two offer more branding potential because we can help the consumer make things turn out better with our brand. Also, the story is more interesting if it has the potential for a better ending. When we write a brand story, the brand positioning statement becomes the conclusion or ending of the story.

In our hamburger example, the following is a brand story linked to a brand positioning statement:

Once upon a time, there was a dad, a mom, and 2.3 children. The kids loved to go out to fast-food restaurants. They liked hamburgers, but they really liked fries, shakes, and the toy they got with their kid meal. Best of all, they could fidget and get up and down and even play around during the meal without getting yelled at.

Dad liked to go out, too. It was fun to be with the kids when they were having fun. And you could really fill up on the burgers and splurge on the kids ("Thank you, Daddy!"). Dad thought to himself, "All this, and it's cheap, too!"

But Mom was not happy. She resisted when Dad and the kids suggested going out for fast-food hamburgers. The food did not appeal to her, and she did not approve of what they ate. By the time they returned home she was in a bad mood, often saying that no one appreciated her cooking.

Our job as marketers is to create a better ending to this story by showing how our brand could solve Mom's problems. So how about Dad and the kids taking Mom out for a break? She could relax and the family could have fun while enjoying each other's company. In this brand story, the hamburgers are not the main point. The point is family togetherness, fun, and Mom being appreciated, with Mom appreciating that the family is having fun together.

In this example, the brand positioning statement can be written as the conclusion to the brand story:

To families where mothers resist going out for fast-food hamburgers, ours is the brand of quick-service restaurant where kids can have fun and the whole family enjoys being together.

This classic example is based on the history of one of the world's great brands. As we can see, the brand story provides context for the brand positioning statement and explicitly ties it to the narrative arc of the targeted consumer experience. It can be a useful device.

Here is another brand story for low-fat cheese:

Becky and Ronn live in an urban area with their two young daughters, Ellie and Maggie. Becky works in an office but is able to leave work at 4:30 to pick up the kids and get dinner ready. Ronn likes to eat early, at about 5:30. Becky always prepares a hot meal for the family with dishes like meatloaf or spaghetti. She prides herself on this. She tries to serve vegetables, but these are not big favorites with Ellie or Maggie. However, both Ronn and the kids always compliment her when she serves vegetables with a cheese sauce. Ronn sometimes cooks on the weekend, and the family really loves his baked potatoes with cheese on top.

Becky's friend Sarah is always mentioning that she is trying to get her family to eat healthier. Mostly they are avoiding high-fat dishes and trying to eat more fruit and vegetables. Recently Sarah expressed surprise when she saw leftover broccoli with cheese sauce in Becky's refrigerator. "Do you know how much fat that has in it?" she exclaimed to Becky.

Becky was dismayed. As a heavy consumer of cheese for cooking, she began searching for a brand of low-fat cheese that could be used to make any dish more appealing to her family without fear of criticism. (Note that the last sentence of the brand story is the brand positioning statement.)

The following positioning statement links directly to this brand story.

To heavy consumers of cheese for cooking, this brand of low-fat cheese can be used to make any dish more appealing without any fear of criticism.

In effect the positioning statement writes the ending to the story.

Becky was dismayed by Sarah's criticism. As a heavy consumer of cheese for cooking, the idea of a brand of low-fat cheese that could be used to make any dish more appealing to her family without fear of criticism was very attractive to her.

As these examples show, a brand story is a powerful tool for communicating and enriching the brand positioning statement.

BRAND POSITIONING STATEMENTS AND THE ORGANIZATION

Brand positioning statements must be written by individuals, but the process of writing them must fit into an organization. So what is the best organizational context for developing a statement? There are two traditional approaches, the *marketing planning approach* and the *advertising approach*. However, there is a third approach that is more comprehensive and effective: the *brand design approach*. We discuss all three.

The Marketing Planning Approach

Writing a brand positioning statement can be approached as part of the strategic planning process. Usually this occurs in the context of the annual marketing plan. Marketing plans vary widely, but usually they are heavy with sales projections and budgeted expenses for marketing activities. The plans include extensive reviews of the market situation, including consumer trends, research, and competitive intelligence. Marketing strategies take the form of "increase distribution in channel X" or "take share from competitor Y" or "spend more for advertising that targets current buyers of Z."

There are three problems with writing brand positioning statements in the context of marketing planning. One is that there is so much information about so many things under review that the statements simply get lost; they do not get the attention they deserve from the presenters or the executives in the room. A second problem is that statements developed in this context often have more of a strategic flavor. They represent what the company *wants* to do as opposed to being consumer-focused. Here's an example of a strategy-oriented brand statement:

> To the companies worldwide operating large truck fleets, this brand of transmission equipment is the first to have fully automatic hybrid electric transmissions that provide industry-leading fuel savings.

The problem is that this positioning statement merely makes the claim that the company's intention is to lower fuel costs through new technology.

It does nothing to make this a meaningful idea to engine manufacturers who sell to fleet buyers (who are very skeptical of large expenditures on new technology).

A third problem is that marketing plans tend to involve a few people in the organization for a specific period of time. Thus, brand positioning statements become associated more with the marketing planning process than with broader management decision-making; they never become ingrained in the company's wider culture.

The Advertising Approach

Brand positioning statements can also be approached as more of a functional activity than a strategic one. Usually this means that branding is considered in the creation of advertising, and this in turn often means that the advertising agency is heavily involved. In many ways this approach to branding is the flip side of the marketing planning approach.

Brand positioning statements can get much more attention in this context. But this can also turn into more of an obligatory exercise, a dance that company managers and the agency perform, an effort that is just a preliminary event to the actual review of advertising creative.

In this context, brand positioning statements often take on more of a communications flavor. They are more an attempt to persuade; they become more about promising rather than convincing. Consider this example:

> To people who expect the best in mobile phone service, this brand makes sure the customer gets the right technology, the right service plan, and the right equipment for their needs.

This statement presents the brand as a promise to the consumer, which is a hallmark of advertising. Therefore, it is natural that statements linked to the production of ads tend to be expressed this way. Whatever the quality of the advertising, done in this context the brand positioning statement itself is often rather hollow and empty.

The Brand Design Approach

If there are limitations to writing brand positioning statements as part of marketing planning and as part of advertising execution, how should we best approach them? The most effective way is the *brand design approach*, which allows us to be fully consumer-focused. We start with the consumer, not with the company's strategy or the advertising creative. This approach is *consumer-focused, design-based*, and is *negotiated through internal dialogue with the entire organization, not just marketing and communications.* Crafting brand positioning statements in this way will lead us to a description of the brand that is neither too abstract nor too concrete, executable but not overly encompassing.

What do we mean by design-based? A brand cannot be consumed in the form of a brand positioning statement. It must take physical form as a design. A design is a look, a feel, a sensibility that captures an underlying meaning. Think of famous designers, such as Ralph Lauren. Many different brands, from clothing to food to jewelry, could reflect Ralph Lauren (yes, there could be a Ralph Lauren hamburger). Ralph Lauren is a brand, an *idea* that can be designed into many things. Design expresses meaning.

Any brand must ultimately be a design, and the design must be based on something. So what better to base it on than the brand positioning statement? The statement can guide design and help express the meaning of the brand concept.

Capturing meaning through design can be expressed in many ways. It can be expressed *verbally* through words (and sounds). Or it can be expressed *visually* through pictures and images. Touch and smell are also possible but more difficult to execute.

In thinking through how to express meaning through design, it is useful to divide the verbal and the visual in order to give them equal attention and then to distinguish among major ways of expressing verbal and visual meaning. Here is a checklist for thinking about expressing brand meaning:

Verbal
- *Naming.* Give descriptive or figurative names to the product and company to reflect meaning.
- *Wording.* Develop a lexicon of words that become a vocabulary having special meaning.
- *Describing.* Compose phrases and sentences that uniquely capture meaning.

Visual
- *Picturing.* Illustrate meaning with photographs or drawings of actual things.
- *Symbolizing.* Signify meaning through more abstract images and graphics, including fonts.
- *Animating.* Convey meaning by the movement and morphing of objects.

Figure 5.1
Brand Design Schematic

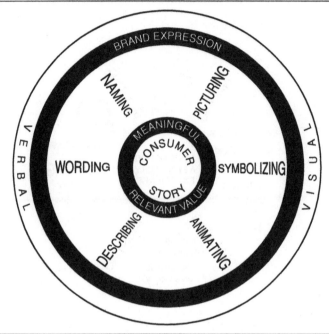

The diagram in Figure 5.1 brings these elements together. By working out the expression of the central meaning of the brand, in any or all of the ways on our checklist, we will have devised a design for the brand.

We return to our brand story about hamburgers and Mom, Dad, and the kids. If meaningful, relevant brand value lies in a break for Mom with a fun family experience, then how can this be expressed through design? With a bow to the history of a very successful brand, the design might be laid out as in Figure 5.2.

McDonald's, as brand design, can be seen as a tessellation—a mosaic—of verbal and visual images that express meaning. Figure 5.2 provides a sense of this tessellation through collage.

By approaching brand positioning statements in the context of brand design, we make them part of the organic process of bringing brand meaning to life. They literally provide the idea for the design. They are "executable" ideas—abstract yet concrete enough to guide design.[3]

The way we get to effective brand design in this way is through *dialogue* with members of the entire organization. Any organization contains many

Figure 5.2
McDonald's Brand Design

groups that may relate to the company's product(s) in different ways. But most will care about the meaning of a product. Engineers in a technical company, medical people in a health-care organization, editorial staff at a newspaper, and the family in a private company all have their own stories and their own values tied to the meaning of the product. If brand meaning is approached in a way that excludes them, these groups will usually ignore branding in the decisions they make and may even actively resist branding efforts. One of the major problems with approaching branding as marketing planning or as advertising is that others will view it as the provenance of a small group of marketing or communications people.

A brand design approach, however, lends itself to an internal communications process. The final brand design must be consumer-focused, but it should be acceptable to internal constituencies that attach different meanings to the product. Arriving at optimal consumer meaning requires dialogue among members of different internal groups (in some cases consumers should even be part of the dialogue).

The word "dialogue" is chosen for a reason. In 1999 Daniel Yankelovich provided an excellent analysis of dialogue as a special type of communication process. Dialogues are not debates or discussions.[4] They represent an effort to listen with empathy to other groups where all groups are on an equal footing and each group makes its assumptions clear. Depending on the level of mistrust among the groups, the process may be more or less elaborate. When there is passionate commitment to product meanings that define a culture within the organization, an extended dialogue over many sessions is required. When dialogue is more about examining the meaning of the product from several points of view (including the consumer's), one or two sessions may suffice.

The crucial point is that it is only after the dialogue process is completed and people have clarified their assumptions and listened with empathy and equality that a brand design is finalized. Negotiation takes place around the brand design. If there are compromises to be made, they are made in full understanding of the different points of view. Branding is freed from misunderstandings and turf wars. This in turn sets the stage for complete buy-in from everyone involved in the process—the people who will be responsible for executing the brand design.

SUMMARY

Writing an effective brand positioning statement is critical to branding. It should capture the meaning of the brand, and it merits considerable effort in its crafting. This is best approached not as an adjunct to planning or advertising, but as part of a *consumer-focused, design-based process negotiated through internal dialogue.*

Brand positioning statements will take on even more importance in the future, as the way that consumers learn about brand meaning is changing. Seeing a brand on television and receiving a promotion for it in a newspaper are becoming only one of many possibilities. Consumers now use a growing array of media, and audiences are becoming more fragmented across media. Increasingly consumers expect to have nonmedia contacts with brands. The challenge of the future is learning how to integrate marketing in a 360-degree way across all of these possibilities so that the brand is not lost in all the complexity. As depicted in Figure 5.3, brand design has an extremely important role to play in this.

The center of any marketing effort must include a clear focus on brand meaning. As we have seen, the well-articulated brand positioning statement is critical to clarifying brand meaning for marketers and consumers alike.

Figure 5.3
Integration through Brand Designs

Bobby J. Calder is the Kellstadt Professor of Marketing and currently the chair of the Marketing Department at the Kellogg School of Management. He is also a professor of journalism in the Medill School of Journalism and a professor of psychology in the Weinberg College of Arts and Sciences at Northwestern University. He has been a consultant to many companies and to government and not-for-profit organizations. His most recent books are Kellogg on Integrated Marketing (John Wiley & Sons, 2003) and Kellogg on Advertising and Media (John Wiley & Sons, 2008). He received his BA, MA and PhD degrees from the University of North Carolina at Chapel Hill.

NOTES

1. Calder, Bobby J. 2008, *Kellogg on Advertising and Media*, New York: John Wiley & Sons.
2. The discussion of the Tiffany brand has benefited from conversations with my Kellogg colleagues Steven Burnet and Richard Kolsky.
3. Backer, Bill (1993), *The Care and Feeding of Ideas*, New York: Times Books.
4. Yankelovich, Daniel (1999), *The Magic of Dialogue,* New York: Simon and Schuster.

CHAPTER 6

CREATING AND MANAGING BRANDS

ALICE M. TYBOUT and GREGORY S. CARPENTER

INTRODUCTION

Brands are one of the most universal aspects of markets. Every organization, whether it competes in consumer markets, has a brand—an identity, a name, a reputation. Goldman Sachs, Caterpillar, Bloomberg, and McKinsey & Company are all focused on business-to-business markets and have brands that are recognized by their customers, just as Under Armour, Coca-Cola, and Mercedes-Benz are known to their consumers. More generally, oxygen, electricity, water, financial advice, and even weather forecasts are distinguished by brands. Even people are brands, for good and bad. Think Tiger Woods. It would be difficult to find a person who is not touched by a brand.

Brands play many roles in buyers' lives: They provide important information about the functionality of a product or service, enable consumers to project desired images to others, and convey the experience that will result from consuming the brand, as in the case of Tide, Ralph Lauren, and Disney, respectively. The value that brands deliver to buyers has, however, evolved over time. When markets were less developed than today, the quality of brands in categories such as automobiles, restaurant meals, and coffee varied widely, creating substantial risk for buyers. Accordingly, brands served primarily as a means of signaling a consistent level of quality that one could expect to receive from a product. McDonald's, Marriott, and Toyota all grew to be important symbols of reliable quality and good value. As the intensity of competition has increased and the quality of products has become less variable, the role of brands has evolved. For many consumers, life is too complicated, time too short, and the array of alternatives too bewildering. In addition, technological advances have resulted in unfamiliar new markets and the redefinition of familiar markets. Mobile telephones, the latest technology in a nearly century-old market, are progressing at an incredible pace, requiring consumers to choose between simple mobile phones and a quickly expanding array of much more sophisticated devices. Brands such as iPhone and BlackBerry instantly convey meaningful information about what to expect from two such complex devices.

Brands continue to serve consumers by saving time, assuring a level of quality, and simplifying choice, but they have evolved to do even more. In many product categories, the brand name, rather than the product, is now the primary basis for choosing one product over another. In the auto industry, for example, benchmarking and intense competition has resulted in products that have achieved near parity in quality, leaving the brand to convey meaning about the product. Similarly, the brand name is a key characteristic distinguishing, say, a Dell laptop from a Hewlett-Packard laptop.

The power of brands is borne out by the annual assessment of the *100 Best Global Brands* as depicted in Table 6.1. This study, which is conducted by Interbrand in collaboration with *BusinessWeek*, reveals that the 2009 most valuable brand in the world was Coca-Cola, valued at $68.7 billion.[1] This figure represents the value of the *brand*, apart from the remaining assets of the

Table 6.1
Brand Value in 2009

Rank	Brand	Sector	2009 Brand Value	Change in Value versus 2008
1	Coca-Cola	Beverages	$68.73 billion	3%
2	IBM	Computer Services	60.21	2%
3	Microsoft	Computer Software	56.65	−4%
4	GE	Diversified	47.78	−10%
5	Nokia	Consumer Electronics	34.86	3%
6	McDonald's	Food	32.28	4%
7	Google	Internet Services	31.98	25%
10	Disney	Entertainment	28.45	−3%
12	Mercedes–Benz	Automotive	23.87	−7%
20	Apple	Computer Hardware	15.43	12%
36	Citi	Financial Services	10.25	−49%
43	Amazon.com	Internet Services	7.86	22%
57	Morgan Stanley	Financial Services	6.40	−26%
72	UBS	Financial Services	4.37	−50%

Selected results from "100 Best Global Brands," *BusinessWeek*, September 28, 2009.

Coca-Cola Company; the brand accounts for more than 50 percent of the company's market capitalization of $132.5 billion. The relationship between brand value and market capitalization is similar for other well-established global brands, such as McDonald's, Disney, and Mercedes-Benz; in each case, the brand value exceeds 40 percent of the market capitalization.

Brands require careful management in order to maintain their value. Top-ranking brands, such as Coca-Cola, IBM, Microsoft, GE, and Nokia, have been built over decades and remain among the world's most valuable brands because they have both shaped and adapted to consumers' evolving needs and lifestyles. Brands such as Google and Amazon, which have gained significant value in recent years, have done so by offering innovative and superior solutions to contemporary problems; they enable time-starved, information-swamped customers to get what they want—be it information or products—quickly and efficiently. By contrast, financial service brands, such as Citi, Morgan Stanley, and UBS, which pursued short-run gains at the expense of long-run stability, lost not only the public's trust but also substantial brand value during the banking meltdown of 2009.

In this chapter, we examine how brands create value. We begin by elaborating on the questions: What is a brand? And, how are brands created? We then turn to an examination of three different types of brands: *functional brands*, *image brands*, and *experiential brands*. We consider how each type of brand is best managed and how it may be leveraged through brand extensions. Finally, we explore three branding strategies—corporate, family, and product—and we relate these alternative approaches to the types of brands.

WHAT IS A BRAND?

Despite consumers' nearly universal experiences with brands, the concept of "brand" remains poorly understood. When queried about why they buy brands such as a Coca-Cola soft drink, Ralph Lauren clothing, or a Mercedes-Benz vehicle, consumers' responses typically reflect little insight into the appeal of brands. "Coke tastes better than Pepsi," some will argue. "Ralph Lauren's clothes fit me best and, besides, they're well made." "Mercedes-Benz is an incredibly well-engineered car; it will last forever." These reasons may or may not be true, but few consumers can reliably distinguish between brands of soft drinks in taste tests, and most consumers keep their cars for only a few short years in the United States. Rather than deriving value from the product alone, buyers often seek and gain much more value from the brand. But what is that value?

On the most basic level, a brand is a name, symbol, or mark associated with a product or service and to which buyers attach psychological meanings.

Salt in a jar is simply sodium chloride. Buyers have few associations with it, except perhaps for some recollections from chemistry class. Morton's Salt, on the other hand, may evoke memories of childhood, baking with Mom, and dependability. Many will easily recall Morton's well-known advertising phrase, "When it rains, it pours." Likewise, a brown, fizzy, sweet soft drink is a product that, as noted earlier, many find difficult to identify correctly in a blind taste test. Coca-Cola, however, is much more than a product. Consumers feel so passionately about Coca-Cola, in fact, that they resist any effort to change it as a matter of principle (recall the New Coke debacle of the 1980s). Without associations and without emotion, Coca-Cola would be just water, sugar, carbonation, and spices.

The number and combination of associations that can be attached to any product to create a brand is infinite. Consider bottled water. Although it is a very simple *product*, bottled water *brands* are much more complex. Perrier is of course seen as French, with all that this implies: European, sophisticated, refined, expensive. On the other hand, the brand associations of Poland Springs (owned, interestingly enough, by Switzerland-based parent company Nestlé) are conveyed by its Maine heritage: honest, independent, and reasonably priced. Similarly, in Sport Utility Vehicles, BMW offers driving excitement, performance, and fine engineering while Toyota offers dependability, quality, and value.

A brand can be represented as a network of thoughts or associations in consumer memory. Recalling every product feature, thought, image, and association linked to any one product would require enormous effort. Instead, consumers develop summaries of these thoughts and associations called *perceptions*, which are useful (if imprecise) simplifications of a more complex reality. For example, consider Jaguar, the traditionally English automaker. Our perceptions of a brand such as this can be reasonably complex: Jaguar has created a modern expression of English luxury reflecting sophistication, tradition, refinement, status, and understatement. Our perceptions can also be relatively simple and straightforward: Walmart is a store with the lowest everyday prices; Toyota has been known for its dependability and quality.

For a brand to have value, its associations must become part of buyers' lives. If there is no evocation of the brand meaning when a consumer walks into a grocery and sees Coca-Cola or Morton's Salt, then the brand has none. Brand meaning or brand equity must ultimately reside in the minds of buyers, though it is shaped through product design, advertising, distribution, and all the other ways an organization touches the buyer. Without equity, a brand is a product with a meaningless name attached to it.

A brand's associations can be remarkably valuable to buyers. In the case of Perrier, water can be obtained easily and inexpensively in most of the world, but the feeling of being French is more difficult to obtain. Jaguar brings the uncommon experience—being transported in British luxury on your daily commute—available to the masses. Rather than simply bottling water or manufacturing fine cars, Perrier and Jaguar make what is the privilege of the few available to the many. For that they are handsomely rewarded.

The distinction between a product and a brand is expressed well by the late Stephen King of WPP Group, London:

> A product is something that is made in a factory; a brand is something that is bought by a customer. A product can be copied by a competitor; a brand is unique. A product can be quickly outdated; a successful brand is timeless.[2]

How Do You Build a Brand?

A common misconception is that building a brand is simply a matter of clever advertising or creating a logo. Certainly advertising plays an important role in building many brands, especially those brands that seek to differentiate from competitors on the basis of their image. However, to be successful, even image brands must have a product, a price, and a distribution channel that support the image communicated through advertising and logos. Advertising is simply the way the brand's value is communicated to potential buyers. For some brands, such as Coca-Cola, advertising plays a central role in building the associations that define a brand. For other brands, such as Amazon, characteristics of the service experience rather than advertising serve as the primary means of building brand equity.

To understand the process of building a brand, consider a brand that was built from scratch: automaker Saturn.[3] Saturn was a bold idea, trumpeted by General Motors chairman Roger Smith as the key to GM's long-term competitiveness and success. It was conceived in the mid-1980s to be a world-class product: a compact vehicle developed in the United States that would be a leader in quality, cost, and customer satisfaction. The Saturn line was engineered to offer reliable, efficient performance and a comfortable ride at a reasonable price. The high quality of the car was conveyed to consumers by offering a money-back guarantee within 30 days or 1,500 miles. This support for the claim that Saturn was a high-quality car was important (perhaps even necessary), in light of consumers' perception at the time of the parent company, GM. However, while the car was well-designed and offered a great value, wisely Saturn did not make functional aspects of the car the basis for brand differentiation.

In the years following its launch in 1990, Saturn quickly became known as a unique U.S. car company that marketed no-nonsense, reliable cars in a friendly way. Consumers who viewed themselves as practical and patriotic might have been invited to choose Saturn as a means of communicating these values to those around them. Saturn no doubt attracted many such customers, but it resisted the temptation to make brand image the primary basis for differentiation.

Instead, Saturn built its brand around a key insight regarding U.S. consumers. It recognized that for most consumers, buying a car is a distinctly unpleasant experience, as are most interactions with car dealers. Saturn sought to change all this. Saturn invited customers into a relationship with a car company that would treat them as a friend—with regard and respect. In contrast to the typical car-buying experience of the time, Saturn created a pleasant shopping environment. Salaried sales consultants, many of whom were hired from outside the auto industry to avoid perpetuating traditional selling tactics, were well-informed and helpful. The company's fixed-price policy eliminated unpleasant haggling over price and reduced the buyer's anxiety about overpaying due to being a poor negotiator. When recalls were necessary, dealers sponsored events such as barbecues and outings to baseball games to entertain customers while their cars were serviced and washed. Dealer-sponsored gatherings of Saturn owners and tours of Saturn plants personalized the experience of owning a Saturn.

Advertising played a critical role in capturing the corporate personality, as reflected in the people who created and consumed the brand. Early ads featured employees talking about how they came together to build the Saturn culture and the pride that they felt in seeing the first car roll off the assembly line. Later ads shifted attention to customers and their passion for their cars. In all advertising, the people who were associated with the product were central, rather than the product per se. Advertising summarized the concept underlying the Saturn brand with the tag line, "A different kind of company, a different kind of car."

Did Saturn build a product that was a leader in quality, cost, and customer satisfaction? Yes, it did. But that description fails to capture the essence of a brand that prompted nearly 100,000 owners from places as far away as Alaska to drive to the Spring Hill plant in Tennessee for the Saturn Homecoming in June of 1994. One couple attending got married during the event, with the president of Saturn giving the bride away!

Although the initial years were golden, the brand began to falter when it came time for customers who bought the first Saturn cars to trade them in for newer models. If they sought to move up to a mid-sized car, minivan, or SUV (as many Saturn owners, as well as consumers in general, did in the mid-1990s), they were out of luck with Saturn. For 10 long years, the only cars Saturn offered were the original S series compacts. Eventually, Saturn did introduce a mid-sized line (the L series in 2000) and an SUV (the Vue in 2002). The Relay minivan (2005) and the Sky roadster (2007) followed. Although these new models were welcomed, by this time the brand had lost critical momentum. The new-model vacuum was the result of many factors; while Roger Smith championed the brand, he retired shortly after the first Saturn rolled off the line. Saturn garnered only mixed support among the leadership team that followed Smith, many of whom were skeptical about the project and preferred to focus on GM's older, more established brands. In addition, GM dealers were resentful of the dollars ($5 billion) invested in the product development of Saturn. Finally, the Saturn culture eroded as the powerful United Auto Workers union leadership eliminated the flexible work rules implemented at the original Spring Hill plant and persuaded GM to shift production of later models to plants elsewhere in the country that were in danger of being shuttered. Ultimately, rather than Saturn transforming GM, GM transformed Saturn into simply another one of its struggling brands. The Saturn experiment came to a sad end in 2009 when GM retired the brand as part of a restructuring following bankruptcy and a massive federal bailout. The lesson: It isn't enough to *create* a brand, even one consumers love. Firms must continually invest in a brand to keep it meaningful and relevant. Without careful management and ongoing support, brands die.

In summary, brands are complex, risky, and require an enduring commitment. The building of a brand is guided by a vision of the desired positioning (see Chapter 4, "Developing a Compelling Brand Position," and Chapter 5, "Writing a Brand Positioning Statement and Translating it into Brand Design"), and is implemented by the organization culture (see Chapter 7, "Making the Brand Come Alive within Your Organization") and *all* the decisions related to the marketing mix.

THE THREE TYPES OF BRANDS

Had Saturn wished to create a *functional brand,* the focus would have been on creating associations based on the physical features of the car and the benefits that they provided. Had the goal been to build an *image brand*, greater emphasis would have been given to creating a personality for the car via advertising and other communications.

Instead, Saturn chose to create an *experiential brand*. Doing so entailed designing a strong product and pricing it fairly. And the brand undoubtedly came to have a personality—that of a thoughtful, friendly, unpretentious person. But the central associations were not to the car per se, but rather to the larger experience of owning a Saturn and to the relationship that owners felt with the company. Let's consider these three types of brands and how they are best managed in greater detail.

Functional Brands

Consumers buy *functional brands* principally to satisfy functional or physical needs—to wash their clothes, to relieve pain, to transport the family. Many consumers' associations with these brands are related to the tangible aspects of the product. Successful functional brands are closely tied in buyers' minds to specific product categories, and they often share many associations with other brands in the same product category. Tide is nearly synonymous with clean clothes, for instance. Beyond serving basic needs, many functional brands differentiate from their competitors by offering *superior performance* or by providing *superior economy*.

Superior Performance   Gillette is strongly linked to the wet shaving category and to the function of products belonging to that category: providing a close, comfortable shave. Gillette built these brand associations over the last 100 years through a series of innovative products. Founded in 1895, Gillette was the first to launch a two-track razor, known as the Trac II, in 1971. Designed to improve comfort, the Trac II sparked a series of innovations that continues today. In 1977, Gillette launched the Atra, which had a pivoting head for its two blades. The Sensor, launched in 1990, offered spring-loaded blades. Three-blade razors replaced two-bladed models in 1998 with the launch of Mach3, followed by the Mach3 Turbo. When Gillette's claim to superior performance was challenged by Schick's introduction of the four-bladed Quattro razor in 2003, Gillette responded first by introducing a new dimension to wet shaving in the form of a battery-powered three-bladed razor, M3Power, and then by launching the five-bladed Fusion in both power and regular formats in 2006. The Fusion Power with a redesigned handle appeared in 2007 followed by the Fusion Power Phenom and the Venus Embrace (designed for women) in 2008. Since the company was founded, each new Gillette product has been positioned as offering superior performance relative to the models that went before it, creating a brand distinguished by its emphasis on superior performance.

Detergents such as Tide (U.S.) and Ariel (Europe) are also functional brands that compete on the basis of superior performance. Tide and Ariel are strongly associated with the detergent category, and these brands strive to differentiate from other detergents in terms of providing the cleanest wash. Procter & Gamble (P&G), which owns the Tide and Ariel brands, as well as Gillette, focuses considerable resources on improving these brands in order to retain their leading position in the detergent category.

Many business-to-business brands also differentiate on the basis of superior performance. Caterpillar, the maker of earth-moving equipment, has built an extraordinary brand on the basis of outstanding customer service. Although competitors like Komatsu may offer equipment that performs as well or costs less, Caterpillar provides unequaled service in the form of replacement parts. If a Cat breaks down anywhere in the world, Caterpillar delivers the necessary parts within 48 hours. This service is incredibly important to companies that operate earth-moving equipment. Even the best-performing and lowest-priced machine is simply dead weight when it is inoperable because of unavailable parts. Cost is important, but productivity is essential. Through excellent service, Cat ensures its customers' productivity. Other equipment, however attractive it seems at the time of purchase, carries a greater risk. Thus, Cat built its brand on the realization that superior performance can be delivered in innovative ways.

Bloomberg Professional service is another business-to-business brand built on superior performance. Bloomberg Professional service provides comprehensive real-time and archived financial and market data, as well as analytic software and trading tools, to banks, investment companies, government agencies, law firms, and news organizations. The company constantly upgrades its product and backs it with outstanding customer service. Despite the hefty price tag of $18,000 for an annual subscription, Bloomberg clients are fiercely loyal. When a skeptical boss at an East Coast money-management firm balked at the high price of the service, he offered to increase his analysts' bonuses by $15,000 if they would give up their Bloomberg service. Eleven out of 12 refused the offer. One analyst went so far as to state that he would prefer to see his bonus cut by $15,000 rather than give up his Bloomberg.[4]

Superior Economy   Offering *superior economy* is another approach to differentiating a functional brand. Superior economy may be provided by saving time and reducing hassle or by saving money. BIC competes with Gillette in the shaving category by offering conveniently available, disposable razors at a lower price. McDonald's is another brand that offers superior economy. When someone says "McDonald's," consumers think "fast food" and "good value." Few think "superior taste." McDonald's is known the world over as the source of a quick, predictable, inexpensive, hot, hassle-free meal. McDonald's competes by striving to satisfy consumers' appetites more consistently and faster than any other fast-food franchise. Similarly, computer-maker Dell offers superior economy by making the purchase of a computer easy and inexpensive.

Due to the lack of strong product differentiation, many business-to-business brands are built on superior economy. One intriguing example is Xiameter, created by Dow Corning, a worldwide leader in silicones. Traditionally a full-line, high-service provider of silicones, Dow Corning faced great pressure from lower-priced rivals offering very similar if not identical products. How could Dow Corning offer a full line, excellent service, and low price simultaneously when faced with lower-priced rivals? In response, Dow Corning created Xiameter, a low-priced brand offering a limited range of products identical to those sold by Dow Corning, but at a 15 percent discount. To make those savings possible, Xiameter offers no service, has substantial minimum purchase requirements, provides limited flexibility in terms of delivery, and accepts few currencies. For large and sophisticated customers, Xiameter offers significantly more value than the traditional full-line, high-service offering, making Xiameter a remarkable success in a very tough market.[5]

Creating and Managing Functional Brands   Functional brands connect with consumers by helping them achieve basic goals related to physical needs, such as the need for food, shelter, health, or safety. Because consumers vary in their focus on these needs and in their ability to pay for products, both functional brands that focus on superior performance and those that focus on superior economy may succeed in a product category. Some consumers may favor the brand of razor that provides the closest, most comfortable shave, whereas others may prefer the brand that performs adequately and is the least expensive.

Building functional brands requires focusing resources on the product (for superior performance) or the place and price elements of the marketing mix (for superior economy). Advertising can reinforce the connection between the brand and the product category, and it can communicate what makes the brand superior to competing products. Advertising per se is not the basis for differentiation, as may be the case for image brands. To sustain a strong position in the marketplace, functional brands must win the race to provide the best functionality or the lowest cost—or both. In many instances, improving performance means doing what the brand does currently even better. Thus, Gillette razors have evolved from one to five blades, with each additional blade increasing the closeness of the shave without compromising comfort.

Expanding functionality may be an attractive strategy in light of several consumer trends. The lines between consumers' work times and recreation/family times are blurring (e.g., parents take children along on business trips, conduct business via a cell phone at a soccer game, and shop online at work) and many consumers report experiencing "time famine." Thus, products and services that help them cope with these changes are likely to be well-received. For example, Net-a-Porter.com has enjoyed rapid growth in recent years. The site, which targets cash-rich, time-starved "fashionistas," combines a weekly online glossy magazine that decodes the latest fashion trends with a boutique where such fashions can be purchased. In London and New York, purchases can be delivered the same day to a customer's home or office by handsome male couriers.

Similarly, many new technology-based products, such as smart phones, are based on the assumption that more functionality in a single product is just what consumers need. However, it is still a challenge to sustain any competitive advantage that is created. Designers such as Gucci have their own e-commerce sites, and a number of smart phones offer similar e-mail access, web surfing, and picture-taking capabilities. Moreover, there is a risk that some consumers may feel overwhelmed or intimidated by products that seem smarter than the user. Indeed, Jitterbug phone has built its business on the premise that some people want their cellular phone to be just that—a phone. For $14.99 per month, Jitterbug customers get 50 anytime minutes on a phone that doesn't take pictures, play music, surf the Web, or organize their lives—and they love the simplicity. In the end, brands succeed by providing the "right" level of functionality for a targeted group of buyers, rather than by simply adding functionality.

Yet another strategy for growing a functional brand is to extend it into a new product category. Conventional wisdom is that brand extensions should involve a new category that is closely related to the core brand so that the extension will be viewed as appropriate. For functional brands, this implies that extensions should be made into product categories that have similar features or that relate to the same need or function at a more abstract level. Thus, the Tide brand successfully extended into the portable laundry stain-treatment product with Tide-to-Go, and the Mr. Clean brand successfully extended into a chain of Mr. Clean Performance Car Washes. By contrast, extensions that contradict core associations or that are based on more peripheral associations are likely to fail and, thus, are potentially damaging to the core brand. For example, abrasive scrubbing is a core association for SOS cleaning pads, making the brand extension into a window cleaner (SOS Glassworks) inappropriate. Likewise, Sleeping Beauty is a damsel in distress in the classic children's fairy tale, making the launch of the Disney Sleeping Beauty executive fountain pen (priced up to $1,200), a questionable decision at best.

Image Brands

Image brands create value by projecting a desirable image. Although they may be based on an extraordinary product, these brands are distinguished from competitors because buyers see them as offering a unique set of associations or image. Image brands are often created in categories where products are relatively undifferentiated or quality is difficult to evaluate (i.e., consulting services), or where consumption of the product is highly visible to others (e.g., cars, shoes, clothing, alcoholic beverages). In these cases, the images attached to the brand add value by distinguishing it from other brands, or by serving as a "badge" to inform others of the consumer's group membership or accomplishments. In either case, it is the set of images attached to the brand that define the brand's uniqueness and create symbols that are highly valued by buyers. Some brands that begin as functional brands may evolve into image brands if efforts are made to interpret functional features more abstractly and link them to more emotion-laden consumer goals (see Chapter 4, "Developing a Compelling Brand Positioning").

Image brands have become increasingly important as competition in many markets has eliminated tangible differences in products. In many categories such as consumer electronics, appliances, or automobiles, traits such as reliability, durability, prices, and even styling have become strikingly similar. Faced with a lack of differentiation, prices have been driven down, and in response, organizations have turned to image and the broad array of the options this branding approach affords.

Image brands may be created in many ways—by adding product features that evoke images or make an emotional connection with buyers, by associating a brand with particular types of users, or by clever advertising campaigns.

Feature-Based Image   One good example of feature-based image building is Viking kitchen ranges. As a result of intense competition, fine kitchen ranges are available at a wide range of prices. All of these ranges generate heat in a sufficiently consistent, reliable way to cook well. Viking is no different in this respect. What truly distinguishes Viking ranges is their restaurant-style design. Viking ranges are stainless steel and have little, if any, painted surface. They offer an industrial look and are priced at a premium level, out of "range" of many consumers' pocketbooks. Viking has enjoyed remarkable success. Ironically though, those who purchase Viking and other premium ranges typically do less cooking than those who buy lower-priced kitchen equipment. The appeal of a restaurant-style range is to make a personal statement to those who visit the home that the owner truly appreciates food—indeed, only the best in food and food preparation.

Waterman pens offer yet another example of image differentiation. Waterman pens certainly perform the writing function, but that alone would not justify the price in the Edson line, which can cost $600 to $1,100. Rather, choosing an Edson pen is a means of conveying status and refined taste. Indeed, the pen is depicted as being of heirloom quality, something that might be handed down from one generation to the next. Further, by offering a broad array of finishes, Waterman pens enable the users to express their personality in a subtle, sophisticated manner. "Which Waterman are you?" they ask in their advertising. A Waterman pen is more than a fine writing instrument; it is a statement about the user's taste and style.

By contrast, Toyota's Prius has features that convey a different image than Viking or Waterman. Unlike other hybrid vehicles that are distinguished from nonhybrid versions of the same brand by a small badge on the trunk or side panel, the Prius is a strictly hybrid model with a distinctive look. As a result, the Prius driver can be assured that everyone will recognize his commitment to the environment and economic good sense.[6]

User Imagery   Brands also create images by focusing on *who* uses the brand. Often this approach takes the form of hiring celebrity spokespeople to represent the value of the brand. Nike has utilized this approach to great effect. Through the endorsement of superstar athletes such as Michael Jordan, Tiger Woods, LeBron James, Derek Jeter, and Maria Sharapova, the Nike brand has come to stand for extraordinary individual athletic performance, winning, and uniqueness. By contrast, Under Armour, the brainchild of Kevin Plank, a former walk-on football player at the University of Maryland, has adopted a different approach to user imagery. Under Armour is depicted as the brand worn by warrior athletes—challengers rather than established superstars. These athletes are shown engaged in team-building, strenuous training, and gritty battle on the playing field, all activities familiar to kids who are passionate about playing sports. Interestingly, the user imagery employed by Under Armour implies (intentionally or unintentionally), that established brands such as Nike are athletes whose primary accomplishments are in the past rather than the future, a potentially undesirable association.

The Apple brand has also been built on the basis of user imagery. Apple was launched as a "different" type of computer by virtue of its unique operating system. However, this functional differentiation per se was not the basis for the brand. Rather, Apple presented its computers as being for the iconoclast, someone who worked smarter rather than harder and got ahead by creating the rules, not playing by them. This user imagery was introduced by the infamous "1984" Super Bowl ad. In the ad, a young, vibrant, female athlete put an end to the droning presentation being delivered by an establishment-type leader to his passive audience of followers by throwing a sledgehammer at the screen. Her move was a thinly disguised reference to IBM's stronghold on computing in corporate America. Subsequent advertising employed the tag line "Think Different," again implying that Apple was for the iconoclast and drawing an interesting, if unintentional contrast to the classic IBM by saying: "Think." More recently, Apple has challenged Microsoft by personifying the two brands: a rumpled John Hodgman of the Daily Show represents the PC as old, out-of-touch, and hopelessly uncool, while a young, hip Justin Long portrays Mac as fresh, tech-savvy, and easygoing. Although Apple's share of the overall PC market is modest, the compelling use of user imagery has enabled the Mac to dominate the premium retail PC market in the United States (PCs over $1,000), and command a substantial price premium.

Image through Advertising   Another way to create image brands is through advertising, which often manages to create vivid associations with little reliance on either product features or celebrity users. Among the classic examples are Coca-Cola and its rival Pepsi, as well as a wide variety of brands of beer. Pepsi offers perhaps the most informative example. As a follower in the market to Coca-Cola, Pepsi sought at first to steal share from the leader through a low-priced, me-too strategy. "Twice as much for a nickel," was one long-ago advertising slogan that focused on greater value for the same price. These efforts only served to reinforce the dominance of Coca-Cola. Pepsi subsequently adopted a strategy of asserting that it is the beverage for the younger consumer through advertising campaigns such as "The Choice of a New Generation" and, more recently, "Generation Next." By creating the image of being associated with younger users, Pepsi cast Coca-Cola as the beverage of older consumers, thus gaining an advantage. The parallel to Under Armour's challenge of Nike is evident.

Absolut Vodka is another image brand built through clever advertising. Its long-running print advertising campaign is based on an arguably irrelevant product feature, the shape of the bottle, and a play on the brand name. The ubiquitous ads, many of which were created by well-known artists beginning with Andy Warhol, feature the bottle or a bottle-shaped object and the tag line "Absolut _____ " (fill in the blank). By using advertising to link the brand with pop culture and artistic vision, Absolut has achieved a dominant position in the premium vodka market.[7]

Brands built solely on advertising can be remarkably successful. Creating them, however, requires heavy, sustained spending on advertising. When new consumers enter the market, if current users do not reinforce the images of the advertising, more advertising dollars must be spent to educate these new buyers. That constant education process is expensive. However, the rewards can be a sustained uniqueness, a price premium, and a larger market share.

Business-to-Business Image Brands   Although image brands are more commonplace in the consumer realm, they also occur in the business-to-business world. Business-to-business brands that are based on image fall into two categories: those built exclusively for business customers (i.e., other firms) and those that are focused on end-users or consumers, who are the customers of the firms to which the company's products are sold.

Many business brands are built with an eye on customers. As concerns about global warming and other environmental issues have grown, General Electric (GE) developed a branding initiative focused on environmentally friendly innovations. Long advertised as bringing "good things to life," GE has a tradition of innovation in both consumer and business markets. Over the years, its emphasis has shifted to business markets, though it has continued to focus on innovation. Since 2001, its branding theme reflects its innovative tradition in its advertising tag line: "imagination at work." From this imagination platform, GE launched an initiative focusing on environmental issues. Dubbed Eco-Imagination, the brand focuses on new products and other innovations across GE businesses with valuable environmental benefits, such as hybrid locomotive engines, low-power consumption appliances, a new water business, and wind turbines to generate power. The innovations offer functional benefits but also provide their customers image advantages. A railroad concerned about improving the image created by diesel engines spewing columns of black smoke may now purchase more obviously environmentally friendly hybrid locomotives.

Professional services firms have created valuable business-to-business image brands. Although McKinsey & Company, Boston Consulting Group, and Accenture may not be widely known among consumers, these firms have unique associations in the minds of the senior executives who are their customers. For such brands, image is often a central concern, reflecting a firm's position as a powerful, confident, stable thought leader. Advertising, in the form of "tombstones" in the financial pages listing the deals that the firm has successfully consummated with prestigious clients, has been the traditional approach to building and reinforcing the image of professional services firms. However, Accenture (formerly Andersen Consulting), has taken a more innovative and somewhat riskier approach. The company has employed vivid imagery (i.e., scenes from the animal kingdom, comedic actors such as John Cleese, and sports figures such as Tiger Woods), in its television ads and airport billboards to establish itself as a forward-thinking, innovative firm—a firm that understands the problems of business and delivers solutions that will ensure a company's high performance. Accenture's commitment to using advertising to build its brand has been largely successful, though the company summarily (and probably, wisely) dropped the use of Tiger Woods in the wake of the 2009 scandal surrounding his personal life.

In the past two decades, more traditional business-to-business companies have adopted a direct-to-consumer approach. As part of those efforts, these firms have developed consumer brands. The logic for such an approach might at first seem a bit odd. If DuPont is selling nylon fiber to carpet mills, what relevance does a DuPont consumer brand have? The carpet mill selects the fiber; the consumer's choice is limited to the carpets available at retail, much the way that an automaker chooses the plastic for the dashboard and the consumer is left to choose among different vehicles. However, by building a meaningful brand with the end-user, the manufacturer can generate *end-user pull*. Consumers may demonstrate a clear preference for DuPont Stainmaster carpet, putting pressure on the mills to choose DuPont fiber. By generating consumer pull, a manufacturer such as DuPont achieves greater influence over its *customers' customers* and, hence, a much more favorable negotiating position—obvious evidence of the power of a brand.

Direct-to-consumer business brands have proven remarkably successful, and that success has fueled interest in branding and blurred the traditional distinction between consumer and business brands. Since the launch of Stainmaster carpet, DuPont, a fairly traditional chemical company, has embraced branding. Teflon, Tyvek, Kevlar, Lycra, and others followed Stainmaster. This is sometimes called an "ingredient" branding strategy. This type of approach has found its greatest success in microprocessors and pharmaceuticals. Intel employed its "Intel Inside" campaign to differentiate from a direct competitor, Advanced Micro Devices (AMD), with stunning effect. At one point, Intel earned $10 billion in one year, whereas its rival earned about $1 billion, even though both made a virtually identical product and AMD priced its product significantly below Intel's. Consumers the world over sought computers with "Intel Inside." In the U.S. pharmaceutical business, the direct-to-consumer approach is popular and has played a role in the success of many well-known brands, including Lipitor and Viagra. The success in a growing number of direct-to-consumer brands suggests that this approach will continue to grow.

Creating and Managing Image Brands   Image brands succeed when they make an emotional connection with consumers. They address consumers' desires to belong to a larger social group, to be held in esteem by others, or to define themselves according to a particular image. Advertising and other forms of communication (e.g., publicity, event sponsorship, promotions) play a prominent role in developing image brands because their value stems from a shared interpretation of what the brand represents rather than the product features per se.

An examination of consumer trends may reveal opportunities for creating new image brands. As noted earlier, many contemporary consumers experience time famine. Often this means that there is limited opportunity to express certain aspects of their personality or self-identity. Image brands allow people to believe that a part of their identity remains alive. For example, driving a Sport Utility Vehicle (SUV) rather than a minivan may allow soccer moms and dads to express their desire for an adventurous lifestyle without ever having to venture from the comforts of suburbia. And driving a luxury SUV, such as a Porsche Cayenne, conveys not only adventure but also material success.

Building image brands can take time and considerable resources. The images that define these brands must be created in the minds of consumers. In the case of a global brand like Coca-Cola, this means creating images that are meaningful and valuable to consumers around the world, a challenging and endless task. New consumers are born every day who have never heard of Coca-Cola. For the brand to have continued success, those new consumers must somehow be introduced to and accept the images that Coca-Cola offers.

If a firm is successful in building and maintaining an image brand, it is likely to enjoy a significant competitive advantage. The most obvious benefit is that duplicating the images associated with one brand is difficult, expensive, and of questionable competitive value. Why would a competitor seek to copy the Ralph Lauren image when an infinite array of alternative images can be created that might provide a meaningful basis for competitive distinction? Thus, image brands offer a considerable degree of insulation from competitors. Moreover, once established, image brands can create some insulation from price competition. When buyers value a brand's image, price becomes less of a consideration in the purchase decision.

A key threat to an established image brand is that its future success is tied to the continued attractiveness of the associations that have been built. Michael Jordan has retired from basketball. Although he is still familiar and held in high esteem, his market power as an outstanding athlete fades as his seasons off the basketball court increase, and thereby diminishes his value to brands he endorses. Tiger Woods is still the unquestioned leader in his sport, but his activities off the golf course have added unwanted associations to his personal brand and are potentially damaging for brands such as Gillette, Nike, and Accenture, which he helped to build. Conspicuous consumption in the form of $1,000 pens, BMWs, and fur coats is viewed less favorably when economic conditions are tight than when the economy is booming.

Further, images related to badge products often have limited appeal across generations. If Jaguar offers a taste of the traditional English luxury, this association may be seen as outdated and be rejected by youth in favor of an alternative, contemporary concept. As a case in point, Toyota is suffering as a result of its success with the baby-boomer generation in North America. It has come to be seen as mom's or dad's car. As a result, younger car buyers are seeking a more modern alternative; some are turning to Honda, others to Volkswagen. Toyota's challenge is to retain its positioning as an affordable, dependable car while connecting with the lives of younger buyers. If Toyota fails to achieve this balance, it may suffer the same fate as Buick, which has an aging customer base and an increasingly unattractive image to new buyers. But Toyota's Prius, with its green image, and the hip, relatively affordable RAV4 SUV, are helping Toyota attract younger buyers.

One effective growth strategy for image brands is to launch brand extensions. A strong image brand may be extended to any product that might be linked to the general image that the brand portrays. Ralph Lauren, for example, has successfully extended his brand from clothing to furniture, linens, and even a restaurant. All of these products depict a common lifestyle and, thus, reinforce the Ralph Lauren image. Of course, extending image brands can be carried too far. Neither Donna Karan bottled water nor a Kanye West trip-booking web site were able to generate significant sales. And brand extensions that contradict core associations, such as Crystal Pepsi, seem doomed to failure.

The Internet and social media can also be effective tools in building strong image brands because they enable consumers to deepen and personalize their connection to the brand. Martha Stewart wannabes may log onto MarthaStewart.com, where they can ask questions, share ideas, buy products, and generally learn more about how to emulate their idol. Likewise, fans of celebrities or supporters of political candidates and causes may opt to receive text messages and "tweets" to remain up-to-date and connected to brands that are important to their identity. Indeed, Barack Obama, arguably an image brand, succeeded with young voters in part through his effective use of social media. Young supporters were encouraged to subscribe to text messaging that offered up-to-the minute information about the campaign and ways to help Obama. Subscribers' commitments to the brand were also rewarded by ensuring that they were the first to receive breaking news, such as Obama's selection of Joe Biden as his running mate. Those who signed up for MyBO.com also received a questionnaire in which they were asked to vote on their policy priorities, and the results were rolled into the "Organizing for America" movement. To the degree that social media create communities of like-minded brand enthusiasts and deepen consumers' passions for the brand, they move it in the direction of the type of brands that we discuss next—experiential brands.

Experiential Brands

Experiential brands differ from image brands in terms of their emphasis. Whereas image brands focus on what the product *represents*, experiential brands focus on how consumers *feel* when interacting with the brand. The brand experience is co-created by the brand and the consumer at the time of consumption and, consequently, it is unique and highly personal. Indeed, such a brand may be experienced differently by the same individual at different points in time.

An experiential brand may include a tangible product, but this is not required. Moreover, if a product is part of an experiential brand, ownership of it may never be transferred to the consumer. Instead, products, environments, and services are combined to create temporary multisensory encounters with the brand. These encounters may be recurring or may involve extended contact with the customer. Consequently, the "place" and "people" components of service delivery are particularly important in creating strong experiential brands.

Disney is a classic example of an experiential brand. Visitors to Disney World buy the experience of seeing delight on the faces of their children and, perhaps, a chance to regress to the carefree fantasies of their own childhood. Souvenirs may be purchased, but they are valued primarily for their ability to evoke memories of the larger experience and not in and of themselves.

On a more everyday level, QuikTrip has built an experiential brand in the convenience store industry. The company, which owns and operates more than 500 stores located in the Midwest and the South, is dedicated to providing its customers with a superior shopping experience. QuikTrip stores are clean, well-organized, and brightly lit while offering a range of high-quality, freshly prepared beverages and foods. Further, the company provides a money-back guarantee on everything it sells, including gasoline. It refuses to stock adult magazines and strictly enforces laws related to the sale of tobacco and alcohol. However, the employees truly make shopping at QuikTrip special. QuikTrip only hires individuals who are judged to be patient, extroverted, and "nice." They also must exhibit a willingness to work in a team and learn from others. The company then provides them with extensive training and pays the highest wages in the industry. The company promotes from within, providing a career track and resulting in turnover that is lower than the industry average. As a result, QuikTrip has been named one of *Fortune* magazine's 100 best companies to work for six years running. And, its satisfied employees are critical to the company's success in building an experiential brand.[8]

Although it is always important that a brand offer consistency, the range of experiences around which a brand may be built is enormous. Experiences can be viewed as varying on three dimensions: *valance* (positive, negative), *potency* (mild, intense), and *activity* (passive, active).[9] The valance associated with many experiential brands is positive. Brands such as Disney, the Chicago Symphony Orchestra, and Elizabeth Arden compete by offering pleasurable experiences. However, some brands focus on experiences that are less serene. For example, bungee jumping or roller coaster rides may strive to outdo competitors by offering the most frightening, death-defying experience.

Experiential brands also differ in terms of the potency of the experience. Although a stop at a favorite local café may evoke mild, positive feelings, a massage and facial at Elizabeth Arden may lead to more intensely pleasurable feelings. Likewise, a horror film may create a mild fright, whereas a ride on the world's largest roller coaster may create a heart-stopping one. The potency of an experiential brand may be affected by both the intensity of a single sense and by the number of senses that are stimulated.

Finally, experiential brands vary in terms of whether the consumer is a passive observer or an active participant. Brands associated with traditional venues of entertainment, such as movies, concerts, and theater, historically have offered a relatively passive experience. The consumer reacts to the material being presented rather that interacting with it. However, driven in part by advances in technology, these forms of entertainment are finding ways to heighten consumers' involvements with their brands. Devotees of the teen-based soap opera *Gossip Girl* are encouraged to visit the web site and download music featured on the show, as well as blog and offer feedback. Similarly, the *Star Wars* brand engages viewers by licensing Lego to create construction toys and video games based on the characters and themes in the movies.

Other experiences go beyond heightening consumers' mental involvement and engage their bodies. Snowboarding and extreme sports require such active participation that uncoordinated or mature consumers are at high risk of bodily harm should they choose to participate.

Experiential brands connect with consumers' desires to move beyond a self-presentation and focus on self-enriching experiences and causes. Interacting with the brand is an end in itself, rather than being a means to some other goal. Situational and individual differences are likely to influence consumers' affinities for different types of experiential brands. Most consumers may seek positive experiences most of the time. However, segments of consumers who need to test and to define themselves (e.g., young adults), or who are deprived of control in other aspects of their lives (e.g., economically disadvantaged), may embrace negative and extreme experiences because surviving such experiences creates feelings of mastery and control. Similarly, the constraints of work and family obligations may prevent the consumption of intense and active brands on a daily basis. Instead of an afternoon of snowboarding or a trip to Disney World, consumers must settle for more mild (and often more affordable) experiences, such as a manicure or a trip to Starbucks, in order to indulge themselves on an everyday basis.

Creating and Managing Experiential Brands   In the face of rapid competitive imitation, brand differentiation on the basis of product features becomes more difficult to sustain. Thus, companies may avoid commodity status by conceiving of their brands as representing a larger experience. Consider the category of electricity providers. One company's kilowatt is indistinguishable from another's. As a result, differentiation (and, thus, the ability to charge a price premium) might seem impossible in this industry. However, Texas-based Green Mountain Energy has proven that an experiential energy brand can be created and that customers will pay a price premium to purchase it. Capitalizing on deregulation and the fact that electric energy production is the single greatest source of pollution, the Green Mountain brand offers residential and business customers in Texas and selected other areas of the United States an ecologically superior alternative—clean electricity generated by wind, water, and sun. Although customers do not experience any difference in their electricity (and in regulated markets, the energy may still be delivered by a traditional provider), customers choose Green Mountain Energy because it makes them feel good knowing that they are reducing their carbon footprint and contributing to a cleaner environment.

Marketers of many image brands also are trying to increase their brands' experience factors. The Nike Town retail store expands associations to the Nike brand beyond those that are based on status or the image of athletic excellence. Visiting Nike Town is an experience. Although Nike Town does not charge admission (after all, it is a retail outlet), it might be possible for it to do so, particularly if the store were to stage events that enabled visitors to interact with star athletes. Similarly, Mattel's American Girl Store does not charge admission. However, if it did, there are undoubtedly many girls and parents who would be willing to pay for the experience of viewing all the artfully displayed dolls with their themed furniture and accessories (all for sale, of course).

Experiential brands face two key challenges. The first is the ability to create the brand experience consistently. Experience brands are typically labor-intensive. Without careful recruiting, clear standards and training, and the right incentive system, employees will lack the ability and motivation to create the brand experience reliably. As a result, companies with successful experiential brands spend a disproportionate amount of their time on hiring and training their personnel, as the QuikTrip example illustrates.

Virgin Atlantic Airways is another good example of the role that employees play in creating a successful experiential brand. Virgin provides air transportation, but the brand is based on creating memorable experiences that extend well beyond the flight. For the upper-class passenger, the Virgin experience starts with a ride to the airport via motorcycle or chauffeur-driven limousine. It continues in the Clubhouse lounge, where the guest may visit the hair salon, library, or game room while enjoying complimentary beverages and snacks. The in-flight experience may include surprises, such as discovering that a masseuse is available or that ice-cream sundaes accompany the movie. And, on arrival, the Virgin passenger may visit Arrival Clubhouse and freshen up with a sauna and shower, or work off jet lag in the swimming pool and gym. At every stage, Virgin employees play a critical role in ensuring not only that the operation runs smoothly, but also that even the most mundane activities are instilled with a bit of fun and theater. Accordingly, rather than hiring those who aspire to a career in the airline industry, Virgin recruits outgoing individuals, such as aspiring actors.

The second challenge to experiential brands is the potential for satiation. Can the third trip to Disney World possibly match the first one? One strategy for addressing this issue is to continuously expand and enhance the experience. The danger with this strategy is that expectations may rise along with the experience, making them ever harder to meet. If Nordstrom's continues to upgrade the level of service, can it meet the expectations that it creates reliably and profitably?

An alternative strategy is for a firm to create multiple, maximally different experiential brands within a category. Lettuce Entertain You Enterprises Inc., which owns more than 30 restaurants in the Chicago area, has enjoyed considerable success with this strategy. Want to be transported to Italy? Try Lettuce's Scoozi. Have an urge for Chinese? Dine at Lettuce's Ben Pao. Longing for Paris? Visit Lettuce's Mon Ami Gabi. Seeking an over-the-top dining experience that wins bragging rights with fellow foodies? Book a reservation at Lettuce's Tru. In each instance, the experience will be authentic, unique, and memorable because the decor, menu, and waitstaff will embody the particular theme.

Experiential brands are easily extended into tangible reminders of the consumption experience (as in the case of Disney). They may also succeed in other brand extension efforts that are unified by a common target audience and understanding of that audience (Disney with movies, theme parks, and video games). However, experiential brands cannot stray outside the bounds of the type of experience they have created. Disney is punished when adult themes or overly suggestive clothing appear in its movies. To sidestep this problem, the company uses a different brand, Touchstone Pictures, for motion pictures targeted at adult audiences. Similarly, Lego, long loved by parents as a toy that fosters nonviolent creative play, is careful to soften the violence in its video games; when a player dies, the Lego bricks from which he is made collapse into a pile. Further, players can be quickly "reassembled" for more fun.

Conversely, a seemingly mundane, functional product may be the foundation for building an experiential brand if the product acquires its meaning through use and customization. Such is the case with Moleskin notebooks. These simple notebooks inspired Armand B. Frasco to create a blog, Moleskinerie, dedicated to "places and adventures, life's little dramas, and other forgettable events that otherwise would have been lost were they not scrawled between the pages of these little black books (armandfrasco.typepad.com)."[10] Moleskin notebooks are also the inspiration for an annual art exhibit and a curated, traveling group show in which artists, architects, film directors, graphic designers, and writers share their work in Moleskin notebooks.

Experiential brands benefit from judicious use of the Internet and social media to extend and enrich the consumption experience among groups of common followers. These vehicles are important venues for enriching the Star Trek experience among the show's fans. Trekkies, as avid fans of the television show are called, gather online in a variety of chat rooms to discuss the TV show episodes and movies, engage in interactive role play, and buy and sell memorabilia. For these devoted fans, Star Trek represents a philosophy or religion, and the Internet is a valuable means of integrating the show into their everyday lives.[11]

The Brand Continuum

We have discussed three types of brands that vary in their basis for differentiation and marketing mix emphasis. As a result, these brands connect with different consumer needs and evoke different levels of consumer involvement. Moreover, sustaining these brands presents unique challenges to management. The Brand Matrix in Table 6.2 summarizes these distinctions.

Table 6.2
The Brand Matrix

Brand Type	Basis for Differentiation	Marketing Mix Emphasis	Consumer Needs and Involvement	Management Challenges
Functional (e.g., Tide, Gillette, McDonald's, Xiameter)	Superior performance or superior economy	Product, price, and/or place	Physiological and safety needs, relatively low involvement	Sustaining the basis of superiority
Image (e.g., Waterman, Nike, Apple, Coke, Pepsi, Eco-Imagination)	Desirable image	Communications	Social and esteem needs, moderate to high involvement	Balancing the brand heritage with the need for relevance in a dynamic environment
Experiential (e.g. Disney, Saturn, QuikTrip, Virgin Atlantic Airways)	A unique, engaging experience	Service delivery (place and people)	Self-actualization needs, moderate to high involvement	Consistency in delivery, risk of consumer satiation

These types of brands have been presented in terms of three discrete categories. However, it may be more helpful to think of them as lying on a *brand continuum* ranging from a focus on the product to a focus on the consumer. At one extreme lie functional brands, which are created in the factory and may be purchased by consumers for consumption at whatever time they might desire. At the other extreme are experiential brands, which are created at the time of consumption with the active participation of consumers. Image brands fall in the middle. They are created at the factory but their value stems, in large measure, from their display by consumers.

Further, although we have classified specific brands into one of the three categories, it is also important to recognize that brands may evolve in ways that shift their categorization. Consider, for example, Volvo. Volvo began as a functional brand that focused on features such as reinforced steel beams in the car's roof and side panels, which offered drivers a higher level of crash protection or safety. However, over time, by design or by default, Volvo evolved into an image brand. It became the car for caring parents. This association was reinforced when the company aired an advertisement in which a young woman announces that she has purchased a Volvo as a means of informing her husband that she is pregnant. The image of Volvo as the car for caring, well-educated, affluent parents served the company well for many years. But eventually this image proved to be limiting; Volvo was tied to a generation (baby boomers) and a lifestyle (conservative) that excluded or did not appeal to many car buyers. In an effort to reconnect with a broader target of consumers, particularly Generation X buyers, Volvo launched a campaign with an experiential theme. Volvo claimed to provide cars that would "save your soul." Of course, this claim would not be credible without significant modification of the car's physical features. The lines of the classic Volvo "box" have been softened, and there is even a Volvo convertible (hardly a design that reinforces the association to safety). Thus, not only has the meaning of the Volvo brand moved from being functional to being more experiential, but the physical features of the car have evolved as well.

A final point worth noting is that although the general population may view a brand as belonging to one of our three categories, this view need not be universally held. Whatever the brand and the product category, heavy users of it are likely to be more emotionally involved, and thereby view the brand as having more image or experiential characteristics than lighter users.

BRAND ARCHITECTURE

Although we have focused on single brands so far, most organizations operate with multiple brands. Creating a logical structure to best utilize these assets is

Table 6.3
The Relationship Between Type of Brand and Branding Strategies

Type of Brand	Corporate	Family	Product
Functional	Sony, Caterpillar	Gillette (Fusion Mach3, Sensor, Atra)	Tide, Cheer, Era (P&G)
Image	Ralph Lauren, Under Armour, Accenture	GM (Chevy, Buick, Cadillac), BMW (3, 5, 8 series, Z-3, X5)	Coke, Sprite, Fanta (Coca-Cola)
Experiential	Saturn, Starbucks, Green Mountain Energy	Lettuce Entertain You (Scoozi, Ben Pao, Mon Ami Gabi, Tru)	Ritz-Carlton, Fairfield Inn (Marriott Corp.)

an extremely important aspect of brand management. Broadly speaking, three approaches are common in creating an architecture or structure for brands: *product branding* (using unrelated brand names for several products in the same product category); *family branding* (using multiple brands in a product category and linking them to a common family name); and *corporate branding* (using one corporate brand for all products). Each of these three branding strategies can be considered in light of the three types of brands discussed in the previous section. Some examples are shown in Table 6.3.

Product Branding

The *product branding* structure is common in traditional consumer goods companies. Markets for consumer products are divided into segments of similar buyers seeking similar value. Across segments, buyers seek different value. To address these differences, firms offer multiple brands, each targeting a distinct segment of consumers. To the buyer, each brand is distinct and has no obvious common affiliation to the parent company. P&G uses this approach in marketing its line of laundry detergents. Few consumers think of Tide, Cheer, and Era as related brands, though P&G makes them all. Coca-Cola uses a similar strategy in marketing Sprite, Fanta, and Coke, as does Miller Brewing in marketing Red Dog versus the Miller brands. Finally, experiential brands may also be marketed using a product approach. Few consumers are aware that Marriott Corporation owns Ritz-Carlton and Fairfield Inn, brands that are at opposite poles of the hotel price spectrum.

A product branding strategy can enable a firm to attract distinct segments of consumers who may not wish to be affiliated with each other. For example, some beer drinkers may prefer the image associated with small microbreweries and disdain more mass market brands, such as Miller and Bud. In launching the Red Dog brand, Miller sought to attract beer drinkers seeking a microbrew image, while continuing to serve the mass market with its mainstay Miller-branded products. Product branding can be highly successful because it creates distinct, powerful, clearly defined brands. It requires deep pockets, however, to build multiple, independent brands, sometimes requiring massive advertising spending to sustain. Of course, no matter how much a company spends, it cannot prevent consumers from learning about the parentage of brands, as Miller discovered when the press publicized the fact that Red Dog was a Miller brand. Such disclosures are more likely to be damaging when the brand is based on image rather than function.

Family Branding

An alternative approach is to adopt a *family branding* strategy. Under this approach, a corporate or umbrella brand name may be combined with more specific product-based names. Traditionally, auto manufacturers have used this branding strategy. For example, Toyota markets Corolla, Prius, and RAV4, among others, each targeted to a different segment of consumers and each having unique associations, but all sharing an affiliation with Toyota to varying degrees. Many family brands begin as product brands, with the company then leveraging the equity in the product brand through line extensions. A good example is Coca-Cola, with extensions such as Coca-Cola Light, Classic, and Zero. Gillette also takes a family branding approach, but does so for a line of functional products. Lettuce Entertain You Enterprises Inc. adopts a family branding strategy for its set of experiential brands. In general, the family branding approach works best when relatively distinct segments of users (or use occasions) exist and, thus, the common affiliation is not likely to increase cannibalization markedly. Instead, the familial affiliation provides an assurance of a certain level of quality. Employing the family brand in this way can bring added power to a new product brand of an existing family brand. This benefit is not without a cost, however. The family brand may impose a constraint on the range of meanings that can be created at the product level.

Corporate Branding

Corporate branding employs the simplest brand architecture: one brand dominates. Such a structure is quite common in business markets. With the exception of NBC Universal, for example, General Electric uses one brand for the vast majority of its businesses. Similarly, Boeing, Dow Chemical, and McKinsey & Company use a single brand for all of their product lines. Like purchasers of product brands, the buyers of these companies' products may differ in the value they seek, creating different segments. As professional buyers, however, the relationship between organizations becomes very important, and it's often not possible to create unique brands without any meaningful link to the corporation.

In the case of consumer markets, image brands such as Perrier may find the corporate branding approach appealing. Having multiple products with a common name may help to clearly define the experience buyers can expect and enrich the brand image. Even functional brands, such as BIC and Sony, may successfully adopt a corporate branding approach. Often companies are attracted to a corporate branding approach for the efficiency that it provides; advertising expenditures can be concentrated on building a single brand name. However, this efficiency carries a price. All products under the corporate brand must be compatible with the associations that the brand evokes, a lesson that BIC learned when it launched a line of perfumes bearing the BIC name.

SUMMARY

Brands are a ubiquitous part of modern markets. They exist because they provide value to consumers. Brands assure a level of quality, simplify choice, and help consumers achieve a wide range of goals from meeting basic, functional needs to self-actualization. Brands also benefit the companies that create them. They support higher margins than strict product differences might permit and thus protect firms against competitors who imitate their products. Brands also may allow the firm to gain leverage over its customers, as DuPont and Intel have demonstrated. In sum, brands serve as a bridge between a company and its customers—they are symbols of the value that the company creates.

Brands must be built, and this is a time-consuming and costly process. When first launched, many brands are simply names with no inherent meaning—Sony, Mercedes-Benz, or Ben & Jerry's meant little at first. Over time, these names and the brands that they symbolize came to represent a rich set of associations in consumers' minds. This observation points to the central idea that at their core, powerful brands reside not with the company, but rather with consumers. The thoughts, memories, and feelings that people have about a brand are, at an individual level, the essence of brand equity.

However, how that equity is created and maintained is often overlooked by organizations that believe value arises only from products, or that value is created in the factory. The companies that we have discussed illustrate that success requires creating value in the factory *and* in the minds of buyers. This process of creating and maintaining brand equity can simultaneously enrich consumers' lives and the company's bottom line.

Alice M. Tybout is the Harold T. Martin Professor of Marketing and a former chairperson of the Marketing Department at the Kellogg School of Management. She is also co-director of the Kellogg on Branding Program and director of the Kellogg on Consumer Marketing Strategy Program at the James L. Allen Center. She is co-editor of Kellogg on Branding (John Wiley & Sons). She received her BS and MA from Ohio State University and her PhD from Northwestern University.

Gregory S. Carpenter is the James Farley/Booz Allen Hamilton Professor of Marketing Strategy and a former chair of the Marketing Department at the Kellogg School of Management, Northwestern University. He is also director of the Kellogg School's Center for Market Leadership, a research center focused on understanding competitive strategy and competitive advantage. He received his BA from Ohio Wesleyan University and MBA, MPhil, and PhD degrees from Columbia University.

NOTES

1. "100 Best Global Brands," *BusinessWeek,* September 28, 2009.
2. www.bizcommunity.com/Quote/196/11/866.html.
3. Aaker, David A. (1994), "Building a Brand: The Saturn Story," *California Management Review*, 36 (2, Winter), 31–50.
4. http://money.cnn.com/magazines/fortune/fortune_archive/2007/04/16/8404302/index3.htm.
5. Anderson, J., N. Kumar, and J. Narus (2007) *Value Merchants: Demonstrating and Documenting Superior Value in Business Markets*, Harvard Business School Press, Boston: Massachusetts.
6. Maynard, Micheline, Nick Bunkley, and Mary M. Chapman contributing (2007), "Say 'Hybrid' and Many People Will Hear 'Prius,'" *New York Times,* via nytimes.com, 07-04.
7. www.marketwatch.com/story/pernod-ricard-snaps-up-absolut-vodka-parent-for-83-billion.
8. Bendapudi, Neeli, and Venkat Bendapudi (2007), "Creating the Living Brand," *Harvard Business Review,* May 2007, 124–132, www.quiktrip.com.
9. Osgood, Charles E., Succi, George J., and Percy H. Tannebaum, (1957) *The Measurement Meaning*, Urbana: University of Illinois Press.
10. http://armandfrasco.typepad.com/moleskinerie/2004/01/first_post_1.html.

11. Kozinets, Robert V. (2001), "Utopian Enterprise: Articulating the Meaning of Star Trek's Culture of Consumption," *Journal of Consumer Research*, 28, 67–89.

ADDITIONAL READING

Keller, Kevin Lane (2007), *Strategic Brand Management*, 3rd edition, Upper Saddle River, NJ: Prentice Hall.

Tybout, Alice M., and Tim Calkins (2005), *Kellogg on Branding*, New York: John Wiley & Sons.

IMPLEMENTING THE STRATEGY

CHAPTER 7

MAKING THE BRAND COME ALIVE WITHIN YOUR ORGANIZATION

LISA FORTINI-CAMPBELL

INTRODUCTION

Despite the best intentions and the expenditure of a great deal of effort and money, many corporate branding initiatives fail to truly change the way customers see a company. In most cases, following a brand initiative, very little about the company actually changes to conform to the new brand direction.

This chapter examines that problem and argues that any branding initiative designed to "come alive" outside the organization must "come alive" inside the organization first. Brand planners must take the nature of the internal organization into account, because the current organization's structure, reward system, culture, and leadership are already sending powerful messages about what the company values and how employees are meant to behave at work every day. If the inconsistencies between the intentions of the new brand direction and the status quo are not discovered and corrected before the new brand is rolled out, employees become confused at best and cynical at worst. In either case, they fail to execute the new brand direction.

This chapter takes a close look at four key dimensions of the internal organization: *hiring; cultural storytelling; job design, rewards, and incentives;* and *leadership*, all of which are powerful communicators about the company's current values. Any marketer hoping the new brand direction will live inside the organization must examine what values are living there now, then help the company identify how it must change to ensure that employees will behave consistently with the new brand vision.

YOUR CULTURE IS YOUR BRAND

Imagine that, after many months of hard work, your organization has just completed a major corporate branding initiative as part of a commitment to transform the company. Perhaps you've branded the organization for the first time. Perhaps you've refreshed a long-standing brand with a new and more relevant position for today's marketplace. Perhaps you've done the most radical thing of all and completely rebranded the company as it moves in a new direction.

This accomplishment has come at great effort and expense. You've assessed customer needs, benchmarked the competition, completed stakeholder interviews, and conducted countless strategic planning meetings. You've worked with outside consultants to craft a precise statement of your brand's unique position and brought in design and advertising agencies to make it come alive visually as well as verbally.

A monumental effort in marketing communications has been completed and new advertising, sales materials, packaging, and web interfaces have been produced. The new brand has been announced at a company-wide meeting with great fanfare. Employee newsletters, coffee talks, and town hall meetings make sure everyone understands the new direction and buys into it.

You're justifiably proud of your work. Your new brand is sharp, compelling, relevant to customers, and well expressed in every way, shape, and form. Yet, after all that work, you're feeling a little disappointed and frustrated. You've helped point the company in a new direction, but every day when you come to work, it still feels like the same old place. Despite the new position, employees are doing everything they used to do in pretty much the same old way.

The inconsistencies between the fresh brand promise and stale employee behavior are starting to bother you. For example, maybe the company has staked itself firmly in the "green" arena, and, while there are a few specific green programs you can highlight on your web site and to the press, a sense of environmental responsibility hasn't permeated the day-to-day behavior of people throughout the organization.

Or, perhaps your B2B organization has branded itself as one thoroughly committed to innovation, and although you have filed for a record number of patents in the last year, there's not much innovation in product design or in business operations. Or, you've branded yourself as a truly customer-centric company, yet customer-facing people are still treating customers in the same way they always have.

Something is wrong. People just aren't taking up the challenge to do what management has asked them to do—that is, to live the promise of the new brand. Maybe, you think, people just don't completely understand what the brand is and what they're supposed to do about it. So, you embark on a concentrated program of "internal branding" designed to educate the workforce—complete with workshops, DVDs, brochures, and takeaway tools to remind everyone of the brand's key values and how they should behave to work consistently with those values. And still very little changes.

You begin to worry that if people don't fully engage in living the brand positioning, then all that branding work will simply become attractive but empty window dressing rather than what it was intended to be—a banner under which the company transforms itself.

Many well-intended and well-planned branding initiatives founder on the shoals of such problems. The nagging suspicion you've had for months that something isn't right eventually becomes a reality. The brand that could have been transformative doesn't take root and passes into history as a hopeful but unfulfilled promise, like many a corporate initiative before it.

But let's assume people do understand the brand position and that you've done your best to make sure they understand their role in it. So why isn't their behavior changing? Is your "internal branding" program failing in some way? Is the amount of internal communication insufficient or misdirected?

What, exactly, is going wrong?

The Culture Credibility Gap

Between the essential first step of employees understanding a company's brand positioning and the final step of doing something to act on it is the important and oft-neglected step of *ensuring that people believe it*. This is called the culture credibility gap.

But, you may ask, why wouldn't people believe something that their company's leaders have spent millions of dollars on, telling employees just how important it is? What undermines an initiative's credibility within the workforce? What causes employees to mistrust what they are being asked to do?

Credibility is undermined because somehow, employees are receiving inconsistent messages from the organization. One set of messages encourages them to adopt new ways of approaching their work, aligning it with a brand position that represents an important future direction for the organization. Another set of (possibly unintended) messages encourages them to maintain the status quo. To employees, no amount of effort spent on increasing their brand understanding or giving them tools to implement a new brand vision will change their behavior if something else is contradicting what you tell them.

So where do the undermining messages come from?

They come from what we could call the "body language" of the organization: all those dimensions of organizational structure, processes, hiring practices, job design, rewards, management style, and leadership that result in the large concept we call "culture." Just as we all trust what people do more than we trust what they say, employees will respond to what the culture's "body language" is directing them to do, rather than to what a new brand initiative is telling them to do, especially if those two forces are at all inconsistent.

If, for example, a new brand positioning stresses the company's commitment to building long-term relationships with customers, yet the sales force is disproportionately rewarded for bringing in new business, a contradictory message is being sent. With this "old" incentive structure, salespeople will keep focusing on acquiring new business rather than on cultivating current customers, despite the new brand direction coming down from above.

If a company's brand stresses a commitment to environmental sustainability, but employee recommendations about how to accomplish that goal are rejected because they "cost too much," an inconsistent message is being sent. Employees receive the message that cost is more important than the new organizational imperative.

If an organization's brand position stresses values of authenticity and transparency, but management is reluctant to communicate the reasons behind its decisions and is unwilling to listen to employee questions about those decisions, an inconsistent message is being sent. Employees realize that management doesn't mean what it says.

It's easy to see how cynicism can take root throughout an organization. In fact, a strong flavor of cynicism in response to a new branding initiative is a clear sign that there are undiscovered or uncorrected aspects of the organization's culture that are fighting against the goals of the new direction.

Therefore, making a brand come alive inside an organization ultimately means that marketers must do more than design and deliver communication programs to teach people what the new brand is. They also must assess what messages are *already* being sent about what the company values, in terms of its structure, processes, rewards, and leadership—in other words, by its entire culture. The marketer must then point out the places where employees could reasonably see contradictions and help the organization overcome these challenges.

Questions of organizational structure, leadership, and culture are usually beyond the scope of a marketer's job description. However, the messages being sent through all aspects of a company's culture are critical to determining whether employees step up to the challenge of living the brand inside the organization. Therefore, a responsible marketer must at least be a voice for pointing out the practices that could render the money and time spent on a new branding initiative worthless. Sometimes, characteristics of the organization's culture haven't been explicitly considered and can be easily changed, sometimes not. In any case, a valuable discussion results when the marketer takes up the challenge to start one.

Living the Culture

Disney Theme Parks, Southwest Airlines, the Mayo Clinic, Zara, and Zappos.com are good examples of truly living brands. Despite the differences in their products, services, price points, and business models, they all have one thing in common. Like flowers that bloom because their healthy root systems feed them well, their brands, lived at every point of contact with the customer, are fed by internal organizations that support—and importantly, do not contradict—the direction of those brands.

Zappos, an Internet shoe and clothing retailer, is an excellent example of the principle in action. Zappos was founded in 1999 and sold a negligible amount of merchandise that year. But, nearly 10 years later, it reported almost $1 billion in gross sales and sold itself to Amazon for $928 million. Zappos achieved this level of success by focusing on building customer loyalty through a brand position focused entirely on customer service. As the first of their 10 core values states, the goal is to "deliver WOW through customer service." Zappos directs all their effort to ensuring that after any interaction any customer has with them, the customer will say, "That was the best customer service experience I've ever had!"[1]

That strategy is supported with tactics like a 365-day return policy, free shipping both ways, and a call center open 24/7. But by themselves, those tactics wouldn't result in enthusiastic and loyal customers if the company's entire culture didn't support that brand identity.

As founder Tony Hsieh said:

> At Zappos.com, we decided a long time ago that we didn't want our brand to be just about shoes, or clothing, or even online retailing. We decided that we wanted to build our brand to be about the very best customer service and the very best customer experience. We believe that customer service shouldn't be just a department, it should be the entire company.

So what's a company to do if you can't just buy your way into building the brand you want? What's the best way to build a brand for the long term?

In a word: culture.

At Zappos, our belief is that if you get the culture right, most of the other stuff—like great customer service, or building a great long-term brand, or passionate employees and customers—will happen naturally on its own.

We believe that your company's culture and your company's brand are really just two sides of the same coin. The brand may lag the culture at first, but eventually it will catch up.

Your culture is your brand.[2]

FOUR ASPECTS OF CULTURE

Culture can seem like a nebulous and amorphous concept, but it rises out of the behaviors that are encouraged or discouraged by the organization's concrete structure, processes, system of rewards, management style, and leadership. When addressing the culture is integrated into new brand initiative planning, then that brand has a better chance of thriving inside the organization so that it can live outside the organization, building the relationship with customers it was designed to build.

Although there are many aspects of an organization's culture, we focus on the four that are essential to consider whenever a company is planning a new brand initiative: Hiring and employee assessment; cultural storytelling; job design, rewards, and incentives; and leadership.

Hiring and Employee Assessment

Because a brand is lived by people, it is clear that a marketer should first consider what kind of people are already working in the organization. Do they have the attitude and the skills needed to deliver the brand the company aspires to?

All best practitioners of living brands place an extraordinary emphasis on hiring. At Southwest Airlines, a U.S.–based low-cost carrier, the brand depends on delivering a fun, customer-oriented airline experience. Southwest makes sure that they "hire for attitude and train for aptitude." Managers at Southwest know that they can always train a person to be a better pilot, flight attendant, reservations agent, or ramp operator, but they can't make someone into a nice, happy, cooperative, problem-solving, and fun-loving person. So, a large part of the assessment of potential new employees is the search for exactly those qualities. As a low-cost carrier, Southwest could simply hire people willing to work for a low wage, regardless of the attitude they bring to their jobs. But it would be impossible for them to deliver a brand widely regarded as the most customer-friendly in the industry.[3]

At Mayo Clinic, a health-care organization consisting of medical schools, hospitals, and clinics, the goal of the brand is to fully live the promise that the "patient always comes first." Strategically, Mayo works toward that goal with a workforce that excels at collegiality and cross-functional cooperation. Because many health-care professionals are trained in highly specialized areas of expertise, Mayo's hiring practices are focused on determining the ability of every potential employee, including doctors, nurses, technicians, and other professionals to cooperate with each other and take suggestions from people outside their area of expertise in the name of higher quality patient care. Mayo seeks to deliver the best in complete patient care, so if they were to hire people exclusively for their technical excellence, ignoring whether they could practice cross-functional cooperation, it would be impossible to live up to a brand that cares for the whole human being rather than just treats disease.[4]

At Zappos, all prospective employees go through two sets of interviews. One, conducted by human resources, is charged with determining the candidate's cultural fit with the company. The other, conducted by the departmental hiring manager and his or her team, looks for relevant experience, technical ability, and fit within the team. Candidates must pass both sets of interviews in order to be hired for an open job. Even when the company desperately needs a technical skill, as rapidly growing companies often do, Zappos will forego the opportunity to hire a technically skilled person who doesn't fit the culture. Zappos takes its culture seriously and protects it in order to protect its brand.

In fact, once a person has been hired at Zappos, he or she works for four weeks in the customer-service center, the "nerve center" of the brand. After four weeks of work and four weeks of pay, Zappos offers every new hire $2,000 to leave the company. This extraordinary offer is a fail-safe device. It recognizes that if someone who is not fully customer service–oriented gets through the hiring process, such a person would be likely to accept such a large financial incentive to leave. Zappos management believes that it is better to pay $2,000 out of pocket to someone who has been mistakenly hired than to allow that person to contaminate the customer-service culture that is central to the external brand.[5]

Of course, it's impossible to rehire the entire organization when a new brand initiative is being developed, but it is equally disastrous to ignore the fact that current hiring or assessment systems may not be looking for the very qualities that will make the new brand initiative a reality. Therefore, the sophisticated marketer will consider the nature of the employee base as a new brand initiative being developed to make sure the workforce has the attitude and skills to carry it off. And, if not, then the marketer must point out that the company's hiring and assessment practices don't align with the brand's aspirations. Such a scenario sends an inconsistent message, and the brand initiative will begin to struggle as soon as it is launched.

Therefore, a marketer eager to make the brand live inside the organization should ask:

- What qualities do our current hiring practices seek out?
- What kinds of people do those practices bring into our organization?
- Are those characteristics consistent with the goals of our brand?
- If we could build criteria into our hiring process (or our system for assessing current employees) that would ensure people were aligned with our brand direction, which criteria would we include?

Cultural Storytelling

The stories a company tells itself, both internally and externally, form the "self-consciousness" of the organization and teach employees in a variety of subtle and not-so-subtle ways how they should think of themselves, how they should behave, and what the company truly values.

For example, every new employee at Mayo Clinic is greeted with, "Welcome to patient care," whether that person is a physician, an accounts payable clerk, a food service worker, or a telephone receptionist. The idea that everyone's job directly touches the patient experience is seeded during training and reinforced throughout the workday. A nurse will openly congratulate a technician at a team meeting for having noticed something about a patient's condition that helped improve the patient's care. Stories about the extraordinary feats of the staff working to care for the whole well-being of a patient, like arranging a daughter's wedding to take place in a patient's room, are told in employee newsletters, shared at staff meetings, and celebrated at all employee events. A cherished "Karis" (Greek for "caring") award is given quarterly to any employee for exceptional service to the company's mission to put patients first.[6]

This type of brand behavior is called cultural storytelling. Internally, an organization describes itself formally in orientation programs, training, and employee celebrations, and informally as people who are socialized on the job by their peers and managers. People talk about what they're proud of about the company, they praise each other for behaving in certain ways, and they celebrate successes and react to failures.

Because this kind of storytelling is pervasive, it is critical for a sophisticated brand marketer to pay close attention to what the company is currently saying about itself and to ask, "Do we have a self-image consistent with the direction of our brand initiative? Are the stories we tell ourselves now consistent with the goals of our brand or are they perpetuating a different set of values?"

Organizations with good reputations for instilling desirable cultures—such as Nordstrom, Southwest, Google, Disney, or Hewlett-Packard (when it was run by Bill Hewlett and Dave Packard)—pay careful attention to the ways in which the company talks to itself about itself, particularly in making sure that no subtle, contradictory messages creep in to undermine the more formally expressed ones.[7]

At Disney, for example, new hires are paired with more experienced "mentors" in order to fully absorb their responsibilities as performing Disney "cast members" under the care of a person fully immersed in the company's brand values. If a new hire expresses skepticism about any of the company's practices or traditions, a more experienced person is right at hand to help explain why the company does what it does. This helps to keep the socialization process of a new employee moving along in a direction that supports the brand.[8]

In the years when Leo Burnett ran the advertising agency that bears his name, managers nipped in the bud the impulses of young employees to vent frustration by criticizing clients. "We don't talk that way about our good clients," was the agency mantra. The company had a stated dedication to client service. What message would have been sent if informal griping were allowed to contradict this explicit mantra? Rather than tolerate such undermining, managers were charged with keeping the water-cooler conversation aligned with the formal brand message of loyalty and respect for clients.[9]

The formal and informal stories a company tells about itself—to new employees and veterans, in formal settings and informal conversations—are the most important expressions of the company's living culture. These stories must be consistent with one another and consistent with the brand's goals; if not, a creeping lack of authenticity infects the culture. This dimension of organizational behavior is so important, and best practitioners are so thoroughly committed to managing it, that some of these companies are called "cults." That pejorative word confuses clarity and intensity of culture for something mindless, and it tends to be used by those who have a weak, vague culture themselves. The important lesson is that those who manage their business culture only half-heartedly risk having uncommitted, cynical employees who nod in the direction of the new brand direction while doing little to fulfill it.

Therefore, a marketer eager to make the brand live inside the organization should ask:

- What do we tell ourselves about our company in the myriad ways we talk to each other formally and informally throughout our organization?
- Is our current organizational self-image consistent with the aspirations of our brand?
- What are we teaching people about ourselves as soon as they join our organization in our orientation programs and in their first months on the job?
- What do we reinforce in our training programs? What do we praise and recognize? What do we celebrate?
- Is anything in our informal communications inconsistent with the values we're trying to reinforce formally?
- If we could change any dimension of our current orientation or training programs, or the employee behaviors we praise and celebrate, which ones would we change to bring our formal and informal storytelling in line with the goals of our brand?

Job Design, Rewards, and Incentives

Companies design jobs to make the work of the company efficient and effective, and they reward people for doing their jobs well. But, it's equally important to consider whether jobs are designed and rewards structured so that it is as easy as possible for employees to live the brand.

At Zara, the fast-growing Spanish clothing retailer and the world's second-largest clothing retailer after Gap, the brand is focused on building a reputation for up-to-the-minute fashion. The company calls its strategy "fast fashion" and aligns every aspect of its organization to make sure that no time is wasted getting designs from the sketch pad to finished garments in the store. As part of that strategy, job structures are designed so that designers do their work sitting among the pattern makers, to allow for plenty of conversation between the two functions as designs are developed. That way, a pattern maker can warn a designer about a difficult-to-execute design before it is finalized—eliminating wasted time on designs that can't be easily made or on countless revisions because a designer doesn't fully understand what it takes to manufacture a garment.[10]

Rewards systems are another way to ensure that the organization is aligned properly with the brand. Indeed, there is no more powerful "body language" in an organization than its reward system. So it is especially important for a marketer launching a new brand initiative to make sure that there isn't anything in the company's current reward structure that explicitly undermines the goals of that new brand.

At Mayo, for example, doctors are salaried, rather than paid by the number of patients they see. That way, there is no conflict between maximizing income and maximizing patient care. At Zappos, customer-service agents aren't measured by how fast they get customers on and off the phone. Of course, they want to take orders, answer questions, and solve problems quickly, but not if a little more time will yield a more delighted customer.

Southwest Airlines keeps its reputation for excellent on-time performance by focusing on exceptionally fast turnarounds between flights. To accomplish that goal, it's the responsibility of all flight crew members, including pilots, to help clean the planes between flights. It's the pilot's job to do more than fly the plane to its next destination; it's to make sure the plane is ready to get back up in the air, on time and in a customer-ready condition each and every time.

It's widely known that Ritz-Carlton, Nordstrom, and Disney make their customer-friendly brands come alive in part because employees are given great discretion to solve customer problems on the spot without checking in with managers about how to handle them. Famously, Ritz-Carlton allows any of its employees to spend up to $2,000 to solve situations that would otherwise be problems for customers.[11] Employees take satisfaction in being trusted to make decisions and in being empowered to take action to delight the customer.[12] Being able to use their own discretion enriches their work and being trusted to do so is intrinsically rewarding. Enabling them to deal with circumstances as they see fit reinforces the idea that they are "ladies and gentlemen caring for ladies and gentlemen" and it makes that slogan come true in practice.

In the years when the Leo Burnett advertising agency was privately held, the company's creative department didn't follow the common industry practice of submitting its work for industry awards. Those awards contests were judged by peers, not by clients: What message would it have sent to tell employees that nothing is more important than creating advertising that builds the client's business, and then turn around and tell them that they should seek the approval of their creative peers irrespective of how well that advertising persuades customers to buy?

Therefore, a marketer eager to make the brand live inside the organization should ask:

- How have we currently designed key jobs in the organization, and does the way of working reinforce the new brand direction?

- Is there anything built into the way key jobs are currently designed that makes achieving the new brand direction more difficult?
- What kinds of behavior does our current measurement and incentive structure reward?
- What values are we creating through that reward system? Are those values and that behavior consistent with the goals of the brand?
- If we could change the design of any key job or any dimension of our current reward system, or add any new measurement to it, how could we create greater alignment between the goals of the brand and the organization's reward system?

Leadership

It goes without saying that ultimately an organization's success hinges on whether an organization's leaders and managers are themselves living examples of the brand's values.

In all the best-practice companies, leaders such as Herb Kelleher, Colleen Barrett, and Gary Kelly at Southwest Airlines, Tony Hsieh at Zappos, Bill Hewlett and Dave Packard at Hewlett Packard, and Denis Cortese at Mayo Clinic all have demonstrated extraordinary personal discipline in making sure that they walk the talk, day in and day out in their organizations.

Tony Hsieh's e-mail to employees in which he explained the acquisition of Zappos by Amazon is just one example of that sort of leadership.[13] Hsieh took great care to reassure his staff that he and the other founders were staying on, that Zappos would retain its independence and cultural identity, and that Amazon hoped to learn from Zappos rather than to chew it up and absorb it. Dry legalism would have been antithetical to the Zappos culture, and Hsieh avoided that entirely. Instead, he kept the tone personal, honest, and humorous where appropriate, while remaining within formal legal bounds. He conveyed the important information coherently and drew his audience into an ongoing discussion about their questions and concerns. Throughout, the written message conveys the authentic voice of a trustworthy leader.

Loyalty to and respect for individuals are part of the culture at successful companies, however much those cultures might differ in particular attributes. And, of course, loyalty and respect are a two-way street. Good leaders win respect and loyalty by demonstrating integrity, commitment, and competence when they are tested. Employees watch their leaders closely to see how they behave, what they praise and reinforce, and what they criticize and discourage. Their behavior tells the truth about what the organization values and what employees need to do to be successful in it. Large (and even small) contradictions between what leaders and managers say and do can undermine a new brand direction more quickly than anything else. On the other hand, a leader who lives the brand builds organizational cohesion around a new direction faster than any other single aspect of an organization.

So, for example, junior accountants or lawyers at large firms absorb the culture by watching senior partners working longer hours than anyone else, orchestrating the efforts of many technical experts, synthesizing complex information, and presenting it in a way that satisfies clients. The overtime a junior is expected to put in seems fair when the boss is working even longer hours and doing it without showing strain. In professional services firms, watching senior practitioners work at the highest level engenders respect while it educates and acculturates.

The master-apprentice relationship does not translate well from professional-services firms to complex organizations in which functions are more highly specialized and diverse, but even in such places, successful leaders find some way to show respect for and to win respect from employees. So, for example, Bill Hewlett and Dave Packard, both engineers themselves, might be found standing over a workbench absorbed in a problem with other technicians and engineers, or participating in a contest to see who could assemble the parts of a computer the fastest. Whatever else it was, HP was an engineering company that valued engineers and recognized good ones.

Similarly, a manager of a Boeing aircraft-assembly plant has been observed establishing rapport with his mechanics by sharing stories about maintaining boat engines. With the ice broken and common interests established, it was easier to sit with them as they brainstormed about how to get the seats installed in the interior of the plane in half the time, or how to create a more efficient way to deliver fuel and coolants to the jet engine; and it was easier to talk with them about why they should participate willingly in continuous improvement efforts.

Ultimately, a good leader depends simply on his or her personality and sincerity to establish a common bond, rather than on technical skills. Herb Kelleher is a famous example. He worked in airports himself on Christmas Day to demonstrate solidarity with employees who had sacrificed their own time with family to make travel easier for Southwest's customers. He dressed himself in funny costumes on Halloween to exemplify the company's egalitarian spirit of fun, and he addressed each 10-year anniversary cohort of employees himself. By showing his own sincere respect for them, he embodied the company's respect for its employees and modeled the attitude that they should have for customers.

New Belgium, the craft brewery, offers another example. In accordance with its explicitly stated culture of transparency and integrity, the CEO, Kim

Jordan, decided to publish the compensation of every employee, including her own, so that each employee could judge the fairness of everyone's pay for him- or herself. In another instance, when the company realized that buying coal-generated electricity was inconsistent with the environmental concerns that are dear to them, Jordan put the issue to the employees and asked them to vote whether to buy cheap coal-fired electricity or to pay more for wind-generated electricity at the cost of reducing the bonus pool. The employees voted unanimously for the green option: wind-power. By giving them the choice, Jordan demonstrated that collegiality and employee ownership were real elements of the company's culture, not just words in a press release.

Although good leadership can build a brand, bad leadership can kill one dead by making every explicit brand message look like a lie. Consider, for example, the message sent by a leader who claims to focus on long-term customer relationships, but who always talks to employees about monthly financials and the daily stock price. Similarly, consider the message sent if a leader says she agrees that the company should be focused on creating loyal relationships with satisfied customers, but can't find the time to make a customer visit or sit in on a customer service phone line. And what message does it send if a company's brand is focused on speed, simplicity, and ease of use but the leader perpetuates bureaucratic, time-consuming, and secretive internal decision-making processes?

A marketer can't change an organization's leadership, nor can he or she change the leader's personal style, but it is important to help the organization's leadership understand just how strongly it affects the believability of any brand initiative. Marketers, with their expertise in communication and persuasion, should step up to the challenge of helping the company's management and leadership realize how important they are to ensuring that all the effort to create a new brand is well-spent. He or she should ask:

- How can I help our leadership understand just how essential their behavior is to the believability of the new brand direction?
- Can I point out qualities and behaviors in our leaders and managers that are consistent with our brand values?
- How can I appropriately point out any that are explicitly contradictory?

SUMMARY

Clearly no marketer, no matter how senior, can change the underlying dimensions of a company's culture all by him- or herself, but he or she performs a great service by helping managers understand just how important that culture is to the company's ability to live the brand.

By helping an organization's leaders examine their practices in *hiring; cultural storytelling; job design, rewards, and incentives;* and *leadership*, marketers can assist companies in better aligning their brand initiatives with their current organization.

This requires marketers to work toward earning an influence far more strategic than they may have today. By uncovering and raising a discussion about the aspects of a company's culture that are unwittingly contradicting the new brand's values, the modern marketer helps to ensure that the brand comes alive inside the organization so that it comes alive outside of it, too.

Lisa Fortini-Campbell is a lecturer in the executive education programs at the Kellogg School of Management, Northwestern University, where she specializes in courses on customer psychology and integrating the customer experience. Outside the classroom, she operates the Fortini-Campbell Company, which conducts research for, consults with, and trains organizations in a variety of industries all around the world. She is the author of Hitting the Sweet Spot and a contributor to Kellogg on Integrated Marketing. She received her BS and MA from Ohio State University and her PhD from the University of Washington.

NOTES

1. http://about.zappos.com/zappos-story/in-the-beginning-let-there-be-shoes.
2. *New York Times* (2010), "On a Scale of 1 to 10, How Weird Are You?" (January 10).
3. www.southwest.com/careers/culture.html; www.southwest.com/about_swa/mission.html; www.uschamber.com/bclc/profiles/southwest.htm.
4. Berry, Leonard L., and Neeli Bendapudi (2003), "Clueing in Customers," *Harvard Business Review* (February).
5. http://blogs.zappos.com.
6. Berry, Bendapudi, "Clueing in Customers," *Harvard Business Review*; www.mayoclinic.org/about/noseworthy-message.html.
7. Packard, David (1995), *The HP Way: How Bill Hewlett and I Built Our Company*, HarperBusiness: New York, New York.
8. Kelley M. Blassingame (2003), "Working Their Magic: Disney Culture Molds Happy Employees," *Employee Benefit News* (September 8).
9. This comes from personal experience having worked there in 1980.
10. Ferdows, Kasra, Michael A. Lewis, and Jose A. D. Machuca (2005), "Zara's Secret for Fast Fashion," *Harvard Business Review* (February 21).

11. ICMR Center for Management Research (2007), "Ritz-Carlton's Human Resource Management Practices and Work Culture: The Foundation of an Exceptional Service Organization."

12. Ritz-Carlton's Service Value 3 is "I am empowered to create unique, memorable and personal experiences for our guests." http://corporate.ritzcarlton.com/en/Careers/YourExperience/OurCulture.htm.

13. *Wall Street Journal* (2009). "Zappos' CEO's Letter to Staff," July 22.

CHAPTER 8

The Sandwich Strategy: Managing New Products and Services for Value Creation and Value Capture

DIPAK C. JAIN

Introduction

Customers today are more informed and demanding than ever before. Fueled by an unprecedented choice of products and services, customer expectations create serious challenges for business leaders in a marketplace rife with competition. At the same time, products and services continue to become increasingly similar—and less differentiated—making it more difficult to develop and extract real value from a brand. As a result, companies today face a formidable task. Firms must find ways to not only launch new products or services that create meaningful differentiation in the minds of their customers, but also to capture and sustain the value they have created for their different target segments.[1] Such dynamics require companies to employ new innovative models if they are to create the necessary conditions for their success. Failure to innovate invites disaster.

As never before, the contemporary market forces business leaders to adapt or fade. Recent dynamics in the industry indicate that this hypercompetitive trend will only increase over time. For astute corporate executives, however, these challenges present a chance to develop or deepen strategic insights. In a competitive marketplace, often the best way to develop market leadership is by revisiting the conventional wisdom to determine novel new product strategies for success. Nothing provides as beneficial an arena for this reassessment as a direct challenge from a competitor. How a firm handles that challenge will mean the difference between losing or gaining ground in the marketplace.

This chapter proposes an approach termed the "Sandwich Strategy," which draws on theory and practice to illustrate how firms can respond to competitive pressures by launching new products and services that create and capture value for themselves, their partners, and their customers. In so doing, the company creates a "triple win" (i.e., "win–win–win") situation.

THE SANDWICH STRATEGY: CREATING CUSTOMER VALUE

Traditionally, companies respond to competitive pressure using the different elements of the marketing mix. The Four Ps of marketing are *product, price, place, and promotion*. Price plays a unique role in managing the marketing mix in the following two ways:

1. Product, place, and promotion are ways of creating value for your customers, while *price* is the only element that allows you to capture that value.
2. Importantly, product, promotion, and place take resources *away* from the firm; *price* is the only element that *brings* resources to the firm.

Therefore, it is important for firms when launching new products and services to use price as a strategic weapon in order to capture the value it creates for its customers, while also enhancing the firm's profitability.

Consider, for example, the scenario where Company A (the incumbent firm) offers a product of quality q and price p, while Company B (a competing firm entering the market) counters with a new product of the same quality Q but decides to price it as P-Y such that P-Y is lower than P. (See Figure 8.1.) How should Company A react to this challenge?

Figure 8.1
Competitive Scenario

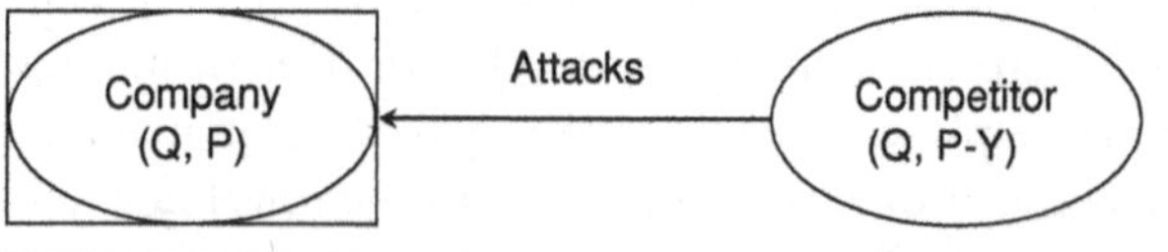

Let's first consider some possible contexts in which this dynamic might emerge, beginning with an example from consumer packaged goods. A company such as Kellogg Co. sells a breakfast cereal at $2.99 per unit. Its customer, the retailer, puts a private label brand next to the "Kellogg's" Corn Flakes on the store shelves and prices the offering at $1.99, undercutting Kellogg by a dollar. The question is, "How should Kellogg continue to capture the value for its breakfast cereal?"

Another scenario involves pharmaceutical companies. A company such as Pfizer has a well-known name-brand drug. The day the patent on this drug expires, however, generic alternatives flood the marketplace, claiming that the generic contains the same active ingredients as Pfizer's offering. A company producing a generic decides to price its product much lower than the brand name. In some cases, the price may be 50 percent to 70 percent lower than the name-brand drug. How should Pfizer respond to ensure an optimal outcome for itself and its customers?[2]

Similar situations arise throughout the telecommunications and wireless industries, where we observe new product competition. Likewise, in the computer software space we have recently seen Linux, the "open source" alternative to existing operating systems, presenting real challenges to long-standing market leaders in a way similar to the way in which a generic drug attacks the profits of the name-brand company.[3] Though all this competition may be good for the customers, firms must act and devise the best solution that is not only best for their customers but for them as well.

So how best to accomplish this goal? Make a sandwich!

New Product Innovation: Using the Sandwich Strategy to Make a Meal Out of the Competition

Under the circumstances above, the last thing Company A should do when a competitor enters the scene is overreact on the basis of price. If the incumbent simply lowers its price to compete, the signal it sends to its current customers is that the company has overcharged them for years—and essentially robbed them. This strategy does nothing to create goodwill with its current customers. The second problem with the price-centric strategy is that it legitimizes the competitor and its offerings. By lowering its price, Company A acknowledges that the competitor's quality is indeed equal—a claim that should be left to the competitor's marketing department to prove.

When the competition grows fierce, smart firms don't get embroiled in a "race to the bottom" rooted in price wars. Instead, to achieve market leadership, companies should try to make a meal of their peers. The "Sandwich

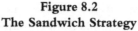

Figure 8.2
The Sandwich Strategy

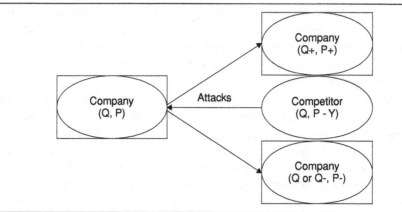

Strategy" represents one new approach: companies faced with severe price competition "sandwich" their competition by innovating new products to sandwich the product positions of their competitors from the top and the bottom. When companies innovate their product lines by using the sandwich strategy to focus on strategic segmentation and positioning, they create expanded market opportunities around their existing offerings, thus creating more value for companies and consumers (see Figure 8.2).

As shown in Figure 8.2, the Sandwich Strategy says that when faced with price competition (represented as Q, P-Y), Company A should create at least two new product offerings. One of these offerings should demonstrate slightly superior quality than the firm's previous offering. As a result, the company should increase the price for this new, improved offering (Q^+, P^+). In addition, the company should create a second product of the same or slightly lower quality than what it offered previously. The price for this product should be reduced or, in some instances, kept at existing rates $(Q$ or $Q^-, P^-)$. Employing the Sandwich Strategy in this way results in the competitor's product becoming sandwiched between the incumbent's two offerings, attracting a different market segment.

One very important point companies must remember is that P- may not have to be lower than P-Y. Instead, P- can actually be greater than or equal to P-Y because the incumbent enjoys a leadership advantage due to its brand reputation, so it can extract price-based value because of that brand. Furthermore, keeping P- ≥ P-Y, will not trigger a price war.

In this instance, the company may not have to go below the price of a competitor but rather remain in the same *general price range* so that customers see little difference between the two offerings, and therefore will likely remain loyal to the established brand.

Under these circumstances, customers might buy the brand leader's current offering at the new price or switch to the incumbent's new offering at a higher price. Either way, the incumbent firm wins.

Reaping What You Sow: The Sandwich Strategy in Action

The Sandwich Strategy in marketing represents a relatively new concept. However, a small number of companies have employed elements of this approach, though they may not have done so explicitly or always extracted maximum value.

The Sandwich Strategy Three-Step Process:

Step 1: **Redefine** the current market.
Step 2: **Resegment** the current market.
Step 3: **Adopt a Sandwich Strategy** for market resegmentation.

We see evidence of the sandwich approach at work in such markets as the one that confronted Federal Express in recent years.

Federal Express   Though most people would consider Federal Express (now referred to as FedEx) a high-quality, reliable leader in the premium overnight delivery service, this company launched overnight service to compete with the United States Postal Service (USPS).

The USPS, in particular, responded to Federal Express's market dominance by creating a product it called Express Mail. USPS priced this service at $8.95 when the average price of a Federal Express delivery was about $12. (See Figure 8.3.) Rather than reacting on price alone, however, FedEx did something more clever: it reacted by redefining its market.

Up until this time, FedEx called its product "Overnight Delivery." But "overnight" does not specify what time to expect that delivery. So Federal Express redefined the market by introducing precision not only in terms of the delivery day, but also in terms of the delivery time. Using this new definition of their business offering, they resegmented the market.

The resegmentation included two deliveries, one in the morning and one in the afternoon. In branding terms, though, rather than calling the new

Figure 8.3
FedEx's Response

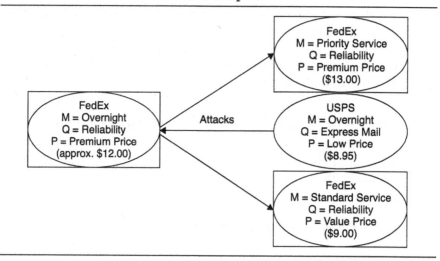

products "morning" or "afternoon" delivery, FedEx labeled the service terms "Priority" and "Standard," terms that send powerful signals to customers about how a client perceives the value of their business. FedEx customers, such as investment bankers Goldman Sachs and JP Morgan Chase, were happy to pay for this service distinction, seeing it as an additional tool to help them manage better relationships with their own clients by providing them with a more convenient and timely service.

Most importantly, FedEx increased the price of its Priority service to $13, slightly more than the amount the company had already been charging for overnight delivery. At the same time, it kept the lower-end Standard service at $9, virtually identical to the price of the USPS Express Mail product—actions perfectly in accordance with the Sandwich Strategy.[4]

This approach not only helped FedEx gain market share, but also increased its profitability. Why? Because its current clients migrated upward from the company's existing offerings to its new Priority offering, paying an additional premium. Meanwhile, FedEx also acquired an entirely new customer segment at the lower end of its enterprise—a segment that would have otherwise taken business to the USPS. What were the necessary circumstances that enabled FedEx to achieve this feat? Its technology investment. FedEx had invested in technology that featured parcel tracking, which was not at that time available to the USPS. Tracking proved to be a powerful incentive for customers.[5]

Examining this scenario from an operations or logistics perspective, it is apparent that FedEx is not going to send a truck twice to the same destination—one for morning delivery and another for afternoon delivery—because that would increase the operations cost. The customer's Standard package may reach the destination at the same time as the Priority package. Given this fact, many people ask why FedEx customers moved from paying $12 to the higher price of $13, and not from $12 to $9?

The short answer is that FedEx really understood its customers, especially clients in the professional marketplace such as Goldman Sachs and McKinsey and Co.[6] The value proposition FedEx offered these companies went beyond price. FedEx went to the customer and said, "We can help you become more client-focused because now we can guarantee delivery by 10:00 A.M. The message you can send to your clients is that you consider their time so valuable that you won't force them to wait until the afternoon to receive a delivery and act on its contents."

So, essentially, what FedEx told companies like Goldman Sachs is that their firm can help their clients manage their time better. And as we know, *time* is the most critical resource for customers today.

Indeed, some of these companies' clients have told us that, when they receive a package, the first thing they do is look to see whether the package was sent Priority or Standard. This information tells them whether the company treats them as an *important client* or an *ordinary client*. It's a signal that helped FedEx capture its value for the overnight delivery of the packages.

The essence of "value capture" through new products for the customers is as follows:

$$\text{Value Perceived} \geq \text{Price Paid}$$

It is unclear whether FedEx thought explicitly in terms of the Sandwich Strategy when considering changes in their business, but the changes are consistent with the sandwich model. In this sense, the sandwich approach became a win for FedEx, for their clients sending packages, and for their clients' clients receiving packages. It's a win–win–win situation.

The Pharmaceutical Industry   Another example of the Sandwich Strategy at work appears in the pharmaceutical industry, as illustrated by the work of Professor Morton Kamien at the Kellogg School of Management and Professor Israel Zang from Tel Aviv University.[7]

If a pharmaceutical company has a well-known drug in the market, the company knows that the day the drug loses its patent, generics will emerge to threaten profits, because these generics will be priced below the brand-name drug. How should a pharmaceutical company react under these circumstances?

Just before the patent expires, the company should launch its own generic and increase the price of its branded product. This will ensure that the brand-loyal segment will still buy the product because, for them, the brand has higher value than the actual price they have to pay for that drug. Furthermore, the price-sensitive segment (for whom the insurance company is not going to reimburse the cost of the branded drug) can buy the company's generic offering. In the end, both segments win, as does the company (win-win-win). Who is worse off? The other generic manufacturers, because they cannot enter the market before the patent expires.[8]

The original company, however, is free to create a generic at any time, because it owns the patent. Kamien and Zang, in essence, are suggesting that the Sandwich Strategy may not simply provide a *reactive* strategy; it can also serve as a *proactive* tool.

This represents a sea change in thinking, and is a much more sophisticated way of launching new products and services than has historically been observed.

NECESSARY CONDITIONS: CAN YOU CREATE A SANDWICH?

The Sandwich Strategy clearly offers companies significant opportunities to create and capture value for themselves and their customers by expanding the market. Before it can deliver the desired results, however, this approach requires several necessary conditions—including leadership in such areas as cost, innovation, execution, marketing creation, and customer relationship management. There are three conditions under which companies should elect to execute a Sandwich Strategy: *cost leadership, market expansion capabilities*, and *speed of execution*.

Cost Leadership

For a company to create a successful low-priced alternative, it is essential that the firm enjoys a position of cost leadership. This means that before the company strives for product or market leadership, as FedEx did, it must ensure that it can maintain cost efficiencies. FedEx knew it could transform its business and offer greater value to customers without the company incurring significant extra costs in providing that value.

The airline industry provides another example of why this first condition is so important. Many airlines, including Delta and US Airways, have tried to create a low-cost alternative to compete with companies such as Southwest Airlines. US Airways produced a product it called *Metro Jet*, which was to compete with Southwest and other low-priced peers. Metro Jet went broke. United Airlines tried executing a similar product extension on the West Coast with its *Shuttle by United*. United ultimately withdrew it. More recently United launched TED to compete nationally with Southwest and JetBlue. TED has also been discontinued.

Common to both of these examples is that US Airways and United had large cost structures. If a company does not enjoy a cost advantage, they cannot easily occupy the lower half of the "sandwich" in the market dynamics we have outlined, and, in fact, this position may prove dangerous and may not help them gain any competitive advantage. For companies to employ the Sandwich Strategy, it is essential they establish the proper cost structure. It is not easy for airlines to create a separate low-cost structure with a low-cost offering. Airlines would be better off resegmenting their current offerings under the existing structure by providing value-added services.

Market Expansion

To successfully employ the Sandwich Strategy, a company must have developed, and then leveraged, its market creation/expansion capabilities that enable it to create innovations in its offerings. This "innovation advantage" demands an innovative mindset throughout the organization.

For example, many consumer packaged goods companies compete with private-label brands not only on price, but also on product variety. When a company offers variety, it is offering a customized product that closely fits a consumer's needs. Most customers would not mind paying slightly more for a product that is closer to their needs than another common product that fails to meet those needs as well.

The ability to innovate helps a company achieve speed-to-market and customization. Procter & Gamble has more than a dozen different offerings just in its Head & Shoulders shampoo line. They offer shampoos and conditioners for oily hair, dry hair, normal hair, "no hair," and so forth. As a result, customers walking into a store can find a hair product that is close to their needs. Consequently, Procter & Gamble can extract value from this brand and charge a greater average price for this product than the price another company could charge for a less customized product.

It is important to remember that there is an upper limit with regard to product variety. A company cannot extend the length of its line beyond the cost-benefit tipping point, where the cost of producing more variations exceeds the benefits perceived by customers. There is always the danger of having too many product offerings, which can then lead to brand dilution, customer confusion, and product cannibalization.

However, while brand dilution and customer confusion remain important factors, product cannibalization is becoming less of a concern because, as many business leaders know, it is better to do to yourself something that your competitor is trying to do to you. Or, put another way: *"Keep the cannibal within the family."*

Speed of Execution

The company must also demonstrate superior speed-of-execution capabilities. Companies should create a portfolio of products, especially in their research and development division. But rather than launching these products simultaneously, the firm can launch a smaller number of them to gauge market reaction from competitors, then quickly react to developments by using other offerings waiting on the platform.

Although speed is indeed critical, some research shows that a company does not need to react immediately to a competitor.[9] In product categories where a new competitor attacks with a low-priced alternative, firms must ask themselves whether there currently exists a market at the lower end. Furthermore, the company must intelligently craft a strategy for *market creation* or *market expansion*, expanding the pie rather than grabbing merely a piece of the pie.

The circumstances surrounding Toyota's entry into the luxury car market with its Lexus offering proves illustrative of the dynamics at work here. When Toyota launched the Lexus model to compete with Mercedes-Benz and BMW, neither of the luxury brands immediately designed lower-end products—because it was unclear whether there existed a lower-end luxury car market. With Lexus, Toyota was conducting market research for its competition. The competition, meanwhile, elected to wait for the results of that research before entering a new market.

Today, of course, we see both Mercedes-Benz and BMW operating successfully in the lower-end luxury arena: Mercedes-Benz with its A Class offering and BMW with its Mini series. It's too early to say whether Mercedes-Benz and BMW waited too long to enter this market or whether they deliberately waited to launch their new offerings. However, the costs of entering the market later may have proven much higher for these firms than the costs of entering earlier.

If the market does not exist and if a company reacts to the challenge based on price, that company is actually helping the competitor *create* the lower-end market, which would otherwise prove difficult for the competitor to create on its own. A company never wants to end up doing its competitor's work, and may prefer to wait and have a delayed reactive strategy.

HOW TO CAPTURE VALUE: CREATING THE RIGHT SANDWICH

We have discussed the theory, practice, and necessary conditions of the Sandwich Strategy; now let us consider how to create an appropriate sandwich.

Three Types of Value

To answer this question we first must understand how customers value a product offering. Research into this area shows that customers evaluate any product or service along three primary dimensions: economic, functional, and psychological/emotional, or what we have termed the "customer value triangle." See Figure 8.4.[10]

Since the value capture model fundamentally relies on the interplay between the values of quality (Q) and price (P), it is essential for marketers to understand how customers think in terms of Q and P to properly capture the value created by the firms.

Figure 8.4
Customer Value Triangle

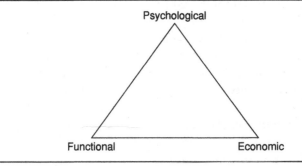

Psychological

Functional   Economic

Economic Value   Customers evaluate the product or service quality in terms of *price*:

$$V = \frac{Q}{P}$$

If a customer perceives the quality of two products to be identical, the offering with the lower price would give higher value. However, economic value does not necessarily mean that lower price always produces higher value. A company may well have a higher-value product, but before that value may be captured, the company must demonstrate the *savings* to the customer. Therefore, economic value really focuses on customer savings. Savings may be defined in terms of *dollars* (such as in the case of Southwest Airlines), or in *time* or *human resources*, especially related in terms of what we may call reducing customer "cost of thinking."

Jiffy Lube, with its 15-minute oil change promise, is among the firms that illustrate the power of reducing cost-of-thinking for its clients. Consumers may perceive a product or service as being slightly expensive, but if what the customer saves by using this product is greater than the price, then the customer will still purchase the product.

In the pharmaceutical industry, for example, there is often a more sophisticated way of looking at the cost savings dynamics by analyzing the *total cost* of completed therapy. So even though the cost of a given chemotherapeutic drug may have been higher than the cost of a competitor's offering, the pricier drug may still represent the greater value in the long run (if, for instance, the lower-priced drug produced side effects strong enough to result in longer, total patient hospitalization). Observing the total cost under these kinds of circumstances shows that frequently the lower-priced option can result in less long-term cost savings for the consumer.

Functional Value   Here, customers equate the product or service quality not just in terms of price, but also to the number and kinds of available features. Functional value emphasizes *sophistication*, not *savings*, and sophistication translates into a product with more and enhanced applications. Laptop computer models, for example, are becoming increasingly popular in proportion to their robust functionality—lighter weight, better battery life, and more modular features that enable customization by the end-user. We see a similar dynamic operating in the cellular phone industry, as well as in many industries where companies—such as Microsoft or Intel—are differentiating themselves by making Q a function of design features.

Psychological/Emotional Value   Some customers evaluate the quality of the product or service in terms of its brand image. Along this dimension, customers are most connected *emotionally* with a product and are willing to explore a brand's image in order to cultivate a relationship with it. Quality here is driven more by intangibles than by tangible features, with the end objective being to achieve "total satisfaction" or "peace of mind." Ritz-Carlton Hotels stands as a perfect example of such value.

Apple's iPod: Capturing All Dimensions of Value   Below is a more detailed example of a product—Apple's iPod—that captures all dimensions of value: economic, functional, and psychological/emotional.

Apple's strategy was to introduce a flagship product in a new market with a premium price. It differentiated through integration with content (iTunes + iPod), industrial design and simplicity, and ease of use. Apple expanded the market by introducing improvements to the product quickly (four generations of iPod in four years), allowing the company to maintain demand and margins. Also, Apple introduced lower-priced models with less capacity and/or fewer features (e.g. Nano, Mini and Shuffle) to expand the market and squeeze the competition all while maintaining the basic model with minor changes in features and price.

In response, Microsoft decided to offer the 30 GB Zune in the $230 to $250 price range. Apple reacted by offering a 30 GB iPod at $250 but also an 80 GB iPod at $350, together with a variety of iPods.[11] This looks like a clear example of the Sandwich Strategy, as the company captured all elements of value while squeezing out the competition. Apple's products are functionally superior to competitive offerings, provide value compared to competitors, and also provide an emotional appeal to its customers.

Creating the Right Sandwich

How does a firm create a sandwich? The rule is that a company should first move in the direction of its strength (i.e., its core value proposition). When pursuing the Sandwich Strategy, companies need to think about the three value dimensions above and determine which side of the value triangle represents their firm's strongest asset. Then, they must leverage that market strength as the first step.[12] If we return to the FedEx example, we can discover how that company took this initial step.

Move in the Direction of Strength   Customers perceived the quality of FedEx to reside in the firm's *reliability*. This reliability, because it translates into "peace of mind," can be mapped along the *psychological/emotional* dimension of the customer value triangle.

In addition, FedEx had developed the technological feature of tracking, which can be mapped along the *functional* dimension of the value triangle. FedEx was not, however, considered to be a cheap product, but rather premium priced. So the company's strength along the *economic* dimension of the value triangle was comparatively weaker than their dominance along the other two sides.

By understanding these facts, and by possessing an important functional tracking feature, FedEx initially reacted to the USPS competition by attempting to deliver an even higher quality product at a slightly increased price (Q^+, P^+). This was its "Priority" morning delivery service. At the same time the company provided this higher quality product, it also modified its current offering as a "Standard" service, effectively forming the bottom portion of the sandwich.

Move Existing Customers Up the Value Chain   So then what should the Postal Service do to respond to FedEx under these circumstances? The answer is that the USPS should also employ a Sandwich Strategy. However, it should move in a direction consistent with what the organization can best deliver along the customer value triangle.

What was the positioning of the USPS at the time of the competitive threat? It excelled along the *economic* dimension of the value triangle by offering customers a low-priced shipping alternative. This was its value proposition.

As a result, the USPS strategy created an even lower-priced offering and then used its current offering as the upper end of the sandwich, rather than competing with FedEx along a dimension—such as functionality—in which the USPS may not have enjoyed market superiority. The new lower-priced offering became the bottom part of their sandwich.

The USPS followed a sandwich approach by redefining their market, just as FedEx did regarding overnight delivery. The USPS redefined the market not by calling their product "overnight," but instead calling it "two-day priority delivery," supporting it with advertising calling out "two days, two pounds, $2.95." Guess what happened? USPS eventually outsourced its $8.95 Express Mail service to FedEx. USPS recognized that it did not have to compete with them. Why compete for another firm's customers when you can deepen and make more profitable your relationships with your own existing customers?

The customers who shifted to the new USPS service priced at $2.95 were the same customers who were already sending letters by lower-priced airmail and other delivery options. While mail delivered via USPS services such as

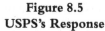

Figure 8.5
USPS's Response

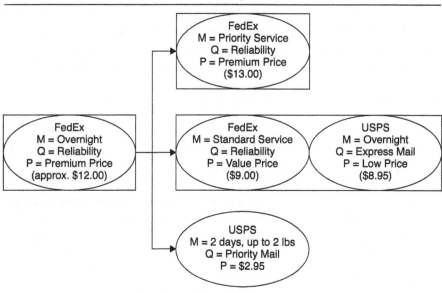

Priority Mail often arrived at their domestic destinations in about two days, the charge to the customer was only the cost of the First Class stamp—a fraction of the new $2.95 service charge that many customers now happily shifted to. Why? Because although the USPS did not absolutely guarantee delivery in two days, it promised two-day delivery, and it succeeded in the vast majority of cases. (See Figure 8.5.) As a result, customers perceived the enhanced quality at the more expensive (though still modest, compared to FedEx) pricing.

Here is the key point that the USPS learned. The game of value capture is not to acquire your competitors' customers, but *to move your current customers up the value chain*, creating better service for them while reaping the financial rewards for providing this service. The USPS did this beautifully in this case.

Compete Against Yourself Rather than be competition-focused, companies can create value by competing against themselves. The pharmaceutical industry provides a perfect avenue to do just this.

When faced with possible competition from generic drug makers, pharmaceutical companies should devise a new indication for their existing drug before they launch their generics, then price the two accordingly so that customers can see the differences between the two offerings.

For example, AstraZeneca's first-in-class $6 billion blockbuster proton pump inhibitor (PPI) drug, originally known as Prilosec (approximately $4/20 mg pill), was facing patent expiration and aggressive generic cost-based competition in 2001. The management challenge for incumbents like AstraZeneca was to figure out how to survive the loss of monopoly protection.

Several years before the patent expired, AstraZeneca formed a team to examine all tactical options to avoid losing the significant PPI revenue stream. AstraZeneca decided to phase out prescription Prilosec and introduce a PPI drug of slightly better efficacy (brand+) in early 2001. The drug was called *Nexium*, priced at $5/pill.

AstraZeneca also introduced a nonprescription, over-the-counter offering of its PPI compound, launched as Prilosec OTC and priced at approximately $0.71/20 mg pill. Prilosec OTC's active ingredient, omeprozole, substituted perfectly for the higher-priced generic prescription offerings. With proactive planning, AstraZeneca effectively sandwiched the generics on price and quality dimensions. The availability of Prilosec OTC at the very low price point (no doctor office visit or prescription required) completely undermined the value proposition of the generic, cost-based competition.

Did this strategy help AstraZeneca? Four years after patent expiration and three years after multiple cost-based competitors began offering omeprozole, AstraZeneca's sales in the PPI market reached an all-time high of $6.4 billion in 2005. Direct advertising and intellectual property management are additional factors in AstraZeneca's success, but it applied Sandwich Strategy basics.

Deciding on the Layers of the Sandwich

The next consideration when capturing value is deciding the type of "layers" of the sandwich a company needs to have. Layers are the number of differential offerings, or brand extensions. When and how should a firm differentiate a new offering from its existing line?

To find the answer we must appreciate and leverage the logic of value capture along two primary dimensions: horizontal and vertical. The horizontal dimension concerns itself with *variety* rather than *quality* differentiation. For example, Coca-Cola produces a number of products to suit customer taste—Coke Classic, Diet Coke, Caffeine-Free Coke, Diet Caffeine-Free Coke, and so on. But there is no differentiation in price along this horizontal product dimension. The company is providing customization. There are, however, important limits to how far the product line can be usefully extended. (See Draganska and Jain, 2003, which employs an econometric model derived from a game-theoretic perspective to analyze firms' uses of product-line length as a competitive tool.)[13] When the company maintains the same quality of price, it can then keep the same brand, rather than creating a differentiated product. The essence of horizontal extension is to capture a higher average price by offering customers a greater set of choices such that customers feel they have a product or service customized to their needs.

With vertical extensions, on the other hand, the goal is to target a different customer segment through the value capture strategy. Here, the quality does vary, and as a result, so does the pricing.

A great example of such an extension is Toyota's launch of Lexus to capture value from luxury car buyers. The Lexus strategy was not to target current buyers of Mercedes-Benz or BMW, but to focus on customers who are looking to enter the luxury car market but are unable to afford the price of a Mercedes-Benz or BMW.

Lexus's approach captured value in the following way. It launched its LS 300 series with an average price of $35,000. The price of a lower-end BMW or Mercedes-Benz at that time was in the low $40,000 range. The quality of Lexus was superb, and as a result it captured the economic value dimension by providing substantial savings to customers. Mercedes-Benz and BMW could have followed a Sandwich Strategy and created cars at the market's upper end and lower end to meet Lexus's sandwich. But they did not do this.

Lexus also captured the psychological value dimension by telling customers that the company was not simply selling them a car, but offering them a *total customer experience*. They did this by creating separate Lexus dealerships and focusing on customer service.

Therefore, the value capture approach allows firms to pursue strategic advantages along either dimension. With the horizontal line, the company provides more varieties to the same customers. In turn, instead of switching to the private label brand with more limited customization, the customer chooses to stay with the brand-name company because it offers more variety. With innovations along the vertical line, the company can work to capture the price-sensitive segment with one product and capture the quality-sensitive segment with another product.

Building Loyalty: Blending Customer Acquisition and Retention

An important value proposition for companies today is to reduce what we call customer "cost of thinking." Why? Because the most critical resource for customers is time. Indeed, the new marketing paradigm involves focusing not only on customer needs, but also on customer resources—such as time.

Consequently, new product offerings should help customers manage their time and resources by reducing customer cost of thinking.

But if a company reduces customer cost of thinking, it must impose a cost to the customer in exchange for this value-added service. This is called the customer "cost of switching." A firm does not want customers to learn everything from them and then actually go buy the product or service from someone else. This scenario was common among many of the dot-com firms, where customers came to a web site to educate themselves, only to then purchase from a competitor.

Customer cost of switching represents another name for the concept of capturing customer value and loyalty. The airlines are a good example of customer cost of switching. Mileage programs provide an incentive related to cost of switching. It is not the mileage program itself that serves as the incentive, but rather the program segmentation linked to the frequency of travel. Airlines offer different levels of mileage programs. The higher the frequency of travel, the more benefits that accrue to the customer. From the customer's perspective, it is more optimal to be at the top level of one airline than to be at the bottom level of five different airlines.

To leverage this cost of switching and build loyalty, the airlines have instituted a number of incentives, such as offering double miles. Further, with a good cost of switching structure, a company can, over time, *increase the price of its offerings* because the value the company provides customers through that cost of switching is greater than the additional price the customer must pay for it.

For firms to capture value through new products today, they need to think of value capture in terms of maximizing as follows:

$$\text{Customer Value} = \frac{\text{Customer Cost of Switching}}{\text{Customer Cost of Thinking}}$$

The company wants the customer's cost of thinking to go down through its new offerings, and the cost of switching to go up.

One example familiar to frequent visitors to India is the famous Bukhara restaurant at Maurya Sheraton in Delhi. If customers visit this Bukhara restaurant they find a simplified menu—only four or five items—but each item is a signature piece. So customers enjoy a low cost of thinking, realizing that whatever their choice, it will be very good. As a consequence, Bukhara has developed a great deal of brand loyalty among its clients, and so the restaurant can extract additional value from this.

SUMMARY

The concept of value creation through innovative products and services has always been intrinsic to the core of marketing. In today's hypercompetitive environment, it is no longer enough to differentiate products and services just based on their core attributes. The value capture strategy presented in this chapter, called the Sandwich Strategy, offers a powerful way to beat the competition while expanding the company's market share. But the approach demands that firms cultivate the necessary conditions for success, including deepening their understanding of customers' needs (both articulated and unarticulated) and adopting a more sophisticated perspective on market segmentation and positioning.

In June 2001, for example, FedEx introduced a higher-quality priority service for $18, promising delivery by 8:00 A.M. The key in this case was to clearly differentiate the service from existing ones. So FedEx specifically appealed to the financial services industry, enabling those customers to promise their own clients delivery before the stock market opened. Similarly, for nonfinancial industries, the FedEx value proposition was to offer customers a tool to help them manage their time more effectively.

Thus, FedEx—which began as an overnight delivery company—*redefined the market* and today can be seen as a firm in the business of *time management* for its clients. By defining the market in this way, FedEx is able to extract more value from its clients. Apple has also continued its innovative strategy begun with the iPod by launching iPhone, which created a splash in the marketplace and changed the dynamics of the cell phone category.

Innovation may seem like an age-old solution to value creation, but the goal here is to capture customer value by "sandwiching" the competition—attacking from different ends of the value chain. Rather than react brashly by cutting price (a move that can send powerful, negative signals to customers about both the quality of a company's product and how it has treated customers in the past), the underlying goal of the innovative new product value-capture approach is to create better value for customers, the company and its partners/collaborators.

Dipak C. Jain is the Sandy and Morton Goldman Professor in Entrepreneurial Studies and Professor of Marketing at the Kellogg School of Management, Northwestern University. He served as dean of the Kellogg School of Management from July 2001 through August 2009 and as the associate dean for Academic Affairs from July 1996 to June 2001. Additionally, he is a visiting professor of marketing at the Sasin Graduate Institute of Business Administration at Chulalongkorn

University, Bangkok, Thailand. He is the coauthor of Marketing Moves: A New Approach to Profit, Growth and Renewal (Harvard Business School Press) and he received his BS and MS from Guwahati University in India, and his PhD from the University of Texas at Dallas.

NOTES

1. Ritson, M. (2009), "Customers Are Suddenly Hyperconscious of Value, and New Low-Promise Competitors Are Nipping at Your Heels: Should You Launch a Fighter Brand?" *Harvard Business Review*, (October), 87–94.
2. The names of these firms are used for illustrative purposes only.
3. Kerstetter, J., Hamm, S., and S. E. Ante (2003), "The Linux Uprising," *Business-Week*, 3 (March), 78–86.
4. The pricing numbers are used for illustrative purposes only.
5. I recall first appreciating the advantages of tracking and reliability when shipping a parcel. Several years ago, when the USPS first offered its Express Mail service, I went to the Evanston, Illinois, post office to send a package to Vancouver. And I can tell you that package is still circling the globe. Consequently, like many customers, I soon realized why more and more people were attracted to FedEx: better reliability delivered at a price only marginally higher than that of the USPS.
6. The names of these firms are used for illustrative purposes only.
7. Kamien, M. I., and I. Zang (1999), "Virtual Patent Extension by Cannibalization," *Southern Economic Journal,* 66(1), 117–131.
8. Koretz, G. (1999), "When Patents Expire: Makers Find Ways to Keep Profiting," *BusinessWeek*, (3656), 18.
9. Kalra, A., S. Rajiv, and K. Srinivasan (1998), "Response to Competitive Entry: A Rationale for Delayed Defensive Reaction," *Marketing Science,* 17(4), 380–405.
10. Anderson, J. C., D. C. Jain, and P. K. Chintagunta (1993), "Customer Value Assessment in Business Markets: a State-of-Practice Study," *Journal of Business-to-Business Marketing,* 1(1), 3–29.
11. The iPod Mini was introduced in January of 2004. The initial line was formed by a 4 GB unit costing $249.99 ($50 below the lowest capacity iPod 15 GB). Two generations of the product have been launched with the following improvements: Generation one had a new touch sensitive click wheel with multiple colors and was significantly smaller than the iPod. Generation two had two capacity models which were the original 4 GB priced at $199.99 and a new 6 GB priced at $249.99. The iPod Nano was introduced in September 2005 substituting for the Mini. It was 62 percent smaller in volume than the Mini. It had two models of 2 GB for $199 and a 4 GB model for $249. Color LCD can display pictures, and there were two colors—black and white. The iPod Shuffle was introduced in January 2005. The iPod Shuffle had an extremely simple design and no screen, hence, limited options for navigating between music tracks.

12. The common practice we observe today is that companies move more toward where they are weaker than their competitors rather than stronger. This approach, known as being competition-centric, leads to becoming more like competitors and hence lack of product differentiation.

13. Jain, D., and M. Draganska (2005), "Product-Line Length as a Competitive Tool," *Journal of Economics and Management Strategy*, 14 (1).

CHAPTER 9

PRICING FOR PROFIT

LAKSHMAN KRISHNAMURTHI

INTRODUCTION

Pricing as a management function has taken on an increasingly important role in many companies. Once largely determined by the finance and accounting departments, marketers have started to influence the prices set on products. The reason for the shift is clear: Costs play a big role in the eyes of the finance and accounting specialists, whereas customer value plays a big role with marketers.

For any company, pricing decisions are complex because they require consideration of both macro and micro factors. First and foremost, a marketer must understand the firm's strategic objective (a macro factor). Pricing depends on whether the strategic objective is profitability or market share. Once the overriding goal is established, it is important to consider five more specific (micro) factors: *costs; competition; customer value and price sensitivity; distribution channel;* and *regulation*. Optimal pricing requires balancing all of these factors; it is a blend of art and science.

SHARE OR PROFIT: UNDERSTANDING THE FIRM'S STRATEGIC OBJECTIVE

A company's strategic objective is often described in terms of market share and profitability. However, strategies that grow market share can and sometimes do hurt profits. For example, when consumers are price sensitive, a price cut may increase market share, but profits may decline. Similarly, investing in a large-scale advertising campaign may build brand awareness and attract new customers, but the expense also may erode short-term profits. Consider U.S. airline companies, which have engaged in fierce price competition over the

182

last few years in an effort to increase their market share, only to see profits sink. And, significant fuel price increases have further compromised profits. Many of these airlines are now engaged in creative pricing in the form of charging for baggage, food service, and preferred seating, as well as for calling the reservation line to purchase a ticket in an effort to refocus on profits rather than market share. Meanwhile, airlines that have not instituted such fees may gain share from consumers who balk at these additional charges.

The tension between market share and profitability is also illustrated by the dilemma of consumer packaged goods companies during tough economic times. Procter & Gamble's (P&G) brands have always enjoyed dominant market share with premium-priced products such as Pampers diapers, Tide detergent, Gillette blades, and Duracell batteries. The prices are justified on the basis of superior functionality. However, P&G is also one of the largest advertisers in the world, adding significantly to the cost of its products. Concern about maintaining market share during the 2008-09 recession led the company to reduce prices on some of its flagship brands and introduce lower-priced versions of these brands (Tide Basic). P&G was forced to forego some profit in order to preserve its market share.

By contrast, some luxury product companies, such as Bose and Coach, responded to the recession by holding firm on their prices while their competitors discounted heavily. These brands made the choice to risk market share losses rather than erode profitability.

In summary, typically companies have both share and profit objectives. However, often it is not feasible to maximize both profits and market share in highly competitive markets. Thus, the primary objective—share or profits—will have the dominant role in setting price. If profitability is more important than market share, then a company will price less aggressively and seek those market segments that are willing to pay premium prices rather than cut prices to appeal to a larger segment. Conversely, if for strategic reasons it is more important to increase market share than grow profits (at least in the short term), a more aggressive pricing and spending strategy may be adopted to attract a larger number of customers. Once the key strategic objective has been identified, the company considers how to set price based on an understanding of the factors discussed next.

THE FIVE KEY DETERMINANTS OF PRICE

There are five key determinants of the pricing decision: *costs; customer value; competition and price sensitivity; distribution channel;* and *regulation.* Let's take a closer look at each.

The Role of Costs in Setting Prices

A product's *variable cost* is the pricing floor (the lowest possible price at which a product can be offered). Variable costs are those that rise or fall with the volume produced and are constant on a per-unit basis. Typical variable costs are raw materials and production costs (costs of goods sold), as well as inventory carrying costs, shipping, sales commissions, and so on.

The difference between the price and the variable cost of a product is the *contribution margin*. The contribution margin is the proportion of the price that remains after the variable costs are covered. For example, if variable costs account for 60 percent of the price, then the contribution margin is 40 percent. Alternatively, the contribution may be expressed on a unit basis. If variable costs are $0.60 and the selling price is $1, then the unit contribution is $0.40.

Thus, if a product is priced lower than the variable cost, the contribution margin would be a negative number; obviously it is not advisable for a firm to price below its variable cost. A notable exception to this rule might be loss-leader products, where the company hopes to gain later sales by "giving away" something up front.

However, a firm should not set its prices such that it merely covers variable costs. It must also cover *fixed costs,* which are costs that are constant over levels of output and periods of time. Examples of fixed costs include plant overhead, rent, advertising, and so on. The contribution margin contributes to covering fixed costs. Thus, dividing the fixed costs by the contribution margin yields the breakeven volume that a firm must achieve to cover both fixed and variable costs. Any sales above this breakeven level contribute to profit.

The relationship between these factors is captured in the following equation:

$$\text{Profit} = (p - c)^*Q - TFC$$

Here, p = unit price, c = unit cost, Q = quantity or volume in units, and TFC = Total Fixed Costs. The term $(p-c)$ is the unit contribution and $(p-c)^*Q$ is the total contribution. A company is profitable if the total contribution exceeds total fixed costs, and unprofitable otherwise. The breakeven volume is then the volume at which the total contribution equals fixed cost; that is, when the profit equals zero. So, setting profit $= (p-c)^*Q - TFC = 0$ and rearranging the terms we see that $Q = TFC/(p-c)$.

Price and cost information can also be used to think about "breaking even" in a slightly different way. Specifically, it is often useful to consider the increase or decrease in sales needed to offset a decrease or increase in price. Consider the following example, where the price, variable cost (c), and contribution margin (CM) are all represented on a unit basis.

Current	20% Price Decrease	20% Price Increase
Price = $1.0P	Price = $0.8P	Price = $1.2P
c = $0.6P	c = $0.6P	c = $0.6P
CM = $0.4P	CM = $0.2P	CM = $0.6P

It is assumed that the variable costs stay the same as a proportion of the *current price*, regardless of the price increase or decrease. This is a reasonable assumption as long as no changes are made to the product (the same materials are used, the same amount of labor is required to make the product). How much must sales increase in percentage terms to make the same *dollar* contribution as before if price is reduced 20 percent? The formula is:

$$\frac{\text{Old \$CM} - \text{New \$CM)}}{\text{New \$CM}} \times 100$$

Therefore, sales must go up $[(0.4P - 0.2P)/0.2P]*100 = 100\%$. How much of a sales loss can be tolerated when price is increased 20 percent before the new contribution becomes less than the old contribution? The answer is $[(0.4P - 0.6P)/0.6P]*100 = -33.3$. The corresponding sales change for a 10 percent price decrease is 33.3 percent, and for a 10 percent price increase is −20 percent.

Table 9.1 depicts the required sales changes for price increases and decreases for different levels of variable costs. So which is better—a price increase or a decrease? A price increase may be more profitable than a price decrease because the percent sales increase required to achieve the same level of contribution following a 20 percent price cut is greater than the percent sales decline that sustains the same level of contribution following a 20 percent price increase. Casual empiricism, however, indicates that this is not how the market behaves.

Table 9.1
Required Volume Changes to Price Changes for Different Variable Costs

VC as % of Price	20% Price Cut	10% Price Cut	20% Price Increase	1% Price Increase
60%	100%	33.3%	−33.3%	−20%
30%	40%	16.7%	−22.2%	−12.5%
10%	28.6%	12.5%	−18.2%	−10%
5%	26.7%	11.8%	−17.4%	−9.5%

To be read as follows: when VC is 30% of the price, a 20% price cut requires a 40% increase in volume to make the same cash as before; a 20% price increase allows a decrease of 22.2% of volume to maintain the same cash as before, and so on.

Promotion sales are frequent among retailers, and in most cases, these actions are barely profitable. But everybody does it; there is a herd mentality in operation.

Indeed, the 2008-09 recession turned some of the price-value expectations on their head. Many luxury goods companies had to resort to significant price reductions to sell their products; not surprisingly, they posted significant losses.

However, Abercrombie & Fitch, which sells upscale casual clothing to teens, decided not to resort to large sales discounts during the 2008 holiday season. Unfortunately, this company also suffered heavy losses. The interesting question is: Would Abercrombie have lost less money if it had pursued more aggressive discounting? Abercrombie's cost of goods was approximately 33 percent of sales. Therefore, a 20 percent price decrease (which was at the low end of discounting during the holiday season of 2008) would require a 42.6 percent increase in sales to make the same contribution. It is hard to imagine such a large increase during a period when consumers were simply staying away from stores altogether. In this case, lowering prices might not have produced significantly better bottom-line results for Abercrombie.

For many service businesses such as the airlines, variable costs as a percent of the selling price are low. In such cases, price cuts may seem attractive. However, if everyone comes to this conclusion and cuts price, the volume gain of any individual player may not be enough for the price cut to be profitable. Not surprisingly, U.S. airlines have collectively lost billions of dollars over the past few years.

Pricing models serve as a validity check. A manager can plug potential prices into the breakeven formula and calculate the sales required to break even at a particular price. This is a straightforward exercise. However, the critical question becomes one of market analysis: Can the volume of product required to break even be sold at the price proposed? Many factors influence this probability, including the size of the market, product awareness, competition and customer price sensitivity, and customers' perceptions of the value of the product.

Consider the following example. A company manufactures cotton pants, which they sell for $10 per pair. Suppose that the variable costs associated with producing the pants are $5 per pair and that there are additional fixed manufacturing costs of $100,000 and selling costs of $50,000.

From a sale of 50,000 pairs of pants, the manufacturer would realize a total contribution of $250,000 ($10 selling price less $5 variable costs multiplied by 50,000 units sold = $250,000), which would be greater than the fixed costs of $150,000. The company would exceed its break even with this level of sales.

However, let's assume that the manufacturer has total production capacity of 80,000 pairs of pants, which could be produced without incurring any additional fixed costs. Therefore, the company has excess production capacity of 30,000 pairs of pants.

If the company were presented with an offer to produce an additional 20,000 pairs at a selling price of $6.50 per pair, should the company accept this order? They have the capacity, but would the lower price justify taking the sale? From the standpoint of total contribution, the answer is "yes." An additional contribution of $30,000 will result from accepting the order ($6.50 selling price minus $5 fixed cost multiplied by 20,000 units = $30,000), increasing profits in this scenario.

But what are the practical and marketing-related consequences of accepting this special order? What if the first buyer, who paid $10 a pair, finds out that someone else paid only $6.50 a pair? The clothing manufacturer must make sure that there is no spillover from the secondary market into the primary market. Selling to an overseas buyer is one way to do this. Making sure that the special order is sold under a different brand name is another way. Making small modifications to the pants for the special order is a third way.

The issue of whether a firm should accept orders that fill capacity but cannot be sold at the regular price goes beyond this hypothetical example. Major companies like Kraft, Kimberly Clark, and others face this problem every day. From a financial point of view, it makes sense to fill capacity as long as the order covers variable cost. But this is a short-term view.

Suppose a company markets a well-known branded product through the retail channel. This company accepts a special order from a large retailer for a store-brand version, for which the retailer will pay a lower price than the manufacturer-branded product. In turn, the store brand will be sold at a lower retail price than the manufacturer brand. What happens if the store brand version starts to sell well at the expense of the manufacturer brand? In response, the retailer will order less of the manufacturer brand and more of the store brand. Faced with smaller demand for the flagship brand and the possibility of even larger unused capacity, the manufacturer accepts the larger order of the store brand. It is easy to anticipate the ending of this scenario. The manufacturer will destroy long-term profits by chasing short-term volume goals.

Ultimately, all costs must be covered or the firm will become insolvent. Clearly, understanding costs is important because firms cannot compute profitability without knowing costs. But costs should only be a starting point for setting price. Fixed costs, in particular, are not relevant in setting prices. Marketers must keep in mind that the formulas do not take *competitive actions* or *consumer behavior* into account; they are simply formulas to compute the sales increase needed when price is cut, and the sales decrease that can be tolerated when price is increased. Competitive actions and dramatic changes in consumer behavior can drastically affect the outcome of any pricing change, as was evident during the 2008-09 recession.

The Role of Customer Value and Price Sensitivity in Setting Prices

It is important to make a distinction between price and value. Customers always want the best value, but that does not necessarily mean the lowest price.

Consider this definition of value: *"Value is defined as the perceived worth in monetary units of the set of economic, functional/technical, and psychological benefits received by the customer in exchange for the price paid for a product offering, taking into consideration available competitive offerings and prices."*[1]

Thus, the *perception* of a product's value is the result not only of the product's features, but also of service levels, brand name, company reputation, competitive offerings, and other factors.

The value that is attached to a product may vary across market segments. Therefore, the analysis of value begins by identifying the key segments in the market. The personal computer market, for example, can be divided into two large segments: corporate use and home/family use. In order to position a product appropriately, we must start with the benefits desired by each segment. Understanding customer benefits in each segment should lead to appropriate product design, choice of distribution channels, communication media, and price. For example, corporate buyers may value connectivity, compatibility, reliability, security, and low total usage cost as key benefits. The family/home segment might value ease of use, fun, education, reliability, aesthetics, peace of mind, low price, and ability to play games, listen to music, chat, and use social networks. Both segments care about price, but they think about price differently. The corporate buyer is focused on total usage cost over the useful life of the computer, while the family buyer may be more concerned with initial purchase price.

In addition, corporate and family buyers are likely to value specific features of computers differently and, therefore, differ in the price they are willing to pay for them. Suppose the Social Security Administration (SSA) wants to buy 500 computers. Price is likely to be the most important factor in the purchase. A computer manufacturer might try to sell advanced graphic capabilities at a small premium over the cost of the graphics card, but the SSA will most likely reject this feature because graphics are not a central component of their business. On the other hand, the same advanced graphics card might be sold at a substantial premium when it is packaged in a multimedia computer sold to the family/home segment. Both segments are price sensitive, but the family segment *perceives the value* of the graphics card to be much higher than the corporate segment does.

Similarly, the corporate buyer and family buyer may differ in the value they derive from the portability of a laptop computer. Suppose you are a consultant who travels extensively. You may value the portability of a laptop quite highly and be willing to pay a hefty premium for a full-featured but ultralight machine (say, one weighing less than 4 pounds). You reap the benefit of a lighter load day in and day out as you travel from airport to airport. Someone who primarily uses a computer at home might also value lighter laptops for their sleek and upscale appearance. However, such a person probably will be unwilling to pay a significant premium for an ultralight machine because the benefits they will realize from portability are relatively small.

Companies create customer value in a variety of ways. Among airlines, Southwest provides a clear economic benefit in the form of low prices and no baggage charges, whereas United provides more functional benefits, such as class of seating. Flyers pay a premium for the perceived value of being able to choose their seats or purchase seats in first or business class. Similarly, Lexus entered the market with the LS400, which was positioned against the E-class Mercedes-Benz but initially offered at a price several thousand dollars cheaper. By offering a V-8 engine compared to the Mercedes-Benz's V-6, Lexus raised the quality perception. It then achieved product leadership by winning J.D. Power quality awards. The extraordinary reliability of their cars coupled with superior, intimate, customer service paved the way for psychological benefits of satisfaction, comfort, and peace of mind. Over time this allowed Lexus to raise prices, narrowing the price gap between its cars and those of Mercedes-Benz.

As suggested by the above examples, customer value is multidimensional. This view of value is depicted in the value triangle below (see Figure 9.1).

Figure 9.1
Three Aspects of Customer Value

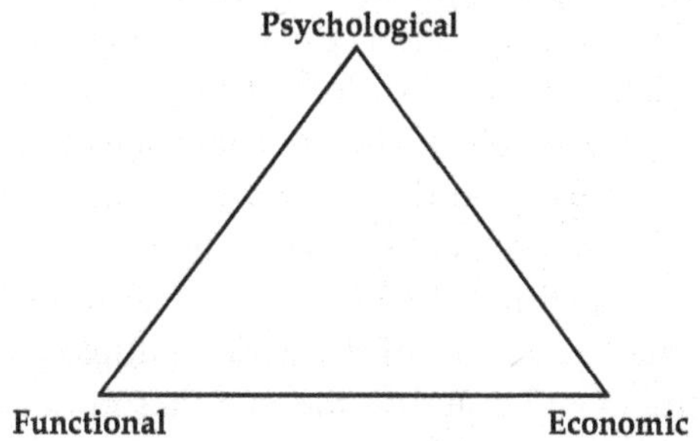

Value may stem from the economic, functional, and psychological benefits provided by the product or service, and pricing is a key factor in the delivery of value. Providing economic benefits goes hand in hand with lower prices. Concentrating on product leadership implies charging a higher price (at least initially) and targeting a segment willing to pay that price for functional or aesthetic superiority. Apple, for example, is regarded as an innovative company. With its Macs, iPods, iPhones, and the recent iPad, Apple has stayed on the forefront of design, aesthetics, and functionality. The company follows a skimming price strategy, where the initial prices are high and appeal to "early adopters"—those customers for whom the products have the highest perceived value right from the start. Prices are brought down through newer models to appeal to a wider audience. Apple also offers psychological benefits of uniqueness and customer delight through its Apple stores. All of these benefits help to keep prices relative to competition high, even though absolute prices drift down over time.

Value is idiosyncratic, making perceived customer value the "art" part of pricing. Value is always relative; there are no absolutes. One person may have high value for a product, but another may have no value for it.

Assessing Value and Price Sensitivity   In light of the importance of value in setting price and the challenge of understanding a product's perceived value in the minds of targeted customers, marketing managers may utilize one or more of the following six techniques:

1. *Managerial judgment.* The managerial judgment approach begins by assembling a team of decision makers within the company who have different perspectives on customers. This team might include product managers, salespeople, and members of the product engineering team. They are asked to estimate how much sales are likely be affected by a certain percentage price increase, beginning at 2 percent and going up to 10 percent. The same questions are then posed for price decreases. In responding to each question, each team member fills out a source of volume model. For example, for a 10 percent price cut, the respondent estimates how much of the sales increase is going to come from current customers, competitive customers, and new customers. For a price increase, the respondent estimates the percentage of sales that will be lost to the competition. In addition, the team members are asked to briefly justify their responses. If there are multiple products in the company, it is instructive to compare the price response (elasticity) estimates across products. Marketers should be able to relate characteristics of the different products to the varying price elasticity estimates. For example,

price elasticity should be greater in more competitive markets, when many substitutes are available, when relative marketing spending is low, and when the expenditure outlay by the customer is large.

2. *Analogous products and benchmarking.* To understand the value of a new generation of an established product, previous generations may be examined. The price of the previous generation serves as the benchmark for estimating the value of the new generation. An analysis of price response of competitive products can also provide an understanding of how the firm's product may be valued. These approaches work best for incremental innovations and when the competitive set does not change.

3. *Focus groups and surveys.* Properly conducted, focus groups can be used to obtain price ranges for products and services. These price ranges will be affected by how the products and services are described, and by what these items are compared to. Therefore, a richer understanding of price response can be obtained by changing the descriptions and the reference products across focus groups.

   Purchase intention surveys can be used to obtain likelihood of purchase at specific prices. Marketers can create a demand curve by using different prices with different random samples. Rather than asking the respondent to react to multiple price points and creating an artificial demand effect, it is better to describe the product and ask willingness to pay a single price and rotate the prices across the random samples. However, the downside of this strategy is that larger sample sizes are required.

4. *Data and experimentation.* With good-quality competitive sales and price data, marketers can estimate a demand curve. If price changes contemplated are in the range of prices in the data, the estimated price elasticity is likely to be a good benchmark. In addition, controlled field experiments are an excellent way to assess price response. Unlike the previous methods, however, experiments are costly, time consuming, open to competitive mischief, and difficult to implement. But when conducted properly, management gets a more reliable measure of price sensitivity. Research conducted by Eric Anderson and his colleagues in the context of catalog retailing provides a good example of the use of field experiments to assess price response.[2]

5. *Value-in-use analysis.* If a new product will replace a product that the customer currently uses, a value-in-use analysis can demonstrate the additional benefits a customer might receive. These additional benefits can then be translated into monetary terms. The price of the product currently used serves as the reference price. The net benefits, which is the difference between the benefits and the additional costs incurred by using the product (training costs, for example), added to the reference price

is the value of your product. The astute marketer returns some of the surplus benefit to the customer and charges a price lower than the value. Combining beta testing and value-in-use analysis is one way of assessing customer value and the price to charge. For example, Xerox used about 20 beta sites in launching their successful Docutech Production feeder product. Value-in-use analysis is more practical for business products than consumer products.

6. *Conjoint analysis.* Conjoint analysis can be used to calibrate trade-offs customers make in terms of price. When price is one of the attributes in the conjoint design, the attribute utilities can be rescaled to reflect how much the customer is willing to pay for specified changes in the attribute levels. Consider the following example. To understand trade-offs among laptop features, a conjoint design was constructed using five features.

1. Size of the hard disk:	60 GIG or 80 GIG or 100 GIG
2. Manufacturer:	Lenovo or HP or Dell
3. Price:	Varies from $1,250 to $2,450
4. Weight:	4 lbs. or 5.5 lbs.
5. Processor Speed:	Intel Centrino running at 1.4Ghz or 1.8Ghz

The respondents were told to assume that they were paying for the laptop out of their pocket, to focus only on the five features, and not to assume that a computer at a lower price is inferior on some other features not mentioned. For example, it was mentioned that the lower price could be because the computer is on sale. By the same token they were told not to assume that a high price signals superior quality on a feature that is not listed. They were also informed that all laptops come preloaded with Windows Vista Premium and are essentially identical on all features other than the five mentioned above. Each respondent was given a set of 18 laptop profiles to rank from most likely to purchase to least likely to purchase. A regression was run to obtain the utilities.[3] Dummy variables were used for all the features except for price, which was treated as a continuous variable measured in thousands of dollars. Here is one respondent's utility function:

$$Y = \text{constant} + 4.10 \text{ (100 GIG)} + 1.47 \text{ (80 GIG)} + 2.19 \text{ (1.8Ghz)}$$
$$+ 1.2 \text{ (4lbs.)} + 1.63 \text{ (Lenovo)} + 2.07 \text{ (HP)} - 9.09 \text{ (Price)}$$

Here, a $1,000 increase in price will reduce the utility by 9.09 units; or one unit of utility is scaled as $110. Thus, a 100 GIG (80 GIG) drive is worth $451 ($162) over a 60 GIG drive; a 1.8Ghz processor is worth $241 over a 1.4Ghz processor; a 4 lb. laptop is worth $132 over a 5.5 lb. laptop;

and a Lenovo (HP) branded laptop is worth $179 ($228) over a Dell laptop. This is a simple problem. There are more sophisticated conjoint methods available, such as Adaptive Conjoint Analysis and Choice-Based Conjoint, which can handle more complex decisions and estimate the price trade-offs.

Using Marketing to Reduce Customers' Price Sensitivities   Customers' price sensitivity is not fixed; it can be influenced by marketing actions. Nonprice advertising, which builds brand image, can reduce price sensitivity.[4] P&G is one of the world's largest advertisers, and their brands are usually priced at a premium in the product categories where they compete. Car manufacturers such as Mercedes-Benz, BMW, and Porsche also use advertising, mostly print, to build a unique brand image. Building image is not just for consumer goods. Investment banks and consulting companies publish white papers and articles to position themselves as thought leaders and subject matter experts. The consulting company McKinsey used this strategy to build a reputation for excellence. Several other consulting companies subsequently followed suit. Companies such as Cisco and IBM use their sales forces to build knowledge differentiation.

In most cases, price sensitivity increases as the dollar volume of the purchase increases, so companies often employ volume discounts. A popular sales promotion is "the more you spend, the more you save." In services, price sensitivity can be reduced by letting the customer experience the product for a limited time for free. This is popular with software but can also be done for physical goods. Creative financing and leasing are other ways of reducing the magnitude of the expenditure. Unbundling is also a way of reducing the size of the dollar outlay. Customers are often less price sensitive to later purchases in a relationship, so unbundled components sometimes can be sold later at prices higher than what may have been initially possible.

Price sensitivity is also affected by the larger purchase context. Customers are less sensitive to price when purchasing items that account for only a small percentage of the overall cost of the product. In the analog device market, many of the components sold are at low unit prices but have healthy margins. These devices are used in products such as oscilloscopes, which cost tens of thousands of dollars. By contrast, price sensitivity is likely to be high when customers are faced with product obsolescence. Buy-back upgrades or leasing program can help address this concern.

When it is difficult to make direct comparisons between products, price is likely to play a smaller role in choice. Accordingly, in the HDTV category, companies like Sony, Samsung, and LG use different terminology to describe their products, making an apples-to-apples comparison difficult. More generally, customers tend to be less price-sensitive when a product is compared to others that are more expensive, and more price sensitive when a product is compared to others that are less expensive.

Finally, in categories where quality is difficult to judge, such as perfumes, vodka, consulting companies, and lawyers, price may be interpreted as an indicator of quality. In such situations, companies may command high prices and margins, while still be perceived as offering a good value.

The Role of Competition

Competition has many effects on pricing. When products are first introduced and during the early growth stages of the product lifecycle generally the size of the market increases, which keeps price pressure relatively low. Typically, prices are high at this stage because of strong demand and fewer competitors. But as customers become more knowledgeable and new competitors enter the market, price pressure increases. Price pressures are generally more subdued when market concentration is high, but pressure increases as market growth slows down and players begin fighting over market share. As a product enters the slow growth and mature stages of the lifecycle relative pricing becomes a pressing issue: The only way to grow is by selling more to current customers, by stealing customers from competitors, or by finding new markets or uses for the product. In addition, excess capacity often contributes to heightened price competition in mature markets, as do low entry costs and high exit costs. In the end, competition forces weaker players out and forces better managed companies to improve.

No company is immune to competition, at least in the long run. The extent to which competitors' price cuts require a response often depends on how well the brand is differentiated along nonprice factors. Brands that offer significant functional and psychological benefits and have loyal customers are likely to enjoy some insulation from competitors' price cuts. A company might also be protected if market conditions make directly comparing prices difficult for the consumer.

In addition to assessing a brand's value in comparison to that of a competing brand that has dropped its price, a company should consider what prompted the competition to change pricing. Are they trying to increase market share or improve profits? Is the price change a strategic move signaling a shift in positioning, or merely a tactical move to address a short-term issue such as excess inventory? The company must also consider how the competitors' price change and any response to that change will impact the channel of distribution. For example, a price cut may both erode retailers' margins (a negative effect) and increase store traffic (a positive effect). A careful analysis of the company's brand position, the competitors' motivations, and the impact on the channel should help companies formulate a sound response, rather than relying on heuristics like simply matching competitors' every move.

The airline industry provides a good example of price competition. Prices are transparent in this industry and customers have many choices. Airlines also suffer from overcapacity. The result has been aggressive price competition. Key players in the industry are now aggressively reducing capacity in an effort to reduce price competition.

Market leaders are generally less vulnerable to competitive pricing actions. Tide detergent is less affected by Surf than vice versa. Smaller players are usually the hardest hit when the leader or one of the major players cuts prices. The "me-too" strategy of the smaller players was founded on price advantage, which is eroded when a major player announces a price cut. Although smaller players generally have lower overhead and administrative costs than larger players, they do not have economies of scale or scope and consequently operate on small margins. When smaller players are forced to cut their prices, they may not have much of a cushion. For these companies, differentiation is the key. If smaller companies cannot differentiate on the basic core product, they may be able to differentiate on benefits such as response time, reliable delivery, customized services, and support. Smaller players also may know their customers better and may be able to react more quickly to changing needs.

In the desktop laser printer market, market leader Hewlett Packard (HP) has a dominant market share, and its printer prices are slightly higher than those of competitors. By constant innovation and extension of the product line to cover a wide price range, HP has created a powerful position in the desktop laser printer market. The company also has invested heavily in its brand, making HP the technical and psychological standard when it comes to laser printers. Thus, the value that the customer derives from the psychological benefit of owning an HP printer is worth more than the additional functional benefits that competition might provide, such as a higher page-per-minute rate from Epson. Thus, product range and brand equity have insulated HP to some extent from pricing actions by competitors.

Competitive prices matter, but the smart marketer builds in brand equity and differentiation (real or perceived) to try to make comparisons across products more difficult. The smart marketer also finds the market segment that will value these differentiating features. Store brands and generics placed right next to name-brand products on U.S. supermarket shelves are quite a bit cheaper yet have not had much success in many product categories. The best examples are in the over-the-counter (OTC) pain relievers and cough and cold remedies market. Bayer routinely outsells its generic counterpart, as does Tylenol. These leading brands have been around for decades, and people have a difficult time trusting generics in medicine. Despite the lower price, the psychological costs of making a mistake is greater than the price difference, so the customer selects the trusted branded product, the one they know will cure their headache.

This principle also applies to the business-to-business market. Psychological benefits are important in business decisions involving the purchase of machinery, mainframe computers, large copiers, selection of consulting companies, and so on. A company not on the preferred vendor list is not likely to be selected. And when the dollar outlay is great, there is often a reluctance to choose the lowest priced vendor or supplier. Reliability (preferred vendor), ease of operation, and technical service may be considered more important than the purchase price.

The bottom line is that for any targeted market segment, companies must stay within a certain price range of their key competitors, and they must differentiate based on added value. It's important to note that competition only benefits the buyer, not the seller (except early in the lifecycle when competition can increase awareness in the marketplace and increase the size of the pie). For example, increasing the number of sellers from one to two reduces the monopoly power of the seller, thus benefiting the buyer. From the buyer's point of view, forcing suppliers to compete on the same terms is the best way of gaining pricing power. As a seller, differentiation relative to competition is the best way of gaining pricing power.

The Role of the Channel

The channel of distribution used to deliver a product to the customer affects costs and therefore price. There are two primary channels: *direct* (manufacturer-to-consumer) and *indirect* (manufacturer-to-retailer-to-consumer). Direct channels have become increasingly popular with the advent of e-commerce and the ability to sell directly over the Internet. Indirect channels typically include some type of bricks-and-mortar storefront (retailer), which introduces additional cost into the equation. Increasingly, companies sell using both channels, and this creates pricing challenges.

A comparison of Dell and HP illustrates how the channel affects pricing and margins. Until recently, Dell only sold its computers direct to the end customer, while HP sold through both direct and indirect channels. Selling through multiple channels is both an opportunity and constraint for HP. The opportunity is in reaching more customers than Dell can. The constraint is in pricing the same products sold both direct and indirect and in sharing margin. HP cannot, without upsetting the indirect channel, sell the same product more cheaply through its direct channel. And, when selling through the indirect channel, HP must share some of its margin with its channel partners. Assuming the same manufacturing costs and ignoring all marketing costs, by using direct channels, Dell could sell a computer to the end-user at the same price as HP but make a higher margin than HP. Dell was successful with its direct-only approach to distribution for many years. However, in order to compete effectively in the home-buyer market, Dell now also uses an indirect channel, distributing through retailers such as Walmart.

By contrast, manufacturers of ubiquitous products like soft drinks, chewing gum, grocery items, batteries, light bulbs, and simple hardware products have little choice but to rely on local retailers. The tangible, low-priced nature of these products coupled with customers' buying patterns (small, frequent purchases to fulfill immediate needs), make it impractical to adopt direct distribution as the dominant approach. As a result, manufacturers must price these products in a way that acknowledges the value (convenient, immediate availability) that retailers add to their end products.

The situation is more complex in the case of products such as books, video, software, or CDs. Direct retailers—through mail order or the Web—have thrived in these categories and have had a major impact on prices of these products. These items are nonperishable and have a relatively higher value per unit weight. They are also easily packaged and shipped. Without the high overhead costs to cover, web retailers can sell these products at a small premium over variable costs.

The lower prices charged by these online retailers impact the bricks-and-mortar retailers. In many cases, the traditional retailer carrying the identical products is forced to match the Web retailer. With higher costs to bear, traditional retailers are finding it difficult to compete. Amazon has led to the demise of many local independent booksellers. Even large national chains like Barnes & Noble and Borders are having difficulty competing with Amazon.

So how should a manufacturer assess the options of using a direct or indirect channel or both? Consider a manufacturer of high-end stereo products such as pre-amps, amps, loudspeakers, and subwoofers. For these products there is typically a manufacturer suggested retail price (MSRP) that allows a healthy margin for retailers. What if the manufacturer were to go direct and sell to end-users at a price lower than what the retailer charges? First, the manufacturer faces the possibility that trusted retailers will stop carrying the stereo equipment. Retailers have knowledgeable salespeople and acoustically designed sound rooms, which facilitate purchases. Second, the manufacturer must be able to reach the target audience without a retail presence, which could entail additional marketing costs.

Because products such as these have high mark-ups to justify the value-added service, the decision to bypass the retail channel could backfire. The manufacturer recognizes that the retailers require the margin to provide the value-added services to customers but fears loss of volume if the retail prices are too high. How does the manufacturer motivate the retailer to lower retail prices? Dual distribution through both direct and indirect channels is one way of rationalizing prices but is not feasible in many cases. Alternatively, the manufacturer can help the retailer by providing customers with certain services where it has a cost advantage relative to the retailer. By sharing in the cost of the services, the manufacturer could influence the retailer to lower prices. For example, the manufacturer might have a web site that provides extensive product information, including comparisons with competitive products, as well as direct links to authorized resellers in the customer's area. The manufacturer could also post new, lower MSRPs, which makes it difficult for retailers to charge higher prices. Of course, the manufacturer could also charge retailers a lower price with the expectation that the retailers would pass the savings to customers.

The manufacturer can also affect retail pricing through advertising. Heavy manufacturer advertising pulls consumers to the stores. This in turn forces more stores to carry the product. This increases retail competition and brings down retail prices, lowering unit margins to the retailer. But total margins can increase because the retailer is now selling more of the product. This outcome is much more likely with the leading brands in the category because they have the greatest pull on consumers. Of course, the cost of the advertising must be compared to the increased revenue that can arise from the higher price to evaluate profitability. Research has shown that although customers select the brand they are loyal to even if the price goes up, they compensate by decreasing the quantity that they purchase. Thus, loyal customers are not price sensitive in the choice decision but are price sensitive in the quantity decision.[5]

In the end, when choosing the appropriate channels of distribution to maximize price, companies may choose to employ both direct and indirect channels. But they must address pricing *across* all channels and strive to maintain some consistency in pricing to consumers.

The Role of Regulation in Setting Prices

The involvement of government in business decision-making affects pricing directly and indirectly.[6] In certain cases, such as the historic treatment of electric and other utilities, government determines the price that will be charged to the end-user, typically in exchange for granting the seller a monopoly or quasi-monopoly. In other situations, government's effect is indirect but often significant. Taxation and tariff policies influence pricing, as do the payment of subsidies and the provision of patents and other forms of intellectual property protection. Government can also affect pricing by deciding how much will be produced (frequently used for agricultural commodities), banning direct sales by producers (common with respect to alcoholic beverages), and regulating the cost of inputs (by setting minimum wages), as well as the creation and disposition of outputs (through environmental laws).

In addition, government can set pricing parameters. United States law in this regard is particularly well developed and has served as a model (both positively and negatively) for other parts of the world, including the European Union and Japan. Indeed, federal antitrust law in the United States has evolved substantially over its 120-year history to account for marketplace changes. At the same time, particular laws still on the books, like the ban on certain types of economic discrimination in the Robinson-Patman Act, are now viewed by many as archaic, a position echoed in the 2007 report of the Antitrust Modernization Commission (chartered by Congress), which recommended its repeal.

Price Fixing   Setting prices to reduce or avoid market risks is instinctively rational behavior that generally has been discouraged by the law, although there has been a substantial softening of public policy in this regard.

There are two types of price fixing—horizontal and vertical. In horizontal price fixing, competitors agree on the prices they will charge or key terms affecting price. In vertical price fixing, suppliers and resellers agree on the prices the resellers will charge, but this only applies where ownership to the products *changes hands*. In other words, vertical price fixing does not cover consignment sales and those through agents or independent sales representatives.

The primary law in this area is Section 1 of the Sherman Act, an 1890 statute that prohibits "[e]very contract, combination ... or conspiracy in restraint of trade." The contract, combination or conspiracy requirement necessarily means that there must be an agreement between or among two or more individuals or entities. As a result, the law does not cover unilateral behavior. Moreover, the Sherman Act does not ban imitating a competitor's pricing behavior (something called "conscious parallelism"), unless there is evidence of communication, such as an invitation to act in concert.

Case law has further refined Section 1 to incorporate two kinds of analysis depending on the activities involved. Some offenses are considered to be illegal on their face, or "per se" illegal, while others are analyzed under the "rule of reason." In general, it is easier to prove a violation under the per se test and more difficult to do so under the rule of reason, because the latter requires detailed economic analysis and a balancing of pro-competitive and anti-competitive effects.

In the horizontal arena, both direct price fixing (competitors meeting in the proverbial smoke-filled room) and indirect price fixing (ambiguous arrangements where a detailed factual review or market analysis is necessary to figure out that price fixing has occurred) remain per se illegal. However, the more lenient rule of reason has been applied in cases when a restriction on price is the incidental effect of a desirable activity ("incidental price fixing").

Vertical price fixing done by agreement was treated as per se illegal in the United States until two Supreme Court cases a decade apart created the modern rule that maximum, minimum, or exact resale prices established by contract are subjected to the rule of reason. However, setting minimum or exact prices by agreement has been controversial since the law changed in 2007, prompting efforts in Congress and at the state level to turn back the clock and once again apply the per se rule to such contracts.

At the same time, whatever happens legislatively, none of the current initiatives changes a 1919 Supreme Court decision that setting maximum, minimum, or exact resale prices without an agreement (i.e., unilaterally) is simply outside the Sherman Act and cannot be challenged as vertical price fixing. As a result, a supplier may announce a price at which its product must be resold (ceiling, floor, or exact price) and refuse to sell to any customer who does not comply. Moreover, even when resellers follow the supplier's resale price policy, there is no agreement. Because of this latitude, many manufacturers of desirable branded products have successfully discouraged the discounting of their products in such diverse industries as agricultural supplies, consumer electronics, appliances, sporting goods, apparel, and automotive replacement parts.

Predatory Pricing   Long-term aggressive pricing that is below marginal cost (or its measurable surrogate, average variable cost) and is aimed at driving rivals out of business can be attacked as "predatory pricing" under Section 2 of the Sherman Act and other antitrust statutes. However, in 1993 the Supreme Court made it clear that a violation also requires that the structure of the market be such to permit the supplier to recoup its losses, an element which severely limits the applicability of the law. In 2007, the Supreme Court established a similarly high standard for "predatory buying," in other words, the process of overpaying for inputs to force competitors out.

Price and Promotional Discrimination   Although economists maintain that the ability to charge different prices to different customers promotes efficiency by clearing the market, U.S. law has focused on ensuring the viability of numerous sellers as a means to preserve competition. Consequently, although price discrimination has been unlawful since 1914, the Robinson-Patman Act amended existing legislation in 1936 so that this entire area is commonly referred to by the name of the amendment. This complex Depression-era legislation was enacted to protect small businesses by outlawing discriminatory price and promotional allowances obtained by large ones, while exempting sales to government or "charitable" organizations for their own use. At the same time, the emergence of contemporary power buyers through consolidation and otherwise, as well as heightened marketplace competition in general, has forced sellers to offer account-specific pricing and promotions by creatively finding ways through the Robinson-Patman maze.

In order to prove illegal *price discrimination*, each of five elements must be present:

1. **Discrimination**

   This standard is met simply by charging different prices to different customers. However, if the reason for the difference is due to a discount or allowance made available to all or almost all customers (like a prompt payment discount), there is no discrimination, something referred to as the "availability defense."

2. **Sales to two or more purchasers**

   The different prices must be charged on reasonably contemporaneous sales to two or more purchasers—a rule that permits price fluctuations. Note that offering different prices alone is not enough. Sales or agreements to sell at different prices must exist.

3. **Goods**

   The law applies to the sale of goods only ("commodities" in the statute), so services are not covered. When a supplier sells a bundled offering, such as computer hardware that includes maintenance services, Robinson-Patman is relevant only if the value of the goods in the bundle predominates.

4. **Like grade and quality**

   The goods involved must be physically the same or essentially the same. Brand preferences are irrelevant, but functional differences can differentiate products.

5. **Reasonable probability of competitive injury**

   The law generally focuses on injury at one of two levels. The first is called "primary line," and permits a supplier to sue a competitor for the latter's discriminatory pricing. But here the law also requires that the discriminating supplier is doing so to drive its rival out of business, and, as is the case with predatory pricing, the market structure must allow the recoupment of losses later through higher prices. Not surprisingly, there are few contemporary primary line cases due to this standard.

Far more common is "secondary line" injury, where a supplier's disfavored customer may sue the supplier. However, the law is clear that only competing customers must be treated alike. Geographic or other legitimate distinctions permit different prices.

Even if all five elements are present there are three defenses: cost justification (price disparities are allowed if due to real differences in the cost to serve), meeting competition (prices may be lowered to meet those of a competitor), and changing conditions (special prices may be provided to sell off perishable, seasonal, or obsolete merchandise).

Robinson-Patman also bans *promotional discrimination* in an effort to deny an alternative means of achieving discriminatory pricing. In general, price discrimination covers the initial sale from supplier to customer, while promotional discrimination relates to the resale of the supplier's products by the customer. This distinction is important because different legal standards apply, and there is more flexibility under promotional discrimination rules.

As is the case with price discrimination, each of three elements must be present to violate the law:

1. **The provision of allowances, services or facilities**

    Here, the supplier grants to the customer advertising or promotional allowances (like $5 off per case to advertise a product) or provides services or facilities (such as demonstrators or free display racks), usually in return for some form of promotional performance.

2. **In connection with the resale of the supplier's goods**

    Again, the law does not reach service providers.

3. **Not available to all competing customers on proportionally equal terms**

    The services or facilities offered or the performance required to earn the allowances must be usable or attainable in a practical sense by all competing customers, something that may require that alternatives be provided. In addition, proportional equality means that the same total benefits do not have to be given to all competing customers. In fact, there are three ways to proportionalize benefits: (1) on unit or dollar purchases (buy a case, get $1); (2) on the cost to the reseller of the promotional activity (a full-page ad in a big city newspaper costs more than that in a neighborhood shopper); or (3) on the value of the promotional activity to the supplier (salespeople dedicated to the supplier's brand have more value than those who are not).

Figure 9.2
Pricing Process

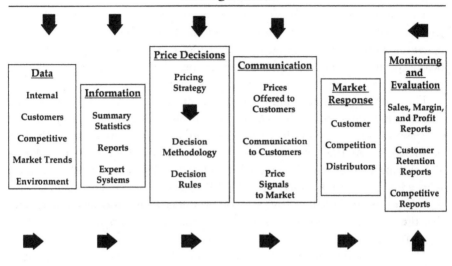

Source: Courtesy of Robert Blattberg, Kellogg School, Northwestern University

Meeting competition is the only defense to unlawful promotional discrimination. Moreover, if the supplier provides promotional allowances to the ultimate reseller, it must also provide them to competitive resellers who buy the promoted product through intermediaries.

The U.S. experience with the regulation of pricing behavior has been a long and evolving one. Although mandating ways of doing business in an effort to ensure a competitive environment, it also has left considerable flexibility to cope with a changing marketplace.[7]

SUMMARY: SETTING THE PRICE

Although picking a precise value for a product's price is ultimately a judgment call, picking a price range should be based on facts and data. Figure 9.2 outlines a process to follow to help set prices.

The first step of the pricing process is to assemble internal data on product sales, prices, costs, and margins as well as equivalent information on competitive products.

The second step is to convert these data into usable information, including the critical indicator of price sensitivity or elasticity (it is not possible to set price objectively without some measure of price response). The Appendix demonstrates how knowledge of price elasticity helps to calculate the profit-maximizing price in certain situations.

The third step is to formulate a price position or strategy based on the data and actionable information. This can take the form of decision rules such as being the premium pricer in the market, being at a certain price point above or below specific competitors with clear rules on what to do when competitive prices change, being the lowest priced player in the market, and so on.

The fourth step is to communicate the prices to end consumers, to the channel, and indirectly to the competition. Proper communication is essential to make channel partners feel included and understand why prices had to be increased. At the same time, the partners must believe that the seller is also sharing in the pain. It cannot be unilateral. Walmart and other retailers who adopt an everyday low price (EDLP) strategy are under a disadvantage when promotional retailers have sales on products. EDLP retailers usually note that their products are priced higher at competing retailers to overcome this disadvantage.

The final two steps involve the actual reaction by the market and monitoring and evaluating the response. Sometimes it takes a while for a pricing action to make its way to the customer. Also, price cuts or increases passed on by the seller to the channel may not actually find their way to the end customer. Therefore, it is important to have a good monitoring system that connects the pricing and other marketing mix changes to sales and market share. In some markets, like the grocery industry, third-party data collection agencies provide extensive data. In other markets, seller cooperation with channel members may be required to collect data.

Savvy marketers will conduct limited experimentation before finally settling on a price. Market testing is always appropriate. Theory will get you only so far in understanding the "science" part of pricing; it is learning by doing that gets at the "art" part of pricing.

APPENDIX
THE ROLE OF PROFITS TO MAXIMIZE PRICE

Mathematically, you can determine the profit-maximizing price as follows. Using the same notation as before with p for price, c for variable costs, and Q for quantity, we have revenue $R = p*Q$, total variable costs $= c*Q$, and total contribution $= (p-c)*Q$. Note this is not profit. You have to subtract fixed costs to obtain profit or operating income before taxes. In order to determine the price that maximizes contribution, it is necessary to assume a relationship between price and demand. Suppose you assume a linear demand curve of the form $Q = a - b^*p$, where a is the intercept and b is the slope. Now, total contribution can be restated as $(p-c)^*(a-b^*p)$. Taking the derivative of this value with respect to p and setting it to zero and solving for p will yield the profit-maximizing price.

$$\partial contribution/\partial price = \partial(ap - bp^2 - ac + bcp)/\partial p = a - 2bp + bc = 0$$

This yields $p^* = (a+bc)/2b$. Substituting this value of p in the contribution formula will yield the maximum contribution possible. For a linear demand curve, the profit-maximizing price is the mid-point of c and the value of p when demand is 0. It is clear that fixed costs play no role in determining the profit-maximizing price. It is a constant that does not vary with q.

Note that b is the price sensitivity coefficient and is *not* the price elasticity. Price elasticity is a dimensionless quantity and is given by $(\partial Q/Q)/(\partial p/p) = (\partial Q/\partial p)^*(p/Q)$. With a linear demand function, this equals $-b^*(p/Q)$. This value will vary along the demand curve. At lower prices and higher quantities, the elasticity will be smaller (less elastic) than at higher prices and smaller quantities (more elastic). From a practical point of view, it is best to compute the elasticity at the current price and use that number to evaluate changes in quantity to changes in price. As long as the price changes are not dramatic this would not lead to any problems.

A different demand curve is given by $Q = a^*p^{-b}$. This will yield a concave-shaped demand curve. Taking logarithms on both sides, you get $\log(Q) = \log(a) - b^*\log(p)$. This is a linear demand function in log-log space. An interesting feature of this demand curve is that the price elasticity of demand is a constant, equal to $-b$. This is most easily seen by rewriting the elasticity formula $(\partial Q/Q)/(\partial p/p)$ as $\partial \log(Q)/\partial \log(p)$, which equals $-b$ from the equation in logs. The total contribution equals $(p-c)(a^*p^{-b})$. Taking the derivative of this value with respect to p and setting it to zero and solving for p will yield the profit-maximizing price.

$$\partial contribution/\partial price = \partial(ap^*p^{-b} - ac^*p^{-b})/\partial p$$
$$= \partial(ap^{-b+1})/\partial p - \partial(acp^{-b})/\partial p$$
$$= (a)(-b+1)p^{-b} + acbp^{-b-1} = 0$$

Rewriting this you get: $(-b+1) + cb/p = 0$, which yields $p^* = cb/(b-1)$

Note that in the demand curve, b is positive, so b has to be greater than 1 to yield a profit-maximizing price. From a theoretical economics perspective, estimated elasticities less than one in magnitude from a multiplicative demand model are not meaningful. This can be confusing. What this implies is that if you estimate the price elasticity using the constant elasticity demand function and get a value less than 1, contribution will increase with increasing price. The usual recommendation is to increase the price when the price elasticity is less than one in magnitude and decrease price when the price elasticity is greater than one in magnitude. These recommendations should not be followed blindly. For example, increasing the price when the price elasticity is less than one can change the reference price of the product and change the competitive set among which the product is being compared. For example, the product whose price is increased may now be compared to other higher quality products. This can increase the price elasticity and result in a much greater loss in sales than suggested by the mathematical model. Strictly speaking, the demand curve assumes that all other things remain fixed as the price is varied. So, the demand curve itself changes in this example. By the same token, reducing the price when the price elasticity is greater than 1 should not be done automatically. It depends on the relationship between the current price and the profit-maximizing price. If the current price is less than the profit-maximizing price, the price has to be increased and vice versa. What will be true is that the optimal price is a decreasing function of the price elasticity. The bottom line is that one needs some estimate of how demand is related to price in order to get a ballpark estimate of a profitable price range.

For any arbitrary demand curve D(p), that is demand D is a function of price p, it can be shown that the profit maximizing price $p^* = [\eta/(\eta + 1)]c$ where η is the price elasticity and is negative, and c is the unit variable cost. The quantity $[\eta/(\eta + 1)]$ is called the markup, and the formula is usually referred to as the markup formula. Here, η has to be strictly greater than 1 in magnitude. For example, when η is -2, the markup is 2; when η is -3, the markup is 1.5, when $\eta = -4$, the markup is 1.33, and so on.

The markup decreases with increasing elasticity, which is reasonable. The more price sensitive the market, the lower the price that can be charged. This formula, however, cannot be used to derive the elasticity for a given price. It only holds at the profit maximizing price. This is a source of confusion and in my experience this formula is misused. For example, an elasticity is estimated from some minimal data about the product in question and the formula is used to compute the profit maximizing price. This is incorrect unless the elasticity is constant (i.e., does not vary by price as in the log-log model), or approximately constant around the profit maximizing price. But how do you know that? To make this concrete, suppose you had gathered data in a purchase intention survey, and you find that 3 percent of customers would buy the product at a price of $150, and 9 percent of customers would buy the product at a price of

$100. A simple elasticity computation is $[(3-9)/9]/[(150-100)/100] = -1.33$. Suppose the variable cost of the product is $50. Then using the formula, the profit maximizing price is $[-1.33/(-1.33 + 1)]*\$50 = \$200$ (approximately). For this to hold strictly, the elasticity at $200 should equal -1.33. It might not, and will not if the demand curve is linear. All of this is approximate, but it is not a bad place to start. Despite these limitations, it is useful because it provides an upper bound on the price. Why an upper bound? A seller in a competitive market cannot charge higher than a monopolist facing the same elasticity of demand.

How does one obtain the price elasticity? If you have sufficient pairs of quantities and prices, you can estimate a demand curve assuming some functional form, and derive the profit-maximizing price. You do not need the markup formula. The formula is most useful when only an estimate of the elasticity is available as shown in the example above, and we believe the elasticity is reasonably constant at the computed optimal price.

Lakshman Krishnamurthi is the Montgomery Ward Distinguished Professor of Marketing at the Kellogg School of Management, Northwestern University. He is the director of the Kellogg on Pricing Strategies and Tactics program at the James L. Allen Center, and served as chairperson of the Marketing Department for 11 years. He is the co-author with Professor Rakesh Vohra of a forthcoming book, Principles of Pricing: An Analytical Approach. He received his BS in engineering from IIT, Madras, his MBA from LSU, Baton Rouge, Louisiana, and an MS in Statistics as well as his PhD in Marketing from Stanford University.

NOTES

1. As defined by Anderson, James, Dipak Jain, and Pradeep Chintagunta (1993), in "Customer Value Assessment in Business Markets: A State-of- Practice Study," *Journal of Business-to-Business Marketing*, 1 (1).
2. Anderson, Eric T., and Duncan Simester (2004), "Long Run Effects of Promotion Depth on New Versus Established Customers: Three Field Studies," *Marketing Science*, 23(1), 4–20.
3. The ranks were first converted so that the most likely to purchase computer was ranked 18 instead of one. Running a regression using rank order data is inappropriate from a statistical point of view. However, in most cases, the procedure works quite well.
4. Krishnamurthi, Lakshman, and S.P. Raj (1985), "The Effect of Advertising on Consumer Price Sensitivity," *Journal of Marketing Research*, 22 (May), 119–29.
5. Krishnamurthi, Lakshman, and S.P. Raj (1991), "The Relationship Between Loyalty and Price Sensitivity," *Marketing Science*.

6. This section was written by Eugene F. Zelek Jr., senior lecturer in marketing, Kellogg School of Management, Northwestern University, and Chair, Antitrust and Trade Regulation Group at Freeborn & Peters LLP, a Chicago law firm. The copyright for this section is owned by Mr. Zelek.

7. For more detailed information on this topic, see Eugene F. Zelek Jr. (2010), *The Legal Framework for Pricing,* in Thomas T. Nagle, John E. Hogan, and Joseph Zale, *Strategy and Tactics of Pricing* (5th edition), Pearson Education Inc., Upper Saddle River: New Jersey.

CHAPTER 10

ADVERTISING STRATEGY

DERECK D. RUCKER and BRIAN STERNTHAL

INTRODUCTION

Advertising is one of a brand's most valuable tools for building equity and creating market success. When a brand is differentiated from its competitors on dimensions important to consumers, advertising provides an instrument to communicate this advantage. For example, in the early 1980s, Reebok (then a small brand by any measure) assumed a leadership position in the athletic shoe market by advertising its greater comfort for women athletes because it was constructed of soft garment leather. In the 1990s, Pantene grew from a minor brand to a leader in the shampoo and conditioner category by advertising the shiny and healthy hair that was made possible by its Pro V ingredient. And in the 2000s, within two years of launch, Dreamery Ice Cream attracted 14 percent of the super-premium ice cream market by advertising it as a brand that offered both the smooth taste that consumers associated with Häagen Dazs and the chunky ingredients offered by Ben & Jerry's.

Advertising also stimulates brand growth when there is parity among alternative brands in the category. Different brands of peanut butter, analgesics, bottled water, and cough remedies typically do not offer unique functional benefits. Yet Jif has a dominant share of the peanut butter market, and Advil is the leading brand of ibuprofen. These brands achieve dominance by using greater advertising weight than competitors to promote the benefit that stimulates category demand. Thus, Jif promotes superior taste and Advil advertises greater pain relief than other brands. However, for many consumers, any brand of peanut butter or any brand of ibuprofen offers similar performance and has similar (if not identical) ingredients.

Another benefit of advertising is that it can help sustain a brand's market position over time. Frosted Flakes has advertised its superior taste by using Tony the Tiger as its spokesperson since the 1950s. Over the same time period, Marlboro has employed images of the old West to reinforce its position of empowerment and maintain its rank as the leading brand of cigarette. And Samsonite has emerged as the number-one brand of luggage by promoting its durability. For these brands, advertising has cemented the link between brand and benefit so that it serves as a barrier to competitive entry.

What makes these advertising strategies so successful? To answer this question, we begin by identifying situations when it is appropriate to use advertising. We follow with an assessment of how consumers use advertising information to evaluate brands and make purchase decisions. On the basis of this analysis, we identify and examine factors that enhance the impact of advertising. For advertising to have an impact on consumers' responses, it typically must engage the consumer. Engagement involves ensuring that people attend to the message, allocate the cognitive resources necessary to process and to elaborate on its content, and link the brand to its benefits. We conclude with a description of strategies for measuring ad effectiveness.

WHEN IS IT APPROPRIATE TO ADVERTISE?

In the late 2000s, advertisers were spending about $270 billion in advertising in the United States and $420 billion worldwide. We have already referenced cases when advertising had a role in establishing, building, and maintaining the equity of a brand. However, there are also situations in which advertising has little influence on consumers' responses or is inefficient in communicating brand benefits or in building brand equity. So when is it appropriate to advertise?

One factor in deciding whether to advertise is the target's characteristics. When the target is substantial and specific target members are not readily identifiable, advertising is a good means of communicating brand information. This is the case when the target can only be described in general demographic terms (such as men 18 to 34), as might be the case for Burger King. In contrast, if the target is composed of a niche group of 2,000 chemical formulators for whom a contact list is available, interpersonal communications are typically preferred because they provide the opportunity for individual feedback to potential customers. Indeed, in many business-to-business contexts, blogs and social media rather than mass media advertising are the primary means of communication among members of a distribution channel.

Another factor that influences whether to advertise is the "news" value of the brand. News is generated when a brand offers some advance over its own or the competition's existing products. For example, TV advertising enhanced the rapid adoption of the iPod, which offered consumers a new way to acquire and to carry their music with them. News is also created when new benefits for existing products are advertised. UPS advertised the news that its service made supply chain management more efficient, a promise that was backed by its record of reliable and timely package delivery. Finally, brands can present news when the brand and its benefits are well established, but the target is unfamiliar with the features because they are about to purchase a product in the category for the first time. Advertising by Huggies disposable diapers and Enfamil baby formula offers news to moms when their first child is born; Visa's advertising of its credit and debit cards is newsworthy to college students who are considering cards for the first time; and Norelco electric shavers present news to teens who are deciding whether their shaving needs are best met by a blade or an electric razor.

Advertising also serves as a vehicle to limit the impact of competitors' initiatives. In some categories, such as athletic shoes or fast foods, the advertising expenditure is so substantial that new entrants may not have the resources to advertise enough to gain a substantial share of advertising voice. In this event, the new entrant's ad expenditure is likely to build the category rather than the brand. Even if new entrants have the resources necessary to compete, important category benefits might be so strongly associated with established brands that the new entrant cannot attract sufficient demand to pay out the ad expenditure.

Finally, advertising might be warranted even though it is not a highly efficient way to communicate brand information. Sometimes simply the fact that a brand is advertising communicates important information to the audience. If a firm is not widely known to consumers, a sudden and aggressive ad campaign can send the message that the company is a substantial entity. Product manufacturers can also use advertising to signal to retailers that a brand will receive significant support to stimulate sales. And advertising can cue investors to a firm's belief that its products and services are sufficiently competitive to warrant an investment in advertising.

HOW DO CONSUMERS USE ADVERTISING TO MAKE DECISIONS?

Once it has been determined that advertising is appropriate for a brand, an effective strategy must be developed. To accomplish this task, it is necessary to understand how consumers use advertising information to make decisions. In some situations, brand judgments are based on consumers' thoughts about information presented in advertising, as well as how this information relates to what the consumer already knows about the brand and its competitors. We refer to such judgments as *deliberative*. In other situations, judgments are based on a rapid assessment of cues such as a brand's color, shape, or spokesperson. These judgments are termed *thin slices*. Finally, brand judgments can be influenced by the subjective experience that occurs in response to how message information was processed. These are *metacognitive* judgments because they rely on thoughts about the message that served as the basis for judgment.

Deliberative Judgments

We depict *deliberative judgments* in response to advertising in terms of a two-store model of memory (Figure 10.1). Consumers exposed to advertising information initially actively represent it more or less faithfully in working memory, which represents what consumers are thinking about at the moment. The defining characteristic of working memory is its limited capacity; it can store only a small amount of information for a short period of time without further processing.[1]

In order for advertising information to be useful in making a judgment, it must typically be represented in a second memory store we refer to as long-term memory. This memory store is the repository of all the information that a person has ever processed but that is not currently active in working memory. An important property of long-term memory is that it stores information in an organized manner for later use in making judgments. One form of

Figure 10.1
Two–Store Memory Model

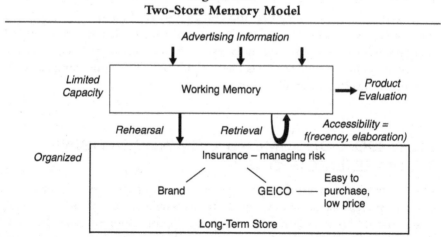

organization that is particularly important to understanding consumers' responses to advertising is hierarchical organization. In Figure 10.1, we depict a two-level hierarchy—a brand level and a category or goal level. In the illustration, GEICO is a brand that is a member of the insurance category. Both brand and category are associated with benefits; the GEICO brand is associated with the benefits of low price and easy to buy, and the category is associated with the benefit of managing risk.

Consumers' judgments of a brand in response to advertising are based on two sources of information: the contents of the advertising, and consumers' prior knowledge. When a consumer is exposed to advertising information, the information is represented in working memory. If the information is relevant, it activates the prior knowledge stored in a consumer's long-term memory. Because long-term memory is the repository of everything consumers have learned, and working memory is a limited capacity store, not all of the information that a person has in long-term memory is likely to be accessible. Rather, the most accessible information in long-term memory is retrieved and represented in working memory. Information is most accessible when it has been processed recently and when it is elaborately represented in memory. Elaboration can be thought of as a rich set of associations that consumers have to a brand. When information presented in an advertising message is rehearsed and stored in long-term memory, it can subsequently be retrieved to serve as a basis for judgment.

To illustrate the two-store model, consider this example. Tom currently owns an HP computer and is considering buying this brand again. But he is also evaluating Acer, Dell, Lenovo, and Apple. He owns an iPhone that he likes very much, and this is prompting him to lean toward purchasing an Apple computer. However, Tom is concerned that with its different platform, an Apple computer might require a substantial investment in time to have the same expertise as he has in using his HP. At the same time, he has had trouble with the Windows Vista platform and wonders whether the next generation of PC software will be more reliable. When Tom sees an ad for an Apple notebook, he learns that he can run Windows on an Apple computer. This prompts him to think that maybe it will be easier to learn the intricacies of using an Apple than he anticipated. In turn, these thoughts prompt Tom to activate (from long-term memory) the fact that his iPhone required only a little intuition to navigate, which increases his confidence that changing platforms will not be difficult. Tom then goes online to check out the different Apple notebook models.

The two-store memory model has several important implications. One is that persuasion in response to advertising is largely *self*-persuasion. Consumers associate advertising claims with their prior knowledge and use this input as a basis for judgment. In Tom's purchase, the information presented in advertising activated his prior knowledge, which influenced his decision. In addition, the model suggests that positioning involves the association of brands to a *category,* which is referred to as the frame of reference, and the association of brands to *each other,* which is termed the point of difference (see Chapter 4, "Developing a Compelling Brand Positioning"). In the context of Tom's decision, the need to buy a new computer activated thoughts about different brands, which are associated with each other by virtue of sharing the same frame of reference (they are members of the computer category). His comparison of category members' points of difference led to a preference for Apple.

Thin Slice Judgments

Not all consumer judgments are as deliberative as the ones represented in the two-stage memory model. In some cases, people make quick, *thin slice* judgments based on a few salient heuristics or perceptual cues. For example, people make attributions about the strength of coffee on the basis of the color of the tin in which it comes: a brown tin signifies that the coffee is strong, a yellow that the coffee is weak, and red that the coffee is rich. Consumers also use shape as a basis for making brand judgments. When mouthwash is packaged in a bottle that has sharp angles it is perceived as stronger than when the bottle is less angular. A round-shouldered bottle that is unique to the vodka category cues consumers to consider Absolut an upscale brand. Advertising that presents white type on a dark background is frequently used when promoting high-tech products because it enhances consumers' perception that the brand offers sophisticated technology. And the use of an attractive spokesperson might signal that the brand is desirable.[2]

The thin slice processing of heuristic or perceptual cues in advertising creates an association with a product that, depending on how favorably the cue is perceived, can enhance brand judgments. Importantly, there is often a trade-off between the influence of deliberative and thin slices processes. As consumers engage in deliberative processing, the influence of thin slices diminishes. And when consumers make decisions on the basis of thin slices, deliberative processing is often absent.

Metacognitive Judgments

Consumers' judgments are not only influenced by the content of advertising messages, but also by the subjective experience that results from how the message information is processed. This is called *metacognitive judgment.* Consider two messages: The first is a positive appeal that presents five benefits of using a brand. The second is a more balanced message that presents these same five benefits along with one negative feature, which detracts from the brand in a minor way. Which message is likely to be more persuasive? It might seem that the more positive appeal would be more persuasive because it includes only brand benefits. However, including a negative feature might make consumers feel more certain about the brand's benefits, because the presence of a negative feature suggests a more complete and balanced presentation of brand information. This feeling of certainty can result in more favorable action toward the brand (e.g., purchase) than if this feeling were absent. Of course, if the negative feature mentioned was central to brand performance, the "certainty" effect might not carry as much weight.[3]

Whether consumers rely on the message content or the subjective experience of processing it to make a judgment depends on their focus. Consider two ads for BMW. In the first, consumers are presented with one reason to purchase the car; in the second, they are presented with 10 reasons. In this case, message recipients are likely to focus on the message content as a basis for judgment. If the reasons presented are equally compelling, they are more persuaded by a message containing 10 reasons than a message specifying one reason to drive a BMW. However, suppose that the first ad asks the consumer to *think* of one reason to drive a BMW and the second ad asks them to think of 10 reasons. In this case, the focus is not on the message content, but on the ease of thinking of reasons. One reason will be easier to conjure up than 10 reasons. Thus, in situations where consumers are focused on the message content, a more favorable judgment of BMW would occur when they are presented with 10 reasons (they don't have to think of them), whereas when they are focused on the processing task their judgment is more favorable when asked to think of just one themselves.[4]

As is the case for deliberative judgments, metacognitive judgments typically require motivation and ability. Whether consumers focus primarily on their evaluation of information, subjective experiences, or both depends on factors such as where consumers' attention is focused, how much thinking is required, and even what product features are emphasized.[5]

WAYS TO INFLUENCE ADVERTISING IMPACT

Whether judgments are deliberative or metacognitive, advertising has a greater impact when it engages consumers. Engagement involves ensuring that people allocate the cognitive resources needed to pay attention to a message and elaborate on the message content. Thus, marketers use communication devices to facilitate positive thoughts related to a brand's features, and particularly to its points of difference in relation to competitive brands. Engagement also prompts a linkage of the brand to its benefits. In the absence of such linkage, consumers might learn about the features promoted in an ad, but they might misattribute the source to some other brand or simply be unable to recall the sponsor.

Creative and Media Strategies

At any moment consumers are bombarded by more information than they can process in detail. Thus, advertising impact is determined first by whether an ad draws enough attention to get noticed so that its content can be processed. Prompting a focus on relevant information through creative and media strategies are two approaches to this problem.

Creative Strategy Presenting information that is incongruous with consumers' current beliefs is one means of drawing their attention to a message. Sometimes this is achieved by presenting brand information that is not expected. For example, consider a message that advocates fewer hours of sleep than the eight that most people believe is necessary. As the discrepancy grows between the message recipients' current beliefs about sleep and the advertising's message about fewer hours needed, consumers' judgments about sleep actually change: They believe that less than eight hours is required. This is especially true if the spokesperson for the message has scientific credentials.[6]

Incongruity was an important factor in the attention-grabbing success of the famous 1984 Super Bowl spot for Apple computer. This TV ad depicted an athletic woman in red shorts and a white tank top (Apple) racing amid workers clad in blue (IBM). They are racing toward a screen on which the Orwellian figure of Big Brother is pictured announcing, "We shall prevail." The athletic woman (Apple) hurls a hammer at the screen just as this pronouncement is made, destroying the screen. This advertisement gained attention because it was unlike advertising for any other brand of desktop computer at the time, which typically described the brand's technical capabilities or illustrated the tasks that could be performed using it. The Apple commercial also drew attention because it contrasted the typical male association to technology exemplified by IBM with the female persona of Apple. Moreover, the use of an aggressive woman as part of the Apple iconography laid the foundation for both the brand's communal or user-friendly orientation and its aggressive pursuit of cutting-edge technology. Today, those brand images are still sustained by Apple's advertising.

Humor is also a frequently used creative device to enhance advertising relevance and attention. When a brand has a strong point of difference, humor can increase the impact of a message by directing attention to this benefit. For example, GEICO's claim that it is so easy to get this firm's insurance that even a caveman can do it gains attention by showing a caveman's irritation at being so marginalized.

Using humor as a device to garner attention requires caution, however. When humor successfully stimulates consumers to focus on the problem addressed by a brand or its point of difference in achieving some goal, the impact of the message can wear out quickly. This is manifested by an absolute decline in advertising impact as exposures to the message mount. One solution to wearout is to use a pool of ads in the campaign that sustain brand news.

In using humor to gain attention, the ad should not simply entertain, as noted, but also direct attention to the brand's benefit. In an ad for Ameriquest, a doctor and his assistant are in the hospital room of a patient who is asleep. As the doctor checks the patient's chart, he waves off a fly that is buzzing around his face. Seeing this, the assistant uses defibrillator paddles to kill the fly, saying, "That killed him" just as the patient's family walks into the room. They are horrified to hear this news. The point of the ad is that Ameriquest doesn't judge too quickly and neither should its clients. But the brand and its benefit are likely to be lost because the humor does not focus on a tangible brand benefit.

Finally, to be effective, humor should not make the target consumer the brunt of a joke, which is likely to result in negative reaction. Greater effectiveness is achieved by making the brand the focus of the humor. Advertising made fun of the Volkswagen Beetle's small size, but its buyers were characterized as sophisticated and economy-minded.

There is a growing trend to include violence in humorous ads in order to enhance attention. A Budweiser ad depicts a young man in a pool hall offering each of his friends a Bud Light. When they accept his offer, the young man offers to fist bump, which is ignored. Instead he receives a vigorous slap on the face. He is told that the face slap is "in" and the fist bump is "out." People in a variety of contexts are then shown face slapping each other violently. In the final scene, the young man's boss initiates a fist bump to acknowledge that his subordinate saved a business account. The young man responds with a forceful face slap that astounds his boss. This execution is highly entertaining and likely to stimulate attention; but the attention paid is not likely to be to the brand or its benefits.

In addition to its questionable relevance, violence in ads can also be problematic because of the escalation factor needed to grab even more attention

Figure 10.2
Two-System Threat Model

with every exposure. In the current climate, consumers need higher forms of stimulation to keep their attention, so the violence quotient must be ratcheted up with each new campaign. It's easy to see why this would quickly become a problem for the brand employing violence as a technique.

Appeals that evoke threats can also enhance the attention paid to advertising. From everyday experience, it might seem that threats would induce attention and motivate compliance. Admonitions given to children such as, "Don't touch the hot stove or you'll get burned" seem to be effective. However, research suggests that without careful calibration, threats might undermine persuasion rather than enhance it.

A two-system model provides a basis for anticipating when threats will be effective and when they will not. As Figure 10.2 shows, a person's danger control system processes information regarding what constitutes danger, who is in danger, and how to control danger. This information can be used to take action that is adaptive in coping with the danger, which should also be specified in the message. For example, an anti-smoking ad might inform people that if they are short of breath after walking up a flight of stairs or have a hacking cough that does not go away, they should place their cigarettes in an inconvenient location so that they will have to consider whether to light up.

The other system pertaining to threat involves fear control. This system processes information related to the dire consequences of noncompliance with a message. Fear control results in the use of a consumer's own repertoire of responses to cope with fear. This might entail drinking, sleeping, running, or engaging in some other coping mechanism. Consider an anti-smoking message that depicts smokers' blackened lungs and suggests that they should have life insurance because it will be needed to send their kids to college. This threat might prompt smokers to control their fear by not smoking. Ironically, though, one response smokers have to fear is to light up a cigarette. This scenario raises the possibility that a fear-based message might activate idiosyncratic responses that are directly opposite to the ones recommended in the message. Thus, advertising involving threats should focus on danger control by identifying what constitutes danger and who is in danger rather than by evoking the dire consequences of noncompliance.

Media Strategy: Moment and Mindset Because it has become increasingly difficult to use creative executions to attract attention, marketers have turned to various media strategies. One such strategy, called "moment," involves presenting an advertising message at a point in time when the category is relevant to target consumers. The other strategy, called "mindset," involves presenting brand information in a context that is relevant to consumers. The premise is that if advertising is presented when people are considering the category and in a context that situates the brand in their lives, they are likely to devote attention to it. For example, AXE body spray attempted to reach people at a moment when personal grooming was relevant to their 14-to-24-year-old male target audience. The company advertised in theaters prior to movies that were popular with this segment, as men are likely to be thinking of dating and about girls while at the movies (i.e., the moment). The choice of movies that are popular with the target segment also implies that there is an appreciation for their taste in movies (i.e., mindset). Relevance created in this manner is likely to enhance attention to the advertising message.

Moment and mindset strategies are often conceived by constructing logical scenarios. For example, the strategist could surmise that the target for luggage would be interested in the category when flying. Thus, advertising Samsonite luggage in airports or in airline magazines would be an appropriate moment strategy. Alternatively, moment and mindset can be empirically based by conducting ethnographies. Along these lines, the selection of media and advertising content for Samsonite might entail having researchers accompany travelers to assess the virtues and difficulties they have with their luggage and the points in time when these products are the focus of their attention.

Message Content

In some situations, the equity of the brand is strong enough that consumers only need be reminded of it without a detailed presentation of arguments via advertising. For example, Toyota has long been associated with reliable transportation. Messages for the brand that remind people of this reliability are sufficient to sustain these brand perceptions among target consumers. In other situations, consumers need detailed information to develop a favorable disposition toward the brand. A variety of content-oriented strategies have been developed to enhance the likelihood that message recipients will activate a rich set of associations to the brand, including *Hard Sell*, the *Big Idea*, *Story Grammar*, *Comparison*, *Spokespeople*, and *Message Repetition*.

Hard Sell   Hard sell was developed by the Ted Bates agency and involves developing a simple associative bond between the brand and its benefit. The hallmark of the hard sell strategy is the claim, "Buy this brand, get this benefit." Thus, the message articulates one benefit with the goal of making this association as direct, clear, and as strong as possible. For example, advertising for the antacid Rolaids claims that "Rolaids spells relief." Hard sell has the virtue of providing a strong link between the brand and the benefit. It is effective when a brand has a point of difference that is important to consumers. When a point of difference is not available, other means of stimulating elaboration are required.

The Big Idea   Developed by the Leo Burnett ad agency, the "big idea" involves identifying a benefit that is important to consumers and, over time, presenting a variety of attributes that support the benefit as a means of sustaining brand news. A good example is advertising for Coors Light beer. Successive generations of advertising promoted the brand's superior cold refreshment benefit by emphasizing the use of Colorado water, cold filtering, and cold-activated cans as reasons to believe this benefit. The big idea can also involve presenting the same benefit and reason to believe but changing the context in which the product works. Along these lines, Coors Light might promote the cold-activated can but create news by showing its use by different segments or in different consumption contexts. In developing a big idea, emphasis should be given to ensuring that there is linkage between the brand and benefit. Coors Light spots enhance brand-benefit linkage by making the cold refreshment benefit the focal point in all ads. Similarly, in Green Giant frozen vegetable advertising, the quality benefit is supported by announcing that the vegetables are fresh-frozen and vacuum packed. Brand linkage is enhanced by always using the Green Giant and the valley in which he lives as the context for presenting the brand's quality benefit.

Story Grammar   The use of story grammar to stimulate elaboration of a brand's benefits was pioneered by Doyle Dane Bernbach in the 1950s (now DDB Worldwide). It is based on the notion that people store information in the form of a goal or problem, solutions to address the problem, and outcomes. In the original DDB executions, an extreme illustration of the problem was shown being solved by the brand. The intent is to have consumers infer that if the brand is effective under dire circumstances, it will also be effective in everyday situations that consumers typically face. For example, in an ad that was created to introduce the Volkswagen in the United States, a person is shown driving a Volkswagen in the early morning after a heavy snowfall. The person's destination turns out to be a garage that houses a snowplow. As the commercial ends, we see the snowplow passing the parked Volkswagen, which we now realize belongs to the snowplow driver. The message is that the Volkswagen's ability to navigate in snow is so good that the person who drives the snowplow relies on a Volkswagen to get to the snowplow.

As the Volkswagen ad illustrates, a story grammar can be an effective means of demonstrating a brand's benefit. This approach is most effective if the benefit illustrated is a point of difference that consumers value. However, a story grammar can be employed successfully even when a brand does not have a benefit on which it dominates the competition. It involves using insight about the problem faced by consumers when using the product category as the point of difference. For example, an ad for Lee jeans showed the lengths to which women go to get into their jeans. Lee was presented as the solution to this problem by showing a woman whose Lee jeans fit perfectly. The reason for this superior fit is not described in the ad. Yet Lee advertising was successful in stimulating sales because women assumed that if Lee understood the difficulty they had in buying jeans that fit well, Lee was likely to make ones that actually did fit.

Although story grammar can provide a vivid demonstration of a brand's performance, a story grammar does not lend itself to the presentation of a substantial number of brand facts. When a list of technical brand features is recited in the context of a story grammar, message recipients often regard the ad as inauthentic. The result is that consumers are more likely to dismiss the ad as unrealistic than they are to learn the brand's benefits. In such situations, a lecture where the brand's features are enumerated and illustrated by visuals is a more effective device. A story grammar can also have limited persuasive impact when it stimulates a focus on the drama at the expense of learning the linkage to the brand. Early identification of the category and brand can be used to address this concern.

Comparison   Elaboration can also be stimulated through comparing the brand to other objects. A frequently used form of comparison involves a side-by-side presentation of a brand's features with those of a competitor. For example, when Crest Pro-Health toothpaste was launched, it enumerated seven features on which it was compared to the leading toothpaste, Colgate Total. Pro-Health had all of these features while the competitor's brand only contained four. The Pro-Health campaign featuring comparison enabled the brand to make substantial inroads on Colgate Total toothpaste.

Comparison prompts a consideration of a brand and its competitor on a feature-by-feature basis. In developing a comparison ad, it is often important to include both features on which a brand dominates the competition as well as ones on which it is at parity. The inclusion of parity features reduces the likelihood that message recipients will believe that there are unmentioned benefits on which competitors dominate the advertised brand.[7]

Some advertisers believe that comparison should be used by category followers and not leaders. For category leaders, comparative advertising is viewed as free advertising for the competitor. However, when a follower is well known, leading brands often do engage in comparison. The persuasive impact of showing brand superiority in a side-by-side demonstration outweighs the likelihood that the advertising will bring to mind an overlooked competitor's brand. When comparison makes salient a competitor's brand that would not be considered without the use of this device, leading brands can compare themselves to a gold standard in some other category. For example, the leading brand of creamers, Coffee-Mate, compares its quality to milk or cream rather than to other creamers.

Not all comparisons in advertising involve competitive brands. In some cases, analogies are used to inform consumers about a brand's features. Analogies involve the transfer of internal knowledge from a base that is known to a target that is being learned. For example, to illustrate how Audi's Quattro enables the car to grip the road, advertising for the brand shows a human hand adopting the appropriate grip for different kinds of objects including a fish, a Ping-Pong paddle, soap, a ball, an egg, and a light bulb. The intent is to illustrate how Quattro varies the tire's grip on the road to reflect driving conditions. This illustration underscores the fact that analogies are particularly useful when communicating complex and abstract information. For this reason, analogies are frequently used to advertise services and technological features of a brand to an audience that has limited expertise in the category.

Spokespeople Advertisers frequently use spokespeople to promote their brands. In some instances, spokespeople are selected simply because they are attractive to the audience. This approach is most likely to be effective when consumers engage in processing the "thin slices" described earlier. Model Paris Hilton advertised for Carl's Jr. fast foods, racecar driver Danica Patrick was a spokesperson for Go Daddy domain registrar, and actor William Shatner was a spokesperson for Priceline.com. The hope is that the positive associations to these celebrities will rub off on the brands they endorse. In addition, the use of celebrities can enhance advertising recall. This effect occurs because message recipients have many associations to these celebrities stored in memory. Frequently, however, this recall pertains to the celebrity and not to the product benefit because there is little association between the two. When this is the case, the use of a spokesperson has a minimal impact on their persuasive impact of a message.

A more insidious problem with spokespeople is that they can undermine the brand's success. This result often occurs when a spokesperson advertises for too many sponsors and thus dilutes the association with some of the brands represents, or he or she engages in behaviors that reflect poorly on the brand. Among the brands for which Tiger Woods served as a spokesperson were Accenture, Nike, Buick, Gillette, Gatorade, and American Express. Brands such as Buick and American Express did not benefit by this association to the same extent as Accenture and Nike. Indeed, the affiliation with Buick and American Express was terminated after several years. Furthermore, when Tiger's personal life was perceived to tarnish his character, Accenture, Gatorade, and Gillette stopped using him as a spokesperson. These brands were placed in a position where they judged that a key representative of the brand's equity, Tiger Woods, was undermining that equity.

Despite these concerns, spokespeople can enhance the perception of the brand they endorse. This is likely when the spokesperson personifies the brand benefit. Tiger Woods was an appropriate spokesperson for Nike and Accenture because he personified exceptional performance, which is the position employed to market these brands. A person who has strong associations with a category in which a brand holds membership can also serve as an effective spokesperson. Alec Baldwin, a well-known TV personality from his appearances on *30 Rock* and *Saturday Night Live*, is an appropriate spokesperson for HULU, an online service that allows the viewer to watch TV shows at no charge. Finally, a person who is perceived to be credible by virtue of being trustworthy and expert can serve to block the negative thoughts people might have and thus enhance the persuasive impact of a message. For example, Stephen Hawking, a world-renowned theoretical physicist, was an effective spokesperson for British Telecom. Not only was he knowledgeable about communication systems, but he was also viewed as being of such integrity that he would only make accurate assertions.

Because using spokespeople can have liabilities, the devices described earlier such as hard sell, big idea, story grammar, and comparison should be considered first. But if it is important to associate a brand with a spokesperson, the use of iconography might be considered. GEICO insurance has had great success in growing its brand by using a gecko as a spokesperson. Similarly, Frosted Flakes has made effective use of Tony the Tiger as a spokesperson, and SpongeBob

SquarePants is a successful spokesperson for both Band-Aid bandages and Kraft cheese. These icons stimulate elaboration of a brand's benefit without running the potential liabilities of using spokespeople.

Message Repetition The elaboration strategies we have discussed require consumers to expend substantial mental resources to associate message information with their prior knowledge. Message repetition offers an alternative to provide the resources necessary for such message processing. However, the number of repetitions must be carefully calibrated. If content is relevant to a consumer's needs, the first several exposures to an ad will prompt that person to learn the message content. At that point, additional exposures are not likely to result in continued processing of the message. In fact, in some instances, message recipients activate their own repertoire of thoughts. These thoughts are often less favorable than those in the message, which is designed to be maximally persuasive. The substitution of message-based thoughts with individuals' own thoughts is likely to result in wearout (a decline in the persuasive impact of the message with repeated exposure). They begin to think, "I already know what they're saying." A good example is the explanation of safety instructions after boarding a plane. Most people have heard these instructions so often that they simply tune out. Interestingly, wearout occurs most frequently in radio advertising, because listeners are typically loyal to a particular station (or small number of stations) and the low cost of placements in that medium result in high-exposure frequencies. Similarly, in business-to-business advertising, the low cost of ad placements results in high frequency of target exposure and thus wearout.

One effective means of managing wearout is to sustain brand news in the advertising. This might be achieved by showing the use of a product in another context or by presenting another reason to use the brand. For example, a campaign for a car battery might illustrate its power by showing it starting multiple cars in cold weather in one ad spot, and in another ad spot showing it continuing to work with the lights, air conditioning and radio on, but the motor off. Alternatively, wearout might be forestalled by discussing the battery's power in one ad and its warranty in another. In this way, the brand's protection benefit would be highlighted by different features that each disseminated news. Wearout can also be forestalled by reducing the resources that people devote to processing message content so that they are unlikely to activate their own repertoire of thoughts. Advertisers who use substantial levels of repetition such as those marketing soft drinks, beer, and fast foods often employ jingles in their ads because the need to process both music and content imposes substantial demands on message recipients' resources that forestall the onset of wearout.

Enhancing Brand Linkage

Many ads are effective in drawing attention and in promoting elaboration, and yet they are not persuasive. Ad recipients can play back a message in detail, but they cannot recall the sponsoring brand or they attribute the ad to the wrong brand. For these ads to have an impact on consumers' behavior, the linkage between the brand and its benefit must be clear.

Brand linkage is facilitated by presenting information about the brand that is consistent with the brand's heritage as developed in prior advertising. For example, retailer Target enhances the brand-benefit linkage by reliably advertising the low prices on fashion-forward items available at its stores and by featuring the Target logo. Sandwich shop Subway stimulates brand linkage by continually promoting its fresh ingredients. In contrast, when the brand walks away from its position, linkage is undermined. Special K had a heritage as a brand of ready-to-eat cereal that was part of a regimen to keep consumers healthy by helping them get or stay thin. When women objected to the advertising on grounds that it objectified women by showing thin models in its advertising, the strategy was changed. Special K announced that women should not be any more concerned about their figures than are men. Although this message resonated with many women, it had little connection to Special K's brand position. In fact, it raised the question of why women would eat Special K if keeping slim was not a goal. After a rapid decline in brand sales, Special K introduced a new campaign that featured model Cindy Crawford, who was known for being fit rather than thin. Thus, a spokesperson was used in advertising to personify the brand's health benefit in a contemporary way, a strategy that helped Special K return to its pre-decline level of sales.

Brand linkage can also be enhanced by the consistent use of executional elements. Along these lines, McDonald's introduces its ads by showing the golden arches, United Airlines commercials reliably include the same eight bars from Gershwin's *Rhapsody in Blue*, Lays ads always end with the claim that "nobody can eat just one," and Vanguard uses associations to tall ships to ensure brand linkage ("The average investor loses 2.5 percentage points of return each year to taxes. That's a lot of water over the bow.") However, when different brands in a category use the same executional element, brand linkage is compromised. For example, print ads for consulting firms that appear in business publications such as *BusinessWeek* and *Fortune* often employ analogies to represent their abstract services. The result of this lack of distinction is confusion about the benefits offered by each firm.

When advertising is presented on radio or TV, early identification of the brand name is a means of enhancing brand linkage. This is particularly the case in the United States, where the sheer number of ads presented and the short duration of most ad campaigns make it difficult for consumers to keep track of the brand being advertised in a particular ad. For example, an ad for a Schick blade razor showed a woman shaving her face to highlight the product's smoothness, but the commercial did not present the brand name until about halfway through. When asked to play back the ad at a later point, consumers were able to describe the ad in detail, but a substantial number of consumers recalled Gillette as the advertising brand, perhaps because it is the leading brand in the category. Also contributing to consumers' difficulties in linking the brand to the benefit was the fact that the ad was on air for only a short period of time. In other countries, where there are fewer ads and campaigns have longer durations, a late identification of the brand name seldom has the deleterious effects found in the United States, and late identification allows the advertising to build suspense and thus foster engagement.

Although early identification of the brand name is generally a good strategy to facilitate brand-benefit linkage, one clear instance when late identification is useful is when consumers have a negative disposition toward the brand. As soon as they are aware of the brand name, they activate their own negative thoughts about it, without processing the ad content. Late identification of the brand in such cases forestalls consumers' dismissals of the brand until after they have learned the brand news. When Gallo introduced premium wines, there was a concern that people's associations of Gallo with its heritage of inexpensive wines would lead them to dismiss Gallo's premium wines without considering their merits. Thus, an ad was developed that first described the product's quality in detail before disclosing that it was a new brand from Gallo.

MEASURING AD EFFECTIVENESS

A variety of measures are available to assess the effectiveness of an advertising message. For TV advertising, most services recruit consumers to evaluate what is ostensibly a new TV program, which in actuality serves as the context for test and control ads. At the outset of the study, participants are asked to indicate their brand preferences in a number of categories, including the ones being tested. They are then shown the program with the test and control ads embedded in it. When the presentation is complete, participants are asked a series of questions about the test ads. These measures tap what message recipients learned about an advertised brand, their beliefs about the brand, their brand preferences, and purchase intentions. In addition, the change in preference after seeing the advertising is assessed. For print ads, measures of effectiveness include target consumers' self-reports of whether they remember seeing the ad, related it to the brand, read most of the copy, as well as the actions taken in response to the advertising. Internet advertising makes use of impressions (were people on the web page where the advertising was presented?), and click-throughs (did they click to a web page for a brand message?). In one way or another these measures tap brand knowledge and brand evaluation.

Brand Knowledge

A frequently used measure of brand knowledge involves asking message recipients who saw a program to recall the content of ads that were presented in as much detail as possible. They are initially asked what ads they saw while watching the program. If message recipients do not identify the target ad, the researcher identifies it for the respondent. Whether they recall or are told the brand name, message recipients are asked to record what the ad showed and what was said. This verbatim recall of ad content is often a poor indicator of brand knowledge. One problem with it is that consumers often have difficulty tracing the origin of their knowledge. As we noted earlier, people respond to advertising by relating what they already know to the advertising content. What is stored in memory is thus a combination of the message information and recipients' own thoughts. When asked to recall the content of a specific ad, people conjure up brand-related information. But they often have difficulty in determining whether the information they retrieve is based on the particular message they are being asked about, some other message they might have seen for the brand, or on self-generated knowledge. Because of this uncertainty about the origin of their knowledge, consumers often do not report some message information that they had learned or might report information from memory as if they learned it from the advertisement.

Even when consumers can recall the content of an ad, the implication for their brand choice is uncertain. Substantial recall of an ad's content might reflect strong opposition to the information presented, and the association of these thoughts to what was said in the ad at the time of recall. For example, if advertising describes the tool kit that comes with a new car, consumers might recall this fact because they may associate the fact that a tool kit will be needed to repair the frequent breakdowns that the brand is reputed to have. This thought will be retrieved when consumers are asked to report the content of an ad and readily associate with the assertion made in the ad. The result is good recall of the advertising content, but also a highly negative brand evaluation.

A more useful measure of recall pertains to message recipients' knowledge about a brand's benefits. Unlike ad recall, which makes explicit reference to a particular source of knowledge, brand recall prompts consumers to enumerate facts about a brand without reference to the origin of that knowledge. To assess whether the brand knowledge consumers exhibit is attributable to advertising for it, an experiment is conducted in which consumers are randomly assigned to see a commercial for a brand or not. Differences in the recall of brand information are attributable to the advertising.

The impact of advertising on consumers' knowledge can also be learned by asking consumers about their brand awareness and top-of-mind awareness. Brand awareness involves specifying the brand name and asking consumers to indicate what functions it serves (what is Tide?). Top-of-mind awareness specifies the category in which a target brand holds membership and asks message recipients to enumerate the brands (list all of the detergents that you can think of). Top-of-mind questions can also pertain to the purchase consideration set (what brands would you consider when next buying detergent?). Poor advertising awareness generally signals the failure to reach the target with the media selected, and thus requires revisiting media selection decisions, whereas low top-of-mind awareness is associated with inadequate message frequency.

In some situations, the primary goal of advertising is to make consumers familiar with a brand name. Billboards and signage at sporting events and on vehicles are often used for this purpose. The hope is that familiarity with the brand name will enhance the chances that people will select the product when they see it at retail. The observation that familiarity with an object is often misattributed to liking for that object is consistent with this notion. To tap this knowledge, message recipients might be asked to perform a word completion task. This entails presenting a word with some letters missing and assessing the extent to which respondents complete the fragment by spelling the brand name. For example, if the word fragment B _ _ l s _ _ _ is completed with the barbeque sauce brand name "Bullseye" more frequently after viewing an ad for the brand than in its absence, there would be evidence that the ad fostered the learning of the brand name.

Brand Evaluation

Advertising effectiveness depends on what people know about a brand, and how they feel about this knowledge. One approach to developing such measures involves asking message recipients to evaluate a brand on general affective dimensions such as like–dislike, good–bad, and superior–inferior, as well as on characteristics such as consumers' feelings about the brand's price and quality. Aggregating responses on these measures provides an overall indication of how favorable consumers are toward a brand, and inspection of responses to individual items offers further insight about why consumers have the brand attitudes they report.

The effect of advertising on brand intentions and choice is another evaluative measure. In lab settings, participants' brand choices before and after viewing advertising for it are used to assess ad effectiveness. The magnitude of switching after viewing an ad is not indicative of the switching that can be expected when the ad airs (participants are aware of the research purpose and may act to accommodate the researcher). However, these procedural demands are a constant when the switching induced by one ad is compared to that induced by another. When studies are conducted in test markets rather than in a lab, not only can the effect of alternative ads be assessed, but the magnitude of this effect can be projected to predict sales outcomes when advertising is rolled out.

For established brands with long-lived positions, such as Kraft's Philadelphia cream cheese, a new ad for the brand is unlikely to have a substantial influence on brand attitudes or choice because message recipients are already knowledgeable about the brand's position. A better indicator of the ad's effectiveness for such brands involves the presentation of an ad in a context of competitive advertising and an evaluation of the extent to which the ad is successful in combating the impact of a competitive attack.

For online advertising, an emerging procedure is to create a substantial number of relatively simple ads for a brand and to place these on different sites. The number of click-throughs serves as a proxy for brand evaluation. The assumption is that if consumers clicked through, it is because they are interested in considering the advertised brand. The ad-site combinations that receive the most click-throughs are considered the most effective, whereas when click-throughs are modest, different ad executions are tried. Although this approach distinguishes more and less effective ads in terms of click-throughs, the strategist is left with limited understanding of why one ad was more effective than another. Thus, learning on the basis of prior advertising is limited.

SUMMARY

Advertising can influence consumers in a number of different ways. It might stimulate them to deliberate about the value of a brand by relating what they know about it to what is reported in advertising. Here, judgments will depend on consumers' predispositions toward the brand and the extent to which advertising provides relevant news about it. In other situations, consumers might base their decision on a quick analysis of thin slices or cues such as the color and shape of a brand offering. In addition, consumers might reflect on the process by which they develop their brand judgments and use this subjective experience as a basis for brand evaluation.

To enhance consumer engagement in processing an advertising message and acting on it, several issues require consideration. One pertains to the development of strategies to attract attention to the message content. This can be achieved by introducing information that is incongruous to consumers' current beliefs and by developing humorous or threatening appeals. In addition, attention can be drawn to an ad by appropriate selection of the advertising vehicle. This entails presenting advertising when the category and brand are relevant to consumers (moment) and in a context with which consumers have resonance (mindset).

Engagement is also fostered by stimulating consumers to represent message information in an elaborate manner in memory. This can be achieved by a variety of devices. If a brand has a strong point of difference, a hard sell that relates brand to benefit warrants consideration. When a brand benefit is supported by multiple attributes, a big idea strategy is likely to be effective. And when brand performance requires demonstration, the use of a story grammar that presents a description of the problem faced by consumers, the steps followed to address the problem, and the demonstration of the brand's success in problem solution is appropriate. Elaboration can also be achieved by comparing the brand to others in the category on dimensions where the advertised brand has dominance as well as dimensions on which it has parity. Comparison to another well-known category in order to teach consumers about the benefits of the advertised brand can also serve as an effective elaborative device. Finally, elaboration can be enhanced by using spokespeople to personify the brand benefit or to reduce the likelihood of counterargumentation.

A final requirement for engagement is that the brand is linked to its benefits. Brand linkage can be undermined by advertising that deviates from the brand's position, uses the same executional elements as those used by other brands in the category, or fails to present the brand name at the outset of the ad. However, late brand identification is warranted when consumers have a negative disposition toward the brand, because this forestalls their activation of negative thoughts about it prior to learning the advertising claims.

The effectiveness of advertising should include measures of what people know about the brand and how they feel about this knowledge. Consumer brand knowledge can be assessed by first having target consumers recall what they know about the brand, then comparing the responses of those who were exposed to advertising and those who were not in order to assess the advertising effect. Recognition of a brand name when given partial cues is useful when the goal is to assess brand name recall. What is less useful is the frequently used verbatim ad recall measure. Consumers' reports of ad recall are often not accurate, and even when they are accurate, they are frequently not correlated with purchase. Measures of consumers' dispositions toward an advertised brand can be evaluated by administering attitude measures, as well as examining their interests in a brand from their willingness to click through on a web site and/or purchase an item. When brands are well-established, the extent to which advertising combats competitive gains offers a good indicator of ad effectiveness.

Derek D. Rucker is the Richard M. Clewett Associate Professor of Marketing at the Kellogg School of Management, Northwestern University. He is a co-author of Advertising Strategy (Copley). He received his BA in psychology from the University of California, Santa Cruz, and his MA and PhD in social psychology from Ohio State University.

Brian Sternthal is the Kraft Professor of Marketing and a past chairperson of the Marketing Department at the Kellogg School of Management. He is also a past editor of the Journal of Consumer Research, an Association for Consumer Research Fellow in Consumer Behavior, and the co-author of Advertising Strategy (Copley). He received his BS from McGill University and his PhD from Ohio State University.

NOTES

1. Baddeley, A. D., and G. Hitch (1974), "Working Memory." In G. A. Bower (Ed.), *Recent Advances in Learning and Motivation,* vol. 8, New York: Academic Press.
2. Gladwell, M. (2005), *Blink: The Power of Thinking Without Thinking,* New York: Little, Brown and Company.
3. Rucker, D. D., R. E. Petty, and P. Briñol (2008), "What's in a Frame Anyway?: A Meta-Cognitive Analysis of One Versus Two-Sided Message Framing On Attitude Certainty," *Journal of Consumer Psychology,* 18, 137–139.
4. Tybout, A. M., B. Sternthal, P. Malaviya, G. A. Bakamitsos, and S. B. Park (2005), "Information Accessibility as a Moderator of Judgments: The Role of Content Versus Retrieval Ease," *Journal of Consumer Research,* 32(1), 76–85.
5. Rucker, D. D., and Z. L. Tormala (in press), "Meta-Cognitive Theory in Consumer Research." In Brinol, P. and DeMarree, K. (eds.), *Frontiers in Psychology: Social Metacognition.* Psychology Press: New York, NY.
6. Bochner, S., and C. A. Insko (1966), "Communicator Discrepancy, Source Credibility, and Opinion Change," *Journal of Personality and Social Psychology,* 4, 614–621.
7. Chernev, A. (2001), "The Impact of Common Features on Consumer Preferences: A Case of Confirmatory Reasoning," *Journal of Consumer Research,* 27, 475–488.

CHAPTER 11

MARKETING CHANNEL DESIGN AND MANAGEMENT

ANNE T. COUGHLAN

INTRODUCTION

Corporate marketing managers worldwide are perpetually challenged by marketing channel design and management problems. A marketing channel structure (sometimes known as channels of distribution) is the set of pathways a product or service follows after production, culminating in purchase and use by the final end-user.[1] The appropriate structure responds to an understanding of not just *what* consumers want to buy, but *how* they want to buy. The resulting organization of channel flows, and overall channel structure, is a key tool in maintaining a competitive edge and increasing a company's profitability.

Distribution channels are complex and can change over time. Consider the following two examples, which suggest both the dynamic pace of change in marketing channel management and the complexity and broad membership that a marketing channel can comprise.

The Distribution of College Textbooks

The distribution of college textbooks used to be an orderly affair. Authors wrote the books; publishers took care of promotion, physical production, storage, and initial shipments; and independent distributors took these shipments and subdistributed them to university bookstores, where students bought their books. A limited and localized used-book market placed only a small damper on sales of new books. Students typically bought all their textbooks, so forecasting sales based on past course enrollments was easy.

232

However, with the rise of Internet bookselling, students learned they could buy their books from sources other than the university bookstore, setting off some price competition and making it difficult to accurately reward publishers' salespeople for book sales (given that many textbook purchases were no longer made locally). Internet selling also made used-book sales easier, in particular through venues such as Amazon.com, which offered independent booksellers the opportunity to "set up shop" under Amazon's "Other New and Used" umbrella. Meanwhile, textbook publishers expanded marketing efforts overseas and in the process created their own "international editions" as well as third-party licensed versions of their products, which sold at drastically reduced prices in foreign markets.[2] It was only a matter of time before enterprising intermediaries in these foreign markets perceived an arbitrage opportunity, leading to wide availability of the reduced-price editions online in the United States. The paper-based distribution of textbooks had become a much less predictable, profitable business than it had been in the past.

By 2010, the textbook market faced a fascinating transformation—from paper to virtual textbooks. With the majority of college students possessing laptop computers, it made sense to foster an electronic marketplace for textbook distribution, for several reasons. First, the cost of distribution drops drastically when a physical product does not need to be produced, inventoried, and taken back as returned goods or overstocks. Textbook prices could therefore fall, leading more students to actually buy their textbooks.[3] Further, the electronic distribution of a textbook could make used-book markets a thing of the past, as temporary electronic licenses could be sold, eliminating the need for a physical book that could be resold multiple times.

Consolidation in the Electric Utility Industry

The ultimate end-user of electricity—a consumer or business that uses it—highly values reliable supply with no interruptions. However, consolidation in the electric utility industry has significantly affected the suppliers and manufacturers of utility infrastructure equipment, compromising the utilities' ability to meet service output demands.

To meet this service output demand, utilities must hold enough safety stock of repair parts so that even a freak ice storm in the wintertime does not unduly interrupt power supply, something that a regional cooperative utility would routinely do. However, as utility companies began to consolidate under publicly held organization structures (rather than as cooperatives), they have become increasingly reluctant to hold large safety stocks due to financial performance pressures from stockholders. These pressures directly conflicted

with their customers' demands for reliable service. As a result, utilities began pressuring distributors upstream to hold the safety stocks instead, thus
increasing distributor cost burdens. In turn, distributors pressured manufacturers to lower their wholesale prices as a means of holding down overall
distribution-level costs. The manufacturers responded to this pricing pressure
by moving production locations from their U.S. bases to the People's Republic
of China.

This cost-cutting move had unforeseen consequences, however. The first
was significantly longer lead times to transport product back to the United
States, due to lengthy physical shipping distances between China and the
United States. Paradoxically, this meant that larger safety stocks would have to
be held by the U.S. manufacturer in order to meet legacy in-stock performance
levels, eating away at the cost savings of producing overseas to begin with.

Distributors found that although manufacturers' foreign sourcing did help
hold costs down somewhat, they experienced out-of-stocks more frequently.
Therefore, some of the larger distributors convinced Chinese companies who
were manufacturing branded U.S. manufacturers' products to make private-
label versions of components that the distributors could source, hold, and sell
themselves without sharing margin with the manufacturer. This cascade of
events has meant that U.S.-branded equipment manufacturers now face both
lower margins and greater competition (from their own distribution partners!)
than they did before consolidation at the downstream utility level. Further,
ultimate end-user consumers of electrical power could face a greater risk of
long downtimes because of an efficiency pressure to minimize safety stock
holdings.[4]

Channel Design Challenges and a Framework for Analysis

Several questions arise as a result of the above examples. Why do marketing
channels change in structure over time? What role do consumer characteristics
and demands play in the appropriate channel design? How should a manufacturer decide what types of intermediaries to use in the channel? What problems
can arise in the ongoing management of complex marketing channels?

This chapter discusses the definition of a marketing channel and the productive purpose it serves in the overall strategy of marketing a product or service.
A framework for analysis is then presented that is robust, widely used, and
helpful in generating insights into both how to build a new channel and how
to modify an existing channel to improve performance in the market. Finally,
the chapter discusses how to apply the framework and concepts to some key
issues facing marketing channel managers today.

DISTRIBUTION CHANNELS: DEFINITION AND MOTIVATION

Marketing channels deliver every product and service that consumers and business buyers purchase everywhere in the world. Yet, in many cases, these end-users are unaware of the richness and complexity necessary to deliver to them what might seem like everyday items. Usually, combinations of institutions specializing in manufacturing, wholesaling, retailing, and many other areas join forces in marketing channels that deliver everything from mutual funds to books, medical equipment, and office supplies to end-users in both businesses and households. A marketing channel can be defined as follows:

> A marketing channel is a set of interdependent organizations involved in the process of making a product or service available for use or consumption.

The definition bears some explication. It first points out that a marketing channel is a *set of interdependent organizations*. That is, a marketing channel is not just one firm doing its best in the market—whether that firm is a manufacturer, wholesaler, or retailer. Rather, many entities are typically involved in the business of channel marketing. Each channel member depends on the others to do its job.

What are these jobs? The definition makes clear that running a marketing channel is a *process*. It is not an event. Distribution frequently takes time to accomplish, and even when a sale is finally made, the relationship with the end-user is usually not over (think about buying an automobile and servicing it over its lifetime).

Finally, what is the purpose of this process? The definition claims that it is *making a product or service available for use or consumption*. That is, the purpose of channel marketing is to satisfy the end-users in the market, whether they are consumers or final business buyers. Their goal is the use or consumption of the product or service being sold. A manufacturer selling through distributors to retailers (who serve final consumers) may be tempted to think that it has generated "sales" and developed "happy customers" when its sales force successfully places product in the distributors' warehouses. This definition argues otherwise. It is critically important that all channel members focus their attention on the true end-user, who is the only channel member who injects new money into the channel and thus funds all channel operations and profits.

The marketing channel is often viewed as a key strategic asset of a manufacturer. For example, direct selling is a method of distribution in which the manufacturer relies exclusively on the efforts of independent distributors to sell its products, rather than relying heavily on advertising to promote its products. Direct selling is frequently organized in a multilevel manner, in which a distributor makes bonuses based on the sales of down-line distributors it has recruited, as well as bonuses and retail markups on its own sales. Many types of products are sold through direct-sales organizations, including cosmetics (Mary Kay, Avon, Amway, Arbonne, etc.), nutritional supplements (Amway, NuSkin, Melaleuca), candles (PartyLite Gifts), books and toys (Discovery Toys), legal insurance coverage (PrePaid Legal), and many others. Direct selling generated more than $30 billion in estimated retail sales in the United States in 2007, with 15 million people participating as independent distributors.[5] Channel efforts by a direct seller's independent distributors are a crucial input, because most of these companies commit to using them as their sole route to market. The Arbonne web site notes that "Leading traditional retailers are known to spend 25–30% of every sales dollar on advertising, media, and other promotions, while network marketing uses those same dollars to reward individuals for 'word-of-mouth' promotion."[6] As is true for direct sellers, marketing channel decisions play a strategically important role in the marketplace presence and success of many companies.

A FRAMEWORK FOR MARKETING CHANNEL ANALYSIS

The marketing channel challenge involves two major tasks: first, to *design* the right channel; and second, to ensure successful *implementation* of that design. The design process involves *segmenting* the market through an analysis of the service output demands (SODs) of end-users, and using this knowledge to design (or redesign, in the case of a preexisting channel) the channel structure to best respond to the SODs of the chosen target segments of end-users. The implementation step requires an understanding of each channel member's *sources of power and dependence*, an understanding of the potential for *channel conflict*, and a resulting plan for creating an environment where the optimal channel design can be effectively executed on an ongoing basis. A successful design and implementation process leads to a *channel coordination* outcome.

Figure 11.1 depicts the important elements in the channel design and implementation process. This framework is useful both for creating a new channel in a previously untapped market and for critically analyzing and refining a pre-existing channel. The following sections further explore these concepts.

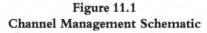

Figure 11.1
Channel Management Schematic

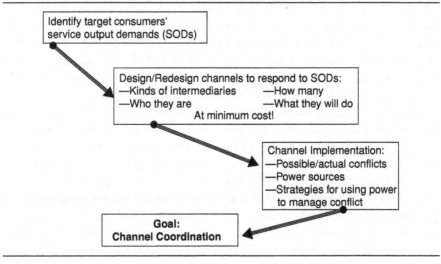

DESIGN OF THE MARKETING CHANNEL: SEGMENTATION, TARGETING, AND POSITIONING

To properly design a product's channel, the channel manager should customize the well-known marketing principles of segmentation, targeting, and positioning to the channel design task. Segmentation and targeting for channel design requires an understanding of end-users' service output demands; positioning for channel design means choosing the appropriate overall channel structure. These ideas can also be used to refine a pre-existing channel structure. Below, we discuss these three issues.

Channel-Based Segmentation and Targeting: Service Output Demand Analysis

One of the fundamental principles of marketing is the *segmentation* of the market. Segmentation means the splitting of a market into groups of end-users who are (a) maximally similar within each group, and (b) maximally different between groups. But maximally similar or maximally different based on what criteria? For the channel manager, segments are best defined *on the basis of demands for the service outputs of the marketing channel*. A marketing channel is more than just a conduit for product; it is also a means of adding value to the product marketed through it. In this sense, the marketing channel can be viewed as another "production line" engaged in producing not the product itself that is sold, but the ancillary services that define *how* the product is sold. These value-added services created by channel members and consumed by end-users along with the product purchased are called *service outputs*.[7] Service outputs include (but may not be limited to) *bulk-breaking, spatial convenience, waiting and delivery time, assortment and variety,* and *customer service.*

End-users (individuals purchasing for personal consumption or business buyers) have varying demands for these service outputs. Consider, for example, the purchase of laundry detergent by consumers in two different segments: the at-home segment and the on-vacation segment. Figure 11.2 outlines the differences in service output demands between the two segments of buyers. The profiled at-home buyer has low demands for all service outputs except product variety, where he or she is relatively brand-loyal and hence demands a particular brand and type of detergent. Meanwhile, the family on vacation, who has rented a condominium for a week, has a relatively lower valuation for assortment and variety, but a much higher relative valuation for bulk-breaking, spatial convenience, and quick delivery (both segments presumably have low relative demand for customer service, so this service output has been omitted from the illustration).

A different marketing channel can survive and thrive by targeting one versus the other segment: the at-home buyer would typically choose to buy detergent at a supermarket or hypermarket, but the on-vacation buyer shops at the small mom-and-pop convenience grocery store in the neighborhood of the family's condo. The on-vacation buyer is aware of, and willing to pay, the higher price that the mom-and-pop store charges, because he or she is cognizant of the value of the extra service being consumed for the exact same physical product.

This example shows how the same product can be demanded with a widely varying set of service outputs, resulting in different demands for the product-plus-service-output bundle by different segments of end-users. A detergent maker that does not distribute through small mom-and-pop outlets misses the on-vacation segment (which has a high willingness to pay and thus offers a relatively high gross profit margin). Similarly, a detergent maker that does not distribute through supermarkets or hypermarkets would miss the at-home buyer segment, which is of substantial size (although lower-margin). Indeed, the same consumer can inhabit different service output–driven segments when in different purchase situations. Thus, an analysis of service output demands by segment is an important input into a manufacturer's distribution channel

Figure 11.2
Service Output Demand Differences
An Example of Segmentation in the Laundry Detergent Market

Service Output	At-Home Use		Family Vacation Use	
	Descriptor	Service Output Demand Level	Descriptor	Service Output Demand Level
Bulk-breaking	"I have plenty of room in my laundry room to store detergent, and I know I'll use it up"	Low	"We're renting a condo for just one week, and won't be able to take extra detergent back on the plane"	High
Spatial convenience	"I drive to the supermarkets in my area to shop"	Low	"I'm not familiar with the area, so I go to the local grocery store down the street"	High
Quick delivery	"I have plenty of detergent at home, so I'm not panicked about getting it on this grocery trip"	Low	"I need to buy detergent right away so that it's there when I need to run a load of laundry"	High
Assortment and variety	"I need a concentrated detergent for my front-loading machine and normally buy Tide"	High	"I can't be too particular about which brand of detergent I buy; it's only for a week, and it's not my washing machine"	Moderate

design and can help increase the reach and marketability of a strong product to multiple market segments.

With an understanding of an end-user's varying service output demand intensities, the channel manager must then decide what segments to target. (Note that this also means that the channel manager will decide what segments *not* to target, as knowing what segments to ignore in channel design and management efforts keeps the channel focused on the key segments offering the most profitable sales.)

Why not target *all* the segments identified in the segmentation and positioning analyses? The answer is that even if all segments have some *sales* potential, the *profitability* of serving them may differ, because of the costs of structuring an appropriate channel to provide desired service output demands. This suggests the importance of understanding how channel costs arise from the channel structure created: in short, understanding the cost of *positioning* the product-plus-service-output bundle appropriately for each potential target segment. We turn next to this issue.

Channel Structure: The Channel's Positioning Task

When the market has been segmented into groups of end-users, each of which can be described by a set of service output demands, the channel manager should next define the optimal channel to serve each segment. This is called "positioning" or "configuring" the channel. Just as positioning a product means setting its product attributes, price, and promotional mix to best fit the demands of a particular segment, so also positioning refers to the design of the distribution channel to meet the target segment's demands.

This exercise should be done even if the channel ends up *not* selling to some of the segments in the end, as the channel analyst may discover that some segments simply do not make reasonable targets because their demands cannot be adequately met with the channel's current resources. Alternatively, the positioning exercise may reveal some unexpectedly attractive segments to target. Unless the optimal channel is defined for each segment, it is impossible to make a thorough decision about what segments to target.[8]

The optimal channel is defined first and foremost by the *necessary channel flows* that must be performed in order to generate the specific segment's service output demands. Channel flows are all the activities of the channel that add value to the end-user. In enumerating the list of channel flows, we go beyond the concept of the mere handling of the product to include issues of promotion, negotiation, financing, ordering, payment, and the like. Figure 11.3 depicts eight classic channel flows and shows the costs that are typically incurred in

Figure 11.3
Marketing Flows in Channels

Marketing Flow	Cost Represented	Typical Flow of Activity in Channel
Physical possession	Storage and delivery costs	Producer ⇒ Wholesaler ⇒ Retailer ⇒ Industrial and/or Household End-User
Ownership	Inventory carrying costs	Producer ⇒ Wholesaler ⇒ Retailer ⇒ Industrial and/or Household End-User
Promotion	Personal selling, advertising, sales promotion, publicity, public relations costs	Producer ⇒ Wholesaler ⇒ Retailer ⇒ Industrial and/or Household End-User
Negotiation	Time and legal costs	Producer ⇔ Wholesaler ⇔ Retailer ⇔ Industrial and/or Household End-User
Financing	Credit terms, terms and conditions of sale	Producer ⇔ Wholesaler ⇔ Retailer ⇔ Industrial and/or Household End-User
Risking	Price guarantees, warranties, insurance, installation, repair, and after-sale service costs	Producer ⇔ Wholesaler ⇔ Retailer ⇔ Industrial and/or Household End-User
Ordering	Order-processing costs	Industrial and/or Household End-User ⇒ Retailer ⇒ Wholesaler ⇒ Producer
Payment	Collections, bad debt costs	Industrial and/or Household End-User ⇒ Retailer ⇒ Wholesaler ⇒ Producer

Notes:
The flows of activity shown here are typical but can vary from channel to channel. For example, a retailer may take orders for products that are shipped directly from the manufacturer to the end-user, causing physical possession to pass directly from the manufacturer to the end-user. Each channel member who participates in the performance of a channel flow bears a cost. Producers, wholesalers, and retailers are collectively called the Commercial Channel Subsystem. End-users are channel members who can perform channel flows but are not considered commercial channel members.

performing these flows. The list is generic and can be expanded and customized to a particular channel's situation; but the activities represented are typical of most channel structures.

For example, the family on vacation described previously has a high demand for spatial convenience and minimal tolerance for out-of-stocks of laundry detergent. This means that good performance of the *physical possession* channel flow (the physical holding of inventory) takes on great importance for such end-users. Each product- or service-selling situation can have its own unique combination of service output demands by segment, implying the differential importance of different sets of channel flows.

Further, the channel analyst must identify the optimal *channel structure* to produce the necessary channel flows (which themselves, of course, result in the generation of the required service outputs that are demanded by a particular segment of end-users in the market). The design of the *channel structure* involves two main elements. First, the channel designer must decide *who* should be the members of the channel. For example, will a manufacturer of a high-performance energy/protein bar seek distribution through large supermarkets, small independent grocery stores, direct selling, and/or high-end athletic product stores? Moving up the channel from the retail level, analysts must decide whether to use independent distributors, independent sales representative companies (called "reps" or "rep firms"), independent trucking companies, financing companies, and/or any of a whole host of other possible independent distribution channel members that could be incorporated into the channel design.

Beyond this decision, the channel manager must also decide the exact identity of the channel partner to use at each level of the channel. If a line of fine watches will be sold through retail stores, for example, should the outlets chosen be more upscale, like Tiffany's, or should they be family-owned local jewelers? The choice can have implications both for the efficiency with which the channel is run and the image connoted by distributing through a particular kind of retailer. In a different context, if a company seeks distribution for its products in a foreign market, the key decision may be which distributor is appointed to carry the product line into the overseas market. The right distributor may have much better relationships with local channel partners in the target market, which can significantly affect the success of the foreign market entry.

The other main element of the channel structure is the decision of *how many* of each type of channel member to include in the channel. This is the *channel intensity* decision. In particular, should the channel for a consumer good include many retail outlets (*intensive* distribution), just a few (*selective* distribution), or only one (*exclusive* distribution) in a given market area? The answer to this question depends both on efficiency and on implementation factors. More intensive distribution may make the product more easily available to all target end-users, but may create enormous competition among the retailers selling it, resulting in destructive price wars among them. The price wars may negatively affect their margins, which in turn may cause them to be less interested in promoting or supporting the product.

The channel structure decisions of type, identity, and intensity of channel members all should be made with a mind toward minimizing channel flow costs. That is, each channel member is allocated a set of channel flows to perform, and ideally the allocation of activities results in the reliable performance of all channel flows at minimum total cost. This task is very important, particularly because it involves comparing activities across different companies who are members of the channel; but a careful channel audit can lead to cost savings in the channel that produce direct profitability results.

This exercise results in one channel profile for each segment that was identified in the market segmentation stage of the exercise. Each of these channel profiles is called a *zero-based channel*, because it is designed from a zero base of operations—that is, as if there is no preexisting channel in existence in the market. The concept of a zero-based channel means that (a) the segment's service output demands are met, and (b) they are met at minimum total channel cost.

So why should the channel designer not then target any and all channel segments that offer revenue potential? The answer is that channel members face *bounds* on their ability to build the appropriate channel design for every segment both efficiently (at low enough cost to be profitable) and effectively (to create high end-user satisfaction).

Both internal channel factors and external environmental factors are instrumental in defining these bounds. Internally, *managerial bounds* may constrain the channel manager from implementing the zero-based channel (for example, top management of a manufacturing firm may be unwilling to allocate funds to build a series of regional warehouses that would be necessary to provide spatial convenience in a particular market situation). Externally, both *environmental bounds* and *competitive benchmarks* may suggest some segments as higher priority than others. For example, legal issues and constraints can affect channel design and hence limit targeting decisions. Alcoholic beverage distribution is highly regulated in the United States; many states license only a limited number of alcoholic beverage distributors and enforce "two-step distribution." This means that alcohol cannot be sold from a manufacturer directly to a retailer, but must be sold through one of the limited number of distributors in the state market. Meanwhile, wineries face restrictions on whether they can sell directly to consumers who live out of state, and if so, in what quantities. This constrains them from targeting wine-lovers who may have visited their winery on a vacation but live out of state, forcing them to try to gain independent distribution through the two-step distribution model.

When superior competitive offerings do *not* exist to serve a particular segment's demands for service outputs, the channel manager may recognize an unexploited market opportunity and create a new channel to serve that underserved segment. Meeting previously unmet service output demands can be a powerful competitive strategy for building loyal and profitable consumer bases in a marketplace. But these strategies are impossible to identify without knowledge of not just *what* consumers want to buy, but importantly, *how* they want to buy, and the necessary response in terms of channel flow performance and channel structure.

This element of the channel analysis seeks to identify a subset of all the segments in the market that the channel plans on targeting, based on the channel designer's segmentation and positioning insights.

Establishing or Refining the Channel Structure

The channel manager has now identified the optimal way to reach each targeted segment in the market, and has also identified the bounds that might prevent the channel from implementing the zero-based channel design in the market. If no channel exists currently in the market for this segment, the channel manager should now establish the channel design that comes the closest to meeting the target market's demands for service outputs, subject to the environmental and managerial bounds constraining the design.

If there is a preexisting channel in place in the market, however, the channel manager should now perform a *gap analysis*. The differences on the demand and supply sides between the zero-based and actual channels constitute gaps in the channel design. Gaps can exist on the demand side or on the supply side, as Figure 11.4 suggests.

On the demand side, gaps mean that at least one of the service output demands is not being appropriately met by the channel. The service output in question may be either undersupplied or oversupplied. The problem is obvious in the case of undersupply: the target segment is likely to be dissatisfied because these customers would be willing to pay for more service than they are getting. The problem is more subtle in the case of oversupply. In this case, target end-users are getting all the service they desire—and then some—so end-user satisfaction is not an issue. However, the fact that that service is costly to supply implies that reducing service output provision would close a demand-side gap by reducing costs by more than the corresponding loss in revenue,

Figure 11.4
Types of Gaps

PERFORMANCE LEVEL: COST:	Demand-Side Gap (SOD>SOS)	No Demand-Side Gap (SOD=SOS)	Demand-Side Gap (SOS>SOD)
No Supply-Side Gap (Efficient Flow Cost)	Price/value proposition=right for a less demanding segment!	*No Gaps*	Price/value proposition=right for a more demanding segment!
Supply-Side Gap (Inefficiently High Flow Cost)	Insufficient SO provision, at high costs: price &/or cost too high, value too low	High cost, but SO's are right: value is good, but price &/or cost is high	High costs *and* SO's=too high: no extra value created, but price &/or cost is high

generating a net profit gain. Clearly, more than one service output may be a problem, in which case several demand-side gaps may need attention.

On the supply side, gaps mean that at least one flow in the channel of distribution is carried out at too high a cost. This not only wastes channel profit margins, but it can also result in prices that are higher than the target market is willing to pay, leading to reductions in sales and market share. Supply-side gaps can result from a lack of up-to-date expertise in channel flow management or simply from waste in the channel. The challenge in closing a supply-side gap is to reduce cost without dangerously reducing the service outputs being supplied to target end-users.

When gaps are identified on the demand or supply sides, there are several strategies available for closing them, as Figure 11.5 suggests. But once a channel is already in place, it may be difficult and costly to close these gaps. This suggests the strategic importance of initial channel design. If the channel is initially designed in a haphazard manner, channel members may have to live with a suboptimal channel later on, even after recognizing channel gaps and making best efforts to close them.

MANAGEMENT OF THE MARKETING CHANNEL: POWER, CONFLICT, AND COORDINATION

Even with a well-designed channel structure, the channel manager faces the ongoing task of coordinating the actions of all channel members. This section

Figure 11.5
Closing Channel Gaps

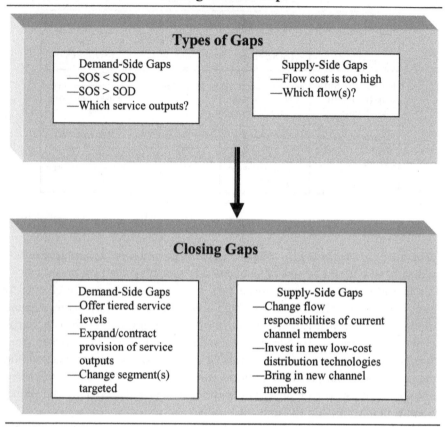

discusses how the concepts of channel power and channel conflict help the channel manager improve overall channel coordination.

Channel Power

The channel manager's job is still not done, assuming that a good channel design is in place in the market. The channel members now must *implement* the optimal channel design, and indeed must continue to implement an optimal design over time. The value of doing so might seem to be self-evident, but it is important to remember that a channel is made up of multiple entities (companies, agents, individuals) that are interdependent, but that may or may not all have the same incentives to operate in the desired manner.

Incompatible incentives among channel members would not be a problem if they were not dependent on each other. But by the very nature of the distribution channel structure and design, specific channel members are likely to *specialize* in particular activities and flows in the channel. If all channel members do not perform appropriately, the entire channel effort suffers. For example, even if everything else is in place, a poor-performing transportation system that results in late deliveries (or no deliveries) of product to retail stores prevents the channel from selling the product. The same type of statement could be made about the performance of any channel member doing any of the flows in the channel. Thus, it is apparent that inducing *all* of the channel members to implement the channel design appropriately is critical.

How then can a "channel captain" implement the optimal channel design in the face of interdependence among channel partners, when not all have the incentive to cooperate in the performance of their designated channel flows? The answer lies in the possession and use of *channel power*. A channel member's power "is the ability of one channel member (A) to get another channel member (B) to do something it otherwise would not have done."[9] A's power over B is greater, the more *utility* A can offer to B, and the *scarcer* is the utility that A can offer to B for complying with A's requests.

In particular, these two forms of power are complementary to each other: the more of one type of power A has over B, the more valuable on the margin is an increment in the other type of power. Further, A lacks power over B unless A has at least some of both types of power: for example, if A were the only potential channel partner to have personnel who speak French, this would endow A with *scarcity*; but, if B seeks to enter the Japanese market, French-speakers are unlikely to provide much *utility*, and therefore the scarcity of knowledge of French endows A with no real power. Alternatively, if A were a transportation firm that could offer reliable trucking services to B, but if there were many similarly capable transportation firms, A would be able to offer *utility* to B, but not *scarcity*—again, resulting in no real power of A over B.

Scarcity is an intuitive criterion for power: it corresponds to the notion of monopoly power in economics. Utility, however, is less immediately actionable from a channel management point of view. What sorts of utility could A offer to B? One approach posits five kinds of channel power, each of which influences the utility A can offer to B. A is said to have:

- *Coercive* power over B if B does what A wants because of the threat that A will withhold something of value from B if B does not comply with A's request.

- *Reward* power over B if B does what A wants because B will get a (financial or other) reward from A for complying.
- *Legitimate* power over B if B does what A wants because B perceives that A has the right to tell B what to do.
- *Expertise* power over B if B does what A wants in order to gain access to A's knowledge or proficiency.
- *Referent* power over B if B does what A wants in order to "look like" or benefit from the brand equity of A.

Notice that with each of these power sources, B expects some reward (or a failure to take away a reward) from A; these can all therefore be thought of as types of *utility* power in the utility/scarcity dichotomy.

Channel power can be used to further one channel member's individual ends. But if instead channel power is used to influence channel members to do the jobs that the optimal channel design specifies that they should do, the result will be a *coordinated channel* that more closely delivers demanded service outputs at a lower cost.

Channel Conflict

Channel conflict is generated when one channel member's actions prevent the channel from achieving its goals. Channel conflict is both common and dangerous to the success of distribution efforts. Given the interdependence of all channel members, any one member's actions have an influence on the total success of the channel effort, and thus can harm total channel performance.[10]

Channel conflict can stem from differences between channel members' goals and objectives (*goal conflict*); from disagreements over the domain of responsibility and benefit in the channel (*domain conflict*); and from differences in perceptions of the marketplace (*perceptual conflict*). These conflicts directly cause channel members to fail to perform the flows that the optimal channel design specifies for them, and thus inhibit total channel performance. The management problem is twofold. First, the channel manager needs to be able to *identify* the sources of channel conflict and, in particular, to differentiate between poor channel design (which can of course also inhibit channel performance) and poor performance due to channel conflict. Second, the channel manager must decide on the *action* to take (if any) to manage and reduce the channel conflicts that have been identified.

In general, channel conflict reduction is accomplished through the application of one or more sources of channel power. For example, a manufacturer may identify a conflict in its independent distributor channel: the distributorship is exerting too little sales effort on behalf of the manufacturer's product line, and thus sales of the product are suffering. Analysis might reveal that the effort level is low because the distributorship makes more profit from selling a competitor's product than from selling this manufacturer's product. There is thus a *goal* conflict. The manufacturer's goal is the maximization of profit over its own product line, but the distributorship's goal is the maximization of profit over *all* of the products that it sells—only some of which come from this particular manufacturer. To resolve the goal conflict, the manufacturer might use some of its power to reward the distributor by increasing the distributor's discount, thus increasing the profit margin it can make on the manufacturer's product line. Or, the manufacturer may invest in developing brand equity and thus pull the product through the channel. In that case, its brand power induces the distributor to sell the product more aggressively because the sales potential for the product has risen. In both cases, some sort of leverage or power on the part of the manufacturer is necessary to change the distributor's behavior and thus reduce the channel conflict. Besides obvious bases of power such as coercion and reward, leverage can also be gained through expertise, legitimate authority (e.g., contracts), and the accumulation of brand equity, an example of referent power.

Channel Coordination

After following the steps of the channel management schematic in Figure 11.1, the channel will have been designed with target end-user segments' service output demands in mind, and channel power will be appropriately applied to ensure the smooth implementation of the optimal channel design. When the disparate members of the channel are brought together to advance the goals of the channel, rather than their own independent (and often conflicting) goals, the channel is said to be *coordinated*. This term is used to denote both the coordination of interests and actions among the channel members who produce the outputs of the marketing channel, and the coordination of performance of channel flows with the production of the service outputs demanded by target end-users. This is the end goal of the entire channel management process. As conditions change in the marketplace, the channel's design and implementation may need to respond; thus, channel coordination is not a one-time achievement, but an ongoing process of analysis and response to the market, the competition, and the abilities of the members of the channel.

APPLICATION OF THE CHANNEL DESIGN/ MANAGEMENT FRAMEWORK TO CURRENT ISSUES IN MARKETING CHANNEL DESIGN AND MANAGEMENT

This framework is useful in evaluating currently existing channels as well as in creating new ones. However, it is also important to recognize that the framework for analysis we propose will be implemented by channel managers operating in a constantly changing environment. This section presents two issues of particular importance for channel management that illustrate how these concepts play out in real channel management situations: (1) how to efficiently and effectively distribute to low-income consumers with innovative channel strategies; and (2) the strategic choice of whether to attack demand-side gaps or supply-side gaps first, when both limit channel performance.

Distributing to Low-Income Consumers with Innovative Channel Strategies

Low-income consumers are frequently ignored because channel managers believe that their buying power is too limited to be profitable. However, across various markets and various product purchase situations, this segment does indeed have money and does buy a great deal of product—and in many markets, low-income consumers vastly outnumber middle-income and wealthy ones. The question becomes how to *efficiently* target and distribute to this segment, subject to generating the right service outputs—at the right intensity levels—that will permit this segment to buy at a price it can afford.

Checking demand-side gaps should be a first priority in evaluating the market and profit potential of a low-income segment. Very often, low-income consumers lack storage capacity, and by definition they lack the disposable income to buy in bulk. Thus, *bulk-breaking* demands are typically high in this segment. Similarly, because low-income consumers frequently do not have reliable transportation (e.g., they are unlikely to own cars), *spatial convenience* demands are also intense. Further, because low income is correlated with lower educational levels, these consumers are likely to need specialized *customer service* to learn how to use or even assemble certain products. Overlaid on these typically high-service output demand levels (which as a consequence are expensive to provide) is the overall low willingness to pay in this segment, simply due to income constraints. The demand-side gaps challenge the channel designer to develop low-cost ways to offer the service outputs that this segment must have in order to purchase.

On the supply side, typical channel arrangements also suffer from serious gaps, because the established channel structure has been designed to appeal to the service output demands of a higher-income segment. Correlated with the need for bulk-breaking is the fact that low-income consumers do not have large homes or storage spaces in which to *inventory* bulk purchases (i.e., perform the *physical possession* flow). This means that a low-price hypermarket retail offering, for example, is out of their reach despite the attractive price points, because they have nowhere to store large quantities of product, and no way to reach these spatially inconvenient retail locations. Standard channels are also generally built on the implicit assumption that consumers will perform part of the *financing* channel flow, by *paying* for product at the point of purchase or even in advance (for special-order products). However, low-income consumers lack the financial wherewithal to front significant amounts of cash to make major purchases or to buy in bulk, and they often do not even have access to standard financial outlets such as banks or credit cards to obtain loans or smooth out payment cycles for larger durable purchases. Targeting these consumers therefore can require a new and creative approach to sharing financing and payment channel flow costs. Additionally, *risking* can be burdensome for low-income buyers, because they have insufficient financial depth to recover from any purchase mistakes.

It is no wonder that these consumers are not often at the top of the list of segments to target. However, low-income consumers as a group actually have considerable purchasing power, although it may be in smaller chunks per household unit and available at less than regular intervals. The channel designer who can structure a route to market to efficiently *and* effectively target these consumers, however, can enjoy solid sales and significant loyalty, given the limited competition for this segment's purchasing power.

For example, CEMEX, the Mexican cement company, found an innovative solution to the challenge of targeting the poor that illustrates both the challenges and benefits of this strategic channel initiative.[11] CEMEX recognized that low-income consumers in Mexico constituted a large untapped market for its cement products. With many Mexican families migrating to the outskirts of major cities from the countryside, there was not enough housing to accommodate them; they further could not afford to buy property outright. Instead, a family simply occupied open land on the outskirts of an urban area and started to build a home, one room at a time. The goal was to build one room per year until the family had a true home.

However, building even one room required considerable capital to buy all the inputs (including not just cement, but also windows, doors, electrical wiring, flooring, roofing materials) and to purchase them in the right quantities, appropriately bulk-broken. The buyer also required several other key elements: storage space to hold product until it would be needed (for example, a bag of cement left outside is likely to spoil in the rain and damp, or to be stolen—thus, a need for risk management); expertise in how to build a sturdy room to which one could add other rooms in a sensible sequence (thus, a high demand for customer education); transportation help to get the raw materials to the building site from the dealer (thus, a high demand for spatial convenience); and help in actually building the room (i.e., demand for another element of customer service, because these consumers of course could not afford a contractor and building crew to do this for them!).

Juxtaposed against these service output demands was the consumer behavior of this segment in Mexico. Although the notion of building a home for one's family was revered (the home was called the family's *patrimonio*, or patrimony to be handed down to one's children), this long-term goal seemed to be all too frequently interrupted by the short-term cultural demands placed on consumers' disposable cash. Many events in the life of the community required sharing expenses; for example, a friend was arriving from the countryside; a family member had a new baby; a daughter or niece reached her 15th birthday. And, because these consumers were not generally employed in the formal economy, they did not have reportable income and therefore lacked access to banking services such as loans. These factors combined to make it seem impossible to close the large demand-side gaps while controlling supply-side costs.

However, CEMEX hit on a creative strategy for helping this segment save their money for building materials and assisting in the establishment of their *patrimonio*. It recruited women in the target segments' areas who ran *tandas*, small groups of consumers or families who agreed to contribute a fixed amount of money per week to a common pool; each week, one family got all that week's money. The *tanda* was thus a means of enforced savings. CEMEX's *tandas*, however, were organized to pay out in building materials rather than cash to the *tanda* members, thus guaranteeing that saving would go to the building of rooms, rather than to community or family celebrations.

CEMEX also hired architects to create design specifications for simple rooms of various types (living room, kitchen, bedroom, bathroom, etc.), and worked with other building materials manufacturers to design "kits" with everything in them to make a room. Finally, CEMEX arranged for help in actually building the rooms until local expertise could develop. Cost savings from lower materials waste, and an increase in total market demand, covered the cost of providing all of these value-added service outputs.

As a result, CEMEX has been able to make a viable business out of what looked like a hopeless one; but in order to do this, it had to make sure that valued service outputs would be provided that had previously been missing (everything from providing the right assortment and variety to helping with financing). The channel's structure and the way channel flows were performed had to change dramatically as a result; CEMEX took over many functions that had either not been done before for this segment or had been previously done by dealers. Such creative solutions are the hallmark of other similar efforts to target poor consumers, as exemplified by the help of microfinance firms in less-developed countries. (For further discussion on this topic, see Chapter 13, "Marketing to Consumers at the Bottom of the Pyramid.")

Should Demand-Side Gaps or Supply-Side Gaps Be Attacked First?

When both supply-side and demand-side gaps exist in the channel structure, which should be addressed first? It is possible to close gaps on the supply side without affecting demand-side provision of service outputs; conversely, it is also possible to seek to close demand-side gaps without focusing on maximizing efficiency on the supply side of the channel. Clearly, if channel partners have the commitment and wherewithal to attack both sets of gaps simultaneously, the channel will approach coordination faster; but it is often crucial to start with one set of problems and only later attack the other. Which, then, is the most compelling set of gaps to deal with first: supply-side (that is, cost management) or demand-side (that is, service output provision)?

The answer is not uniform in every circumstance or market. Attacking the supply side gaps first is a good idea when doing so not only helps the channel control costs, but also enables better processes for meeting target end-users' service output demands—that is, when the supply-side gaps themselves help to *cause* the demand-side gaps. For example, if end-users are intolerant of out-of-stocks in retail stores (that is, have a high demand for *quick delivery* once they enter the store), but in fact a retail channel suffers from poor inventory processing and shipping (that is, faces a supply-side gap in the *physical possession* channel flow), then it might not be possible to solve the demand-side gap without first improving inventory handling processes on the supply side. On the other hand, when a supply-side focus is costly (e.g., requiring the development or adoption of new and expensive technology), channel partners may be unwilling to support the effort if demand-side efforts that improve sales are not also forthcoming.

For instance, Guarantee Mutual, an employee benefits insurance company, worked on improving back-room operational capabilities in its channel, but it had to battle impatient salespeople who did not see an immediate improvement to sell to their corporate customers.[12] In this situation, the channel captain must decide how long the demand-side improvements can wait before not only end-users, but also possibly one's own channel partners, become disenchanted with the lack of service output excellence in the channel.

In some situations, channel members may not have the will or commitment to invest in closing gaps, despite the fact that end-user satisfaction would increase (as would channel profits) if gaps were closed. When this is the case, it is sometimes possible to enlist the support of end-users themselves to demand that the supply-side improvements be undertaken. Suppose improving on-line ordering or payment technologies could help close both supply-side and demand-side gaps, but high-level support and funding for investments to do this are not forthcoming. In this situation, an entrepreneurial channel member could offer some of the benefits of improved ordering and payment directly to end-users (whatever is possible given a constrained budget), to demonstrate to other channel members the true payoff of making gap-reducing investments—in effect, to use "pull demand" from end-users to convince the channel to undertake these investments. This type of "skunkworks" effort was used in the Mary Kay Corporation to show the value of increasing electronic communications abilities with Mary Kay distributors. After the distributors experienced the benefits of improved reporting through the generation of timely electronic productivity reports, and started demanding them from the company as a whole, more broad-based support for IT investments was forthcoming.[13]

In short, some general principles for prioritizing the attack on gaps in channel design are:

- Seek to fix the most fundamental gaps first—the ones that themselves cause other gaps to occur ("get the biggest bang for the channel investment buck").
- Focus on end-user demand-side gap reduction first when this will help "sell in" the rest of the gap reduction effort throughout the channel.
- Recognize that channel gap management is an ongoing and time-intensive process that often requires sequential rather than simultaneous gap-reduction activities.

SUMMARY

Creating and managing a marketing channel system is an enormous and strategic undertaking. Once created, it is often extremely hard to change or to dismantle. The "lumpy," high fixed-cost nature of many channel investments necessitates careful consideration of how the channel should be structured and managed when it is initially created or whenever any major change is contemplated.

Creation of the channel structure starts with an understanding of the end-user's demands for the service outputs of the channel. Service output demands vary for different end-user segments of the market, and this suggests the value in developing a customized channel for each segment's demands. The mapping between demanded service outputs and the channel flows necessary to produce those service outputs must be understood, so that the type of channel (e.g., direct to consumer, through independent distributors or retailers) as well as the specific identity of channel members can be established. Finally, each channel member's responsibility for channel flow performance must be clearly delineated and an appropriate management system put into place to guarantee that channel members actually perform their respective channel flows.

In the case of preexisting channels, a channel analysis is still a useful exercise, as it can uncover important channel gaps that inhibit growth of sales and profits. Gaps can exist on the demand side (through insufficient or excessive service output provision) or on the supply side (through excessive cost of performing channel flows). When demand-side gaps exist, the product's sales are likely to experience immediate ill effects. The negative impact of a supply-side gap may be more subtle but can be just as harmful: performing adequate channel flows, but at too high a cost, produces a high price for the bundle of product and service outputs that consumers demand. As a result, competitors with better channel management skills may find an opportunity to steal sales by offering comparable (or even superior) levels of service outputs at comparable (or even lower) overall prices.

Even with a good channel structure, the channel members may have difficulty implementing the design. Channel conflicts can arise from differences in goals, disagreement over domains, or differing perceptions of reality. Any of these can prevent the best channel structure design from succeeding in a market. Judicious application of relevant sources of channel power can reduce channel conflicts to manageable levels. Ideally, channel managers seek "channel coordination," a situation where all channel members strive for the unique goal of providing demanded service outputs at minimum cost.

The channel design process takes place in a complex and ever-changing environment. Channel members who do not recognize this may succeed in the short term, but they will face difficulties as the marketplace changes in fundamental ways around them. A constant vigilance and willingness to respond are the keys to successful ongoing channel management.

Anne T. Coughlan is the John L. & Helen Kellogg Professor of Marketing in the Marketing Department at the Kellogg School of Management. She is the academic director of the Distribution Channel Management: Bridging the Sales and Marketing Divide program at the James L. Allen Center, and the lead author of the leading textbook on distribution, Marketing Channels. She holds a BA and a PhD in Economics from Stanford University.

NOTES

1. For greater detail on any of the issues developed here, please refer to: Coughlan, Anne T., Erin Anderson, Louis W. Stern, and Adel I. El-Ansary (2006), *Marketing Channels*, 7th edition, Upper Saddle River, NJ: Pearson Education.

2. For example, the third-party licensed Indian version of the *Marketing Channels* textbook sold for the equivalent of about US$4, while the U.S. edition sold at a list price of about $140. The arbitrage opportunity could thus be enormous.

3. In one survey, only about 50 percent of required textbooks were bought (either as new or used books) by MBA students see: Shulman, Jeffrey D., and Anne T. Coughlan (2007), "Used Goods, Not Used Bads: Profitable Secondary Market Sales for a Durable Goods Channel," *Quantitative Marketing & Economics*, 5, 191–210.

4. For a discussion of similar consequences of distribution consolidation in other industries see: Fein, Adam J., and Sandy D. Jap (1999), "Manage Consolidation in the Distribution Channel," *Sloan Management Review*, 41 (1, Fall), 61–72.

5. See www.dsa.org, the web site of the Direct Selling Association, for information on member companies and on direct selling in general. www.dsa.org/pubs/numbers/ provides a summary Fact Sheet on direct selling in the United States. An overview is also contained in Coughlan et al. (2006), see Note 1, pp. 454–460.

6. Viveiros, Beth Negus (2009), "Mary Kay's Rhonda Shasteen Works on a Brand Makeover," *Direct Magazine*, January 1, which notes that Mary Kay "can't sell directly to end users. Consultants get credit for every sale." Also see: Coughlan, Anne T., and Erica Goldman (2004), "Mary Kay Inc.: Direct Selling and the Challenge of Online Channels," Kellogg School of Management Case number KEL034. Similarly, the Arbonne web site says, "At Arbonne, innovative products are only half of the story—the other side of our success is found in the most important ingredient of all . . . our remarkable people! Join this spirited legacy of individuals today." (www.arbonne.com/company/opportunity/people/ and www.arbonne.com/company/opportunity/industry.asp, viewed on September 25, 2009).

7. See Coughlan et al. 2006 (Note 1); Chapter 2 provides a detailed discussion of service outputs.

8. See Coughlan et al. 2006 (Note 1); Chapter 3 for a discussion of channel flows, and Chapter 4 for a discussion of channel structure and intensity of distribution.

9. See Coughlan et al. 2006 (Note 1); p. 197; Chapter 6 discusses channel power sources and uses in depth.

10. See Coughlan et al. 2006 (Note 1); Chapter 7 provides a detailed discussion of channel conflict.

11. Segel, Arthur, Michael Chu, and Gustavo Herrero (2006), "PatrimonioHoy," Harvard Business School case # 9-805-064 and "Cementing Family Futures," April 17, 2009, at www.changemakers.com/en-us/).

12. Coughlan, Anne T., and Richard Kolsky (2006), "Guarantee Mutual: Group benefits," case, Kellogg School of Management.

13. Coughlan, Anne T., and Erica Goldman (2004), "Mary Kay Inc.: Direct Selling and the Challenge of Online Channels," Kellogg School of Management Case # KEL034.

CHAPTER 12

BUILDING A WINNING SALES FORCE

ANDRIS A. ZOLTNERS, PRABHAKANT SINHA, and
SALLY E. LORIMER

THE SALES FORCE: A POWERFUL CUSTOMER-FACING ORGANIZATION

Sales forces are important for manufacturing and service companies alike. By our estimates,[1] the amount invested in sales forces in the United States exceeds $800 billion a year, close to three times the $269 billion spent on all media advertising and more than 34 times the $23.4 billion spent on online advertising in 2008.[2] According to a *Selling Power* magazine survey, computer and office equipment manufacturers such as Microsoft, Xerox, Cisco, and IBM each have more than 14,000 salespeople in the United States.[3] Manufacturers of consumable goods such as PepsiCo, Sysco, and Interstate Bakeries each have more than 10,000 salespeople, and medical products manufacturers such as Schering Plough, Johnson & Johnson, and Pfizer each employ more than 7,500. Service businesses also use sales forces as an important marketing channel. Insurance company Hartford Financial employs 100,000 U.S. salespeople, telecommunications giant Verizon has 35,000, and financial company American Express employs a force of more than 23,000. On average, companies invest about 10 percent of their annual revenues in their sales forces to pay for salaries, benefits, taxes, bonuses, automobiles, travel expenses, computers, and other administrative and field support for salespeople and their managers.

The significance of the sales force goes beyond its cost. The sales force is perhaps the most highly empowered organization within many companies. Usually working alone and unsupervised, salespeople are entrusted with a company's most important asset—its relationship with its customers. Often, salespeople have considerable control over this relationship; to some customers, the salesperson *is* the company. Because of the sales force's critical impact on customer relationships, its effect on company revenues and market share is significant. Through interactions with corporate sales leaders and executives in a wide range of businesses around the world, we have observed that in any given situation, a *very good* sales force—one that has talented salespeople who engage in the right selling activities—will produce at least 10 percent more revenues in the short term than an average sales force of the same size. In the long term, the revenue impact is much greater—typically 50 percent or more.

A good sales force is a powerful asset for a company, but the source of its power also makes it difficult to control, direct, and manage. The sales force consists of people, each with his or her capabilities, motivators, and values. People bring creativity, flexibility, and the ability to listen to customers and respond to their concerns. But at the same time, they bring egos and the need for security and meaning. Unlike advertising, salespeople cannot be turned on and off, and unlike a web site, they cannot be expanded and upgraded overnight. Creating, maintaining, and continuously improving a successful sales force is a significant challenge for any company, a challenge that requires the constant attention of company leaders to ensure that decisions, processes, programs, and systems that affect salespeople—the *sales effectiveness drivers*—are well-managed and in alignment with company business strategies.

In this chapter, we describe the role of the sales force in executing a company's business strategy, identify triggers for adapting and improving the sales force, provide a framework for understanding and increasing sales force effectiveness, and show how the framework can help companies that face numerous challenges and opportunities develop strategies and tactics for creating a more effective sales force.

THE ROLE OF THE SALES FORCE

As a key link between the company and its customers, the sales force plays an important role in executing a company's business strategy and driving customer satisfaction and company results.

The Sales Process

Connecting successfully with customers requires many diverse and often complex tasks. Developing strong customer relationships can involve activities such as identifying, contacting, and qualifying prospective customers; understanding

Figure 12.1
A Typical Sales Process and Examples of the Activities

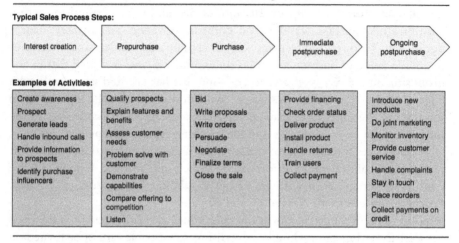

Typical Sales Process Steps:

Interest creation	Prepurchase	Purchase	Immediate postpurchase	Ongoing postpurchase

Examples of Activities:

Create awareness	Qualify prospects	Bid	Provide financing	Introduce new products
Prospect	Explain features and benefits	Write proposals	Check order status	Do joint marketing
Generate leads	Assess customer needs	Write orders	Deliver product	Monitor inventory
Handle inbound calls	Problem solve with customer	Persuade	Install product	Provide customer service
Provide information to prospects	Demonstrate capabilities	Negotiate	Handle returns	Handle complaints
Identify purchase influencers	Compare offering to competition	Finalize terms	Train users	Stay in touch
	Listen	Close the sale	Collect payment	Place reorders
				Collect payments on credit

customer needs, proposing solutions, and showing advantages over competitive offerings; persuading, negotiating, and closing sales; bringing together appropriate company resources, coordinating work across multiple departments to ensure that an appropriate solution gets delivered, and collecting payments; and keeping in touch with customers to ensure that solutions meet their needs and to seek opportunities for future business. Customer connections are most effective when companies take a systematic approach to accomplishing all of this work by organizing the activities required to attract and retain customers into a defined sales process. Figure 12.1 shows some typical steps in a sales process.

Although Figure 12.1 represents a basic overview of the sales process, the best approach for any company depends on a variety of factors, including product and market characteristics, the industry and economic environment, and company strategies and culture. Often, the best sales process varies by customer segment. For customers who understand the product and know what they want, the right sales process emphasizes the *purchase* step in Figure 12.1, making transactions as inexpensive and painless as possible for customers. For customers who want help solving complex problems, an appropriate sales process focuses on the *prepurchase* step so that salespeople add value by listening to customers, assessing their needs, and jointly developing solutions. For customers who require help with financing or installation, the *immediate postpurchase* step becomes more salient. By focusing on customer needs, an effective sales process results in many sales at an appropriate price.

When Should a Company Use Personal Selling?

The personal connection that salespeople establish with customers can have a large revenue impact. Face-to-face selling is generally believed to be more effective than less personal ways of doing business, but it is also more expensive—it costs a company much more to make a face-to-face sales call than it does to contact customers via e-mail or telephone, for example. Consequently, a sales force is most appropriately deployed to target select customers, products, and selling activities—specifically, those where the gross margin on the incremental sales that personal selling generates (above what less-expensive selling channels could generate) exceeds the incremental cost of making face-to-face sales calls. Generally, these include:

Customers/prospects that:

- Have good potential or strategic importance for the company and are responsive to face-to-face sales force coverage.
- Value creative problem-solving, discussion, demonstration/installation, and other selling activities that benefit from live personal interaction.
- Have complex buying processes.

Products/services that:

- Have good potential or strategic importance for the company and are responsive to face-to-face sales force coverage.
- Are complex or require solutions to difficult customer problems.
- Involve customizing the offering and message to a specific customer's needs and buying process.
- Have complex buying processes.

Sales activities that:

- Benefit significantly from personal interaction and discussion between the buyer and seller, including listening, understanding the customer's decision-making process, assessing needs, educating the customer, performing demonstrations, customizing the offering, solving problems, handling objections, and negotiating contracts.
- Require working cooperatively with multiple people at the customer site or with other selling partners.

When deployed against the right customers, products, and selling activities, an effective sales force performing the personal selling function is an invaluable asset for a company—a powerful customer-facing force that can be a source of considerable competitive advantage.

When Should a Company Outsource the Sales Function?

Personal selling can also be accomplished by outsourcing the sales force. Instead of hiring salespeople who are employees of the company, companies can outsource all or part of the sales function by contracting with independent individuals or selling organizations (selling partners) to sell the company's products and services. The type of selling partner varies by industry and includes agents, brokers, distributors, manufacturers' representatives, independent contractors, wholesalers, dealers, and value-added resellers (VARs). Sometimes selling partners sell a company's products and services exclusively; other times they sell complementary or even competitive products from different manufacturers.

Several aspects of a company's situation determine whether it is best to keep the sales function in-house or to outsource it.

Keep the sales function in-house when:

- The company wants close control of selling activity, ensuring that all effort is devoted to its own products; that effort is allocated appropriately across products, activities, and customers; and that effort can be redirected quickly if needed.
- The company wants ownership of salesperson quality by controlling the hiring profile, the recruitment process, and salesperson training and coaching.
- The company wants sales activity coordinated closely with other company departments, such as marketing, customer service, and operations, making personnel throughout the company better informed about customer needs and competitor's capabilities.
- The company wants to know its customers and wants to control the total customer experience; it sees ownership of the customer relationship and understanding of customer needs as a significant source of competitive advantage.

Outsource the sales function (either fully or partially) when:

- A selling partner has capabilities—such as established relationships with key customer decision makers—that would be hard for the company to replicate.
- The company wants to gain rapid entry into a market.
- The company's products are part of an assortment of products in a selling partner's portfolio (for example, paper clips sold by an office products distributor).
- A selling partner can combine the company's products with other products to create a complete solution for customers (for example, a computer

industry VAR that combines hardware and software components to sell as an integrated product).

- A selling partner makes it affordable to reach more customers than the company could manage to pay for on its own (for example, small accounts in rural areas), usually because the partner shares its costs with multiple manufacturers.
- The company wants to control costs and limit risk exposure by linking sales expenses directly to sales volume.

Companies that use selling partners need mechanisms to encourage their partners to use sales time and other assets effectively to support the company's products and services. These mechanisms can include partner incentive programs, marketing programs, partner managers, sales process assistance, sales analytics, and end-user pull-through programs that act as levers if not to control, at least to influence how effectively selling partners operate.

Companies that employ their own salespeople will generally have greater ability to influence the effectiveness of their personal selling efforts. The remainder of this chapter focuses on how such companies can create, maintain, and continuously improve an excellent sales force.

TRIGGERS FOR ADAPTING AND IMPROVING THE SALES FORCE

Because of the high cost and significant revenue impact of a sales force, most companies that employ their own salespeople take an active interest in maximizing sales force effectiveness. Companies can build and maintain sales force excellence by reacting effectively when *events* that occur externally to the sales force bring about a need for sales force change. In addition, opportunities for effectiveness improvement are driven by a company's desire to *constantly innovate* to improve the sales force. Event-driven and innovation-driven sales force improvements are described further here.

Event-Driven Sales Force Improvement

Sales forces frequently need to change when events external to the sales force require an appropriate reaction. Some examples are:

- The company launches a significant new product line.
- An economic boom or bust creates new opportunities or challenges for the sales force.

- The company has acquired a firm with a sales force that covers many of the same customers.
- Customers are consolidating, so the current selling process is no longer effective.
- Competitors have launched new products and have increased their investment in their sales forces to attack the most profitable market segments.
- The sales force needs to provide unique value as increasing numbers of similar products and services come into the marketplace.

How effectively a sales force responds to major events has a large profit impact. Figure 12.2 describes two companies that faced challenging external events and summarizes how their sales forces responded and the results they achieved. The examples demonstrate that the quality of the event response by the sales force can have a significant effect on company results.

Figure 12.2

A Comparison of How Two Sales Forces Responded to Challenging External Events

An *Unsuccessful* Response to External Events at a Large Financial Services Company

Event	Sales Force Response	Company Results
• The company acquires several smaller financial service firms. • Salespeople at the acquired firms make more money than the company's current salespeople for doing similar work.	• Avoid sales force disruption by allowing the acquired sales forces to continue to operate independently. • Minimize loss of salespeople from the acquired firms by continuing to pay them their current high compensation.	• When salespeople discover that others with similar jobs are getting paid more, they are upset by the unfairness. Sales force morale suffers. • Some of the best salespeople leave the company and take customers with them. • Administrative costs increase because the company has to manage dozens of sales compensation plans. • Once the acquisition phase is over, gaining sales force acceptance for integrating the sales forces becomes even more challenging.

A *Successful* Response to External Events at United Airlines

Event	Sales Force Response	Company Results
• Air travel declines following 9/11/01. • High fuel prices and inflexible labor agreements increase industry costs.	• Replace the "price and relationship" sales approach used with corporate travel departments and travel agencies with a new value-based, consultative sales model. • Use a structured process to implement the new selling model. • Gather input from customers and involve both the sales and marketing teams. • Develop a new sales force competency model and revise the hiring profile. • Re-interview salespeople for jobs; retain only those who have capabilities needed for success in the new environment. • Revise sales force training and establish mechanisms for best practice sharing. • Develop a suite of technology products to assist salespeople in their interactions with customers. • Revamp goal setting and performance management systems to reinforce the new selling model.	• Salespeople find the new sales approach to be more strategic and professional. • Customers believe the new sales approach is more tailored to their needs and priorities. • Sales results are strong following implementation of the new model. United establishes contractual partnerships with many high-priority new accounts and renews contracts with many high-priority existing accounts. • Company leaders feel that the new sales model makes substantial performance contributions worldwide.

The Figure 12.2 examples illustrate how *vision* is often a critical element of successful sales force event response. United Airlines responded successfully to its external challenges by first developing a vision of what its sales force should look like in the new business environment. This enabled the company to create a cohesive implementation plan for aligning sales force systems, processes, and programs around that vision. The financial services company, on the other hand, responded to its external event—the acquisition of multiple smaller companies—without a strong vision of what its ultimate sales organization should look like. Had the financial services company developed such a vision up front, it could have taken steps to move the sales force toward that vision with each new acquisition, which would most likely have created a more favorable long-term outcome.

The Effectiveness Hunt: Constantly Innovating to Improve the Sales Force

The best companies do not limit their focuses on sales force effectiveness to times when major marketplace or company events compel change. Instead, they engage in *ongoing effectiveness hunts* designed to improve aspects of the sales force on a continuous basis. Many successful companies will undertake formal initiatives to improve sales force effectiveness. Novartis, a global healthcare products company, conducts a sales force effectiveness review every year using structured processes and analytic tools to reveal high-priority opportunities to enhance global sales force effectiveness. Some companies have full-time employees who are responsible for improving the competence and productivity of salespeople. At GE a "Director of Commercial Excellence" has responsibility for global sales force effectiveness and is charged with developing consistent frameworks and best practices for GE sales forces and propagating them across the company's numerous businesses.

Companies can get a sense for the extent to which sales force effectiveness improvement can impact the bottom line by comparing the results achieved by top-performing and average-performing salespeople. Top performers— those who have achieved the best results relative to the potential in their territory—demonstrate what level of performance is possible in a sales force. Substantial improvement in sales force effectiveness can be made by investing in sales force programs, systems, and processes that enable average salespeople to learn from the best salespeople and as a result, increase the average sales force performance level.

At Novartis, as part of the sales force effectiveness review process, sales leaders identified high-performing and average-performing salespeople and then observed salespeople from these two groups on typical sales calls in order to identify how they influenced the customer buying process. Novartis identified a set of success behaviors differentiating top-performing salespeople and incorporated these behaviors into a training program for the sales organization. The company also implemented new coaching tools and realigned the performance management process to reflect the success behaviors. Salespeople who had been trained and coached to emulate the behaviors of top performers had a more favorable perception among their customers. A survey asked customers to select the best industry salesperson that they interacted with; the results showed that the company's salespeople who had completed the training were selected 46 percent of the time, compared to only 22 percent of the time for salespeople who did not complete the training. The customer's preference was also linked to better sales results.

Sales leaders at other companies have implemented various sales force changes aimed at propagating the behaviors of top performers. Companies have changed hiring profiles so that job candidates are screened for characteristics and skills discovered among their best salespeople. Others have shared data and tools developed by the company's best performers throughout the sales force. The corporate commercial excellence group at GE recommends that as a "best practice," all GE businesses should use the performance of top-performing salespeople as a benchmark for setting goals for all salespeople, thereby challenging everyone to strive to be the best they can be.

We have seen opportunities to improve sales force effectiveness at hundreds of companies around the world. Consider a few examples.

- A chemical company conducted an assessment of its sales management team by asking salespeople to complete 360-degree evaluations of their managers on important competencies, such as leadership, communication, and coaching. The company discovered that approximately 40 percent of its sales managers were rated "below expectations." Realizing that in time, an ineffective sales manager brings down the performance in all of the territories that he or she manages, the company initiated a serious effort to upgrade the quality of its sales management team.
- At an insurance company, more than 60 percent of new salespeople left the company before completing their first year of employment. For years while the market was growing, this high level of sales force turnover was an expected part of the company's successful business model. The company recruited thousands of new salespeople every year, knowing that those who discovered that they were unsuited for the job would leave quickly. Yet as the market became saturated, the model stopped working

well. With less-favorable market opportunity, too many people with good long-term potential were leaving too quickly, and the company's investment in recruiting and training was no longer paying off because not enough people stayed long enough to produce significant results. When the company discovered that salespeople who made their first sale quickly were much more likely to stay than those who struggled for months to make a sale, it launched an effort to improve the early success of new recruits by developing a more targeted profile for screening candidates during the recruiting process and by providing better training, coaching, and account assignments for new salespeople.

- At a pharmaceutical company, analysis revealed that personal sales calls were profitable only for the top 30 percent of physicians who wrote 90 percent of the prescriptions for the types of drugs the company sold. Yet close to half of the sales force's time was spent unprofitably with the bottom 70 percent of physicians. The company launched a major effort to educate the sales force about how to spend its time more effectively and provided each salesperson with data showing how smarter targeting could improve performance.

- Analysis of territory account workload data at a cosmetics company revealed that the majority of sales territories either had too much work for a salesperson to handle effectively (25 percent of territories) or had too little work to keep a salesperson fully busy (32 percent). The company increased sales force effectiveness and customer coverage significantly by reassigning undercovered profitable accounts from high-workload territories to salespeople who had time to call on them.

A Framework for Understanding and Improving Sales Force Effectiveness

Discovering ways to enhance sales force effectiveness starts with understanding the various components and linkages that explain how a sales force influences company results. At the beginning of a course that we teach at Northwestern University's Kellogg School and other venues, entitled "Accelerating Sales Force Performance," we ask the sales leaders in attendance a simple question: "How do you know when you have a successful sales force?" Their answers, both spontaneous and reflective, span a wide range of topics. Figure 12.3 provides some typical responses to our question, organized around several dimensions of sales force effectiveness that link logically to one another. Sales leaders tell us that in a successful sales force, *salespeople* with strong skills,

Figure 12.3

How Sales Leaders Describe a Successful Sales Force: The Dimension of Sales Force Effectiveness

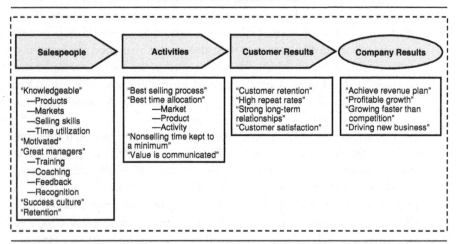

capabilities, values, and motivations engage in the right kinds of *activity* to drive *customer results*, and customer results ultimately impact *company results*.

Sales leaders can make sales forces more effective through their decisions, and through the various processes, systems, and programs that they are responsible for. We call these the *sales effectiveness drivers*. As shown in Figure 12.4, the sales effectiveness drivers form the root of the chain of components that link salespeople to company results. Sales leaders can build an excellent sales force by doing an excellent job of managing the sales effectiveness drivers.

Sales Effectiveness Drivers

The sales effectiveness drivers are organized into five categories, with Figure 12.4 providing several examples of drivers for each category. The categories affect the sales organization in different ways, as described here. The drivers listed within each category are defined and discussed in more detail later in the chapter (see Figures 12.11–12.15).

Definer drivers—such as sales force size and structure—*define* the sales organization by specifying the right sales force investment and giving salespeople a straight line of vision by setting up a logical organizational structure with clear roles for salespeople.

Figure 12.4
The Five Categories of Sales Effectiveness Drivers and Their Impacts

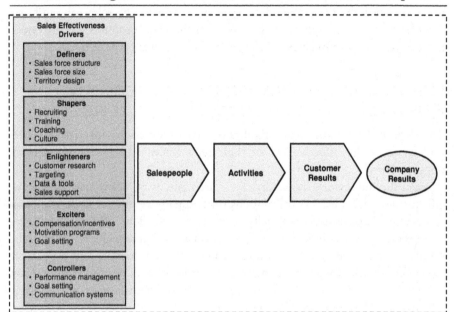

Shaper drivers—such as sales force hiring and training programs—*shape* the members of the sales force by ensuring that everyone has the skills, capabilities, and values needed for success.

Enlightener drivers—such as sales data and tools—*enlighten* the sales force by providing the information salespeople and managers need to understand customers and to be successful.

Exciter drivers—such as sales compensation and incentive programs—generate *excitement* within the sales force by motivating salespeople to work hard and inspiring them to achieve.

Controller drivers—such as sales force performance management systems—*control* and direct sales force activities to ensure that the sales force stays on course to achieve company goals.

Individual sales effectiveness drivers can have influence in multiple ways, yet for simplicity, the framework lists them in the driver category where they generally have the most significant impact. For example, the driver "compensation/incentives" is categorized as an exciter because the right compensation and incentive plan motivates salespeople to work hard to achieve challenging goals. However, compensation and incentives can also have impact as a *shaper* because they help attract the right type of person to the sales job, and as a *controller* because by aligning incentives with the right products or customers, the company communicates to salespeople what it wants them to do.

USING THE FRAMEWORK TO ASSESS AND ENHANCE SALES FORCE EFFECTIVENESS

The Figure 12.4 framework highlights two observations for helping sales leaders assess the effectiveness of their sales forces and find improvement opportunities.

First, the framework shows that there are many ways to evaluate sales force effectiveness. Sales leaders often focus on company results—a sales force that achieves goal consistently is usually considered "excellent." But goal achievement is only a partial indication of how good a sales force really is. Making the numbers is a sign of success, but it can also be a sign of luck. A comprehensive assessment of sales force effectiveness requires looking at multiple dimensions. Sales leaders need to ask questions that focus on each dimension of sales force effectiveness in the Figure 12.4 framework.

- Are our goals being achieved across product lines? (Company results)
- Are our customers' needs being met? (Customer results)
- Are our salespeople engaged in the right activities? (Activities)
- How good are they? (Salespeople)
- Are we implementing best practices with each of the sales effectiveness drivers? (Sales effectiveness drivers)

A second observation evident in the framework is that the roots of an effective sales force are in the sales effectiveness drivers. Excellence in the drivers creates strong salespeople, encourages quality sales activity, and generates strong results. Sales leaders should seek solutions to sales force issues, challenges, and concerns by looking to the decisions, processes, programs, and systems for which they are responsible. By ensuring that all the sales effectiveness drivers are well-managed and are in alignment with company business strategies, sales leaders bring excellence to a sales force.

By guiding a logical and comprehensive decision-making approach, the framework can help companies that face different challenges and opportunities take appropriate action to ensure that their sales forces are as effective as they can be. Four situations when the framework is helpful are described here.

Situation 1: When Events Occur Outside the Sales Force

Events in the industry and environment or within the company often create new challenges or opportunities for sales forces. Sales leaders often tell us that the major issues they face originate outside of the sales force—for example, *customers* are changing their buying processes, *competitors* are becoming more aggressive, an economic downturn has created a less-favorable *environment*, or a new *company strategy* has shifted the company's product portfolio and target market emphasis. The framework helps sales leaders assess the impact that these types of events have on the sales force so they can determine what sales effectiveness driver adjustments are required to keep the sales force on a track to success.

Figure 12.5 shows a decision-making process for determining what sales effectiveness driver adjustments are needed to help a sales force adapt successfully to external and company events.

Situation 2: When Specific Sales Force Issues Emerge

The best sales leaders are constantly on the prowl for loose nuts and bolts. They often find specific issues or concerns that reside within the dimensions

Figure 12.5
A Decision-Making Process for Adapting a Sales Force to Major Events

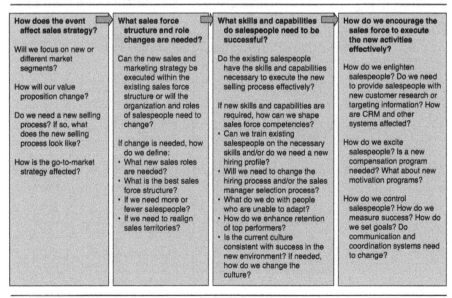

How does the event affect sales strategy?	What sales force structure and role changes are needed?	What skills and capabilities do salespeople need to be successful?	How do we encourage the sales force to execute the new activities effectively?
Will we focus on new or different market segments?	Can the new sales and marketing strategy be executed within the existing sales force structure or will the organization and roles of salespeople need to change?	Do the existing salespeople have the skills and capabilities necessary to execute the new selling process effectively?	How do we enlighten salespeople? Do we need to provide salespeople with new customer research or targeting information? How are CRM and other systems affected?
How will our value proposition change?		If new skills and capabilities are required, how can we shape sales force competencies?	
Do we need a new selling process? If so, what does the new selling process look like?	If change is needed, how do we define:	• Can we train existing salespeople on the necessary skills and/or do we need a new hiring profile?	How do we excite salespeople? Is a new compensation program needed? What about new motivation programs?
How is the go-to-market strategy affected?	• What new sales roles are needed?	• Will we need to change the hiring process and/or the sales manager selection process?	
	• What is the best sales force structure?	• What do we do with people who are unable to adapt?	How do we control salespeople? How do we measure success? How do we set goals? Do communication and coordination systems need to change?
	• If we need more or fewer salespeople?	• How do we enhance retention of top performers?	
	• If we need to realign sales territories?	• Is the current culture consistent with success in the new environment? If needed, how do we change the culture?	

of sales force effectiveness shown in Figure 12.3. For example, they may observe that *salespeople* have grown complacent; there is too little sales *activity* focused on important customers; or that the sales force is not achieving the desired *customer* or *company results*. As sales force issues like these emerge, the framework suggests a diagnosis path that traces the causes of concerns back to the root sales effectiveness drivers, revealing what modifications are needed to create the best solutions.

The Diagnostic Process Figure 12.6 shows, step by step, how one company diagnosed a specific sales force concern—"salespeople are not devoting enough time to new business development"—by linking the cause of the problem back to remedial sales effectiveness drivers. These drivers are defined and discussed in more detail later in the chapter (see Figures 12.11–15).

The diagnostic process involved asking a series of questions that led to identification of probable causes and ultimately solutions. The questions used to

Figure 12.6
A Process for Diagnosing Sales Force Concerns Illustrated
with an Example

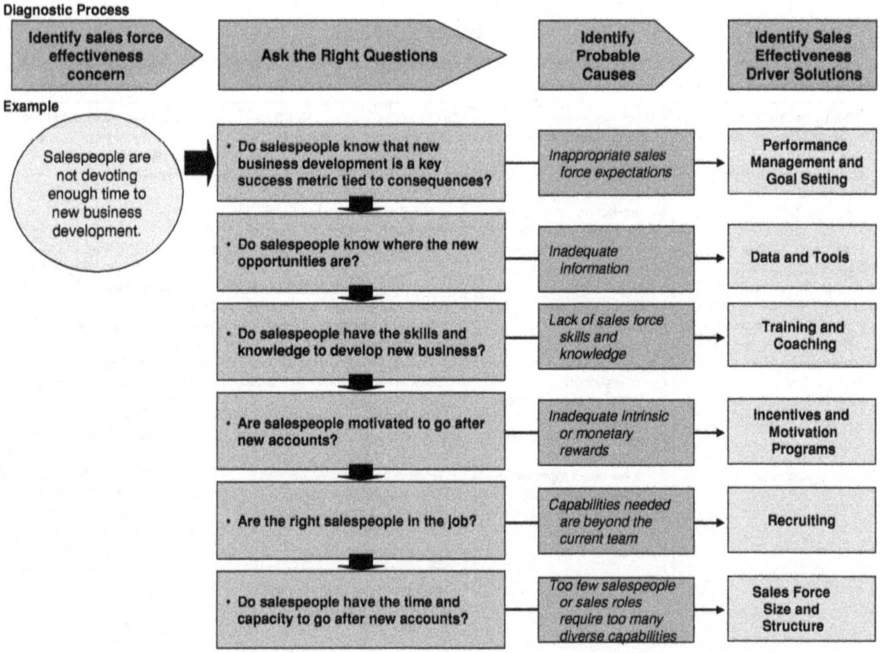

diagnose this particular concern can be adapted to address the variety of challenges faced by sales forces. The questions are sequenced so that those asked first link to sales effectiveness drivers that are easier to change. For example, adjustments to performance management processes, goals, and data and tools can generally be made fairly quickly and without significant disruption to the sales force. The questions near the bottom of Figure 12.6 lead to sales effectiveness drivers that are more challenging to change—the recruiting program and the size and the structure of the sales force. Because these drivers determine the people in the sales force and the assignment of customer responsibility, changing them is generally more disruptive, is harder to implement, and will take longer to have an impact. Some companies will have considerable success effecting change by leveraging the easier-to-change sales effectiveness drivers. Others will have to rely on the harder-to-change sales effectiveness drivers to create an effective solution. Solutions to the most difficult sales force challenges typically involve adjustments to multiple sales effectiveness drivers.

Situation 3: When Companies Want to Boost Effectiveness

Often sales leaders simply want the sales force to get better and need to identify the best ways to go about making improvements. Several diagnostic tools can reveal high-impact effectiveness enhancement opportunities. By analyzing historical data that reflect territory activity, opportunity, and results, sales leaders can gain insights into how well the various sales effectiveness drivers are performing. Benchmarking against competitors and keeping up with industry best practices also can help companies discover opportunities to increase sales force effectiveness.

Using Performance Frontier Analysis to Identify Top Performers   A powerful way for companies to reveal ways to improve sales force effectiveness is to observe the traits and activities of the best performers in their own sales forces (see the Novartis example earlier in the chapter). It's not always obvious how to identify who these "best performers" are. Traditional ways of measuring performance—using sales manager input and territory rankings on metrics such as sales and quota-attainment—do not always provide a complete picture, because they may not sufficiently separate the sales impact of territory factors (such as market potential, market growth, or competitive intensity) from the sales impact of a salesperson's ability and hard work. Many sales forces (including Novartis) have used an analytic tool called *performance frontier analysis* to enhance traditional methods of identifying top performers. Performance frontier analysis (see example in Figure 12.7), looks at historical territory-level

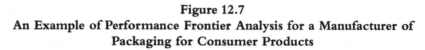

Figure 12.7
An Example of Performance Frontier Analysis for a Manufacturer of Packaging for Consumer Products

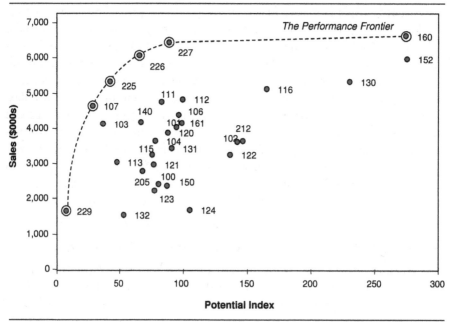

data and isolates the impact of the salesperson on territory performance metrics (in this case, sales) by controlling for territory differences (in this case, in market potential).

Each dot in Figure 12.7 represents a sales territory. Territory potential is expressed as an index (100 represents the average territory) and is based on a combination of account-specific estimates provided by salespeople and business demographic data. The best-performing territories are those with the highest sales relative to their potential.

The dotted curve connecting the best-performing territories at the top of the plot represents the performance frontier—in other words, the sales that can be achieved for territories with different amounts of potential. This level of performance is possible because someone in the sales force has achieved it. Top-performing salespeople include those who are on or close to the performance frontier curve. Sales leaders can compare the traits and behaviors of salespeople in this group to those of others in the sales force, revealing what characteristics and actions of individual salespeople lead to sales success.

They can trace the source of these traits and behaviors back to the root sales effectiveness drivers, revealing what sales force changes are needed to propagate success characteristics and actions across the entire sales force.

Using a Performance Scorecard to Identify Sales Effectiveness Driver Improvement Priorities When diagnosis reveals a large list of sales effectiveness drivers that are candidates for improvement, companies typically get the best results by prioritizing the drivers and focusing improvement efforts on a small number of the most important ones first. A performance scorecard, such as the example provided in Figure 12.8, is a useful tool for assessing sales force effectiveness and prioritizing initiatives based on their likely impact.

The scorecard profiles each sales effectiveness driver in terms of two measures: *performance* and *strategic impact*. A performance score reflects how competent or capable a selling organization is at maximizing each sales effectiveness driver. Companies can derive performance scores using data analysis, benchmarking, and the input of company leaders or other experts. In addition,

Figure 12.8

Example of a Sales Force Performance Scorecard for the Swiss Division of a Health-Care Company

the lists of important driver *best practices* provided later in this chapter (Figures 12.11–12.15) are a useful tool for assessing performance of many of the key sales force effectiveness drivers. Strategic impact measures the importance of a sales effectiveness driver on an organization's ability to succeed. Most companies rely on management judgment and/or outside experts to derive strategic impact scores.

The performance scorecard provides a snapshot of an organization's performance and the strategic impact of the sales effectiveness drivers at a particular point in time.

The position of each driver on the scorecard suggests an action. A driver with low strategic impact but high performance, such as sales force size in the example, can be maintained at current levels. Sales effectiveness drivers with high strategic impact and high performance, such as motivation programs, need to be monitored closely to ensure that their performance stays high. Drivers with low strategic impact and low performance, such as indirect marketing support, can be monitored to see whether their impact increases over time. Sales effectiveness drivers with low performance and high strategic impact, such as training, sales manager development, targeting, and sales force tools, present the greatest opportunity for effectiveness gains and as such could be top priorities for sales leaders.

The performance scorecard is specific to a company and its condition at the time the assessment is conducted. Sales effectiveness drivers move to the right as the sales force's performance improves and to the left as performance slips (usually when changes in the environment render current practices less effective or when sales leaders and individual salespeople fail to maintain high performance standards). Drivers move up or down as their strategic impact changes due to modifications in environmental conditions and company strategy. Sales leaders gain particular insight when they conduct assessments on a regular basis and track changes over time.

Situation 4: When Companies Identify an Issue or Concern within a Specific Sales Effectiveness Driver

Quite often, sales leaders focus on single-driver solutions for their effectiveness enhancement initiatives—for example, "our *territory alignment* needs to change: large differences in territory potential are creating unfairness in the sales force," "the sales force needs more accurate and timely *information:* there are too many gaps due to IT problems," or "morale is low because our *goal-setting process* results in unfair sales targets." Yet we have observed that most difficult sales challenges require multiple sales effectiveness driver solutions. Often, sales leaders turn to drivers that are highly visible (such as compensation), nonthreatening (such as training), or that offer new hope (such as CRM), while overlooking sales effectiveness drivers that are less obvious and more difficult to change, such as culture, leadership, and recruiting. The thinking framework described in this chapter links sales force issues and concerns with potential solutions.

IMPROVING THE SALES EFFECTIVENESS DRIVERS

Once sales leaders have identified which sales effectiveness drivers need renewal, they need to take action to change and improve the problematic drivers. In order to have the desired impact on salespeople and their activities, sales effectiveness driver decisions need to align closely with a company's *sales strategy*. Here, we describe the key elements of a sales strategy, and then provide advice on how to get maximum impact from a sales force by aligning each of the categories of sales effectiveness drivers with that strategy. Additional frameworks and insights on these topics are provided in Zoltners, Sinha, and Lorimer (2009).

In order for a company to achieve excellence in its sales effectiveness drivers, it needs a cohesive and well-communicated *sales strategy* that aligns sales force goals with company goals. As Figure 12.9 shows, the sales strategy creates an important link between a company's business strategy, goals, and objectives and the sales force.

A good sales strategy includes three critical components. First, it defines target *market segments* and specifies which segments the company will serve with personal selling (and which it will serve with other selling channels). Second, it specifies what *value proposition* needs to be delivered to each segment. Third, it defines the best *selling process* for delivering the value proposition, including

Figure 12.9
Linking Company Business Strategy to Sales Force Activity and Results

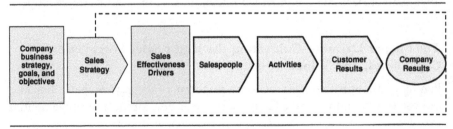

Figure 12.10

Some Important Best Practices for Developing an Excellent Sales Strategy

Best Practices

| Sales Strategy Design and Implementation

A plan for who the company's customers are, what the value proposition is, and how the selling is done. | 1. Marketing and sales develop a sales strategy jointly using a defined business process.
2. Meaningful, actionable customer segments are defined and a product/service offering is tailored based on the needs of each segment.
3. A sales process for each customer segment is developed that aligns with the value proposition strategy and mirrors the customer buying process.
4. The company selects selling channels to deliver the sales process to different market segments based on effectiveness and cost.
5. The sales force communicates compelling value propositions to each customer segment, specifying the benefits and economic worth customers will realize relative to alternatives. |

the role of personal selling in executing the sales process for each segment. Sales and marketing teams work together to develop sales strategy decisions, continually fine-tuning them through market segmentation, customer offering and value proposition development, and sales process refinement.

In an excellent sales force, all of the sales effectiveness drivers reinforce the company's sales strategy. Figure 12.10 provides a list of some important *best practices* that companies can use to determine how effective they are at developing an excellent sales strategy.

The Definer Drivers: Setting Up the Right Organizational Structure

Definer decisions should be consistent with and reinforce a company's sales strategy, and generally need to be made before decisions in the other categories of sales effectiveness drivers. Figure 12.11 provides a list of some important *best practices* that companies can use to determine how effective they are at developing and implementing excellent decisions for several key sales force definer drivers. Additional frameworks and insights for making good sales force definer decisions are provided in Zoltners, Sinha, and Lorimer (2004).

The Shaper Drivers—Cultivating the Right Sales Force Skills, Capabilities, and Values

Figure 12.12 provides a list of some important *best practices* that companies can use to determine how effective they are at developing and implementing excellent decisions for several key sales force shaper drivers.

Figure 12.11
Some Important Best Practices for Sales Force Definer Decisions

Best Practices

Sales Force Structure

The definition of sales roles (generalist vs. specialist) and sales force reporting relationships.

1. The company uses sales specialists (market, product, or sales activity) when the complexity of the selling process requires greater capability and skill than a generalist salesperson can acquire.
2. The sales force structure is both efficient and effective and also considers fit with corporate strategy and manageability of the structure.
3. Large strategic accounts receive special attention.
4. The company clearly defines each sales role and specifies the knowledge, skills, and competencies most critical for success in the role.
5. The company defines sales force reporting relationships for clear accountability.
6. The sales force structure adapts to evolving business needs.

Sales Force Size and Resource Allocation

The number of salespeople and how they divide their time between customer segments, products, and selling activities.

1. The company understands how the sales force should spend its time across activities, customer types, and products and can estimate the effort required to execute the sales process for different customer segments.
2. The company can estimate the incremental sales that will result with different levels of sales force effort for different customer segments, including carryover sales (e.g., sales that result in future years due to current year efforts).
3. The company makes sales force sizing and allocation decisions based on analysis that considers opportunity and impact of sales coverage.
4. The company considers risk and uncertainty inherent in the business environment when making sales force sizing decisions.
5. The company considers performance across the portfolio of opportunities when making resource allocation decisions, and is not biased by the individual interests of particular product, market, or regional teams.

Sales Territory Design

The assignment of responsibility for customers and prospects to salespeople and teams.

1. The company designs sales territories to match customer coverage needs to the capacity of the salesperson or team assigned to cover each territory.
2. Territory and region boundaries are set based on business criteria (workload, potential, and travel) and not on the needs of specific individuals.
3. The sales force uses a formal, centralized process to evaluate territory design changes while incorporating sales manager input to address local market needs.
4. The sales force audits territory design every 1–2 years and conducts a full evaluation when a major event (such as a new product launch) affects territory workload and potential.
5. Efficient alignment tools are used to derive and maintain very good alignments.
6. The company has a specific transition plan for managing any disruption to salesperson-customer relationships that occurs when the territory design changes.

Figure 12.12
Some Important Best Practices for Sales Force Shaper Decisions

Best Practices

Recruiting

The process of profiling sales jobs, and finding, selecting, and attracting the best talent for the sales force.

1. The company has defined the objectives of the sales job and has an up-to-date job description and ideal candidate profile for each sales role.
2. The company develops a high-quality pool of applicants using multiple sources (referrals, campus recruiting, internal placements, etc.) and tracks results by source so it can continuously improve the applicant pool.
3. The evaluation and selection process includes behavioral interviews and/or ability testing that checks for the behaviors candidates need to succeed.
4. The evaluation and selection team includes strong sales managers who are trained on interviewing skills.
5. The recruiting team looks for the personal characteristics that lead to job success, understanding that experience alone is a poor predictor.
6. Sales managers recruit constantly, maintaining a list of potential recruits to expedite the hiring process in case of unplanned vacancies. Warm-body hiring is avoided.
7. The company has a formal attraction program designed to convince the best candidates who have been extended offers to join the company.

Training and Coaching

Instructional programs and manager guidance to help salespeople acquire and improve the skills and knowledge needed for success.

1. Training and coaching programs focus on critical competencies that are required to execute the sales process successfully.
2. Training programs are effective (have high impact on critical competencies) yet are efficient (minimize the time salespeople spend away from customers), using a mix of classroom, on-the-job, and self-taught learning methods.
3. The company blends classroom training with continuous reinforcement of learning through coaching, information support, and performance management processes.
4. Particularly when the environment is changing, the company encourages salespeople to be responsible for their own learning and provides mechanisms for sharing knowledge with others.

Culture

The unwritten set of rules, values, and norms that guide salespeople's choices and behaviors.

1. The company has defined an appropriate "ideal sales culture" that aligns with customer needs, treats salespeople with respect, and reinforces company objectives and strategies.
2. There is strong culture consensus within the sales force—salespeople make consistent choices about how to behave when they face specific dilemmas.
3. The culture has intensity. Corporate slogans and mission statements are more than words—salespeople live them with passion and use them routinely to guide choices.
4. Sales leaders continuously communicate ideal culture choices to the sales force, reward appropriate behaviors, and ensure that their actions are consistent with their words.
5. Sales leaders serve as role models for the sales force; there is a clear connection between leaders' stated values and their actions.
6. All the sales effectiveness drivers are clearly aligned to reinforce the ideal sales culture.
7. The company periodically conducts sales force surveys to evaluate the sales culture. If gaps exist between the current and ideal culture, it takes steps to bring things in line once again (such as conducting workshops with sales managers to discuss and resolve culture gaps).

Figure 12.13
Some Important Best Practices for Sales Force Enlightener Decisions

Best Practices

Targeting, Data, and Tools	1. Sales systems are designed to assist and enhance sales force work processes; they are not just instruments of control for sales managers.
The management of customer information and tools that help the sales force plan its time and be more effective with customers.	2. Sales reports and tools help salespeople and managers assess and improve performance by providing only essential information in a visual, customized, and relatively simple format.
	3. The sales force has good data measuring account and/or territory potential and uses it to improve goal setting, targeting, performance management, and sales force deployment.
	4. The company segments customers according to their potential and their needs, and provides salespeople with data and guidance enabling them to tailor the offering and sales process appropriately for each segment.

The Enlightener Drivers—Providing the Information Salespeople Need to Be Successful

Figure 12.13 provides a list of some important *best practices* that companies can use to determine how effective they are at developing and implementing excellent decisions for some sales force enlightener drivers.

The Exciter Drivers—Motivating Salespeople to Achieve

Figure 12.14 provides a list of some important *best practices* that companies can use to determine how effective they are at developing and implementing excellent decisions for two key sales force exciter drivers. Additional frameworks and insights for making good sales force definer exciter decisions are provided in Zoltners, Sinha, and Lorimer (2006).

The Controller Drivers—Keeping the Sales Force on Course

Figure 12.15 provides a list of some important *best practices* that companies can use to determine how effective they are at developing and implementing excellent decisions for several key sales force controller drivers.

SUMMARY

Sales forces have high impact on both revenues and costs, yet managing a sales force successfully is a significant challenge for any company. An excellent sales force has talented *salespeople* who engage in the right *activities* to meet

Figure 12.14
Some Important Best Practices for Sales Force Exciter Decisions

	Best Practices
Compensation and Incentives *The way that the sales force is paid including both salary and performance-based incentives (bonuses and commissions).*	1. The company defines a target income range for each sales role that is competitive with similar roles at other firms. 2. The amount of variable pay is greater for sales roles that have a greater impact on short-term sales. 3. The sales incentive plan pays for performance by meaningfully differentiating payouts between top and bottom performers. 4. The sales incentive plan encourages sales activities that are consistent with the company's strategy and aligned with the desired sales culture. 5. The plan is simple enough that salespeople understand how their performance impacts their pay and can easily explain the plan to others.
Motivation Programs *Programs that inspire salespeople to work hard and achieve by providing rewards and recognition (outside of the regular compensation plan).*	1. Sales force motivation programs are varied, appealing to a diverse range of individual needs. For example, the company offers sales contests and spiffs that appeal to salespeople's need for *achievement*, sales meetings that appeal to their need for *social affiliation*, and recognitions such as President's Club that appeal to their need for *ego gratification*. 2. All motivation programs align with the desired sales culture.

customer needs and drive *company results*. The best way to create, maintain, and continuously improve an excellent sales force is to ensure that the company decisions, processes, programs, and systems that affect salespeople—the *sales effectiveness drivers*—are well-managed and in alignment with company business strategies.

Andris A. Zoltners is the Nemmers Professor of Marketing at the Kellogg School of Management at Northwestern University. He is a founder and co-chairman of ZS Associates, a global business consulting firm with 1,500 people across 20 offices in North America, Europe, and Asia. He is the co-author of four books on sales force management including Building a Winning Sales Force (2009) and The Complete Guide to Accelerating Sales Force Performance (2001). He received his BS from the University of Miami, his MS from Purdue University, and his MSIA and PhD from Carnegie-Mellon University.

Prabhakant Sinha was a faculty member in the Marketing Department of the Kellogg School of Management from 1983 to 1987 and currently teaches in

Figure 12.15
Some Important Best Practices for Sales Force Controller Decisions

Best Practices

Performance Management

A processes for keeping performance on track by setting objectives, developing action plans, measuring performance, and implementing consequences.

1. The company provides a framework for managers to use when evaluating salespeople based on a consistent classification system and/or sales force competency model.

2. The sales force has a defined performance management process that creates goals and plans for salespeople, measures their performance relative to goals, and provides appropriate rewards or corrective consequences.

3. Sales managers meet regularly with salespeople to provide ongoing feedback, coaching and guidance, periodic progress reviews, and/or annual performance reviews.

4. Performance evaluation recognizes differences in territory potential, so that salespeople are rewarded for their hard work and not for having a good territory.

Goal Setting

Processes for establishing territory-level goals for sales, growth, or other results metrics.

1. The company consistently sets goals for the sales force that are challenging, attainable, and fair.

2. The company sets accurate national sales goals, using structured data-based analysis as well as input from both marketing and sales. It does not set excessive stretch goals that can lead to low sales force morale.

3. The company allocates national goals to the territory level using data-based analysis of territory trends and market potential, as well as input from sales managers.

4. The company has a plan for what to do with sales incentive pay if, as a result of market uncertainties, it sets sales goals significantly higher or lower than they should be.

5. In markets with high uncertainty, sales goals have short time frames and/or specify reasonable ranges of performance, rather than single numbers.

executive education programs on sales force effectiveness at the Kellogg School of Management and the Indian School of Business. He is a founder and co-chairman of ZS Associates, a global business consulting firm with 1,500 people across 20 offices in North America, Europe, and Asia. He is the co-author of four books on sales force management including Building a Winning Sales Force (2009) and The Complete Guide to Sales Force Incentive Compensation (2006). He received a Bachelor of Technology from I.I.T. Kharagpur and his PhD from the University of Massachusetts.

Sally E. Lorimer is a consultant and business writer. She was previously a principal at ZS Associates, where she consulted with numerous companies on sales force effectiveness. She is the co-author of three books on sales force management including Building a Winning Sales Force (2009) and Sales Force Design for Strategic Advantage (2004). She received her BBA from the University of Michigan and her MBA from the Kellogg School of Management at Northwestern University.

NOTES

1. Zoltners, Andris A., Prabhakat Sinha, and Sally E. Lorimer (2009), *Building a Winning Sales Force: Powerful Strategies for Driving High Performance*, New York: Amacon.
2. IAB—Interactive Advertising Bureau (2009), "US Advertising Spending: The New Reality," (May), available at: http://www.iab.net/insights_research/530422/1675/804370.
3. Anonymous, (2009), "America's 500 Largest Sales Forces," *Selling Power*, (October), 51–68.

ADDITIONAL RESOURCES

Zoltners, Andris A., Prabhakant Sinha, and Sally E. Lorimer (2004), *Sales Force Design for Strategic Advantage*, New York: Palgrave Macmillan.
Zoltners, Andris A., Prabhakant Sinha, and Sally E. Lorimer (2006), *The Complete Guide to Sales Force Incentive Compensation: How to Design Plans That Work*, New York: Amacon.

PERSPECTIVES ON CONTEMPORARY ISSUES IN MARKETING

CHAPTER 13

MARKETING TO CONSUMERS AT THE BOTTOM OF THE PYRAMID

BOBBY J. CALDER, RICHARD KOLSKY, and
MARIA FLORES LETELIER

INTRODUCTION

The traditional goal of marketing is to stimulate consumer demand and/or to shift it from one company's product to another. From this perspective, low-income consumers, and especially the so-called bottom-of-the-pyramid (BOP) poor, are of little interest. There is no point in marketing to people who cannot feasibly pay for our product or our competitor's.

It might seem that the problem of poverty is not a marketing problem but a social problem. In a capitalistic economic system, the fact is that some people are marginalized. According to the World Bank, more than 3 billion people live on less than $2.50 a day.[1] In the past, more than a billion people have survived on less than $1.25 a day and the latest global economic downturn could add upward of 90 million people to this number.[2] The problem is compounded in that, with the extreme poverty of many rural areas around the world, the poor migrate to urban slums where they are unprepared to participate in economic activities. The population of the world has fairly recently changed from a mostly rural one to a mostly urban one, and most of this change has occurred in the poorer countries. Poverty prevents these urban poor from even participating in markets that provide basic necessities such as housing.

Whereas in rural communities there exist social practices that help people cope, in urban slums there is only the catch-22 option of the markets that offer transactional relationships in which the poor cannot participate. Thus, in the case of housing, the urban poor often reside on plots of land for which they cannot demonstrate proper legal documentation (which itself in some countries might require many years to resolve). Most of this population lacks bank accounts and credit histories. Mortgage loans are out of the question. People are forced to construct piecemeal housing on their own, leading to overcrowding and a deep sense of despair. And, with inadequate housing, children become entrapped in a cycle of poverty, unable to study in crowded, unlit rooms and living in blighted communities surrounded by the dangers and lures of crime.

Poverty is no doubt a social problem. That said, it is also a marketing problem and an opportunity. To contrast the two views, before addressing marketing to the BOP, we provide a background sketch of how companies currently approach issues like poverty as social problems rather than as marketing opportunities.

CORPORATE SOCIAL RESPONSIBILITY AND RELATED APPROACHES

Companies increasingly respond to social problems such as poverty through Corporate Social Responsibility (CSR) programs. Although CSR programs can take myriad forms, they have in common the effort to spend money to do good. One way to do this is to fund charities. Another is to avoid or ameliorate harmful practices (e.g., avoiding child labor).

More recently, CSR programs have begun to address problems more directly and in ways that benefit others and the company itself. The mantra of this trend seems to be "making money by doing good." It is based on the idea popularized in 2002 by C. K. Prahalad that the private sector could alleviate global poverty by approaching CSR as an opportunity and embedding it in their business operations.[3] In effect, the ideal is to create a double bottom line. So a milk producer in India might solve its supply problems by building village collection centers that draw on small farmers who each may have only one or two head of cattle. The company gets a large-scale supply chain and at the same time benefits millions of small farmers who could not otherwise have sold their milk in this way.[4] Once the company has earned the trust of the farmers, it can then help them to improve the health of their cattle and boost their milk production, which in turn gives the company a better quality product and larger supply of milk.

In 2006 Porter and Kramer added to this approach by calling for more strategic CSR efforts.[5] Their idea was that companies can gain a competitive advantage by analyzing how they are affected by social problems and then designing programs that address these problems. They cite the example of Toyota faced with the problem of automobile emissions. By investing in the hybrid-engine technology of the Prius, Toyota was able to lower emissions and attain a technological lead over other companies that in the end could be very profitable.

However, there are many critics of CSR, because corporate charity funds are limited and needs limitless. Critics contend that social problems can be more effectively addressed by governments or NGOs than by individual companies. Critics point out that even at the governmental level there are many problems with charitable aid. Much of it is wasted through inefficiency and corruption, and aid may breed dependency. Another criticism is that with strategic CSR, if CSR is good business, companies would be doing it anyway. So there is nothing special about CSR.

Against this backdrop, there is increasing interest in "social entrepreneurship" as exemplified by Bill Gates and the Gates Foundation. The idea is to invest in disruptive technologies or social enterprises that actually solve problems like malaria.

An early well-known example of social entrepreneurship is the work of Muhumad Yunus and the Grameen Bank. Since 1983 the bank has been extending credit to people living in rural poverty, first in Bangladesh and then in Africa and Latin America. Grameen makes its borrowers bank members and achieves higher repayment rates than most banks receive for collateralized loans. The recipients, mainly women, normally use the loans to finance small businesses, such as producing handicrafts or homemade cheese. This work has created a model for raising living standards through microfinance institutions (MFIs).

A typical example is Desarrollos Agropecuarios Bravo, producer of branded organic products Aires de Campo. Founded in 2002, the company began with organic lettuce, spinach, and arugula, and now produces a wide variety of organic foods across Mexico by employing people in the local communities in which they operate. MFIs come in different forms—for profit, nonprofit, and hybrid—but the main purpose is to encourage the start of small businesses that will lead to higher incomes and contribute to living standards. This model has been praised for making low-interest loans available to the poor, but some MFIs such as Compartemos in Mexico have been criticized for making money for their investors through high interest rates.

In recent years, social entrepreneurship has often been coupled with social investing. For example, the Acumen Fund is a venture capital operation that accepts below-market returns to start initiatives like maternal health-care facilities in India or a company in Tanzanian making anti-malaria bed nets. It often lends capital to a partner. The Skoll Foundation, the Schwab Foundation for

Social Entrepreneurship, and Ashoka are other examples of organizations that encourage and praise this type of social entrepreneurship.

Thus, the current lay of the land for how companies approach social problems such as poverty is this: Corporate social responsibility has expanded, at least in theory, to be more strategic. The idea is to turn social problems that affect a company into opportunities. By solving a social problem, the firm gains increased advantage in the marketplace and profit potential while at the same time doing good. Ideally CSR becomes integrated into the business as a sort of broadened outlook and heightened sensitivity that informs ordinary decision making. It is a matter of being on the lookout for social problems that are adversely affecting the company but that might be turned to the company's advantage in technology, supply chain, distribution, or some other area. Otherwise social problems are better left to the public sector or to social entrepreneurs that can develop specific technological or financial innovations to solve problems, albeit typically (and perhaps hopefully) at below-market returns.

In this chapter we examine how a company can integrate CSR into its business in a way that informs decision making, specifically in the area of marketing. We believe that focusing on consumers at the bottom of the pyramid can lead a company to develop new competencies in marketing.

BEYOND SOCIAL RESPONSIBILITY: PATRIMONIO HOY

By treating social problems as marketing problems, companies can truly begin to integrate CSR into their businesses. The question then becomes, "How do you market to the bottom-of-the-pyramid consumer, who is often marginalized by companies and not addressed by traditional marketing?" To design marketing strategies for these consumers, we must take a fresh look at the way we think about marketing strategy.

A recent CSR initiative provides a good illustration of how to rethink marketing to these consumers. The Patrimonio Hoy program of CEMEX, one of the largest cement companies in the world, was developed more than a decade ago to assist with housing for the urban poor of Mexico. We have been involved since its inception (one of us [ML] was one of the leading developers of the original concept). Our thinking about marketing to BOP consumers has evolved from this experience, and we will use Patrimonio Hoy here to illustrate our thinking. Following, we provide relevant background information about Patrimonio Hoy and describe the lessons learned. Lessons learned, in its original military sense, means that we often learn more from struggling to get things right than from when things go well. There are always many causes for success, and often luck is one of them. At different points in its history Patrimonio Hoy has tried different approaches and no doubt will do so in the future. This case is far from one stock textbook example; it is a rich source of lessons learned.

The original concept of Patrimonio Hoy is described at length in C. K. Prahalad's book, *The Fortune at the Bottom of the Pyramid* (2004), and updated by Israel Moreno Barcelo, general manager of the initiative, in the latest edition of the book (2009). At the same time it is held up as an innovative case of CSR, it is also cited as a successful business case that illustrates designing channels of distribution around added value service outputs such as financing (see Chapter 11, "Marketing Channel Design and Management").

In 1998, led by Fancisco Garza Zambrano, CEMEX set out to address the auto-construction ("do-it-yourself") segment of the cement market in Mexico. The segment lives in urban slums and is more than 40 percent of the population. These consumers account for 30 percent to 40 percent of cement consumption but could consume more.

At the outset, a team of CEMEX employees and consultants immersed themselves for more than a year in the urban slum of Mesa Colorada in the state of Jalisco, where they converted a tortilla shop into a "garden" (pilot) office. The goal was to understand this segment of consumers and to learn how to market cement and other building materials to them. Previous efforts had met with failure. The company had originally tried to market smaller-than-normal bags of cement to this segment in order to offer a more affordable product. This failed because it was not suited to the population's construction practice of accumulating materials over time. Consumers were building rooms for their houses, not doing small projects.

CEMEX realized that it needed to rethink marketing to this segment based on insight into how people were living and how they thought about construction.[6] Thus, the team signed up a small group of local people to help them conduct a number of learning experiments that they monitored for the year.

Most accounts of the Patrimonio Hoy story focus on the financing challenge faced by people living in slum conditions. People do not have enough money saved at any one time to construct even one room. Most will purchase small amounts of materials and collect these over time. Much of the time the materials will spoil. They are also vulnerable to theft when left outside. If people could have access to credit, so the thinking goes, then they could purchase all of the materials they need to construct a room all at once. Although there is truth in this logic (and merit in microfinancing), it is not the most valuable takeaway from the Patrimonio Hoy story.

In-depth qualitative interviews and ethnographies (see Chapter 3, "Marketing Research and Understanding Consumers") revealed that the main barrier to building homes in this area was not financing but the inability to save money over time to collect all of the materials required to build a room. It was found that even when these consumers came into larger sums of money (such as year-end bonuses), they spent these funds either on unforeseen emergencies (such as health care), items required for festive celebrations, or consumables that provided immediate gratification. As one Patrimonio Hoy participant put it:

> When you have the money in your hand, you spend it. I would think about whether to spend on cement or beer, and beer was much more satisfying than a bag of cement standing out in front of my home, and the bag of cement would make me work yet the beer did not. So the money would be spent.[7]

One manifestation of the inability of these consumers to commit to saving over time is the practice of *tandas*. *Tandas* are a communal savings/credit mechanism where a group of people, usually 10, join together for some determined amount of time and pool their money. Weekly, each *tanda* member contributes a designated amount, such as 100 pesos, which one person would receive each week according to a lottery or an internal agreement about who is most deserving. The major insight was that although people did receive large sums through a *tanda*, most of the time the money was already spent on unforeseen "emergencies" or goods before receiving it. On the surface the *tanda* might appear to be a savings tool, but in effect it was a spending tool for immediate gratification.

Lesson No. 1: The Strategy Must Address Social Values

The team was determined to explore the insight around the *tanda* further. So the team members conducted an experiment with 50 families (and then later with more than 200) where instead of receiving money from a *tanda*, the families would receive the right to construction materials. If they extended the *tanda* for a longer period of time, they could accumulate the amount of material needed to construct a basic room.

From the experiment, the team learned that the major barrier to housing construction is that people have difficulty in not only committing their spending to a determined objective, they have difficulty committing to a future that requires being consistent in any way. The marketing lesson learned was that the strategy had to do more than motivate the consumer to accumulate building materials in a more productive way. It had to do even more than emphasize the goal of having better housing. The strategy also needed to take into account that the traditional social values of the BOP poor are different from other consumers.

The social values of these consumers emerged from the experiment.[7] Participants confessed that they would rather not tempt fate by making long-term commitments that required planning. They were unsure about how long any current employment would last and therefore feared the burden of major expenses. Worse, when people had some sort of family emergency that required them to take off from work, they lacked the practices for renegotiating their time off, preferring to leave the employer without any word and then dealing with the consequences of unemployment later. This lack of commitment resulted in a typical home taking up to 25 years to build and a room taking anywhere between three and seven years, depending on whether the consumer had a mason in the family. The team learned from the experiment that a major challenge was to get people to commit to enough *tanda* cycles, because this required planning for the future. This represented a conflict with traditional values, a conflict that needed to be bridged before the goal of accumulating materials and having better housing would seem relevant.

From this garden experiment, CEMEX learned that it needed to create a program that would focus people on the goal of building their homes without completely adopting a planning perspective. Rather than emphasizing the construction material *tandas*, the team determined to organize around building patrimony, or the handing down of the home to one's children. The ethnographic immersion revealed that people viewed their homes as patrimony. Selling a home implied failure; the goal was to construct a home that would be passed down to one's children. Patrimony created a bridge to the future that minimized the conflict with planning.

No one had ever offered patrimony to people in the urban slums before. In Mexico, patrimonial banking refers to private banking, a service reserved for the wealthy. The idea of a complete room, let alone a complete home, felt like a far-off illusion to these consumers. There was an overwhelming sense of resignation that this was an admirable goal, but just a pipe dream. It did not seem like something that could really happen, even in their imaginations.

To engage these consumers, CEMEX adopted the theme "Patrimony Today" to focus people on the goal of building their home as patrimony, something they could think about in the future and envisage by taking concrete measurable steps *today*. The company promoted the idea of a home as something long-lasting, consisting of durable materials such as block, concrete, and cement, rather than wood and aluminum, cardboard, or corrugated sheet metal, which were common materials used in urban slums. The key was to get people to commit to the goal in a way that would be consistent with their values. Once they committed, the program allowed them to build a room in 70 weeks, three times faster than the average building time.

CEMEX today continues to experiment with new ways to keep people focused on the goal of building their homes as patrimony. One major challenge for the program is getting people to continue building more rooms once they have built a single room. Inevitably consumers' traditional values conflict with this longer-term perspective. Only about 38 percent of members go on to build another room once they have completed the first. To incent consumers to build more rooms, CEMEX has introduced an upgraded offer for those who have a good record with the program. *Patrimonio Hoy Te Impulsa* allows certain members to receive materials earlier in three installments before a customer is done making payments. The idea is to get members to feel like they are being rewarded for having established an impeccable payment record so that they are motivated to continue building faster.

CEMEX has also begun to offer financing for building with a mason as part of its program, a service that could accelerate construction significantly for the 55 percent of families who do not have a mason in the family. Still, it has been difficult to increase the number of consumers returning to build multiple rooms. The patrimony strategy of making construction more consistent with a future perspective has not been able to fully overcome this. The company must find new strategies that more strongly bridge the conflicting values of fate versus planning. Overcoming the resignation of the poor with their present circumstances is the key.

Lesson No. 2: The Strategy Must Produce a New Consumer

The urban BOP often lives in extended families but in many ways are socially isolated. Certainly they do not typically engage in transactional exchanges based on the rights and responsibilities of both parties. Hierarchical client-sponsor relationships are the norm. Even within their communities, peer-to-peer relationships are often weakened by suspicion and distrust. And even within household units, communal-style living may not encourage strong families. The lesson is that marketing strategies need to overcome this isolation by creating social links. The socially isolated consumer cannot see a product as relevant to someone like himself.

Early on, Patrimonio Hoy formulated a strategy that would generate social support around the product in order to negate the adverse effects of social isolation. The company began by establishing transactional relationships between Partimonio Hoy staff and consumers. For example, an interactive sales process was instituted that would generate conversations about people's challenges and goals for constructing their home. CEMEX sales representatives drew people to local offices or to a community gathering place, where they held a 90-minute discussion regarding the challenges of building a home. Potential members were asked how many rooms they had already built, how long it took to build them, what the difficulties in building were, and whether they had joined *tandas* with the intent of building. The discussion went on until there was a public declaration of a commitment to the goal of building one room. These meetings provided much-needed social support, as people began to recognize all the barriers to building that they had experienced. They also listened to testimonials of those who had built and heard the aspirations that came along with building. These initial forums turned out to be crucial for activating people's desire to build.

Out of this early experience with interactive selling, the second major lesson of Patrimonio Hoy began to emerge. Rather than approaching the BOP directly as individual consumers, it would be better to market to them as social units and through social linkages, both existing and created. So CEMEX structured the program as a club with membership dues, instead of incorporating a service fee into the materials price. (The garden experiment revealed that pricing the services into the material made participants focus on the materials rather than on all the steps required to build their homes.) Participants were asked pay weekly membership dues (around 15 percent of the total paid) to receive the benefits of building faster. They would pay another weekly fee that would go toward paying for the materials they needed for the room.

CEMEX recognized the communal nature of the low-income group. The club membership system reflected how important group interactions were to making progress. Members felt obligated to save weekly with the knowledge that if they did not contribute, other members would be affected. In earlier versions of the materials *tanda*, another member would not receive his allotment for that week if a member failed to pay. At a later point CEMEX aggregated members into larger units so that members would motivate each other and be responsible for the other members.

The team designed social links that would keep people focused on the long-term goal via links to specific CEMEX support individuals. Thus, members would have access to a technical advisor that would help them envision what their home could potentially look like in the context of the room being built. About 45 percent of the population already had a mason in the family, but they still lacked a plan for building. It is common for the do-it-yourselfer to build in an ad hoc way, as needs arise. Within the community, the team observed many half-built rooms that had been abandoned as people found that they no longer wanted the room in that particular place. Or, there were rooms that had to be taken down because they were getting in the way of a second floor or some other needed infrastructure. The technical advisor's role was designed to guide people in their thinking about the room they were building. How does it fit in with other rooms they might want to build in the future? Do they envision their children getting married and settling down on the same lot of land? Based on the conversation, the technical advisor provided a design of the room. Moreover, the advisor could break down the list of materials in terms of the steps required to build the room. The materials for building the floor, the walls, and the roof were bundled together, giving people a path to building their room.

Consumers were also linked to a contract manager who would explain the mutual responsibilities of the company and club members. Club members committed to regular payments. In return, Patrimonio Hoy committed to freezing material prices during the 70-week time frame so that people could plan their spending accordingly without the threat of inflation. In addition, home delivery would allow them to receive the large quantities of material needed for building at one time. Finally, although a person had the right to receive a lot of materials at any time after the fifth week during the process, they could opt for a voucher for storage of materials. When they were ready to build, they could exchange their vouchers for materials. These transactional relationships based on mutual promises were a new form of interaction for the consumer and facilitated new norms of behavior.

Besides these transactional relationships, Patrimonio Hoy forces participants to take social responsibility when they become members. It is uncommon in low-income communities for people to sign contracts that detail their responsibilities. Small print is distrusted, and people fear detailed paperwork. Still, CEMEX knew that participants needed to understand the commitment they were making and the consequences involved. When the formal initiation into the program occurs, participants begin to understand that their home will only be built if they take on the role of producers. They must sign a simple document that details their responsibilities and the program's responsibilities. In some cases, participants describe having conversations with family members about who will take on another job to contribute to the home. This is also reflected in relationships within the family as illustrated by the consumer quotes below.[8]

My kids did not want to continue their education; we only had one room. They had just finished junior high and they decided they did not want to go on. When they saw that the house was growing and that they could have a space for themselves, they decided that they wanted to continue with their education. (Guadalajara, 2007)

My son now has a personal computer, which was not possible before because the space is limited and everyone has things to do. My husband gets up at 6 A.M. to go to work and my girls are watching TV, or they are listening to music. It is not possible to study when we are all in one room. (Morelia, 2007)

My daughter is always with her books now; she is the one who most uses the new room, because the TV is always on over here. (Morelia 2007)

The goal is to build linkages between the company and consumers, linkages among the extended family, and linkages with other consumers. In this way CEMEX also engaged the participation of its own members to recruit new members. These members, or *promotoras* (mostly women from the community) went through a training course where they learned not only about the company's products, but were also introduced to the value of working for themselves. They acted as ambassadors for building with Patrimonio Hoy, motivating others in the community to build while simultaneously earning an income. *Promotoras* were paid a commission based on the number of members they recruited and on the retention of those members in the program. They were taught how to create an identity for themselves in the community.

Another way CEMEX increased community linkages was through engaging its local dealers with consumers. Patrimonio Hoy worked with CEMEX's distribution network, but it managed the relationship with dealers directly. Rather than pushing the materials through the distributors to members, Patrimonio Hoy changed the structure of the relationship by creating demand for its dealers through purchasing the program's building materials from local dealers. The dealer takes a lower margin but in return receives a steady flow of demand for building materials, including higher-margin building materials. By participating in Patrimonio Hoy, dealers doubled their sales volume and came to value their relationship with members.

These activities indicate how Patrimonio Hoy has sought not only to sell building materials in a better way but also to allow BOP consumers to function better as consumers and as a community.

Lesson No. 3: The Strategy Must Be High Level

Patrimonio Hoy could be viewed as a marketing strategy for reaching a separate segment of consumers of construction materials. Or it could be operated as a stand-alone business with its own marketing strategy. It has become increasingly apparent, however, that a broader strategic view is desirable. This is because a program like Patrimonio Hoy inevitably faces high transaction costs. With 84 offices, each with contract managers and technical advisors and *promotoras*, it is difficult to demonstrate short-term ROI. For this reason, CEMEX has recently scaled back the number of Patrimonio Hoy offices because they no longer "break even" to CEMEX, and the company has also limited the number of employees in other offices. However, this unfortunately limits the impact of the program. We estimate that Patrimonio Hoy presently serves 40,000 families a year, less than 0.4 percent of the number of families in the urban poor auto-construction segment.

A broader perspective is needed. Viewing Patrimonio Hoy as a market segmentation or stand-alone business marketing strategy does not take into account the total return to the CEMEX brand across segments. Historically local CEMEX brands such as *Cemento Tolteca* and *Cemento Monterrey* have struggled to avoid being categorized as a commodity product and to differentiate themselves from competitors. But marketing research indicated that the local cement brands were rated much higher after the launch of Patrimonio Hoy. Positive word-of-mouth communication spread from the target segment to make customers in other segments more favorable toward the brand.

The company could also realize an added return through market development. This has already been demonstrated. In a previous initiative when members signed up for Patrimonio Hoy, a representative asked them to choose one of three participating schools to sponsor. With each payment, the school accumulated points that were redeemed twice a year for building materials. The objectives of the program were not only to build trust and credibility for Patrimonio Hoy but also to increase demand for building materials. Similar efforts have focused on road construction in communities and helped CEMEX increase sales in the road construction market.

Truly developing low-income markets from scratch is a long-term journey, filled with continuous experimentation and learning. The payoff evolves slowly as consumers learn and spread the word, as the local economy is stimulated, and as scale and experience drive down the costs. Certainly this was the case with Patrimonio Hoy. The lesson learned was that the program must be considered a higher-level business-driven marketing strategy focused on long-term market development and total returns to the business as a whole. If regarded only as marketing segmentation or stand-alone business marketing strategy, it would be chronically underfunded and evaluated too narrowly.

From a more limited marketing-segmentation or stand-alone business perspective, Patrimonio Hoy might not even get credit for the product profit on the incremental cement volume from the segment. CEMEX lacks good metrics on the incremental impact of the program. Similarly, CEMEX has yet to track the impact of the goodwill created by Patrimonio Hoy on the product brands.

The learning we take is that Patrimonio Hoy, and programs like it, should be viewed as high-level, business-driven marketing strategies—and that this has organizational implications. We believe that these programs ordinarily should be managed at the level of corporate marketing rather than product marketing. In terms of organizational structure, Patrimonio Hoy should not report to product marketing but to the corporate level at CEMEX Mexico. This also means that it should not be compartmentalized as CSR.

APPLYING THESE LESSONS MORE BROADLY

The lessons learned from Patrimonio Hoy point up several implications for thinking differently about marketing strategy when targeting bottom-of-the-pyramid consumers. We contrast these differences with conventional ways of thinking about marketing strategy.

From Benefit Laddering to Bridging Social Values

Marketing strategies are fundamentally about making products more mean-ingful to consumers. With conventional approaches to strategy, marketers seek to relate key attributes or features of the product to clear consumer benefits where these benefits satisfy important consumer goals. This meaning is spelled out in a brand positioning statement that is the foundation of the strategy (see Chapter 4, "Developing a Compelling Brand Positioning," and Chapter 16, "Brand-Led Innovation"). The core logic is often referred to as "laddering." An attribute of the product that is highly important to the consumer is identi-fied. In the case of a detergent such as Procter & Gamble's Tide, the attribute might be ingredients that remove dirt. The benefit could be getting clothes as clean as possible ("Dirt can't hide from intensified Tide"). Or a higher benefit might be cleanliness as a substitute for buying new styles of clothing ("Style is option. Clean is not"). A good strategy, conventionally, ladders up to a higher goal associated with more of an emotional response.

Recently Kotler and Lee in *Up and Out of Poverty* (2009) have advocated that marketing strategies targeting the poor should be based on a brand positioning statement in the same way that strategies are for products like Tide.[9] They cite as an example NetMark's marketing of treated sleeping nets for malaria prevention in Africa. The strategy was to position the nets according to the following brand positioning statement:

> We want *mothers* to see insecticide-treated nets (ITNs) as the best way to protect their families from malaria and a better choice than untreated nets, because these nets actually kill mosquitoes. (p. 195)

Note that the attribute "treated" is laddered up to "actually killing mosquitoes" and the greater protection for the family that this provides.

Certainly, marketing to the BOP poor by using brand positioning statements that reflect laddered benefits is a good idea. This represents the application of conventional marketing thinking to marketing to the BOP. The lesson learned from Patrimonio Hoy, however, is that conventional thinking may not be sufficient. Recall that the benefit of constructing a new room was clear to consumers, but this was not enough in itself to cause them to embrace the Patrimonio Hoy program. It was also necessary to overcome the consumer resignation produced by its traditional social values.

BOP consumers may see the benefit of a goal linked to a product and still not believe that that goal is realistic or makes sense for them. The reason is that goals are interpreted in terms of social values. Ordinarily, marketers seek to ladder up to goals that are aligned with prevailing social values. Culture is taken as a given. With BOP consumers, however, culture can be different.

Specifically, the marketer must be attuned to what the philosopher Charles Taylor described as an orienting value. An orienting value is not value in the economic sense. It is a cultural prescription as to what constitutes a worthwhile life. It is a sense of what is estimable. The opposite of an orienting value is inappropriate or even contemptible.

An orienting value for the consumers targeted by Patrimonio Hoy was their sense that life is determined by fate and that planning is not only impossible but an invitation to disaster. They lived in a festive community in which people's status was defined for life at birth. Fate or God determines outcomes, as do patrons and authorities. Attempting to change or overcome one's situation arouses envy and distrust. Planning for any length of time is therefore arrogant. Getting ahead of others represents a lack of respect for others. Instead, respect is attained by participation in family and community festivals. People spend much of their income on things like coming-of-age parties for girls, baptisms, and religious ceremonies. Against the backdrop of this orienting value, consumers could see the benefit of a program for receiving materials more efficiently to build a room in a much shorter time, but they could not see that it was appropriate for them. For them it was culturally inappropriate and to some extent shameful.

Sometimes orienting goals may be so culturally strong as to be virtually intransigent, as with the voodoo religion in Haiti and its emphasis on fate and the futility of planning. However, consumers often hold conflicting orienting values, with strong traditional values in conflict with emerging values. Such was the case with the consumers targeted by Patrimonio Hoy. These consumers lived in a larger society where they were exposed to others who valued getting ahead. Though this conflicted with their stronger traditional values, they nonetheless experienced some tension between the two. The tension arising from value conflicts creates the possibility for change.

The best way to think about using value conflicts to introduce change or new behavior is the notion of bridge practices. If we can find a way to bridge conflicting values in a way that reduces the conflict, consumers will be receptive to change. At Patrimonio Hoy, the idea of patrimony was used to bridge the competing values of accepting fate and rejecting planning versus moving ahead. This was an effective bridge because it was the one way that consumers already thought about the future. It was culturally acceptable to think about the future not in terms of personal advancement or material possessions but in terms of patrimony—doing something for one's family. Moreover, although patrimony spoke to the future, it also was something that could be done in the present. Building only resulted in a room or house in the future. Creating patrimony was something that resulted from what you did today. Hence, the Patrimonio Hoy bridge culturally legitimized the benefit of receiving building materials more efficiently and the goal of a room in the future.

Ultimately helplessness and resignation is the unique challenge of marketing to the BOP. To motivate these consumers, we must not only ladder up from benefits to goals, but also help them overcome their sense of resignation by helping them to recognize a clear bridge to the goal. Metaphorically, we must provide a social bridge that makes it possible and safe to pursue the goal.

Bridging is more than a metaphor. It is a construct that allows us to think about helping the consumer in concrete ways. To underscore the possibilities, recognize that home-building in poor urban communities is, in the parlance of the book *Nudge* (2009), a classic "fraught choice." Consumers, given their orienting values, will quite naturally defer making decisions that involve delayed benefits, are perceived to be very difficult, occur infrequently and involve limited feedback.[10] Therein lies the beauty of Patrimonio Hoy. It provided consumers with a tangible bridge to reach their goals. Patrimony provided immediate gratification, simplified choice, and de-emphasized the obstacles implied by planning.

Our conclusion is that marketing strategies for the BOP should incorporate attempts to bridge conflicting social values as well as benefit laddering in order to create strong brands, especially in cases where strong values prevent recognition or acceptance of benefits and goals. We suspect that value conflicts of the sort described here will be a feature of many efforts to market to the BOP consumer.

From Selling Consumers to Producing Consumers

Marketing strategies conventionally attempt to persuade individuals to believe in the brand benefit by giving them reasons and other supporting information. Salespeople and other consumers may be of strategic importance but they are used as ways of communicating with consumers, conveying messages about the brand benefits. Increasingly, viral marketing efforts are used to influence consumers through word-of-mouth or social media. These channels are essentially used in the same way that paid media is employed for advertising messages. Interactivity is likewise increasingly sought across communication channels.

But marketing to the BOP may require more than this. BOP consumers may feel that they are losing touch with others and becoming more socially isolated as they find themselves moving away from traditional orienting values. Thus, in addition to persuading consumers, we may also need to provide them with social support for their behavior. Letelier and Spinosa (2003) refer to this more broadly as creating and developing "productive consumers."[11] The key idea is that the marketing strategy should allow BOP consumers to transform themselves into consumers who can function better in the social world of a transactional marketplace.

Marketing to the BOP creates new opportunities for them, but in addition to increased isolation, it can lead to resentment. Consumers may lack even the ability to talk about what they are doing. As illustrated with Patrimonio Hoy, this problem is compounded by inexperience with transactional relationships involving dual responsibilities. The marketing strategy must thus seek to "produce" customers as much as sell to them.

We produce BOP customers by interacting with them so that they can better function as transactional consumers. The contract managers of Patrimonio Hoy, for example, were used to teach BOP consumers what it means to enter into a contractual relationship. And salespeople held interactive sessions to get consumers to role-play the experience of moving from being resigned to their present life and lack of housing to committing to building patrimony. Celebrations for consumers who achieved success in the program also helped to substitute for the festive occasions that consumers might have been foregoing.

Ideally, the effort of producing customers can be extended to making the BOP consumer a part of the marketing process. The Patrimonio Hoy program was extended to include training to be a mason as part of the program. The ultimate goal of creating productive consumers is to integrate consumers into their communities better and to strengthen community ties. The school and roads program of Patrimonio Hoy were intended to be not only sales incentives but also community-building efforts in this way.

Thus, the goal of marketing strategy is to create and develop a consumer that can be served better by the company and one that can ideally contribute better to the economic and social capital of the community. The aim is to build productive economic and social capacity.

From Product to Higher-Level Marketing Strategy

A program like Patrimonio Hoy could naturally be viewed as a product segmentation strategy (i.e., how we can sell more cement to the low-income segment of the market in Mexico). Or it could be managed as a small stand-alone business or operating unit with its own product marketing strategy. However, either approach undervalues the program.

There is a better alternative. Marketing is a functional business discipline, and product marketing strategies usually receive the most attention. In fact, most annual marketing plans are product marketing strategies. But an initiative like Patrimonio Hoy demands a broader, higher-level approach. One reason for this is that the program will otherwise be undervalued, but there are two other important reasons that make it even more necessary to distinguish the program from a product marketing strategy.

A second reason lies in complexity. Normally, marketing strategy is viewed in simple terms, such as selling product A to consumer target C, possibly through distribution channel B. This simple ABC view of strategy certainly lends itself to many creative marketing possibilities. But with programs like Patrimonio Hoy, it is important to remember that a more complex ecosystem is in play. As CSR advocates frequently point out, the BOP consumer resides in a complex ecosystem that encompasses many institutions and forces. Housing cannot really be separated from food, nutrition, health care, government, or education. Poverty is multidimensional.

Thus, it follows that marketing must go beyond the ABC approach to strategy to deal with this complexity. Patrimonio Hoy illustrates that this complexity obviously increases the difficulty of the problem faced but that it also increases the opportunity. For example, CEMEX has been able to incorporate housing subsidies from the Mexican government into Patrimonio Hoy. The subsidy money can be used directly to pay for consumer participation in Patrimonio Hoy, which has the potential of creating a more efficient way of getting government housing subsidies to the poor.

By developing Patrimonio Hoy–type marketing strategies around larger ecosystems and partnering with other companies and institutions, it may be possible to generate even more creative strategies. Ideas can arise out of considering such complexity that are more innovative than what a single company might develop on its own, let alone implement. This is all the more reason to approach BOP marketing strategies at a high level.

A third reason for the higher-level strategy approach is related to branding. More and more companies face a particular problem with their entire product line. On one hand they want to offer more and more products and even customize products for smaller segments or even individual consumers. On the other, this proliferation of products runs afoul of business synergy. It is difficult to support all these products with adequate marketing budgets. The result is that the company loses economic leverage in its marketing efforts. To combat this problem, companies are developing high-level branding strategies. These strategies do not call simply for parent brands (or branded houses), where products are held together by a common positioning statement (as with Tide), so that products can be supported as a group. Rather, disparate products are held together more loosely in terms of a shared perceptual essence or similarity (see Chapter 16, "Brand-Led Innovation"). The key to this solution is to create a shared essence for a diverse set of products, each of which has it own distinct brand positioning.

The creation of such brand systems of products linked by a shared essence is an opportunity for linking programs like Patrinomio Hoy to high-level marketing strategy. The programs, and specifically themes like patrimony, could be the basis for associating distinct brands under a larger perceptual umbrella. In the book *Good for Business,* marketing executives Benett, Gobhai, O'Reilly, and Welch argue for just this creation of authentic corporate brands on marketing grounds.[12]

A current example of such branding would be GE's "ecomagination" strategy. GE has created a branding umbrella out of its environmental initiative. Recently it has extended this to "healthymagination," based on an initiative to improve health care through technology. Although this branding is based more on internal initiatives, there is no reason that programs like Patrimonio Hoy cannot be used in the same way for umbrella branding purposes. This is not the same as so-called "cause" marketing efforts, such as P&G's Live, Learn, and Thrive initiative to improve the life of children in need by supporting things like Special Olympics. Cause marketing generally seeks to use CSR to improve corporate reputation. Linking programs like Patrimonio Hoy directly to a high-level branding strategy goes beyond reputation. It speaks to corporate opportunities.

SUMMARY

Perhaps the biggest lesson of Patrimonio Hoy is the need for companies to move beyond CSR and instead learn to market to the poor.

Marketing to the poor requires more expansive thinking about marketing strategy. It requires moving beyond focusing on making product benefits clear and relevant to the goals that consumers are actively pursuing. It requires bridging traditional values that produce resignation about the futility of goals. It requires going beyond selling product to creating consumers who can take a more productive role in a transactional marketplace. And it requires new ways of thinking about marketing strategy at a higher level than the individual product.

In the end, the value of learning to market to the BOP poor may not be just a new source of customers but better marketing in general.

Bobby J. Calder is the Kellstadt Professor of Marketing, and currently the chair of the Marketing Department at the Kellogg School of Management. He is also a professor of journalism in the Medill School of Journalism and a professor of psychology in the Weinberg College of Arts and Sciences at Northwestern University. He has been a consultant to many companies and to government and not-for-profit organizations. His most recent books are Kellogg on Integrated Marketing (John Wiley & Sons, 2003) and Kellogg on Advertising and Media (John Wiley & Sons, 2008). He received his BA, MA and PhD degrees from the University of North Carolina at Chapel Hill.

Rick Kolsky is a lecturer in executive programs at the Kellogg School of Management, Northwestern University. He is also the founder and President of Kolsky & Co., a marketing strategy consulting firm. Rick has worked in the White House and consulted to and taught clients on five continents, in businesses ranging from life insurance to citrus processing to legal services. He received a joint BA-MA in engineering and economics from Brown University and a PhD in economics from Yale.

Maria Flores Letelier is a consultant who specializes in the development of products and services for new markets. She has particular expertise in helping companies understand and enter low-income Mexican markets and the U.S.

Hispanic market. She has also been the Mexican representative for Cheskin, a marketing consulting firm based in California. She received her BA from the University of California at Berkeley and MBA from the Kellogg School of Management, Northwestern University.

NOTES

1. World Bank Development Indicators, 2008.
2. United Nations Millennium Development Goals Report, 2009.
3. Prahalad, C. K. (2009), *The Fortune at the Bottom of the Pyramid,* Upper Saddle River, NJ: Wharton Publishing.
4. Prahalad, C. K., p. 15, see Note 3.
5. Porter, Michael, and Mark Kramer (2006), "Strategy and Society: The Link between Competitive Advantage and Corporate Social Responsibility," *Harvard Business Review* (December).
6. For a discussion of using marketing research to understand social values, see Maria F. Flores Letelier, Charles Spinosa, and Bobby J. Calder (2000), "Taking an Expanded View of Customers' Needs: Qualitative Research for Aiding Innovation," *Marketing Research* 12 (Winter), 4–11.
7. CEMEX internal document (2007), Market research study (August).
8. CEMEX (2007), see Note 7.
9. Kotler, Philip, and Nancy Lee (2009), *Up and Out of Poverty,* Upper Saddle River, NJ: Wharton Publishing.
10. Thaler, Richard H., and Cass R. Sunstein (2009), *Nudge,* 75–82; A Caravan book, www.caravanbooks.org.
11. Leterlier, Maria F, Flores and Charles Spinosa (2003), "Developing Productive Customers in Emerging Markets," *California Management Review* 45 (Summer), 77–103.
12. Benett, Andrew, Cavas Gobhai, Ann O'Reilly, and Greg Welch (2009), *Good for Business: The Rise of the Conscious Corporation,* New York: Palgrave Macmillan.

CHAPTER 14

THE NEW INFLUENCE OF SOCIAL MEDIA

LAKSHMAN KRISHNAMURTHI and SHYAM GOPINATH

INTRODUCTION

The Internet has had a game-changing impact on the practice of marketing, most recently in the form of social media, or consumer-generated media. When the Internet first came about, companies like Dell, which sold computers direct, saw the Internet as a natural and lower-cost extension of their sales efforts and thrived. Other established technology companies like Cisco, IBM, and Microsoft also used the Internet to inform and interact with their business customers. On the other hand, major consumer packaged goods companies, and even some retailers, were poorly represented on the Web at the beginning. Over time, consumer companies realized the power of the Internet as an efficient way to provide information about products, and bricks-and-mortar retailers saw the e-commerce opportunity of the Internet. Along with these developments came the establishment of web sites devoted to consumers who shared their views of products through postings on web forums.

This led directly to blogs, podcasts, Facebook, Twitter, YouTube, and a number of other social networking sites, giving marketers a different problem to deal with. They began to lose control over their marketing to consumers because consumers could interfere with the communication. Dell could promote its products on its web site and in print, but customers who purchased these products now had many web options to share their positive or negative experiences if they chose. This is called *viral marketing* or *social marketing* because the speed at which news travels is astonishing, creating both positive and negative effects for a company's brand, marketing, and communication efforts. This chapter examines the new influence of social media.

SOCIAL MEDIA: AN INCREASINGLY IMPORTANT TOOL

Recently, pizza-maker Domino's was faced with negative publicity when two employees mishandled the preparation of a pizza and posted the video on YouTube. Reportedly it was seen nearly *one million times* within 48 hours after the video was posted. Consider how much money it would have taken to ensure one million viewers through the traditional method of a television ad. It would have cost a lot of money to buy the publicity that Domino's got for free—and at lightning speed—on YouTube. Unfortunately, though, the publicity was negative, and it took Domino's about two days to respond to the negative video. This is the marketer's challenge.

The lesson is that companies need to use all the available 24/7 media at their disposal, including new social media. They must put in place a rapid-response team to address controversies quickly and effectively. Since the incident, Domino's has created Facebook and Twitter accounts and has learned the power of social media in combating adverse publicity. Domino's also learned that the overwhelming majority of viewers of the video were incensed at the perpetrators and sympathized with the company.

The 1982 Tylenol cyanide poisoning incident in Chicago provides an interesting contrast to today's 24/7 media environment. Seven people died after consuming Extra-Strength Tylenol capsules that had been contaminated with cyanide. Johnson & Johnson (J&J), the maker of Tylenol, warned consumers across the country through the major media available at the time—television and newspapers. The company also issued a $100 million nationwide recall of all Tylenol products, even though only the capsule form was contaminated. In addition, the company offered to exchange all capsule Tylenol products for solid tablets. This incident led to the development of tamper-resistant medicine bottles. J&J did not have the Internet to communicate with consumers; it relied on the standard communications tools of the day. But the company responded swiftly and aggressively to assure the public that it was looking after their interests, and the brand did not suffer a fatal blow, as some worried it might. If the same incident were to occur today, J&J would immediately turn to YouTube for posting videos and employ its blog, Facebook page, and Twitter accounts, then supplement the exposure with television and print advertising. The company now has the ability to respond quickly and comprehensively to consumers' concerns and issues of interest in all media.

Dell is another widespread and effective user of social media. In 2006, Dell launched a major initiative to listen to what consumers and key influencers were saying about Dell in the blogosphere, as well as to interact with customers in whichever channels the customers chose. Tools like Google Alerts can help a company track what people are saying and where they are saying it. There were multiple parties talking about Dell, so the company chose to engage with these parties; otherwise the message is shaped by what these parties are saying. Dell is on Facebook and Twitter and is active on Yahoo!Answers, where customers ask questions about a variety of topics, including technology and Dell computers. Dell started a web site called Ideastorm (www.ideastorm.com), which solicits ideas from customers regarding current and new products and encourages feedback, innovation, and dialogue. The concept behind it, called "crowd-sourcing," harnesses the power of a large number of customers in generating new ideas. The community can also either promote or demote the ideas posted. According to Dell's web site, the customer community had contributed more than 12,000 ideas by 2009, and the company has implemented 372 of them.

In a webinar titled, "How Dell is Integrating Social Media into our Business," Liana Frey, Director of Communities and Conversation at Dell, noted that social interaction with customers has had a positive impact on the company's tech support forum because customers can answer questions posted by other customers. The accepted solutions are green-lighted by the person who posed the question if it is helpful. Frey also noted that this customer interaction has saved Dell money.[1]

Just as Dell has found success with customers answering other customers' technical questions, so has Intuit. Intuit owns and monitors a forum called Intuit's QuickBooks Live community, where users can ask and field questions. It is reported that a significant number of the questions are answered by users themselves, and in some cases better than Intuit's own tech support staff. The company claims that this social interaction saves them money.[2]

It is no longer a question of whether companies should participate in social media. Most companies cannot afford *not* to. The question is in what form. Social media is more than Facebook and Twitter. There are also a large number of third-party web forums, blogs, podcasts, and wikis that are distinct from company-run or -sponsored activities but have a substantial following. All of these inputs can impact companies, both positively and negatively. In addition, companies in different industries might utilize the media in different ways.

For example, financial service companies (such as commercial banks, credit card companies, insurance companies) can leverage social media through participation in discussion forums, where people can ask and answer questions on topical issues of the day, such as credit card fraud and interest-only mortgages.

Or they can take the form of blogs maintained by company experts who can post as well as comment on other blogs. The companies can also monitor social buzz so that they can respond quickly and effectively. For example, 2008 and 2009 saw the reputation of many finance companies shredded because of the financial meltdown. It would be prudent for savvy financial companies to learn how to bolster their presence on social media sites to build their reputations.

In the automotive industry, Toyota is recognized as an innovative user of social media. For example, iCrossing, a U.K.-based digital marketing company, was instrumental in building awareness of the iQ City Car from Toyota. iCrossing used activities such as "The Hypermiling Campaign" that generated excitement among the online community.[3] Toyota's iQ blogging site (www.toyota.co.uk/iqblog) saw an explosive increase in the incoming traffic by more than 212 percent. This enabled Toyota to reach new audiences because of positive coverage by three key social media channels—influential blog postings, Twitter, and Flickr.

On a different front, Toyota integrated its online newsroom with YouTube, Flickr, and Twitter. This allowed easy access for the online community to activities, images, videos, and other material related to Toyota. Building on this already high level of exposure, Toyota's online newsroom allowed password-free live online viewing of the simulcast of the unveiling of the 2010 Prius at the Detroit Auto Show.[4]

The realization of the importance of consumer-generated media is not specific to the automotive industry. In electronics, Best Buy uses Twitter to promote its items, and Research in Motion has a popular BlackBerry page on Facebook with a quarter-million fans. Southwest Airlines is active on Twitter, and so is Comcast. Zappos has a Facebook page to reward fans of the brand with special deals; and JetBlue has used Twitter to promote its $599 "all-you-can-fly-for-a-month" deal.

Social media and viral word-of-mouth also have a major impact on the world of culture, including movie box office sales, plays, and concerts, and gallery openings, all of which have short life spans. Texting and tweeting positive or negative opinions soon after attending an event—or even *during* the event—has an immediate and direct impact that conventional media cannot duplicate. This, of course, does not negate the impact of reviews and ratings by critics and other influential people. Texting and tweeting about shows is currently largely the province of a small, generally youthful segment of the viewing public. Still, research indicates that consumers believe the opinion of people like themselves more than the opinion of the others. The Weinstein Company, producers of the movie *Inglourious Basterds* with Brad Pitt, staged an early screening for people who won tickets via Twitter. They also hosted a Twitter Red Carpet event during the movie's regular premiere, where celebrity "tweeters" walked the carpet. Churches, pastors, and evangelical ministers are testing out Facebook and Twitter with the goal of reaching young people. Even Pope Benedict XVI has his own Facebook page!

The power of social media in shaping public opinion in the political arena is evident. President Barack Obama's campaign used the Internet to great advantage to raise millions of dollars as well as to test campaign ideas and engage in a dialogue with the public. For businesses, blogs provide an up-to-date account of what customers are thinking. For advertisers, customer sentiment on blogs and other networking sites provide a much better read of the immediate impact of the ads than any standard market research day-after recall survey can ever accomplish. Note, however, that the web audience is self-selected, while random samples are sought in good-quality market research; caution is necessary when utilizing self-selected web findings. However, even though the initial sample may have been selected randomly in standard market research, the individuals who respond are not technically random, particularly when a small proportion of the original sample chooses to answer.

CAN THIS MEDIA REALLY HELP COMPANIES BE SUCCESSFUL?

Can social engagement with these new forms of interaction create passionate brand fans that traditional media with its one-way advertising may not be able to? It remains to be seen. As with any new media, there is a lot of early hype, and long-term effects are difficult to measure. Traditional media has done well in building powerful, iconic brands that are decades old and still going strong. Think Ivory soap, Coca-Cola, Nescafé, Vaseline, Mercedes-Benz, Levi's, Harley Davidson, and so on. How will brands like these fare in the rough-and-tumble world of new social media? Will new brands be able to build long lives or will the enormous clutter and noise of the new media landscape lead to short customer attention spans, resulting in the premature death of brands?

Dell has some 20 Twitter accounts managed by Dell personnel. The company is trying to cover every customer touch point. In the short run these touch points will multiply, but it's likely that an equilibrium will emerge. Most of the blogs, forums, wikis, podcasts, and social sites are quite irrelevant. There will always be niche sites, but the main sites will coalesce around those few that begin to dominate.

In fact, sites such as Facebook and MySpace are becoming the default home page for many Internet users, indicating the power of this new media. Facebook users, for example, can interact with Amazon without leaving the site. With e-mail, instant messaging, video-sharing, and ability to post photos, Facebook is a self-contained social community, except that it has 300 million active users and is growing! MySpace also plans to offer e-mail and is a powerful community in its own right. Jeffrey Rayport, founder and chairman of Marketspace and a former Harvard Business School professor, makes some interesting predictions about the future of social networking. He advances the notion that a Facebook user is characterized by social profile—a digital make-up—which can change the way that advertisers spend their money. Rather than buy an ad space on the web, advertisers may choose to buy a certain type of social profile and reach such individuals wherever they show up.[5] This is called *behavioral targeting* and is already being used by advertisers who gather data using cookies on computers to follow a user around and show ads that may be of interest.

However, social media engagement is not for everyone, just like Customer Relationship Management (CRM) is not needed for every company. A company would benefit from CRM if tracking individual-level customer data can be beneficial in addressing customer needs more efficiently and effectively. British grocer Tesco uses customer-level data effectively. Supermarket chains in the United States, on the other hand, do not (many of these chains have "loyalty cards," but the rewards are not customized). Similarly, before a company commits resources to monitor and interact with customers on social networking sites, it must ask some basic questions:

- What information do we currently lack, and how would we use this information if we had it?
- Is this information available via social networking sites such as Facebook and Twitter?
- Is interacting with customers via these media an effective way to communicate the company's message, and are they better than e-mail marketing?
- How do we manage the communication between the company and the social networks?
- Should the company screen Facebook and Twitter postings of company employees?
- How do we measure effectiveness of our social media efforts?
- Do our social media efforts lead to greater awareness? Greater purchase intent? Greater sales? Lower costs? More rapid response to customer inquiries?

A company planning to engage in social media can use the above questions as a checklist to assess how involved it wants to be. It is best to start small and learn as you go along. Once the company solicits feedback from customers it should be prepared to respond, otherwise it risks alienation.

Because social media is a relatively new phenomenon, companies are eager to experiment with it. In some cases there is a natural affinity between a company's products and its customers that can be exploited. Starbucks, for example, can send its Facebook and Twitter followers an e-coupon for a new coffee drink and measure its effectiveness quickly. Dell can do the same for its computers, Apple for specific apps it wants to promote, Zappos for shoes, and so on. In all these cases, effectiveness can be measured. This is simply an e-version of traditional couponing, except the promotion in this case is sent to customers who have some positive affinity with the companies in question, as opposed to a blanket coupon drop. One simply cannot count the number of followers on Facebook or Twitter as a measure of success; it depends on whether this virtual customer base can be motivated to act.

WHAT EARLY RESEARCH SHOWS

Not surprisingly, conclusive research on the impact of new media is still slim. And yet, there is a small body of research to examine. For example, in a study assessing which brands are most engaged with their customers online, Starbucks came out on top, followed by Dell, eBay, Google, and Microsoft. This is rather surprising because Starbucks is not a company with a natural web audience. Eleven marketing channels were examined, including social media, and engagement was measured using several criteria.[6] The analysis shows that companies engaged in six or more channels have higher engagement scores and that companies who include new social media in their mix reach customers more effectively.

Research has shown that reciprocal, meaningful, varied, and evolving relationships can exist between customers and the brands they use.[7] As some consumers have sought out others with similar brand affinities, the concept of a "brand community" has evolved. A "brand community" is a specialized, non–geographically bound group of people that is based on a structured set of social relationships among admirers of a brand.[8] Research on brand communities has shown that these communities can influence the perceptions and actions of its members, speed up the flow of information across the communities, and help members evaluate new products introduced into the market.[9,10] The expanding reach of the Internet is helping to accelerate the growth of these types of communities, particularly online brand communities. For example, *Oraclecommunity.net* is an online site for individuals interested in mainly sharing information about Oracle Corp.'s products. However, the site is more than that. Members can share personal stories, pictures, videos, and birthdays as well. Online brand communities can sometimes be restricted, as in the case of "*Club Nintendo,*" which allows only individuals with a product code to join the online club.[11]

Algesheimr et al. explain how these communities develop.[12] Their research asserts that a customer first develops a relationship with a brand based on product usage, which provides functional and symbolic benefits. This is followed by formation of relationships with brand community members. The nature of the customer-brand relationship influences the customer-customer relationship; that is, his or her interaction with the other members. A key finding from the Algesheimr et al. research is that behavioral intentions (e.g., recommendations, active participation) of the community members are translated into actual behaviors. An important feature of the online forums is that the information that is posted is publicly available. Thus, an individual does not have to post in the forums (i.e., two-way communication is not essential) to get valuable information about a product or a topic.

The focus of online word-of-mouth (OWOM) research has been mainly in the entertainment industry (e.g., movies, TV shows). In the case of the movie industry, a study conducted by Nielsen has shown that consumer-generated OWOM is the second most important source of information for moviegoers.[13] Movie trailers are more important than OWOM, while other box-office demand drivers like star power, genre, critics' reviews, and advertising ranked below OWOM. Yet these latter demand-drivers have been extensively studied in the earlier marketing literature. Now, because of availability of OWOM data, researchers have started to assess its impact both prerelease and postrelease of the movies. This distinction is important, because prerelease OWOM is based on the expectations about the quality of the movie, whereas postrelease OWOM comprises moviegoers' feedback based on actual experiences with the movie.

Although there are some variations regarding which type of OWOM is important, the common finding is that user reviews do play an important part in influencing future moviegoers' decisions to watch the movie. The opening day performance is critical, as it often makes or breaks a movie. However, it must be noted that opening day may not be that critical for sleeper/limited release movies; in other words, movies that are released in a few markets on the opening day, with new sets of markets added in subsequent weeks. The main finding from the Gopinath et al. study is that both blog volume as well as blog valence have a significant impact on box-office performance.[14]

Not surprisingly, urban markets such as New York are more responsive to the volume of the blogging activity, while others such as Tampa are more responsive to studio-initiated advertising. This is one of the few academic studies that makes direct comparison between firm-generated media (e.g., advertising) and consumer-generated media (e.g., blogs).

In a different setting, Godes and Mayzlin sought to understand the impact of forum postings on the ratings of TV shows.[15] They used data from 44 TV shows that premiered in the United States during the 1999 to 2000 season. For viewership data, Nielsen ratings were used, and Usenet newsgroup conversations were used for the OWOM data. They report that both volume (extent of buzz) and entropy (variation in the posts) have an impact on TV ratings.

Chevalier and Mayzlin also examine how the ratings of books on sites such as Amazon.com and barnesandnoble.com affect sales rankings on the two web sites.[16] In Web studies, researchers have also tried to compare the relative impact of positive and negative OWOM. Chevalier and Mayzlin find that negative reviews have a greater impact than positive reviews. In a related study, Shin et al. find that negative buzz leads to price cuts for high-ticket items, whereas positive buzz enables price increases for low-priced items.[17] The adverse impact of negative OWOM has been found in non–web site specific studies as well. For instance, Luo finds that consumer complaints in the airline industry have a detrimental impact on a firm's future stock returns.[18]

Although different measures have been used to quantify OWOM, not much work has been done to understand the nature of these online conversations. However, Gopinath et al. have shown that the impact of OWOM is greatest when the product is relatively new in the market; this high level of impact decreases over time.[19] For a brand with a portfolio of products, this suggests that a greater chunk of the online marketing budget should be allocated to newer products than to the more mature products. The second key finding from the Gopinath study is that attribute-related conversations are more important when the product is new, but conversations related to the emotional aspects take the upper hand once the product reaches the mature stage of its lifecycle. Firms can use this information to develop more effective advertising strategies. The findings suggest a shift in advertising content from highlighting product features in the early stage to emphasizing emotional aspects to build customer engagement in the later stages of the product lifecycle.

Recent research has also focused on the impact of the characteristics of the influencer and the influenced. Forman et al. study how the characteristics of the reviewer influence how community members perceive the review and their purchase decisions.[20] They find that reviews containing self-disclosure are rated more favorably by the community than reviews by anonymous reviewers.

In a movie industry setting, Gopinath et al. find that geographical markets with a greater proportion of the population less than 40 years old respond more to blogs than other markets.[21] This study also finds that the impact is accentuated with the level of broadband penetration and household income in the market. Finally, in the mobile phone industry, Gopinath et al. find that it might be sufficient for firms to track the most vocal posters in order to predict the firm's future performance in terms of sales.[22]

Although academic researchers have not yet investigated all the different forms of consumer-generated media, the depth and rigor of their analyses provide actionable insights for forward-looking firms.

SUMMARY

Social media is changing the way brands and consumers engage with each other. Marketing is now a 24/7/365 activity. It is imperative for companies to evaluate and participate in a wide variety of communication vehicles, from television to print to Web to social media, in order to reach current and prospective customers in all the ways they wish to interact with the company.

From a marketer's point of view, success in the end is measured by sales. High awareness and even preference is not enough if these attributes do not translate to sales. Thus, marketers cannot forget that all the elements of the marketing mix, including price, distribution, and customer service, need to be in place. What these new forms of social media afford is an opportunity to build passion and excitement among current and potential customers, which could give the brand an extra lift. The real measure of loyalty is not just whether a customer buys the same brand most of the time, but whether the customer would recommend the product or buy it under unfavorable circumstances, such as when its price is higher than the competition or when the product is out of stock.

This is the golden age of marketing. Marketing is about creating, communicating, and capturing value. It is about delivering products and services that are consistent with individual customer preferences. The Internet and social media make this one-on-one engagement possible in a unique and all-new way. The winners over the next 10 to 15 years will be companies that use this new media to become good listeners, good engagers, and good closers. Let the future unfold!

Lakshman Krishnamurthi is the Montgomery Ward Distinguished Professor of Marketing at the Kellogg School of Management, Northwestern University. He is the director of the Kellogg on Pricing Strategies and Tactics program at the

James L. Allen Center, and served as chairperson of the Marketing Department for 11 years. He is the co-author with Professor Rakesh Vohra of a forthcoming book, Principles of Pricing: An Analytical Approach. He received his BS in engineering from IIT, Madras, his MBA from LSU, Baton Rouge, Louisiana, and an MS in Statistics as well as his PhD in marketing from Stanford University.

Shyam Gopinath is a doctoral candidate in marketing at the Kellogg School of Management, Northwestern University. His work on consumer-generated content has won him an award and has been featured in BNET and MIT Sloan Management Review. He is an ad-hoc reviewer for Marketing Science, a leading marketing journal. He received his BS from University of Kerala, India. He has MS degrees from IIT Madras and University of Virginia.

NOTES

1. Frey, Liana (2009), "How Dell is Integrating Social Media into our Business," WOMMA webinar (August 27).
2. Jana, Reena (2009), "How Intuit Makes a Social Network Pay," *BusinessWeek* (July 13–20).
3. Jennings, Rebecca, Christine Spivey Overby, and Jennifer Wise (2009), "Case Study: Social Media Helps Toyota Communicate Complex Attributes Of New iQ," *Forrester* (September).
4. Schwartzman, Eric (2009), "Online Newsroom Best Practices with Toyota Social Media Supervisor Scott Deyager," www.ontherecordpodcast.com (May 21).
5. Rayport, Jeffrey (2009), "How Social Networks are Changing Everything," *BusinessWeek* (May 7).
6. Serkin, Tova (2009), "The World's Most Valuable Brands. Who's most engaged?" www.engagementdb.com (October 27). Unfortunately the methodology is not well explained, so it is not clear how engagement is numerically scored.
7. Fournier, Susan (1998), "Consumers and Their Brands: Developing Relationship Theory in Consumer Research," *Journal of Consumer Research,* 24 (4), 343.
8. Muniz, Albert, and Thomas O'Guinn (2001), "Brand Community," *Journal of Consumer Research,* 27 (4), 412–432.
9. Muniz, Albert, and Hope Schau (2005), "Religiosity in the Abandoned Apple Newton Brand Community," *Journal of Consumer Research,* 31, 737–747.
10. Brown, Stephen, Robert Kozinets, and John F. Sherry Jr. (2003), "Teaching Old Brands New Tricks: Retro Branding and the Revival of Brand Meaning," *Journal of Marketing,* 67 (3), 19–33.
11. Dholakia, Utpal, and Silvia Vianello (2009), "The Fans Know Best," *Wall Street Journal,* (August 17).
12. Algesheimer, Rene, Utpal Dholakia, and Andreas Herrmann (2005), "The Social Influence of Brand Community: Evidence from European Car Clubs," *Journal of Marketing,* 69 (3), 19–34.

13. A. C. Nielsen (2007), "American Moviegoing Study."
14. Gopinath, Shyam, Pradeep Chintagunta, and Sriram Venkataraman (2009), "Do Blogs Influence Movie Box-Office Performance?" Working Paper, Kellogg School of Management, Northwestern University.
15. Godes, David, and Dina Mayzlin (2004), "Using Online Conversations to Study Word-of-Mouth Communication," *Marketing Science,* 23 (4), 545–560.
16. Chevalier, Judith, and Dina Mayzlin (2006), "The Effect of Word of Mouth Online: Online Book Reviews," *Journal of Marketing Research,* 43 (3), 345–354.
17. Shin, Hyun, Dominique Hanssens, and Bharat Gajula (2008), "The Impact of Positive vs. Negative Online Buzz on Retail Prices," Working Paper, Anderson School of Management, UCLA.
18. Luo, Xuoeming (2007), "Consumer Negative Voice and Firm-Idiosyncratic Stock Returns," *Journal of Marketing,* 71 (3), 75–88.
19. Gopinath, Shyam, Jacquelyn Thomas, and Lakshman Krishnamurthi (2009), "A Framework for Linking the Dimensions of Online Word of Mouth to Firm Performance," Working Paper, Kellogg School of Management, Northwestern University.
20. Forman, Chris, Anindya Ghose, and Batia Wiesenfeld (2008), "Examining the Relationship between Reviews and Sales: The Role of Reviewer Identity Disclosure in Electronic Markets," *Information Systems Research,* 19 (3), 291–313.
21. Gopinath, Shyam, Pradeep Chintagunta, and Sriram Venkataraman (2009), "Do Blogs Influence Movie Box-Office Performance?" Working Paper, Kellogg School of Management, Northwestern University.
22. Gopinath, Shyam, Jacquelyn Thomas, and Lakshman Krishnamurthi (2009), "A Framework for Linking the Dimensions of Online Word of Mouth to Firm Performance," Working Paper, Kellogg School of Management, Northwestern University.

CHAPTER 15

FROM THE WHEEL TO TWITTER: WHERE DO INNOVATIONS COME FROM?

DAVID GAL

INTRODUCTION

$\mathbf{O}$ne of the most pressing questions managers face today is how to beget innovation in their enterprise. Several factors, including the increasingly global character of competition, the increasingly rapid diffusion of information and technology, and the increasingly professional administration of business, are converging to make the need for innovation ever more salient. Whereas successful new products once ensured companies a lengthy period of relatively uncontested profit, today rapid imitation by competitors means that resting on laurels ensures accelerated profit erosion and obsolescence. Managers are acutely aware of the increasingly Darwinian nature of the marketplace and recognize that the future of their organization depends on their ability to innovate.

As a consequence of the resulting thirst for insights on innovation, hundreds of books and thousands of articles have been written on how managers might foster innovation. Indeed, the number of books and articles issued on the topic appears to be proliferating exponentially. Most tend to focus on a small number of innovative companies, typically those in the technology or design space, such as Google or IDEO. The articles and books attempt to understand how those companies have successfully innovated and to abstract some general lessons on innovation from the experience of the examined companies. Although these insights can often be useful, it is often unclear whether the anecdotal experience of specific companies can be applied to other companies or contexts. For example, Google has been a phenomenal commercial success despite the lack of an initial revenue or business plan, but it is hard to extrapolate the value of having a business plan solely from Google's experience. It might be that for every company that succeeds without a business plan, many more tend to fail because they lack a business plan, a phenomenon that might not be appreciated from examining a single or small sample of companies.

This chapter examines how managers can foster innovation in the enterprise in a novel way, by abstracting insights from Jared Diamond's sweeping overview and analysis of the history of innovation in his book *Guns, Germs, and Steel*. From this broad historical view of innovation, it is hoped that new insights into innovation in the corporate context will emerge.

INSIGHTS FROM *GUNS, GERMS, AND STEEL*

Guns, Germs, and Steel is a 1997 book by Jared Diamond, a professor of geography and physiology at the University of California–Los Angeles.[1] Diamond's book attempts to provide a high-level historical account of human history from the emergence of agriculture to the modern era, with the main goal of explaining why civilizations thrive or fail. One chapter of the book, "Necessity's Mother," details Diamond's account and analysis of the history of innovation and is particularly pertinent to this chapter.

In "Necessity's Mother," Diamond uses the historical record to challenge much of the conventional wisdom regarding the nature of innovation. Here, we distill some of Diamond's conclusions that are of particular relevance to innovation in a corporate context.

Invention Is the Mother of Necessity

Diamond's most counterintuitive observation is that, in contrast to the conventional wisdom, most major historical inventions were not invented to fulfill a pressing need but instead were developed by tinkerers and hobbyists who developed their inventions due to their own curiosity, rather than with regard to customer demand or profit. Diamond provides the automobile as an illustration. At the time the automobile was invented, horses had been accommodating people's land transport needs for thousands of years, and railroads for several decades. There was no sudden shortage of horses or dissatisfaction with rail transport that precipitated the invention of the automobile. Indeed, from Nikolaus Otto's invention of the gas engine in 1866, it took more than 50 years of improvements by a series of tinkerers and hobbyists followed by improvements by entrepreneurs before widespread adoption of automobiles started to take hold. Many other well-known inventions in history, including the airplane, the computer, the camera, the typewriter, the television, and the Yahoo! Internet search engine, can similarly be credited to the efforts of hobbyists and tinkerers.[2]

Diamond also observes that most inventions find their greatest use for a different purpose than that for which they were originally invented. Diamond provides the example of Thomas Edison's phonograph. When Edison invented the phonograph, he listed 10 potential applications it might serve. Of this list, playing music was ranked lower than preserving the final words of the dying, announcing the time, and recording books for the blind. Initially, Edison concluded that the phonograph had no commercial value. A few years later, however, he found that the phonograph had commercial potential as a business dictation device. Accordingly, when entrepreneurs developed jukeboxes based on the phonograph to play music, Edison was concerned that it would detract from the serious business purpose of the device. Only many years later did Edison finally concede that playing music was indeed the phonograph's major application. Diamond also provides the example of the steam engine, which was initially invented to remove water from coal mines, later used to power cotton mills, and ultimately found its greatest commercial value powering locomotives and steam boats.

Although Diamond focuses mostly on inventions that preceded the twentieth century, examples of inventions finding their greatest commercial value in a different application than that for which they were initially intended are just as abundant in contemporary times. For instance, Viagra was initially developed by Pfizer as a treatment for angina until it was incidentally noted by patients that it improved their erectile dysfunction symptoms and was subsequently developed for that indication.[3] YouTube was created on February 14, 2005, by guys with no Valentine's Day dates who thought the service would be a great video dating site. The founders posted ads on Craigslist hoping to attract video daters to the site. However, soon users co-opted the site to post all manner of videos to share with their friends and with strangers. By July 2006, more than 65,000 videos were being posted to the site per day.[4]

Similarly, Jack Dorsey, one of the inventors of the micro-blogging service Twitter, commented—tongue in cheek—in mid-2009 about the unexpected uses of his invention: "Twitter was intended to be a way for vacant, self-absorbed egotists to share their most banal and idiotic thoughts with anyone pathetic enough to read them. When I heard how Iranians were using my beloved creation for their own means—such as organizing a political movement and informing the outside world of the actions of a repressive regime—I couldn't believe they'd ruined something so beautiful, simple, and absolutely pointless."[5]

Diamond also argues that most major inventions tend to find their greatest uses for applications that did not even exist and were not imagined at the time of the inventions. That is, in contrast to the conventional wisdom, individuals do not realize there exists an application that requires an invention until after it has been invented in the first place (hence the title of Diamond's chapter). To illustrate, Diamond provides the example of gasoline. In the nineteenth century, the middle distillate fraction of petroleum was used in oil lamps, whereas gasoline, the most volatile fraction, was discarded. Only after the invention and adoption of the internal combustion engine was it recognized that this waste product was an optimal fuel for engines. A more recent example is the Internet, whose early predecessor was a U.S. Department of Defense network for linking radar stations.[6] Who would have imagined that the Internet would ultimately be used for downloading music, blogging, social networking, and instantly communicating with people all over the world?

Invention Is Cumulative

Diamond's second major conclusion contradicts the "heroic theory of invention"—the hypothesis that unique "great" inventors and scientists are responsible for generating the most significant advances. In fact, Diamond argues, invention is a cumulative process where most inventions are simply incremental but ultimately important contributions to existing inventions, and that the milieu in which innovations arise is often more important for the genesis of an invention than the specific inventor.

As an illustration, Diamond traces the history of the steam engine, which is typically credited to James Watt in 1769. Diamond documents that Watt's steam engine was an improvement of a similar engine developed by Thomas Newcomen 57 years earlier (of which 100 units had been sold), which itself was inspired by Thomas Savery's 1698 steam engine, in turn inspired by a 1680 design of Denis Papin, who had developed his designs from the ideas of Christiaan Huygens. Likewise, Diamond argues that Edison's "invention" of the incandescent light bulb followed 40 years of other incandescent light bulbs developed by other inventors. Similar histories can be traced for the cotton gin, the airplane, and the telegraph.

Although not discussed by Diamond, it is similarly remarkable to reflect on the many scientific discoveries credited to sole geniuses that were discovered more or less contemporaneously by others. Among these are calculus (Isaac Newton and Gottfried Leibniz),[7] special relativity (Albert Einstein and Henri Poincare),[8] evolution (Charles Darwin and Alfred Russel Wallace),[9] the inverse square law of gravitation (Isaac Newton and Robert Hooke),[10] and the structure of DNA, which many groups were racing to uncover before being preempted by Watson and Crick.[11] These observations truly highlight the verity of a quote famously attributed to Newton: "If I have seen far it is by standing on the shoulders of giants." Ironically, the phrase itself, though indeed used by Newton in a correspondence with Robert Hooke, was in common usage in the seventeenth century and had been used at least 500 years earlier by Bernard of Chartres.[12]

The Diffusion of Innovation

In addition to observing *how* specific inventions arise, Diamond also addresses the question of *where* most innovations within a particular society arise. Diamond's answer is that most inventions used by a society come from other societies: most do not invent the majority of innovations that they use, but instead adopt them from other societies.

For example, the alphabet, the water wheel, tooth gearing, the magnetic compass, the windmill, door locks, pulleys, the rotary quern, and the camera obscura were each invented independently only once or twice in world history in Eurasia, and then diffused across the continent. As an illustration of this phenomenon, Diamond cites the history of the wheel. Evidence shows the first instance of the wheel occurring around 3400 B.C. near the Black Sea, with subsequent appearances over the next several hundred years across all of Eurasia. The single independent origin of the wheel is attested to both by its rapid spread after its initial occurrence (too rapid to be accounted for by independent inventions) and by the fact that all the wheels had the same design, consisting of three wooden boards fastened together.

Thus, diffusion of innovation occurs because innovations that give sufficient advantage to a society are observed and adopted by other societies. Further diffusion occurs when societies that refuse or are unable to adopt the innovation are ultimately replaced by those that have adopted it.

Diamond cites two main means through which innovations diffuse: the first is through the equivalent of detailed blueprints for re-creating an invention, whereas the second is simply through inspiration and models of existing inventions. That is, once a particular innovation is observed, the knowledge of what can be invented and models of how the invention operates can allow other societies to imitate or reverse-engineer those inventions.

In the case of acquiring "blueprints" for an invention, Diamond cites four main contexts in which such transfers are likely to occur. The first is *peaceable trade,* for which he cites the acquisition of transistors by the Japanese from the United States in 1954. The second is *espionage,* for which he cites the appropriation by Arabs of silkworms from Southeast Asia in 552 A.D. The third is *emigration,* for which Diamond cites the displacement of the Huguenots from France in 1685 and the subsequent spread of their clothing manufacturing and glassmaking technologies. The fourth is *war,* for which Diamond cites the defeat of the Chinese by the Arabs at the Battle of Talas River in 751 A.D., after which the Arabs took advantage of Chinese captives who were experts in paper making to develop an indigenous paper-making industry.

IMPLICATIONS FOR CORPORATE INNOVATION

There are several important insights from Diamond's book that can be applied to the understanding of innovation in a corporate setting.

Invention versus Innovation

What can be learned from the observation that most inventions are not invented to fulfill a specific need? Often, the conclusion is that the ultimate commercial value of most inventions cannot be determined *a priori,* and so companies should promote invention without regard to specific commercial applications. Because of the serendipitous nature of invention and discovery, companies often surmise that they should create an environment that allows serendipity to operate by directing resources toward inventions without defined commercial applications.

In many discussions of innovation, the Post-it Note is often cited as a prime example to support this line of thought. The story of the Post-it Note is that a scientist, Spencer Silver, working in 3M's labs in 1968, accidentally discovered a reusable, pressure-sensitive adhesive, which ultimately became the adhesive used in 3M's Post-it Notes.[13] Companies then conclude that because the discovery of the adhesive required serendipity, they should promote open-ended research in order to realize serendipitous discoveries.

However, it can be argued that this conclusion is a false one. The reality is that basic research (or research that is otherwise not directed at a specific application) is much more likely to yield commercial failures than successes, and is thus unlikely to provide a sufficient return on corporate investment. Rather, it is precisely *because* of the unpredictable nature of invention documented by Diamond that commercial rewards tend to flow toward *innovators* rather than *inventors.* An invention refers to a new concept. By contrast, an innovation involves the commercial application of an invention. Inventions are relatively numerous, whereas innovations are relatively rare.

To illustrate this point, the U.S. Patent and Trademark Office issues around 100,000 patents annually, with only a small fraction ultimately leading to successful commercial products.[14] Likewise, university technology licensing offices have drawers filled with unlicensed patents as well as technologies they did not even bother to patent; major research universities consider themselves fortunate if they are able to recoup 5 percent of their research budgets via licensing of their inventions.

It is also the case that successful inventors are often unsuccessful innovators. Consider Bell Lab's inventions of the transistor and UNIX operating system and Xerox PARC's invention of the graphical user interface, Ethernet, and the laser printer; all these inventions were adapted by subsequent innovators who realized most of the profit potential of these inventions.

To understand why this is the case, we return to the example of the gas engine. Otto's gas engine was seven feet tall, heavy, and produced little power, making it not particularly useful for a commercial product. Only after many generations of improvements by hobbyists and tinkerers (who received no commercial benefit from their inventions) did the automobile become refined enough by entrepreneurs to be a useful commercial product that provided a reasonable return on investment. Similar stories can be documented for the early versions of most major innovations.

Unlike hobbyists, tinkerers, government, and university-funded R&D labs, corporations do not have the liberty of spending 50 years to develop a technology that does not have clear commercial potential. This lesson has been internalized by many large corporations, such as General Electric (GE), where corporate R&D once managed autonomous projects but where projects are now required to be funded by specific business units.[15]

Because inventions that ultimately lead to useful innovations are rare, relatively unpredictable, and developed cumulatively over long periods of time, the focus of corporations needs to be on *innovation*: that is, on the translation of existing inventions to *specific commercial applications*. This does not mean companies should not invent, but emphasis should be placed on improving existing inventions for a particular application; that is, for innovation.

Indeed, the serendipitous discovery of the adhesive that gave birth to the Post-it Note serves to illustrate this point well. Despite its promotion by its inventor, Spencer Silver, development of the adhesive did not proceed until another 3M researcher, Art Fry, recognized an application for the adhesive six years later. After the application was identified, it took several more years of research, development, and refinement before the Post-it Note product was successfully launched.[16] Thus, it was the *innovative application* of an invention, rather than the invention itself, that was the major factor behind the commercial success of the Post-it Note.

Anticipating Customer Needs

Assuming we accept that companies should put emphasis on innovation rather than invention, *how* should corporations focus on innovation? From the observations that most inventions ultimately find their greatest use in applications they were not invented for, and that most of these applications themselves arise only after the inventions arise, we can surmise that the focus of a successful innovation strategy should be on *creative applications for existing inventions* and combinations of inventions. Thus, the hallmark of successful innovation is the imagination of applications that do not yet exist for inventions that do exist (either in full or partial form).

More specifically, the observation that most inventions do not arise to fulfill a pressing consumer need highlights the role of identifying customers' needs before the customers can identify those needs themselves. Indeed, it is now widely accepted among marketing researchers that customers often have little insight into their preferences, and thus are typically unable to spontaneously express a need for products that do not yet exist. This is particularly true in the case of discontinuously innovative products (i.e., products that offer a discontinuous leap in the value proposition for customers). Stated in the words of Henry Ford: "If I had asked my customers what they wanted, I would have built a faster horse."

Nintendo is an example of a company that successfully identified an application that met customer needs before the customers anticipated those needs themselves. In an era where video-game users and other manufacturers were focused on making ever more powerful machines, Nintendo was able to identify a need for a game system that offered the opportunity for more intuitive controls via physical interaction. Had Nintendo given video-game customers what they were demanding, it would have simply built a more powerful machine with better graphics. However, the interactive Nintendo Wii fulfilled a need that gamers and nongamers alike had not (and likely could not have) articulated. Thus, Nintendo emerged from being an also-ran in the video-game console market to the industry leader following the introduction of the Wii. Seeking to imitate the success of Nintendo, the head of Sony's gaming unit, Kazuo Hirai, declared at the 2009 Tokyo Game Show: "We want to build controllers you can't even begin to imagine could exist."[17]

Other examples of innovators who identified new applications for existing inventions before those applications existed or were demanded by customers include the developers of the Post-it Note and the entrepreneurs who connected Edison's phonograph to a coin slot and a music collection, creating the jukebox. Conversely, when Honeywell developed a home computer in 1969, the only applications the company conceived of for the device were balancing checkbooks and managing recipe cards. They thus marketed the Honeywell Kitchen Computer for more than $10,000 to housewives—and did not sell even one unit.[18] As these examples illustrate, identifying applications to fulfill customer needs that do not explicitly exist (and that the customer cannot articulate) is central to successful innovation.

Looking Outside the Organization

Diamond's observation that most innovations within a society come from other societies is highly relevant to corporate innovation: most innovations that are adopted by successful companies will arise outside the company. This is true because no matter how brilliant and creative the company's employees and how conducive to innovation the corporate culture, the sheer number of brilliant and creative people outside the company will necessarily be greater. Outside innovations will come from multiple sources, including the company's customers, other companies in the same industry, or other industries entirely. Therefore, successful innovation is often about how successful a company is at identifying, adopting, adapting, improving, and integrating outside innovations.

Examples of companies that have successfully adopted and adapted externally developed innovations abound. For instance, Capital One, the credit-card issuer, is well known for its innovative information-based marketing strategy. Prior to the emergence of Capital One, credit card companies traditionally served only the prime market (i.e., consumers with high credit ratings), and all credit cards had a $50 annual fee and carried a 19.9 percent APR. Capital One transformed the market by using information to identify narrow consumer segments and target them with highly customized offers.[19] However, Capital One's innovation is really an adaptation of traditional segmentation and targeting strategies, enabled by improvements in information technology.

Likewise, Harrah's was inspired by Capital One to create its own information-based marketing strategy in a completely separate industry—casinos and resorts. Thus, Harrah's became a highly successful innovator in its industry by adopting and adapting an innovation used in the credit card industry.[20]

AOL provides another example of the adaptation of an existing innovation to a new context. AOL became the largest U.S. Internet service provider largely through a strategy that emphasized getting disks with a 30-day free trial of the program directly into people's hands. Free AOL disks were given away at many large retailers, such as copy store Kinko's, and were also frequently inserted into daily newspapers. On certain days, every major newspaper in the country had an AOL disk inserted in the paper.[21] Of course, as in the case of Capital One's information-based strategy, AOL's basic approach was not new, but it represented an instance of sampling, a marketing practice with a long history.

Likewise, Xerox did not invent the concept of leasing, but when the company failed to both license its technology to large technology firms such as IBM and failed to convince customers to make the upfront investment required for its copiers, the company adopted a business model based on leasing that ultimately formed the basis of Xerox's successful marketing efforts.[22]

Many other successful companies have adopted innovations directly from other companies or acquired them. For instance, Google's AdWords program, the company's auction-based keyword advertising program and the source of almost all the company's revenues, was adopted from competitor Goto.com, which featured a similar program.[23] Goto.com's founder, Bill Gross, had in turn been inspired to come up with this innovation from the traditional paper-based Yellow Pages. Moreover, Google's second-most-popular application after its search engine, Google Maps, was the result of the acquisition of an Australian company that has subsequently been adapted, improved, and integrated with other features. An acquisition is also the source of the fastest-growing consumer product of the Dutch electronics giant Philips, which bought the Sonicare brand and technology for toothbrushes from a Washington-based start-up.[24]

Many companies have recognized the importance of outside innovations as an important source of innovation for their own organizations by explicitly identifying, evaluating, and acquiring large numbers of outside technologies. For example, the network equipment manufacturer Cisco bases its innovation strategy on acquiring outside start-ups and often acquires more than 50 such start-ups in a year.[25] Cisco thus outsources basic R&D to the start-up community and is able to focus on identifying key innovations and then acquiring, adapting, improving, and integrating those innovations into its portfolio. Likewise, in 2001, Procter & Gamble (P&G) CEO Arthur Lafley initiated a program dubbed "Connect and Develop." As part of the program, P&G has 75 technology scouts that scour the globe in pursuit of new innovations that P&G can use and adapt.[26]

Other companies have excelled in integrating a number of externally developed innovations into an innovative product. Apple invented neither the MP3 player nor the smart phone, but the company is particularly skilled at integrating many different inventions to make innovative products, such as the iPod and iPhone. Another example of successful integration of innovations to produce an innovative new product is the recently introduced Jet drink fountain developed over a four-year period by Coca-Cola. The fountain allows for the distribution of 120 drinks from a machine 40 percent smaller than traditional soda fountains, which typically only allow for the distribution of six to eight drinks. Coca-Cola's new Jet fountain incorporates microdosing technologies adopted from the pharmaceutical industry, an operating system used for smart phones, and styling from Italian automakers.[27] Similarly, the Elliptigo device developed by a California startup combines the mechanics of an elliptical machine with those of a bicycle, allowing exercisers to perform elliptical movements on a machine that can be ridden outdoors like a bicycle.[28] Thus, as all these examples serve to illustrate, a critical component of a successful innovation strategy is the identification, adoption, adaptation, improvement, and integration of existing innovations to new, often previously unidentified, applications.

SUMMARY

This chapter summarizes some of Jared Diamond's observations about the history of innovation in the book *Guns, Germs, and Steel* and attempts to identify relevant insights from these observations to the context of corporate innovation. This chapter is not intended to offer a comprehensive treatment of how managers can foster innovation in the enterprise, a task that is well beyond the scope of a single chapter. However, based on Diamond's observation, we can conclude that the answer to the focal question raised in the title of this chapter is that innovations arise from (1) novel applications of existing inventions, and (2) from outside the organization. Thus, the chapter highlights three key insights about innovation in a corporate context:

1. The focus of corporate innovation should be on the novel application of existing inventions rather than on invention.
2. The hallmark of innovation in a marketing context is the identification of unarticulated customer needs and the imagination of applications to fulfill those needs.
3. Most useful innovations will arise outside the organization (and even outside the industry) and their identification, adaptation, and integration are the foundation of a successful innovation strategy.

David Gal is assistant professor of marketing at the Kellogg School of Management, Northwestern University. He received his BS from Penn State University, and his MS and PhD from the Graduate School of Business, Stanford University. He teaches Introduction to Marketing New Products and Services at Kellogg.

NOTES

1. Diamond, Jared (1997), *Guns, Germs, and Steel,* New York: W.W. Norton.
2. Thomson, David G. (2006), *Blueprint to a Billion,* Hoboken, NJ: John Wiley & Sons.
3. Boolell, M., M. J. Allen, S. A. Ballard, S. Gepi-Attee, G. J. Muirhead, A. M. Naylor, I., H. Osterloh, and C. Gingell (1996), "Sildenafil: An Orally Active Type 5 Cyclic GMP-specific Phosphodiesterase Inhibitor for the Treatment of Penile Erectile Dysfunction," *International Journal of Impotence Research,* 46, no. 4, 47–52.
4. Arrington, Michael (2006), "YouTube's Magic Number—$1.5 Billion," *TechCrunch* (September 21), www.techcrunch.com/2006/09/21/youtubes-magic-number-15-billion/.
5. Taylor, Jim (2010), "Technology: The Law of Unintended Consequences," *Psychology Today* (January 27).
6. Kruse, Amy, Dylan Schmorrow, and Allen Sears (2004), "ARPANet." In *Berkshire Encyclopedia of Human-Computer Interaction,* Ed. W. S. Bainbridge, Great Barrington, MA: Berkshire, 37–40.
7. O'Connor, John J. (1996), *The Rise of Calculus,* St. Andrews, Scotland: University of St. Andrews.
8. Poincaré, Henri (1906), "Sur la Dynamique de l'électron," *Rendiconti del Circolo Matematico Rendiconti del Circolo di Palermo,* 21, 129–176.
9. Slotten, Ross A. (2004), *The Heretic in Darwin's Court: The Life of Alfred Russel Wallace,* New York: Columbia University Press.
10. Westfall, Richard S. (1980), *Never at Rest: A Biography of Isaac Newton,* New York: Cambridge University Press.
11. Judson, Horace F. (1996), *The Eighth Day of Creation: Makers of the Revolution in Biology,* New York: Cold Spring Harbor Laboratory Press.
12. McGarry, Daniel D., trans. (1955), *The Metalogicon Of John Of Salisbury: A Twelfth-Century Defense Of The Verbal And Logical Arts Of The Trivium,* Berkeley, CA: University of California Press.
13. Petroski, Henry (1992), *The Evolution of Useful Things,* New York: Knopf.
14. Dematteis, Bob (2004), *From Patent to Profit: Secrets & Strategies for the Successful Inventor,* New York: Square One Publishers.
15. Larson, Charles F. (1999), "R&D in Industry," *AAAS Report XXIV: Research & Development FY 2000.*
16. Petroski, Henry (1992), *The Evolution of Useful Things,* New York: Knopf.
17. Tabuchi, Hiroko (2009), "Apple's Shadow Hangs Over Game Console Makers," *New York Times* (September 25), www.nytimes.com/2009/09/26/technology/26games.html.
18. Cowan, Ruth Schwartz (1985), *More Work for Mother: The Ironies of Household Technology from the Open Hearth to the Microwave,* New York: Basic Books.
19. McNamee, Mike (1999), "Capital One: Isn't There More to Life Than Plastic?" *BusinessWeek* (November 22).

20. Watson, Hugh J., and Volonino Linda (2003), "Customer Relationship Management at Harrah's Entertainment." In *Decision Making Support Systems: Achievements, Trends and Challenges,* Hershey, PA: IGI Publishing, 157–172.

21. Swisher, Kara (1999), *AOL.com*, New York: Three Rivers Press.

22. Kearns, David T., and David A. Nadler (1993), *Prophets in the Dark: How Xerox Reinvented Itself and Beat Back the Japanese*, New York: HarperCollins.

23. Karp, Scott (2008), "Google AdWords: A Brief History of Online Advertising Innovation," *Publishing 2.0: The (R)evolution of Media* (May 27), http://publishing2.com/2008/05/27/google-adwords-a-brief-history-of-online-advertising-innovation/.

24. Smith, Chris (2000), "Philips Agrees to Buy Optiva Corporation," *E-Dental.com* (August 31).

25. White, Bobby, and Vauhini Vara (2008), "Cisco Changes Track in Takeover Game," *Wall Street Journal* (April 17).

26. Huston, Larry, and Nabil Sakkab (2006), "Connect and Develop: Inside Procter & Gamble's New Model for Innovation," *Harvard Business Review*, 84, no. 3, 58–66.

27. Stanford, Duane D. (2009), "Coca-Cola Seeks Edge With 120-Drink Jet Fountain," *Bloomberg.com* (April 6), www.bloomberg.com/apps/news?pid=20601110&sid=aMfTlEvNNSCc.

28. Garvey, Jude (2008), "Run While You Ride on the ElliptiGO Bike," *Gizmag* (September 25), www.gizmag.com/run-while-you-ride-on-the-elliptigo-bike/10076/.

CHAPTER 16

BRAND-LED INNOVATION

BOBBY J. CALDER and EDWARD S. CALDER

INTRODUCTION

There are many successful paths to innovation, yet companies often limit themselves to only one or two of these paths, and therefore they unnecessarily constrain their growth potential. A "path to innovation" is the application of a specific set of disciplines, processes, or frameworks that lead to a positive business outcome. For example, applying the processes and practices of research and development to improve a product would be pursuing the R&D path to innovation. But there are other paths to innovation as well that often go unacknowledged by many companies. Specifically, while market research and technology R&D are powerful drivers of innovation, so too are other paths, such as business model innovation and design-led innovation. Because of misconceptions in the way companies view innovation, they have not fully exploited all the paths to innovation open to them.

As David Gal highlights in Chapter 15, "From Wheel to Twitter: Where Do Innovations Come From?" over time many theories of innovation have become taken as conventional wisdom. For example, he cites the misconception that innovations are primarily internally generated, emerging from within a company, organization, or country. This misconception leads companies to invest inwardly in structures, resources, and processes that improve their own capacities for innovation. In fact, a significant amount of innovation emerges from the diffusion of ideas across boundaries: companies partner and collaborate, employees migrate, and generally there is an ever-increasing flow of information across boundaries. The implication that Gal draws is that corporations must embrace ideas from the outside and leverage these flows of information to help generate innovation.

Some companies are now attempting to transcend this traditional inward orientation and move toward externally generated innovation. Gal points to a leading example, Procter & Gamble's (P&G) Connect and Develop program, which the consumer products company created to refute the notion that relevant innovations only come from internal sources. Connect and Develop allows scientists, engineers, and entrepreneurs to partner with P&G on exciting new technologies and ideas. Indeed, it is a bi-directional portal allowing outside parties to leverage the equally exciting technologies created within the walls of P&G.

In other companies, programs such as "open innovation" and "capability investments" have been developed. In addition, a host of smaller companies have created entire business models revolving precisely around the fact that good ideas can come from anywhere. For example, Innocentive is a company that describes itself as an "open-innovation community." Essentially, Innocentive is a facilitated network that connects people with challenges to people with solutions, wherever they might come from.

If there were ever a time when inward investment was the only clear path to innovation, as these examples show, the world has changed—barriers to knowledge transfer have precipitously declined with advances in information and communications technology. Our approach to innovation should change accordingly. However, theory often lags the real world, and misconceptions persist. Companies lean too heavily on history and generalize lessons from a limited number of successful companies from past eras. The theories championed by such case studies then become enshrined in "conventional wisdom" and are exuberantly reapplied without sufficient consideration of situation-based relevance. Ironically, misconceptions about innovation may actually be limiting the capacity of companies to be innovative.

To be fair, conventional wisdom is not without utility. If we had to evaluate every action individually without any guiding principles or heuristics, progress would grind to a halt. So in many cases conventional wisdom creates efficiencies. The risk, however, is that conventional wisdom is limiting. It removes the burden to think broadly or in new directions. The following section discusses further how conventional wisdom concerning paths to innovation has limited the range of even inward-focused approaches companies pursue when trying to create successful new products and services.

INNOVATION IS MORE THAN MARKET RESEARCH AND TECHNOLOGY

Where do successful new products come from? Ask most executives and they will identify two primary sources of innovation that lead to new products and services. First, innovation emerges from insights into customer needs. Customers create opportunities for innovation through the needs they have in life. If customers want access to their entire music collection on the go, there is an opportunity to create an iPod. If customers want to link up with friends and family and share stories, there is an opportunity to create Facebook. Needs might be functional, but they might also be social or emotional—in many cases, all three. Sometimes customers can articulate their needs, while other times they lie buried beneath frustration and compensating behaviors. The point is that every successful innovation is based on an important, as-yet-unsatisfied need, or at least an unarticulated problem to which people are resigned. Without discovering a new need, or a new way of satisfying a need, there is no possibility of innovation, and so not surprisingly companies invest significant resources in trying to uncover and understand customer needs.

The second answer most executives will provide regarding the origin of successful new products is technological progress. Opportunities for innovation are created when existing technologies are improved or entirely new technologies are invented. These technological advancements allow companies to better satisfy customers who do not even know they have a need. For example, advancements in information technology have allowed us to get access to e-mail, send text messages to friends, see the latest sports scores, and make dinner reservations—all from our mobile phone. Technology is everywhere. It gets us to work. It heats our homes. It enables us to communicate with people halfway around the world. And because it is ubiquitous, technology is often the first choice to not only provide better solutions to consumer needs but also to a large extent create needs. In the past, who would have ever needed a telephone?

Certainly, many innovations do come from deep customer insights and technological developments. Thus, corporations are correct to build market research organizations and R&D groups to exploit these sources of innovation. Large companies have built large organizations around each approach and essentially put them in competition in the effort to optimize innovation. The problem arises when it becomes conventional wisdom that marketing research and technology development are the *only* robust paths to innovation. In fact, there are more paths to innovation, and successful organizations should be open and prepared to use all of them.

BUSINESS MODEL AND DESIGN-LED INNOVATION

Before discussing brand-led innovation as a new and promising path to innovation, we describe two other emerging paths: business model and design-led innovation. Together these paths, along with the traditional paths, contribute to the multipath approach to innovation advocated here.

Business Model Innovation

Innovating by adopting new business models is a path that requires thinking holistically about how companies create value for both the customer and the company itself.[1] In many situations it is not necessary to pull one of the two traditional innovation levers, marketing research or technology. Rather than finding a new need or new technology, companies can offer customers an entirely new way of doing business.

For example, a company could enter a new market with existing technology or technology borrowed from another market if it determines that there is a better business model that offers advantages to customers. An auto insurance company might enter the life insurance market not with any breakthrough insight into why people buy life insurance or some new actuarial model but with a new way of doing business. Agents could sell the life insurance as a bundled option with automobile insurance. The product would supply additional coverage in the event of death or disability from any kind of accident. This would be a convenient, one-stop way of getting supplemental coverage for the consumer and a low-cost way of generating incremental revenue for the company. The need is not new, but the delivery of the product is a new way of doing business.

Innovation of this kind requires thinking about all components of the business model and how they fit together. On the customer side, this would include examining how the customer accesses the product (e.g., home delivery, retail location) or how the customer pays for the product (e.g., cash, financing). On the company side, business model innovation would include consideration of how the company makes profits (e.g., turnover, margin model) and what resources and processes are needed to deliver the solution (e.g., people, equipment).

As an example of business model innovation, consider Dow Corning's creation of Xiameter, a subsidiary that sells bulk silicone online. Dow Corning recognized that the company's premium silicone offering overshot the need many consumers had—in other words, Dow Corning's traditional business

Figure 16.1
Xiameter's Business Design Approach to Innovation

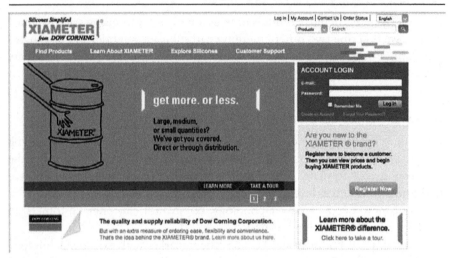

offered *more* quality and *more* service than the customers needed or wanted. A significant segment of the market knew what they wanted and only needed convenient access to cheap silicone. These customers did not need to talk to a sales or technical rep about specific formulations. They did not need help with customizing their order. Furthermore, they did not want to pay for the services and product features that they were not consuming. In response, Dow Corning created Xiameter, a new entity with an entirely new business model. Xiameter sold bulk silicone with no bells and whistles. Xiameter had no custom services. It relied on Internet sales, IT systems, and automation to keep prices low while maintaining margins (as can be seen in Figure 16.1). In this example, the source of innovation is not a new need or technology but an innovative way of doing business.

Two important points can be learned from this example. First, Dow Corning did not really innovate based on some deep consumer insight. The company always knew that some customers bought bulk silicone based only on the best price they could negotiate. Also, Xiameter offered no great technological developments—it is the same basic silicone they have always sold. Instead, the path to innovation was the business model. Dow Corning changed the customer value proposition by making it easy and cheap. The company also changed the delivery model by automating processes and moving to a lower overhead structure. Xiameter delighted customers and became a major success for Dow Corning.

Design-Led Innovation

There is a growing recognition of the importance of design as a robust path to innovation. Certainly design has always played a role in innovation. Abstractly, design is about choices, and every product represents a series of choices (often tacit) made by engineers, marketers, and strategists. However, many companies are now leveraging design principles and design thinking to drive new growth through innovation. This contrasts sharply with the role of design as either an afterthought—something you do once significant constraints have already been placed on a product or service—or design as purely an aesthetic activity left to design professionals.

Consider the household solutions company Oxo. Sam Farber, inspired to create a range of usable products because of his wife's arthritis, established Oxo in 1989. He recognized that many kitchen utensils were functional, but few were well designed. Peelers peeled and knives cut, but utensils were not easy to use, comfortable, or particularly pleasant to look at. He also had a suspicion that the market for well-designed kitchen products was probably much greater than just arthritis suffers. Oxo decided to use design principles and design thinking to create a new line of kitchen products that did not necessarily *do* anything different, but rather provided a different experience. Oxo partnered with New York–based Smart Design to develop the new line of products called Good Grips (see the peeler in Figure 16.2). Oxo designed ergonomic rubber grips that made the utensils easy and comfortable to use. The company improved functionality by optimizing blade thickness and sharpness. It added style elements that not only invited use of the product but also turned the product into something worth displaying. By simultaneously considering

Figure 16.2
Oxo's Design Approach to Innovation (Peeler, www.oxo.com)

form, function, and the entire user experience, Oxo was able to develop a superior product that delighted consumers. Furthermore, through the design-led path to innovation, Oxo extended the company's portfolio to a wide range of household products and in the process realized significant growth.

As with the business model–led innovation of Xiameter, the key to Oxo's success was in following a different path to innovation. Certainly consumer insights played a role in Oxo's success. And certainly new technology (e.g., materials) had an impact on the final products. However, it was design principles and design thinking that drove the effort and dictated how those consumer insights and new technologies were seamlessly blended together. Thus it was design that really created the business opportunity.

BRAND-LED INNOVATION

As the Dow Corning and Oxo examples indicate, the multiple paths strategy pursues innovation through any resource available, whether it is insight into unmet consumer needs, new technology, business models, or design. In this spirit it is curious that companies don't examine their *brand* as a *source* of innovation. In defiance of conventional wisdom, brands are not just the result of innovation—they can be an important *path* to innovation.

On its face, using a brand as a source of innovation may seem synonymous with pursuing unmet consumer needs. After all, a brand is the idea or meaning of a product in terms of some relevant consumer goal (see Chapter 4, "Developing a Compelling Brand Positioning," and Chapter 5, "Writing a Brand Positioning Statement and Translating It into Brand Design"). A strong brand, as represented by a positioning statement, provides the consumer with a distinct means of fulfilling the goal. It's easy to see why a brand might be seen entirely as the result of innovation rather than a source of innovation. But, although it is true that brands arise out of needs, once established, a strong brand becomes an idea in the mind of consumers that guides them to a product and shapes their experience with it. Knowing that McDonald's features the Big Mac both directs you either toward eating there, if you are positive about the brand, and influences what you will actually experience in eating a Big Mac.

Once established, brands take on a life of their own. They exist in the minds of consumers as positive ideas that give direction and expectations. In this sense, brands can be viewed as a source of innovation. Once a company has established a brand in a product category, it has met a need. But the brand then can be used to lead the company into new product categories. Even if the company can find no need or technological advance that would justify entering the category, the brand could allow it to enter and compete.

The brand-led path to innovation thus uses established brands to enter new categories, using the brand rather than relying on new insights or technology to develop a product specifically for that category. The story is a bit more complicated than this, however. Companies currently view cross-category branding as more a matter of consolidation than innovation. So before discussing brand-led innovation further, we must connect it to the related problem of consolidation of products and brand architecture.

Consolidation and Brand Architecture

Companies are increasingly attempting to manage portfolios of products by consolidating them into fewer and fewer separate brands. The principal motivation for this consolidation is to achieve business synergy. It is perfectly possible to manage a portfolio by letting each product (aside from minor product extensions) stand alone as a separate brand. This brand architecture is often referred to as a "house of brands."[2] The brands may carry a common company endorsement identifying the company as the maker, but the brands otherwise are not intended to have any connection in the mind of the consumer. The problem is that this brand architecture is difficult to support. Each brand must have its own marketing budget, and there is no way to leverage spending in one product category with sales of a product in another category.

To solve the problem of business synergy, companies traditionally move to a "branded house" (range brand, parent brand) architecture. The goal is to have brands that have many sub-brands associated with them. By having a smaller number of branded houses with a larger number of sub-brands, the company can support the brands better and gain leverage. The criteria for whether a product can be a sub-brand of a brand should be whether it shares a common positioning statement with the branded house, the parent. So Kraft markets many sub-brands of its Kraft Macaroni & Cheese brand, but all are positioned as the meal kids love because it is so cheesy (i.e., kid-friendly). One sub-brand is The Cheesiest, another is Spirals. If a product does not fit in a branded house—if it must be positioned differently—its sales must justify separate support, or it is a candidate for being pruned from the portfolio.

Although the branded house architecture achieves synergy, the problem is that sub-branding becomes more and more questionable as products move away from close-in extensions like the shape of the macaroni. If Kraft wants to introduce microwavable packets of macaroni and cheese, can this product be positioned as the cheesiest? The branded house architecture helps solve the problem of synergy but at the cost of putting a damper on innovation. It is difficult to enlarge a branded house because the products in it have to fit, which means they have to be positioned similarly. The goal of brand-led innovation is to use the brand to innovate in a way that escapes the resistance produced by consolidation and the use of branded house architectures. There are two types of approaches to brand innovation: The Branded House Approach and the Brand System Approach.

The Branded House Approach

Traditionally companies have been wary of enlarging a branded house, particularly across product categories. Indeed, there is risk in this. If Mom sees using a microwave oven to prepare a quick meal for a child as an unavoidable necessity rather than as a way to make her child happier, then there is a danger in introducing microwavable Kraft Macaroni & Cheese. But this should not obscure the fact that there *is* the potential for innovation within an established branded house. Entering a new category with a branded house implies that the brand positioning will remain nearly the same, but there can still be innovation in the category.

Consider the following example. P&G presently has a branded house of anti-aging face creams named Olay Total Effects. It is positioned around consumer needs like improving skin elasticity, brightening dull skin, and fighting dryness. The Olay branded house consists of several sub-brands of face cream, but the company would like to enter the body wash category. The category is price sensitive with strong competition from private label brands. If P&G has no new insight or technology, it would seem difficult to innovate in this category. But it does have the Olay Total Effects brand, which represents a way of thinking about wrinkles. Applying this idea to the body wash category brings innovation. The consumer might well resist a pricey body wash purporting to fight wrinkles without a specifically articulated need to remove wrinkles with a body wash. But the idea of having Olay Total Effects in another form as way of fighting wrinkles is a different matter. The difference is subtle but very significant. Think of it this way—the consumer knows the brand as a positive idea. P&G's innovation is to provide a new way of using the brand. If the consumer can be said to have a need, then the need is more for the brand than for any unmet or unarticulated need.

Could P&G innovate in any category this way? No, it would be difficult to translate Olay Total Effects into, say, the deodorant category. But in a situation where the current brand positioning can be translated into a new category (in this case, from fighting wrinkles on the face to fighting wrinkles on the body), the brand becomes a powerful force for innovation, without the necessity of breakthrough insights or technology.

Let's look at another example to pin down this logic. The Mercedes-Benz brand uses a branded house architecture, for which the flagship is the S-Class automobile. Its brand positioning can be stated in the following way:

> The revolutionary S-Class is the definitive automotive experience, having an unparalleled and forward-thinking combination of sheer driving pleasure, charismatic styling, intelligent innovation, and sumptuous elegance that provides unprecedented safety.

The Mercedes-Benz branded house architecture has many sub-brands in the automobile category (perhaps too many). But what are the possibilities for brand-led innovation in other categories? One potential category is driver-training instruction, which is a high-growth category and might be attractive for Mercedes-Benz to enter. The goal would be to use the Mercedes-Benz automobile brand positioning to determine how the brand could be implemented on the driver-training platform. Note that the brand calls for "sheer driving pleasure" and "unprecedented safety." Mercedes-Benz realized that this translated into a school where students learn to have fun by driving safely.

Thus, a good target for Mercedes-Benz would be consumers who want to train their teenagers not just to drive, but to drive with pleasure safely before they can develop bad habits. Hence the positioning for the child could be stated as:

> To drivers as young as 12, you can learn to enjoy driving safely and well in a fun and rewarding environment.

The result was an innovation called the Mercedes-Benz Driving Academy. It covers not just the basics but more challenging things like night driving, highway driving, driving with friends, bad conditions, and things that are likely to be "fun" for the target age and that increase their skills (see Figure 16.3).

We could take the view that Mercedes-Benz has found an unarticulated need: to train children in driving in an enriched, more fun way. But, again, in this case the brand has created the need. Sending a child to the Honda driving school probably makes much less sense to the target consumer than sending them to the Mercedes-Benz Driving Academy. It is the Mercedes-Benz brand that creates the need to start your child with a Mercedes-Benz driving experience.

Figure 16.3
Mercedes-Benz Branded House Approach to Brand-Led Innovation

As this example shows, the branded house approach to brand-led innovation is a matter using an existing brand positioning to think through what the same brand could mean in a new category. The brand positioning remains essentially the same and dictates how the brand is implemented in the new category. There's no need to worry about confusion or dilution of the brand, because the brand positioning in the two categories is entirely consistent. The consumer can see that the two categories are just different ways in which the brand can be consumed.

The Brand System Approach

There is another approach to brand-led innovation that is even more powerful and more generally usable. It is also related to brand architecture and managing portfolios of brands. As discussed earlier, the traditional brand architecture decision is between a house of brands, where each brand essentially stands alone, and a branded house, which is made up of sub-brands with the same positioning. Although the branded house is one way of leveraging the marketing, it does not allow much deviation from the common positioning.

There is an third, emerging alternative to the traditional brand architecture choice between a house of brands and a branded house, called the Brand System Approach. Rather than use the brand positioning of an existing branded house to enter a category, a new brand positioning is developed for the category. However, this new brand positioning is associated with the existing brand position at a higher level, called a *common essence*. The common essence might be a shared underlying experience or simply a set of perceptions that color both brands.

An example is the Virgin brand. Virgin is an airline, a music store, a cola, a cell phone carrier, and more. The brand positioning in each category is not the same. As a cell phone in the United States, Virgin is positioned for younger people as an affordable way of paying for mobile service. But across all categories, Virgin connotes the experience of being different and the perceptions of freedom and individuality. This is the defining characteristic of a brand system.

The underlying principle has to do with similarity. How can two things that are quite different be seen as similar or related? If we have a different brand positioning in each category, how can the brands be similar? But after all, even if we have apples and oranges, we can see similarity between them. Apples and oranges are both fruit, they are both round, and they are eaten in similar ways. So given some basis of similarity, things that are different can still be seen as related.

A brand system is predicated on establishing some basis of similarity for a brand positioned differently in different categories. As shown in Figure 16.4, the logic is to link the differently positioned brands through a common higher-order essence defined by a shared consumer experience or set of perceptions. As noted by the dual arrows in Figure 16.4, this essence comes from the different brand positions but also adds to them. A strong brand positioning

Figure 16.4
The Logic of Brand Systems

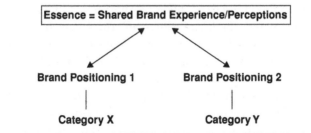

in one category that contributes to the essence of the system thereby can reinforce a brand positioning in another category.

Consider a maker of baby formula with a brand in Asia that is strongly positioned as follows:

> To status-conscious moms with high expectations for their newborns, this brand of infant formula is doctor-recommended for ensuring your infant develops to his or her fullest capacity because it contains a major scientific advance.

Obviously the positioning is around credibility and authority and a scientific ingredient. The same company also has a line of drinks for young children, positioned as follows:

> To status-conscious moms trying to give their toddlers a treat that is good for them, this brand of nutritional drinks will be loved by your child and will ensure that he or she keeps on growing and developing because it is nutritionally advanced.

The positioning in this category is around taste that children will enjoy and that moms can feel good about. Note that positioning differently in the two categories would seem to call for two different brands, or branded houses, in order to avoid confusion and dilution. The positioning is tasting good on the one hand and a medical/scientific benefit on the other. A brand system solves this architecture problem by relating the differently positioned brands through a common essence. In this case, the company realized that both speak to the experience of wanting a better life for your child than you have had and of looking at your high expectations for your child as a badge of honor for yourself. Common perceptions would involve being proud, ambitious, and dedicated. The resulting brand system is depicted in Figure 16.5.

This example illustrates how a brand system solves the brand architecture problem of allowing a brand to be differently positioned in different categories. The design of the brand, the brand names, and the visual characteristics would reflect the similar essence but call out the differences in positioning as well.

A brand system not only expands the options for brand architecture beyond the house of brands and branded house choices, but it also creates a path for innovation. Take another look at Figure 16.5. With an established brand system, the question immediately arises as to what other categories the brand could enter. The company is no longer constrained to supporting a product in

Figure 16.5
Example of Brand System Approach to Brand-Led Innovation

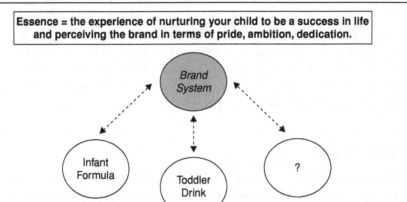

Essence = the experience of nurturing your child to be a success in life and perceiving the brand in terms of pride, ambition, dedication.

a new category as a separate investment or to entering the new category with a similar positioning. The question becomes, using the essence of the brand as a strength, "How can the brand be positioned in a way consistent with this, but taking the unique characteristics of the category into account as well?"

In the example of the infant formula, consider whether the company should attempt to enter the product category of vitamin supplements for pregnant or lactating moms. On its face, entering this category might be attractive but highly daunting. Introducing an entirely new brand would be expensive. Moreover, it would be difficult to find an untapped consumer need or improved chemical formula. If this company were only a branded house, offering pregnant, adult women a supplement from a maker of infant formula would invite confusion and dilution. The brand system, however, not only solves the architecture problem but also points to innovation in the category.

Without a marketing research or technology breakthrough, it would be difficult to see how to position a new brand of vitamin supplements. The brand system suggests that even a modest, me-too positioning around completeness can be given extra impact by connecting it to the essence of the system: the experience of nurturing a child to be a success in life and perceiving the supplement in terms of pride, ambition, dedication. Driven by this essence, the positioning for the vitamin supplement becomes:

To pregnant or lactating moms with rising expectations for their family, this brand of vitamin supplements covers all your nutritional needs with

one pill and is the nutrition supplement that gives your child a head start
in life before birth and while breastfeeding.

Here, the innovation is in the tie between the supplement and the experience and perceptions that is the essence of the brand system. The system
creates a new way of consuming the brand. This approach carries powerful
implications for companies looking to innovate beyond the traditional market
research or technology-driven avenues.

SUMMARY

Traditionally, companies have been both rewarded and limited by approaching
innovation through discovering new unmet consumer needs or new technological advances. Without disputing that these are potentially worthwhile paths
to innovation, they should not be taken as the *only* paths. Any resource, both
internal and external, can potentially be used as a path to innovation. As we
have seen, both business models and design can be pursued as new internal
approaches to innovation. Established brands are another resource and should
be added to companies' overall quest for innovation.

Brand-led innovation has been overlooked, however, because of brand architecture considerations. The real risk of confusion and dilution in expanding
a branded house, along with the expense associated with expanding a house
of brands, has stood in the way of realizing the potential of brands to guide
innovation. Even in the absence of any great new consumer insight or technological breakthrough, people will still respond to being able to consume more
of a brand they value in a different way. Companies can tap into this growth
potential either by finding new categories where a product can be branded in
nearly the same way (the branded house approach) or by finding a common
brand essence that allows a company to enter a new category with a different
positioning (the brand system approach). In either case, brand-led innovation
should be part of a multiple-path innovation strategy.

*Bobby J. Calder is the Kellstadt Professor of Marketing and currently the chair
of the Marketing Department at the Kellogg School of Management. He is also
a professor of journalism in the Medill School of Journalism and a professor
of psychology in the Weinberg College of Arts and Sciences at Northwestern
University. He has been a consultant to many companies and to government
and not-for-profit organizations. His most recent books are Kellogg on Integrated
Marketing (John Wiley & Sons, 2003) and Kellogg on Advertising and Media*

(John Wiley & Sons, 2008). He received his BA, MA, and PhD degrees from the University of North Carolina at Chapel Hill.

Edward S. Calder is a consultant at Innosight, a leading management consulting firm that enables organizations to achieve continuous growth through innovation. He has worked with many leading companies in a broad range of industries, with a focus on engineering, technology, and health-care organizations. He received his BS from Northwestern University and MS from the Massachusetts Institute of Technology.

NOTES

1. Johnson, Mark, Clayton Christensen, and Henning Kagermann (2008), "Reinventing Your Business Model," *Harvard Business Review*, 50–61.
2. Aaker, David A. (2004), *Brand Portfolio Strategy*, New York: Free Press.

CHAPTER 17

MANAGING PRODUCT ASSORTMENTS: INSIGHTS FROM CONSUMER PSYCHOLOGY

RYAN HAMILTON and ALEXANDER CHERNEV

INTRODUCTION

Conventional wisdom suggests that variety facilitates choice. There are many reasons for this. The most intuitive explanation, featured prominently in economics research, is that larger product assortments offer an opportunity for a better match between an individual's preferences and the available alternatives in a choice set. Larger assortments also facilitate choice because they allow consumers the flexibility to change their minds when making a future purchase decision. Consumers might prefer larger assortments simply because choosing from more alternatives increases the perception of freedom of choice.

Larger assortments increase the likelihood that the available choices adequately represent all potentially available options. Indeed, consumers may delay their purchasing when they feel that the available options do not adequately represent the entire roster of possibilities. For example, consumers might be more likely to choose when selecting from a retailer that offers a larger assortment because it is less likely that a potentially superior alternative is not represented among the available choices.

However, evidence has begun to accumulate that, despite the perceived advantages for consumers, larger assortments are often not worth the extra time and effort required to make a choice. In fact, adding more options can be detrimental to profits because of choice overload. When faced with too many choices, consumers may become overwhelmed and react by making no choice at all. Managers have taken notice and reacted accordingly. Many large consumer packaged goods companies—including Procter & Gamble, Colgate-Palmolive, and Unilever—have embarked on large-scale contractions of their product lines, trimming brands in an effort to streamline their product portfolios. These companies have found that, far from driving customers away, smaller assortments have actually led to increases in sales and customer satisfaction.

In this chapter we take a consumer's perspective in discussing the advantages and disadvantages of larger assortments. We begin by exploring the most important factors that drive consumer preference for larger or smaller assortments. We then highlight a number of specific solutions and decision rules that managers can use when making assortment decisions.

THE PARADOX OF LARGE ASSORTMENTS

Recent behavioral research has documented an interesting paradox. When choosing among assortments (e.g., choosing a store in which to shop), consumers tend to prefer larger assortments. Yet they often are less likely to make a choice and are less confident in choices made from larger rather than smaller assortments. Often, they fail to make a choice at all from large assortments. This inconsistency between consumers' initial preferences and their subsequent behaviors implies that consumers cannot accurately predict their need for variety and tend to overrate the attractiveness of large assortments. Numerous studies demonstrate that this paradox occurs not only in relatively low-involvement decisions like choosing grocery items, but also in decisions as consequential as whether to participate in an employee retirement plan.

Why do more options lead to a lower likelihood of making a choice? Three primary factors contribute to choice overload: increased cognitive costs of evaluating available options, increased cognitive costs of making a choice, and increased consumer expectations.

Increased Cognitive Costs of Evaluating Available Options

One reason why more options may reduce the likelihood of making a choice is that as the number of options increase, so does the effort needed to evaluate them. As "cognitive misers," people are often unwilling or unable to put forth the extra effort required to make choices from larger assortments. Each alternative to be considered comes with new information that must be processed and evaluated, including information about product performance, price, size, color, and brand. As the number of alternatives increases, so do the cognitive costs of choosing.[1]

The increased cognitive costs associated with larger assortments can lead to counterproductive outcomes, even in situations where consumers are faced with important decisions such as managing their investments. For example, it has been reported that retirement accounts offering a larger number of investment options tend to result in lower levels of participation than plans with fewer options. On average, every 10 additional funds a plan provides is associated with a 2 percent decrease in participation rates.[2]

Increased Cognitive Costs of Making a Choice

In addition to processing the information describing each of the available options, consumers have to make choices by selecting one (or a subset) of the available options and rejecting the others. The larger the number of available alternatives, the more difficult the decision. This is because as the number of available options increases, so does the number of attribute dimensions on which they need to be compared and, more important, the potential benefits that a consumer has to give up when choosing a particular option. Thus, by offering a greater variety of attractive options, larger assortments can complicate consumer choice when consumers are forced to give up potentially important benefits.[3]

Consider Gillette's assortment of shaving gels, each highlighting a specific benefit: moisturizing, skin renewal, protection, comfort, and sensitive skin. Given the choice of only two products, one offering extra protection and one promising moisturizing, a consumer would simply have to decide whether it was worth trading off extra moisturizing for a slightly more abrasive shave. Adding more options, however, makes the decision much more difficult. How much does one value skin renewal relative to extra comfort, ultra-moisturizing, protection, and sensitive skin formulations? Unless the consumer already knows which type of gel he prefers, he may end up picking one of the options at random or choosing a brand that offers less variety than Gillette (e.g., Nivea or Barbasol), and thereby requires making fewer tradeoffs.

Increased Consumer Expectations

A third problem with larger assortments is that they often increase consumers' expectations of finding an option that is exactly what they are looking for. These increased expectations might well lead a consumer to walk away empty-handed from a larger store—even if the available options are a closer match than are the options available elsewhere. Thus, when a small store fails to offer an exact match for a customer's preferences from its limited selection, consumers might be nevertheless satisfied with the selection because it confirms their expectations of limited variety.

However, when shopping at a massive superstore, consumers might be less satisfied with the available options because of the increased expectations of finding the "ideal" option.

Retailers that position their large assortments as a key advantage may be setting up expectations that they cannot meet.[4] Stores that lure in consumers with promises of the largest selections or the most options can be encouraging their customers to set unrealistic expectations. Thus, based purely on a difference in expectations, a consumer who might be perfectly happy with a pair of shoes chosen from the relatively limited selection at a department store might be a great deal more picky when choosing from the much larger assortment available at a specialty shoe store—and ultimately he or she may be unwilling to settle on a pair of shoes from the extremely large selection found online. This same logic explains why it can be easier to find a romantic partner in small towns than in large cities. Small-town residents may just be looking for the best partner out of a small, well-defined group of prospects, whereas residents of big cities may set a much higher standard, reasoning that they should be able to find their perfect match from such a large group of potential mates. Thus, a man or woman who might be perfectly acceptable within the limited selection found in a small town could be evaluated as unacceptable in the expanded lineup of singles in a big city.

Implications for Choice

Increased cognitive costs, increased choice difficulty, and increased consumer expectations associated with larger assortments can lead to negative outcomes for both retailers and consumers. One of the consequences of choice overload is the increased difficulty of making a choice, often leading to a decrease in consumer satisfaction with the option ultimately chosen. In addition, the availability of many appealing options can lead to less confident decisions, leaving consumers unsure of whether they selected the best option or whether they left a better choice on the shelf. The choice overload associated with larger assortments can also result in an increased likelihood that consumers will postpone choice or even fail to make a purchase at all. In this light, identifying strategies for managing choice overload has important implications not only for consumers but also for many manufacturers and retailers. We identify several approaches to effectively managing product assortment, focusing on strategies to minimize the negative impact of choice overload.

STRATEGIES FOR MANAGING CHOICE OVERLOAD

Our research suggests several strategies for managing choice overload. These strategies can be grouped into two categories: (1) strategies for optimizing the assortment, and (2) strategies for optimizing the consumer decision-making process.

Optimizing the Assortment

The set of products a firm offers or a retailer carries tends be more important than simply the sum of all the individual options. As such, the assortment as a whole needs to be optimized to create the most value for consumers—by reducing the risk of decision overload—at the least cost to the company. Optimizing the assortment involves three key aspects: optimizing assortment size, streamlining the assortment structure, and improving the differentiation of options comprising an assortment.

Optimizing Assortment Size   One strategy for minimizing the negative repercussions of too much choice is to optimize the size of the assortment. The most obvious solution is to reduce the assortment size to a point where the advantages of adding another option are lower than the disadvantages of complicating the consumer decision process. Consider the case of a large online grocery store that dramatically reduced the size of its assortments (by an average of 54 percent) in almost all categories. Although one might expect the result to be disgruntled customers who could no longer find what they wanted, in reality there was an average 11 percent increase in sales across the categories with reduced assortment sizes. After the assortment reduction, 75 percent of customers actually increased their spending.[5]

In looking to reduce assortment size, which options should go? How can a manufacturer or retailer reduce assortment size in a way that minimizes the negative consequences for consumers? One approach involves considering the attractiveness of the options comprising these assortments. Studies have shown that consumer choice among assortments depends on the attractiveness of each option. So consumers tend to prefer smaller assortments when choosing among assortments comprised of relatively more attractive options than when browsing relatively less attractive options.[6] To illustrate, when choosing between a retailer carrying a larger assortment and one carrying a smaller assortment, consumers are more likely to go for the smaller assortment when both stores carry more attractive options than when they both carry less attractive options. This suggests that retailers can compensate for some of the perceived disadvantages of smaller assortments by carrying more attractive options. For example, the ice-cream industry confirms that flavor assortments are indeed correlated with quality, such that higher-end manufacturers (e.g., Häagen-Dazs) tend to offer less variety than lower-end manufacturers. From the standpoint of managing the perceived benefits and costs to consumers, the optimal assortment size will tend to be smaller for stores carrying more high-quality merchandise than for stores carrying more low-quality merchandise.

There are three common strategies for increasing the overall attractiveness of an assortment: enhancing quality, carrying best-seller items, and focusing on niche markets.

Enhancing quality boosts attractiveness. Assortments that comprise higher-quality options are more likely to be perceived as more attractive, whereas those that comprise lower-quality options are likely to be perceived as relatively less attractive. The downside is that increasing quality can be costly, meaning that enhancing quality is typically the most expensive strategy for increasing the attractiveness of an assortment.

A less expensive strategy is to carry only those options that are preferred by large segments of the market. To illustrate, assortments comprised of bestseller items that are likely to appeal to the majority of consumers are usually perceived as more attractive than assortments comprised of less popular items. This suggests that stores with fewer offerings that carry only bestsellers may have an advantage over stores with larger assortments of middling options. Borders recently implemented this strategy by reducing the number of titles sold in their brick-and-mortar stores and carrying only the best-selling books.

Catering to the needs of a niche segment can also be a good strategy. Some assortments contain items that, while relatively unappealing to the general consumer, are a good match for the tastes of a specific consumer segment (e.g., book stores that cater to specific ethnic, lifestyle, or language preferences). By stocking a smaller inventory that appeals to a niche market, these retailers can create assortments that are quite alluring to a particular customer set. As with assortments consisting of higher quality items and bestsellers, tightly targeted assortments also allow retailers to increase their customers' preferences for smaller assortments.

Streamlining the Assortment Structure   In addition to managing the number and attractiveness of options comprising an assortment, decision overload can be reduced by organizing the available options, thereby reducing some of the cognitive costs associated with larger assortments. There are three common approaches to organizing options within an assortment: taxonomic, goal-derived, and idiosyncratic.

Taxonomic Organization   Managers can reduce choice overload by organizing their assortments based on their physical properties, such as manufacturer, size, or type. Making an assortment easier to search increases the likelihood that consumers will select an item for purchase rather than forego making a choice. Because choice complexity increases with assortment size, it is especially important to have a clear organizational structure as the assortment gets larger.

On the other hand, while large assortments obviously benefit from a clear organization, smaller assortments may sometimes benefit from lack of organization, because disorganized assortments tend to be perceived as offering more variety than organized assortments.[7] Since greater variety is one of the reasons consumers prefer larger assortments over smaller ones, disorganization can increase the attractiveness of a smaller assortment. Thus, strategic disorganization sometimes can make smaller assortments more appealing without actually increasing the number of items offered.

Goal-Derived Organization   Another approach involves using a goal-derived, rather than taxonomic, organization of options. This alternative organization groups options according to the underlying consumer goal they serve. For example, most city guides group activities taxonomically (restaurants, theater, music, etc.). But this same set of potential activities could also be grouped according to consumers' goals: things to do on a first date; places to go to impress a client; or ways to kill an evening for less than $20.

Goal-derived categories may reduce consumers' search costs by providing a more intuitive or natural way of searching through assortments. Because most consumer shopping is goal driven, goal-derived categories frequently provide a better match for consumers' thinking processes as they wade through the decision process. In addition, goal-derived categorization can save consumers time by grouping complementary items together. For example, a grocer might group everything needed for breakfast in one place rather than in four or five scattered locations in a store. Rental car company Hertz recently began to use goal-derived grouping, placing cars into "prestige," "fun," and "green" categories. For customers who are looking for a fun car to rent on vacation, searching by size can be cumbersome; after all, both a large convertible and a tiny Mini Cooper could be considered fun cars. In Hertz's new configuration, both types would be classified under the "fun" category, giving consumers an easier way to find what they are really looking for.

Some retailers have begun to layer taxonomic and goal-derived organization strategies on top of one another. Rather than retrain customers who have grown accustomed to the largely taxonomical organization at most grocery stores, some grocers have started stocking the same item in both taxonomical and goal-derived locations. For instance, bananas can often be found in both the produce section (taxonomic) and next to the milk (goal-derived), making shopping easier for those who like to eat bananas with their cold cereal.

Idiosyncratic Organization Other companies employ an idiosyncratic organization scheme that groups options in order of their attractiveness to a particular individual. This strategy can reduce search costs by making it more likely that consumers will find what they're looking for early in their search. By ordering an assortment based on a customer's own preferences, retailers increase the likelihood that each customer will find an acceptable option early on, thereby avoiding the cognitive costs of searching. Because this requires maintaining the diversity of a large assortment that can match the preferences of a significant number of consumers, preference-ordered assortments obviously are most likely to be found in online environments, where changing the organization of options is the result of just a few mouse clicks. In brick-and-mortar stores, knowledgeable sales clerks can serve this function by assessing potential customers' preferences and then leading them to the options they are most likely to prefer.

Improving Option Differentiation

Another approach to managing choice overload involves optimizing the differences in options comprising the assortment. Both insufficient differentiation as well as over-differentiation can exacerbate choice overload.

Consider two brands of toothpaste, each offering several variations. The first assortment offers four toothpastes differentiated by flavor: cinnamon, banana, lemon, and mint. The second assortment offers four toothpastes differentiated by functional attributes: cavity prevention, tartar protection, teeth whitening, and breath freshening. The two assortments in our example differ in terms of the degree to which the features of each option complement one another. In the first assortment, combining two or more noncomplementary product features does not necessarily increase their overall utility. For example, blending cinnamon and mint flavors does not create a superior combination.

2566356

In contrast, in the second assortment the differentiating features of the options do complement one another, and mixing them could provide more functionality than each option considered separately. For example, combining cavity prevention and tartar protection leads to a superior combination.

Which of the two assortments—comprised of complementary (e.g., functionality) or noncomplementary (e.g., flavor) options—is more likely to be preferred by consumers? Our research shows that consumers express an initial preference for assortments comprised of complementary options. However, when asked to make a choice, they are more likely to choose an option from an assortment comprised of noncomplementary (e.g., flavor) than complementary (e.g., functionality) options.[8] Thus, increasing product assortment by adding options differentiated by complementary features tends to *lower the attractiveness* of all alternatives in that assortment. This is because adding an option differentiated by a complementary feature highlights an attribute dimension on which the original product is inferior, thus decreasing its overall attractiveness. Consequently, each new complementary feature used to extend the product line ultimately makes the existing products less attractive because they are trumped on the attribute defined by the newly added feature. As a result, complementary assortments ultimately lead to a decline in the probability of choosing any option. The conclusion for marketers looking to increase sales volume is that although complementary assortments are initially perceived as more appealing than noncomplementary ones, to increase sales volume manufacturers and retailers should focus on developing assortments comprised of noncomplementary options, such as those differentiated by flavors.

Confusion can be caused by *over-differentiation*. This occurs when products are differentiated on multiple dimensions without all possible combinations being available. For example, consider two restaurants: one where desserts vary in price and one where desserts are equally priced. Consumers who are unsure which dessert they would most enjoy might use price to make a selection (e.g., choosing the least expensive when on a budget and the most expensive for a special occasion). Those with established preferences, however, might find it difficult to choose when the price of their most preferred option conflicts with their spending goals (e.g., the most preferred option is also the most expensive one for those on a budget). Such preference-inconsistent pricing might complicate the consumer decision process and lower the overall choice probability from an assortment where options are differentiated on multiple dimensions.[9] The practical implication of this finding is that companies need to identify the key attributes on which to differentiate choice options, and that differentiating on too many attributes can hurt rather than help sales.

Optimizing the Consumer Decision-Making Process

In addition to optimizing the design of their assortments, companies can assuage choice overload by optimizing the consumer decision-making process. In particular, there are three approaches to simplifying the consumer decision process: (1) reducing preference uncertainty, (2) providing a default option, and (3) structuring the decision process.

Reducing Preference Uncertainty   Because most of the potential negative consequences of larger assortments are associated with consumers' confusion concerning their own preferences ordering of the available options, reducing preference uncertainty should also reduce the likelihood of choice overload. One particularly effective approach to reducing preference uncertainty is to help consumers define an attribute combination that represents their "ideal" option before they are shown the options available.[9] Indeed, in the absence of an ideal attribute combination, consumers have to construct their attribute preferences (i.e., figure out what attributes they find important and what attribute values they find desirable) *while* they are searching for the option that incorporates these attributes and delivers the highest utility. The problem is that as the assortment size increases, so does the task of articulating one's ideal combination of attribute values. Thus, the choice process is likely to get quite a bit more complicated in the context of larger assortments. As a result, when faced with a larger assortment, consumers without a readily available ideal point are likely to shy away from the rather daunting task of simultaneously forming their ideal attribute combination and searching for the option that best matches their ideal point—often leaving without making a choice at all.

Thus, companies can reduce consumer confusion and nip choice overload in the bud by having consumers construct their preferences *before* they start evaluating the available options. For example, prior to presenting all customization options, computer-maker Dell's web site asks consumers to answer several basic questions aimed at helping them articulate the most important attributes they want in a computer. Such prechoice preference articulation can help companies simplify the search process and reduce the negative consequences of carrying a large assortment.

Providing a Default Option   Companies can also help consumers deal with larger assortments by providing a default option. A default option may make choosing from larger assortments much easier because it changes the nature of the consumer decision task in two subtle but important ways. First, the default option serves as a reference point for evaluating the other options in the set. Deciding whether each option is better or worse than the default option is much easier than evaluating each option relative to all the other options available. Second, a default option gives consumers a low-effort way of making a choice without having to expend the energy needed for a thorough search and evaluation.

Even for very consequential decisions, such as whether to become an organ donor or participate in a company's retirement saving plan, making the default decision to opt in or to opt out can have a dramatic impact on people's choices. For example, when the default decision is participating in the retirement plan and consumers can opt out, participation rates are substantially higher than when the default is nonparticipation and consumers must opt in.[10] Retailers may engage in a default option strategy by prominently displaying one option from a larger assortment, thereby encouraging customers to consider that option before the others.[11] In addition to simply increasing the sales of the displayed item, retailers that draw consumers' attention to one alternative may also be making it easier for consumers to evaluate and choose options from the rest of the assortment.

Structuring the Decision Process   One strategy for helping consumers avoid the negative effects of larger assortments is to shift their focus from choosing the assortment itself (choosing the retailer) to choosing an option (choosing the product within the store).[12] Indeed, when choosing a retailer, the advantages of larger assortments are likely to loom large, while the potential disadvantages—such as the difficulty of selecting a single option—seem less important. In contrast, when choosing an option the disadvantages of a large assortment become very prominent. Thus, it can be effective to draw consumers' attention to the ultimate choice of the option itself.

For example, a retailer carrying a relatively small assortment might remind consumers through its advertising of past (confusing) experiences shopping from expansive product lines, which should reduce the appeal of larger assortments. As consumers focus more narrowly on making their choices within a store, the perceived advantages of larger assortments should diminish.

SUMMARY

The strategy of giving customers what they want, although intuitively appealing, has resulted in a proliferation of product line extensions and ever-increasing product assortments. Yet, giving consumers more options is not always better when it comes to managing product assortments. In fact, sometimes offering more options can actually backfire, leading to lower sales when consumers fall victim to choice overload. We outlined two ways for managers to overcome choice overload: (1) by optimizing the assortment through the size, structure, and differentiation of its options, and (2) by optimizing the consumer decision process through reducing decision uncertainty, facilitating choice, and refocusing consumers' attention from choosing an assortment to choosing an option from the to-be-selected assortment. Understanding the psychology of assortments gives companies a competitive advantage, allowing them to design assortments and product lines that maximize benefits to consumers while simultaneously minimizing costs.

Ryan Hamilton is assistant Professor of Marketing at the Goizueta Business School, Emory University. He received his BS in applied physics from Brigham Young University and his PhD in marketing from the Kellogg School of Management, Northwestern University.

Alexander Chernev is associate Professor of Marketing at the Kellogg School of Management. He received an MA and PhD in psychology from Sofia University, as well as a PhD in business administration from Duke University. Both authors contributed equally to this chapter.

NOTES

1. Iyengar, S., and M. Lepper (2000), "When Choice Is Demotivating: Can One Desire Too Much of a Good Thing?" *Journal of Personality and Social Psychology*, 79 (December), 995–1006.
2. Sethi-Iyengar, S., G. Huberman, and W. Jiang (2004), "How Much Choice is Too Much? Contributions to 401(k) Retirement Plans." In *Pension Design and Structure: New Lessons from Behavioral Finance*, O. S. Mitchell and S. Utkus, (Eds.), Oxford: Oxford University Press, 83–95.
3. Chernev, A. (2003), "When More Is Less and Less Is More: The Role of Ideal Point Availability and Assortment in Consumer Choice," *Journal of Consumer Research*, 30(2), 170–183.
4. Diehl, K., and C. Poynor (2010), "Great Expectations?! Assortment Size, Expectations and Satisfaction," *Journal of Marketing Research*, 47(2), 312–22.
5. Boatwright, P., and J. Nunes (2001), "Reducing Assortment: An Attribute-Based Approach," *Journal of Marketing*, 65(3), 50–63.
6. Chernev, A., and R. Hamilton (2009), "Assortment Size and Option Attractiveness in Consumer Choice Among Retailers," *Journal of Marketing Research*, 46 (June), 410–420.
7. Kahn, B., and B. Wansink (2004), "The Influence of Assortment Structure on Perceived Variety and Consumption Quantities," *Journal of Consumer Research*, 30(4), 519–533.

8. Chernev, A. (2005), "Feature Complementarity and Assortment in Choice," *Journal of Consumer Research,* 31(4), 748–759.
9. Chernev, A. (2006), "Differentiation and Parity in Assortment Pricing," *Journal of Consumer Research*, 33(2), 199–210.
10. Thaler, R., and S. Benartzi (2004), "Save More Tomorrow: Using Behavioral Economics to Increase Employee Saving," *Journal of Political Economy,* 112(1), S164–S187.
11. Hamilton, R., and A. Chernev (2009), "The Impact of Product Line Extensions and Consumer Goals on the Formation of Price Image," *Journal of Marketing Research*, 46(3), 410–420.
12. Chernev, A. (2006), "Decision Focus and Consumer Choice among Assortments," *Journal of Consumer Research,* 33(1), 50–59.

CHAPTER 18

GOAL-DRIVEN MARKETING RESEARCH: THE ANSWER TO A SHRINKING BUDGET

ANGELA Y. LEE

INTRODUCTION

All managers would agree that making good decisions requires having good information. Sometimes managers think they already have the information they need. Other times they feel that they have to make the decision based on what they know, even though they do not have all the information they would like to have. And then there are times when they feel they need to have more information before making the final decision. Companies spend billions of dollars on marketing research every year to help managers make better decisions, yet they are quick to cut back on marketing research spending in challenging times. These actions seem to suggest that marketing research may not be delivering good value.

Indeed, not every marketing research report that comes back provides information that managers can use. Often managers receive the report and are disappointed with the findings. The research either tells them things they already know or leaves gaps that necessitate a lot of guesswork or arbitrary decisions to map out and implement strategies. But there is another way for companies to increase the return on their research dollars besides reducing the marketing research budget—by making sure that the research does what it is supposed to do; that is, to provide useful inputs for managers to make informed decisions.

This chapter is not about the pros and cons of gathering more information. That line has already been crossed. This chapter is about how to gather the usable information that managers need. Refer to any marketing research handbook or textbook to see the marketing research process clearly outlined:

- Define the research purpose and objective.
- Determine the research design.
- Specify the sampling plan and the sample size.
- Gather the data.
- Analyze and interpret the data.
- Report the results and provide recommendations.

This process reflects the science of conducting market research. It follows a perfectly logical order, starting with the reasons for conducting the research, followed by the type of research to be conducted, and finishing with the final document that reports the results. So what can go wrong?

The biggest trap is that managers often overlook the importance of clearly defining the objective and boundary of the research; as a result, they may end up with a lot of "nice to have" information while lacking the key inputs to help make the decision. Even with the most methodical approach to data gathering, the acquired information can be quite useless unless it can be used to support the recommendations. Successful marketing research that delivers useful information requires close collaboration between the user of the information (the decision maker) and the creator or compiler of that information (the researcher). For example, a company that is considering lowering prices of its machines to increase profit could ask the researcher to find out how many machines the company can sell if it lowers prices to different price levels. The required research can usually be carried out quickly and efficiently. But the researcher who understands the objective of the research would be in a better position to interpret and follow up with information relevant to the decision. For example, she may pick up on how customers value certain features while getting their responses to a price cut. The additional information may enable the company to increase profits by coming up with a new lower-priced model with just the key features.

Thus, if the researcher understands the reason behind the research, the quality and usefulness of the findings will be significantly improved. For this reason, a strong collaborative relationship between the decision maker and the researcher is an important prerequisite for gathering useful data. However, having a good understanding of the business problem and the reasons for conducting marketing research is not enough. The researcher must also clearly and narrowly define the objective of the research so that it will bring in useful information, and not waste resources on collecting the "nice to have" information that does not serve much purpose in the decision-making process.

To render the research findings useful to the manager, the researcher needs to practice the art of *goal-driven* marketing research planning. The idea is to start planning the research where the goal has already been achieved and work backward. This ensures that each stage of the process is guided by what comes after it rather than on what comes before it. Here's how it works.

STEP 1: START BY PREPARING THE REPORT

To help managers meet their objectives, the researcher should start focusing on the *end* of the marketing research process when the goal of the research is achieved—preparing the report first, then working backward. Knowing the nature of the recommendation (e.g., whether to invest in a business) allows the researcher to foresee the kind of arguments that should be presented (e.g., profitability analysis), which in turn helps to define what information is required (e.g., consumption data, market share, pricing, fixed and variable costs) and to specify how the data will be analyzed.

The final report cannot be produced without the research, and the recommendations cannot be made without the data. But the outline of the report can be prepared in advance so that when the data become available, all the researcher needs to do is to fill in the blanks. This procedure of first preparing the shell of the report ensures that the marketing research dollar is well spent—that the right kind of data will be collected and the wrong kind of data will be ignored. In essence, preparing the report helps to fine-tune the objective of the research.

STEP 2: CONSIDER HOW TO ANALYZE THE DATA

Knowing how the data will be analyzed helps determine how to collect the data and the format in which the data should come. Should the data be qualitative or quantitative, or both? Should consumers' preferences be measured using a rank order scale (e.g., "Please rank the following brands in terms of how much you like them, with 1 being the most liked"), a rating scale (e.g., "Please rate each of the following brands using the scale provided, with 1 = dislike very much and 7 = like very much"), or by making a choice (e.g., "please select the brand that you like the most")?

To illustrate, imagine that the purpose of the research is to conduct a segmentation study for a men's clothing store. The goal is to better understand the needs of the store's current and potential customers, with the final report containing a description of the different segments. This would include information on each segment's values, lifestyle, interests, usage and shopping patterns, and demographics. The research instrument should include items that tap into these different topics, and the responses should yield numerical data that could be put through a *factor analysis* (a statistical data-reduction technique used to detect interrelationships among a large number of variables and to explain these variables in terms of their common underlying dimensions) or a *cluster analysis* (a statistical technique in which people are classified into "clusters" where those within a cluster are similar to one another and different from those in other clusters). Such numerical data may be obtained by asking respondents to indicate a degree of agreement or disagreement with a series of statements about certain topics (e.g., "I dress for fashion, not comfort"). Typically the response scale has five to seven categories ranging from "strongly disagree" to "strongly agree," and a numerical value is assigned to each category (e.g., 1 = strongly disagree, 5 = strongly agree). And if the final report is to include respondents' descriptions of their shopping experiences, then the research instrument should include open-ended items that allow comments to be reported verbatim.

Thus, knowing how the data are to be analyzed informs the researcher as to how the data should be gathered. If qualitative data are desired, then media such as personal interviews, online focus groups, and so on (which allow the recording of rich, contextual information) should be used. If quantitative data analysis is intended, then a survey-type instrument is appropriate.

Knowing the kinds of quantitative analysis to be performed also helps to determine how questions should be phrased and how responses should be measured. Responses typically include demographics, values and attitudes such as perceptions and preferences, purchase intentions, and past behaviors, each represented by one or more variables. A variable can potentially be measured using one of four different types of scales: nominal, ordinal, interval, and ratio. The type of scale used determines the kind of analyses that can be performed. *Nominal-scaled variables* are the most restrictive in terms statistical analyses (usually limited to frequency, percentage, and mode), followed by ordinal-scaled variables (median is permissible) and interval-scaled variables (mean and standard deviation are meaningful); and *ratio-scaled variables* are the least restrictive (usually include a wide range of variables, such as frequency, percentage, mode, median, range, percentile ranking, mean, standard deviation, geometric mean).

For example, the editor of a magazine may wish to survey readers to find out what magazines they like to read. Reader preference can be measured in different ways. Respondents may be presented with a list of magazines and asked to indicate which magazines they have read in the last 12 months. This check-all-that-applies measure produces a nominal-scaled number for each magazine (1 = Yes, 0 = No), which can be summed across all respondents. The result can then be reported in a statement such as: "85 percent of our readers have read X, which makes it the most popular magazine among our readers." Alternatively, respondents may be asked to rank the magazines in the order of their preferences. Such ranking data produce an ordinal-scaled number for each magazine and can yield statements such as: "X is the most popular magazine, as it is ranked the #1 most preferred magazine by most of our readers." Another way to assess popularity may be to ask respondents to rate how much they enjoy reading the magazines on a scale of 1 to 5, with 1 being the least enjoyable and 5 being the most enjoyable (with an additional column marked "have never read this magazine"). Data collected using this interval-scaled measure could be reported this way: "X tops the chart with an enjoyment rating of 4.75 among its readers, while Y comes in last with a rating of 2.3." However, it is important to note that it will be incorrect to make a statement about the two magazines involving ratios based on the readers' responses to this question; that is, you cannot say: "Readers consider reading X to be twice as enjoyable as reading Y." To make this kind of direct comparison statements, a ratio-scaled measure is needed. For example, readers could be asked to indicate how much they would be willing to pay for a one-year subscription to the magazine. Their willingness to pay in terms of dollars reflects a ratio-scaled number, which could be reported this way: "X has the most appeal among its readers, as its readers are willing to pay on average $36 for a one-year subscription for the magazine, which is 1.5 times higher than what they are willing to pay for the magazine with the next highest subscription rate."

Thus, the kind of statement you wish to make dictates the type of data analysis to be performed, which in turn helps to specify how the data should be collected, what questions to ask, how to ask, and what types of scaling should be used.

STEP 3: DECIDE HOW TO GATHER THE DATA

Knowing how the data are to be collected helps to specify how many respondents are needed and how to recruit them (i.e., the sampling method). The researcher can choose between random (or probability) sampling and nonrandom sampling methods. Random sampling methods require that each unit in the population (e.g., current customers) has a known chance of being included in the sample. The sample is drawn using some method of random selection, such as a list of random numbers generated by a computer. By contrast, nonrandom sampling methods do not depend on random selection and are influenced by feasibility considerations such as availability of respondents, costs, and time constraints. The key benefit of random sampling is that by relying on statistical theory of random samples, you can compute the size of the sampling error (i.e., the extent to which the estimate from the sample is likely to be different from the measure for the population as a whole). This allows the researcher to make generalizable statements about the population based on the research findings. The sampling error is not applicable to nonrandom samples. However, this does not mean that findings from a nonrandom sample cannot be informative of the population of interest. Nonrandom samples are typically less expensive and less time-consuming to recruit than random samples, and they can be effective depending on the objectives of the research.

For example, generating different positioning ideas would not require a representative sample of target consumers, nor does it call for many respondents. The objective of the research is simply to come up with different ideas to be further developed, considered, and eventually tested. Hence, gathering ideas from a small number of respondents recruited using a nonrandom sampling plan is appropriate. However, if the marketing research objective is to come up with a recommendation for a positioning strategy—supported by quantitative data showing how appealing different positioning ideas are to the target consumers—then a random sampling plan should be implemented. And the appropriate sample size should be determined after taking into consideration the heterogeneity of the target population, the magnitude of the sampling error, and the desired confidence level. Thus, knowing what to ask helps the researcher determine the sampling plan and the sample size.

STEP 4: DETERMINE THE RESEARCH INSTRUMENT AND THE DESIGN

Knowing how to collect data—by using either a random or a nonrandom sample—informs the researcher of the research design and the type of research instrument (e.g., in-depth interview, focus groups, observations, mail survey, online survey, telephone survey) that is most appropriate. A research design is a blueprint or plan for how the research objectives will be accomplished; and there are three types of research designs—*exploratory, descriptive,* and *causal.*

It is not unusual that the researcher employs different designs at different stages of the project. By working backward, the researcher is assured that the type of research design that is most suited to the objective of the research is in play.

Exploratory designs are the least structured and most flexible. As data are gathered, they allow the unexpected to emerge and the information requirements to adapt. For instance, open-ended question formats enable the researcher to probe respondents in focus groups and one-on-one interviews. Therefore, exploratory methods such as qualitative research are most useful at early stages of the research process. Qualitative research is good for idea generation and hypotheses formulation. It can also help managers understand quantitative research findings. However, the interpretation of the findings is based on judgment. The techniques rarely provide precise quantitative measurement, and the ability to generalize the results is limited. An exploratory research design is implicated when nonrandom samples are used.

By contrast, descriptive and causal methods are more structured and inflexible. Once data collection begins, there is little opportunity to change the information being gathered. These methods presuppose that the researcher already knows a lot about the problem being studied. Hence, they are typically employed at later stages in the research process. Descriptive research is conducted to quantify certain market characteristics or functions. It is used when managers want to develop profiles of different segments, estimate segment size, predict sales, and so on. Basically this type of research provides answers to questions about who, what, when, how, how often, and how many, and requires a good deal of prior knowledge about the phenomenon being studied. For example, the researcher adopting a descriptive research design needs to know who the target respondent is and what information is to be collected. If the researcher does not have this information, then it is clear that exploratory research should first be conducted.

When the research aims to provide an understanding of certain cause and effect relationships, then causal research comes into play. Consider a sales force decision facing a pharmaceutical company: How many calls should sales representatives make on physicians each quarter? The answer to this question requires an understanding of the effect of the number of sales calls on the prescription behavior of physicians. Similarly, consider a pricing question facing a consumer packaged goods manufacturer: Should the company increase price by $0.50 per unit? The answer depends on the effect of this price change on sales, market share, and profits generated by the product. In both of these examples, the goal of the researcher is to determine the magnitude of the effect of a marketing mix variable (number of sales calls, price) on some variable of interest (prescription behavior, sales). When random samples that allow for the findings to be generalized are used, then the research would either involve a causal or descriptive design.

The choice of research design should be iterative in nature, and the most appropriate research design depends on the researcher's current knowledge and understanding of the problem, which changes as the research progresses. By working backward, the researcher knows whether he or she has the knowledge of the specific questions to ask, how to ask, and whom to ask. Hence, he or she can determine which research design would work best.

It is useful to begin a project with a specific plan—that's the science of marketing research. But researchers and decision makers must be willing to modify and update the plan based on what they have learned from going backward in the process—that's the art of goal-driven marketing research.

A Case Study: Vive La Crepe

To illustrate these steps, we examine the case study of Vive La Crepe, a three-month-old restaurant in Evanston, Illinois, which wanted to know if it should expand current services to include breakfast on weekdays. Vive La Crepe's current business hours were Tuesday through Friday from 11:00 A.M. to 10:00 P.M., Saturday from 9:00 A.M. to 11:00 P.M., and Sunday from 9:00 A.M. to 9:00 P.M.

The management had limited budget for market research, but it did not want to act blindly and so approached a team of Kellogg students who took on this case as a class project. The research team members knew that their recommendation would have to be based on an understanding of the demand for breakfast in the local community and how much of this demand Vive La Crepe was likely to get. To conduct the research, the team employed the four marketing research steps described above.

Step 1: Identify What Information Is Needed

To assess the market demand for breakfast in Evanston, the research team decided that the following information would be useful:

- Evanston residents' demographics and food spending statistics.
- A listing of Evanston restaurants with information on which restaurants are open for breakfast.
- Information on breakfast traffic at competing restaurants during the week.

To assess the demand for breakfast specifically at Vive La Crepe, the research team thought that the following information would be relevant:

- Factors driving weekday breakfast customers' decisions of where to go for breakfast.
- Weekday breakfast customers' perceptions of Vive La Crepe and their likelihood of going to Vive La Crepe for breakfast.
- Current Vive La Crepe customers' perceptions of Vive La Crepe.
- Likelihood of current Vive La Crepe customers to come for breakfast during the week.

Having identified the information needed for the final report, the research team members then considered the specific format of the information to help them decide how to collect the data.

Step 2: Think About How to Analyze the Data

The goal of the research was to assess whether people would go to Vive La Crepe for breakfast during the week. The research team anticipated that the final report would contain a statement such as: "X percent of the respondents surveyed indicated that they definitely would go to Vive La Crepe for breakfast on a weekday." With this in mind, the team developed the following question to be included in the survey:

Vive La Crepe is a new restaurant located in downtown Evanston. For weekend brunch they serve a variety of breakfast food items, including crepes, omelets, waffles, pancakes, and eggs. If Vive La Crepe were open for breakfast during the week, how likely would you be to go there for breakfast on a weekday?

[] Definitely would
[] Probably would
[] Might or might not
[] Probably would not
[] Definitely would not

Thus, knowing the specific information they needed enabled the research team to specify how the data should be collected and what question should be asked.

Step 3: Consider How to Gather the Data

Given that the goal of the research was to assess the potential demand for weekday breakfast at Vive La Crepe, the research team designed a question to quantify the likelihood of people going to Vive La Crepe for breakfast on a weekday. Because the researchers needed to be able to generalize the purchase intent data to other restaurant-goers not included in the surveys, they knew they had to recruit two random samples: one sample of respondents who currently ate breakfast at a restaurant on a weekday, and a second sample of respondents who were current Vive La Crepe customers.

The research team decided to conduct intercept interviews outside the restaurants to assess how often customers eat breakfast at a restaurant and how likely they would be to go to Vive La Crepe for breakfast during the week. The team members had identified four main restaurants in Evanston that served breakfast during the week, and they set up a schedule to go to each of these locations on different days of the week to conduct intercept interviews. The plan was to approach every third person leaving the restaurant to invite them to participate in the survey.

Date	Time	Location
Saturday, 5/17	9:00–10:00 A.M.	Vive La Crepe, Clarke's, Le Peep
	10:00–11:00 A.M.	Lucky Platter, Walker Brothers
Sunday, 5/18	9:00–11:00 A.M.	Vive La Crepe, Clarke's, Le Peep, Lucky Platter, Walker Brothers
Tuesday, 5/20	9:00–10:00 A.M.	Clarke's, Le Peep, Walker Brothers
	10:00–11:00 A.M.	Lucky Platter, Walker Brothers
	5:00–6:00 P.M.	Vive La Crepe
Wednesday, 5/21	9:00–10:00 A.M.	Le Peep, Clarke's
	6:00–8:00 P.M.	Vive La Crepe
Thursday, 5/22	9:00–10:00 A.M.	Le Peep, Walker Brothers
	10:00–11:00 A.M.	Clarke's, Lucky Platter
Saturday 5/24	9:00–11:00 A.M.	Vive La Crepe

The team understood that they had to make projections of the demand for weekday breakfast business at Vive La Crepe based on the survey results. Thus, they set up a schedule to systematically sample from the populations of weekday breakfast patrons and current Vive La Crepe customers.

Step 4: Determine the Research Instrument and Design

It was clear that the purchase intent data had to come from a random sample of current Vive La Crepe customers and customers patronizing other restaurants for breakfast. Thus, the research team decided to conduct an intercept survey on the street outside the different restaurants. However, a survey was not necessarily the right instrument for all the data that the team needed to collect. Other data collection approaches were identified to be more appropriate for the other pieces of information identified in Step 1.

- Evanston residents' demographics and spending statistics should be available from the U.S. Census Bureau and Bureau of Labor Statistics.
- A listing of Evanston restaurants with information on their opening hours would be available online.
- Information on breakfast traffic at competing restaurants during the week could be collected by conducting on-site observations to take note of the number of tables occupied, size of dining parties, average check size, and menu selections.
- Factors driving weekday breakfast customers' decisions of where to go for breakfast would require a survey administered to competitors' breakfast customers.
- Weekday breakfast customers' perceptions of Vive La Crepe and their likelihood of going to Vive La Crepe for breakfast could be included in the same survey recommended in the fourth bullet point above.
- Current Vive La Crepe customers' perceptions of Vive La Crepe would require a survey administered to current Vive La Crepe customers.
- Likelihood of current Vive La Crepe customers to come for breakfast during the week could be included in the same survey recommended in the sixth bullet point above.

The research team started with the final report and worked backward in its planning of the research. This goal-driven market research planning process ensured that the right research design was in place, the appropriate research instrument used, the critical questions asked, the right people sampled, the proper analyses conducted, and the objective of the research fulfilled.

SUMMARY

The marketing research process is a logical, scientific way to think about how to conduct marketing research. Researchers need to understand the flow and the sequence of steps in conducting good research. But following the sequence in this logical manner is not enough. The master researcher is one who understands and practices both the *science* and the *art* of marketing research. Once the research plan is laid down, the master researcher reverses the planning process. By starting with the report and going backward, the researcher ensures that the objective of the research will be optimally served—by sampling the right people, asking the critical questions, using the appropriate measurement scales, and applying the proper analytical techniques to the data. Thus, by starting at the end where the goal of the research is achieved and going backward in the planning of the marketing research, the researcher ensures that the manager is provided with the right information needed to make the decision. There will be no more surprises and no more disappointments in the adequacy and usefulness of the findings.

Angela Y. Lee is the Mechthild Esser Nemmers Professor of Marketing at the Kellogg School of Management. She is co-editor of Kellogg on China: Strategies for Success. She received her BBA from the University of Hawaii at Manoa, her MPhil from the University of Hong Kong and her PhD from the University of Toronto.

CHAPTER 19

ALIGNING SALES AND MARKETING TO ENHANCE CUSTOMER VALUE AND DRIVE COMPANY RESULTS

ANDRIS A. ZOLTNERS, PRABHAKANT SINHA, and
SALLY E. LORIMER

INTRODUCTION: A SUCCESSFUL CUSTOMER-FACING ORGANIZATION

Sales and marketing work closely together to pursue a common objective: *drive company results by delivering value to customers*. Well-aligned marketing and sales teams create a powerful, unified, customer-facing force that enables a company to successfully differentiate its products and services from competitors as well as sell value, consistently reinforce its brands, and drive company revenues, profits, and market share.

In order for a sales and marketing organization to successfully deliver value to customers, it must accomplish many diverse and often complex tasks. This requires considerable knowledge and many different skills and capabilities. Some of the work is tactical, while other work is strategic. Tactical work involves serving day-to-day customer needs—for example, answering a prospect's question about a proposal or placing a customer's repeat order. Strategic work focuses on developing marketing strategies that enable long-term success—understanding who the company's customers are, what they need, how they value the company's offering, what advantages that offering has over those of competitors, and how customer needs and competitive offerings are likely to evolve in the future.

A successful customer-facing organization also must bridge the gap between long-term strategies and day-to-day interactions with customers. Salespeople need guidance regarding which customers and prospects are most attractive and require attention, which products and services to emphasize, and what the most effective value proposition is for different customers. The company needs to establish prices, design promotions, produce sales collateral and selling tools, and develop quarterly or annual sales forecasts.

Successful customer relationships can only be created and sustained when all these different activities are accomplished successfully. The bandwidth required to complete all of this work is much greater than the capacity of any single individual. A wide range of skills, knowledge, and capabilities is needed to manage day-to-day interactions with customers, develop market strategies and plans, and at the same time accomplish all the activities that bridge the gap between strategy and tactics. Hence, there is a need for specialization into separate sales and marketing roles. At the same time, because sales and marketing share a common objective and depend on one another to accomplish that objective, there is a clear need for coordination and communication between the two.

A TYPICAL FRAMEWORK FOR DIVIDING WORK BETWEEN SALES AND MARKETING

Figure 19.1 shows a representative division of work between sales and marketing in a typical company, with the intersection of the Venn diagram illustrating the need for effective coordination. In this type of division, marketing takes primary responsibility for executing *upstream* activities—those that occur early in the sequence of tasks that need to be accomplished before prospects will buy and hopefully become loyal customers. These activities include market research, competitive analysis, strategy development, segmentation, product development and positioning, branding, customer communications, and packaging. Marketing is also responsible for ensuring that the necessary collateral and other relevant information created by this work flows to sales.

Meanwhile, sales takes primary responsibility for performing downstream activities that occur further along in the customer connection process, where the day-to-day interactions with customers and prospects take place. These activities include account management, personal selling, competitive market intelligence, distributor management, installation, after-sales service, merchandising, and sales effectiveness programs. Sales is also responsible for ensuring that feedback obtained through this work flows back to marketing.

Figure 19.1
How Work Is Typically Divided Between Sales and Marketing

The joint activities in the intersection of the two circles usually require shared decision making and collaboration between sales and marketing. These activities include customer/prospect selection, product/service prioritization, value proposition development/customer messaging, pricing, sales forecasting, and promotions. These activities necessitate a synchronized effort between both sales and marketing.

For a sales and marketing organization to be successful, all the components of the framework in Figure 19.1 must function effectively. Specifically:

- The company must accomplish the *marketing activities* successfully. Other chapters of this book provide ideas for accomplishing many of these activities.
- The company must execute the *sales activities* effectively. Chapter 12, "Building a Winning Sales Force," provides ideas on how to achieve this.
- *Information flows* must run smoothly from marketing to sales and vice versa.
- Sales and marketing must collaborate and cooperate to accomplish the *joint activities*.

Ways that companies can facilitate the accomplishment of all of these objectives are described later in this chapter.

ALTERNATIVE WAYS TO DIVIDE WORK BETWEEN SALES AND MARKETING

Figure 19.1 provides a generalized framework for assigning sales and marketing work within a customer-facing organization. Depending on customer needs and company goals, each company has its own lists of tasks to be accomplished and its own best way to divide those tasks between sales and marketing. Several dimensions of the ways that companies organize sales and marketing work, and examples of how the framework captures these situations, are described here.

The extent to which the sales and marketing teams need to collaborate in order to accomplish joint activities varies across companies. Figure 19.2 compares two situations: a "low-overlap" situation where there are few joint sales-marketing tasks, and a "high-overlap" situation where sales and marketing must cooperate extensively to accomplish many joint tasks.

Independent Sales and Marketing Teams

In some companies, sales and marketing can succeed by working largely independently. Marketing handles activities such as developing product strategy, creating awareness, and generating leads before handing off execution and customer follow-up to sales. A sales leader at a pharmaceutical company describes this "handoff." When asked how the company determined its market segments, the sales leader replied, "It's marketing's job to come up with the segments. We implement the segment plans for individual customers."

Figure 19.2
Sales-Marketing Organizations with Varied Needs for Collaboration

Collaborative Sales and Marketing Teams

At other companies, sales and marketing collaborate extensively to accomplish many joint tasks—for example, working together to decide how to segment markets, develop value propositions, create common standards for leads and opportunities, determine appropriate pricing, and develop tools to support the sales process. Leaders at a company that provides food services to large institutions estimated that marketing spent approximately half of its time engaged in activities that involved direct collaboration with sales—activities such as creating collateral and presentation materials for sales to use with customers and at trade shows and developing proposals for specific customers and prospects.

Sales-Dominant and Marketing-Dominant Organizations

Some organizations have sales and marketing teams that are roughly equal in terms of emphasis and the importance of their activities for company success. Other organizations have marketing and sales organizations where one side or the other is more prominent, as shown in Figure 19.3.

Sales-Dominant Organizations   Many business-to-business companies—for example, in technology, insurance, health care, and distribution businesses—have historically been sales-dominant. These companies attribute their successes largely to differentiated products, personal relationships between salespeople and customers, and the value that the sales force creates for customers. Consequently, sales-dominant companies place most of their customer connection effort on personal selling and account management. They see marketing as a sales support function that performs activities to help the sales force. Such companies devote less time to marketing activities that have long-term strategic impact. The mindset of sales-dominant companies is reflected in a slogan seen

Figure 19.3
Sales-Marketing Organizations Where One Side Dominates

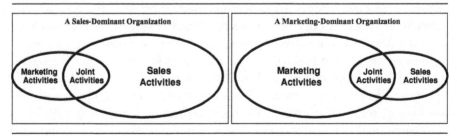

on a poster in the marketing department at a sales-dominant medical technology company in Spain: "The job of sales is to take care of the customer. The job of marketing is to take care of sales."

Marketing-Dominant Organizations   Marketing-dominant organizations include many business-to-consumer companies. In addition to developing marketing strategies, these companies rely on marketing approaches such as advertising, Internet selling, direct mail, and catalogs to connect with their customers and generate demand for their products. At Internet and catalog retailers such as Lands' End and L.L. Bean, for example, salespeople are primarily order-takers who handle inbound calls; increasingly at these companies, customers place Internet orders themselves without requiring assistance from a salesperson. Management expert Peter Drucker summed up the belief of many marketing-dominant organizations when he wrote: "The aim of marketing is to make selling superfluous," and that, "the right motto for business management should increasingly be 'from selling to marketing.'"[1]

Companies with Multitier Distribution   Some companies—for example, consumer goods manufacturers—must connect with multiple tiers of distribution to reach their markets. Procter & Gamble (P&G) sells its consumer packaged goods through food, drug, and mass merchandise retailers (the customer), but the ultimate end-user is someone in a household (the consumer). P&G and other consumer goods manufacturers use sales forces to influence customers (push strategy), and marketing to influence both consumers (pull strategy) and customers. As the power of retailers has increased (with large retailers such as Walmart now controlling a substantial share of the business), consumer goods companies have expanded the role of marketing in connecting with these large customers, requiring stronger alignment of their sales and marketing efforts. Customer-connection work at a consumer goods (or other multitiered distribution) company can be organized as shown in Figure 19.4.

In this environment, several teams are at work simultaneously. A *field sales team* establishes and maintains partnerships with the retail trade. A *consumer marketing team* generates demand among *consumers* by developing brands and differentiating them from competitors. A *field marketing team* develops and helps the sales force execute marketing programs for major retailers (for example, category management programs, trade and consumer promotions, co-op advertising, or customized products). A *strategic marketing team* oversees marketing efforts and guides the activities of both of the consumer marketing and field marketing groups. It is critical that these various sales and marketing teams collaborate and communicate to ensure that their efforts are synchronized

Figure 19.4
An Organization of Sales and Marketing Work in a Multitier
Distribution Environment

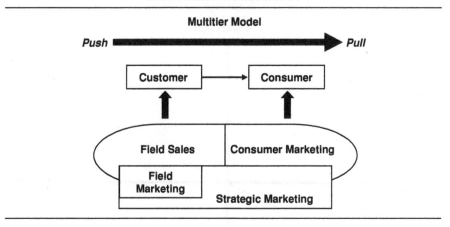

and aligned with consumer desires, customer needs, and company goals and strategies.

THE SALES-MARKETING ALIGNMENT CHALLENGE

A well-aligned sales and marketing organization creates power for a company, but many companies find it difficult to achieve effective alignment. Although sellers and marketers depend on one another to attain the common objective of delivering customer value to drive company results, they often have different thought worlds and points of view about how to go about achieving that objective. Figure 19.5 illustrates three important dimensions of difference between the marketing and sales mindsets.

Customer-Focus versus Product- or Segment-Focus

Salespeople are responsible for a set of specific customers and are expected to deeply understand individual customer needs. Marketing people usually deal with aggregations of customers. Product managers are expected to understand and increase the value of a product or brand across many customer segments. Market segment managers usually look at summarized customer data to develop an overall understanding of the needs of an entire market segment.

Figure 19.5
A Three-Dimensional View of the Sales and Marketing Mindsets

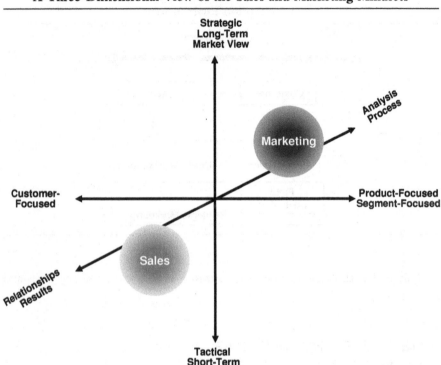

Relationships and Results versus Analysis and Process

Success in sales is driven by salespeople's ability to build relationships with individual customers in order to drive company results. Marketing jobs require analytic capability and success in applying processes for gathering and analyzing data in order to extract a broad view of customer segments and product opportunities.

Short-Term Customer Tactics versus Long-Term Market Strategies

Sales force expectations, recognitions, and rewards are tied to the achievement of short-term financial objectives, such as annual, quarterly, or even monthly sales goals. Marketing people, on the other hand, are charged with building long-term competitive advantage. The impact of marketing projects and decisions is sometimes not evident for many years.

These thought-world differences are both a source of strength and a source of tension for sales and marketing organizations. On the one hand, specialization makes the sales and marketing organization more effective. While sales focuses on building relationships with individual customers and achieving short-term revenue goals, marketing worries about analyzing overall market trends and developing strategies for long-term success. This "divide and conquer" approach allows a company to match people to jobs that best fit with their abilities and at the same time allows people to develop strong skills and deep knowledge as they focus on specific tasks and goals.

On the other hand, thought-world differences can create tension between sales and marketing as the two depend on one another to achieve their common objective. Sometimes tensions arise when one group (either sales or marketing) believes that the other group is not doing its job well. For example, marketing works hard to generate what it feels are excellent leads for the sales force, yet sales believes that marketing's leads are weak and therefore does not follow up. Tensions can also arise when there is perceived unfairness to the work or to the rewards received by either sales or marketing. For example, marketing feels that it gets too little credit for using creative insight to develop programs for the sales force and that salespeople earn all the money simply for closing a sale. Tensions like these are especially likely in areas such as lead generation and pricing, where sales and marketing must cooperate closely to produce good results.

A survey conducted with sales and marketing leaders who attended a 2007 course at Kellogg on integrating sales and marketing strategies shows the difficulty that companies face when trying to align sales and marketing. We asked these leaders prior to attending the course, "What sales and marketing alignment issues do you currently face?" Of the 34 participants who responded (approximately half of which were in sales and half of which were in marketing) 29 indicated that their companies faced difficult challenges in aligning sales and marketing effectively for a variety of reasons, as summarized in Figure 19.6. A more complete list of responses appears in *Building a Winning Sales Force*.[2]

FOUR FACILITATORS OF SUCCESSFUL SALES-MARKETING ALIGNMENT

There are a number of ways that companies can facilitate the alignment of a strong sales and marketing organization—an organization in which both *marketing activities* and *sales activities* are executed effectively, where *information flows* seamlessly between sales and marketing, and where sales and marketing cooperate as needed to accomplish *joint activities* successfully. Figure 19.7 shows

Figure 19.6
Some Common Reasons for Sales–Marketing Misalignment

Alignment Challenge	Example Quote from a Sales or Marketing Leader
Sales and marketing have different responsibilities and perspectives.	• "Marketing has a 30K ft. vision of how things should be in the marketplace and sales has a 3 ft. vision of how things should work with individual customers." (*Marketing leader, media*) • "Sales wants it now and doesn't mind if it's only 80 percent done; marketing wants more time, more research, and more budget." (*Sales leader, exhibit marketing*)
Sales and marketing have different objectives and success metrics.	• "Sales is not held accountable for profits, just revenues. Product management is accountable for both." (*Marketing leader, technology*) • "Sales compensation is not aligned with marketing goals." (*Marketing leader, health care*)
Sales and marketing have conflicts over joint sales-marketing activities.	• "Sales and marketing do not agree on market segmentation, opportunity, and priorities." (*Marketing leader, pharmaceuticals*) • "Marketing lacks credibility with sales. Salespeople prefer to design their own marketing materials that address specific client issues." (*Sales leader, financial services*)
There are breakdowns in sales-marketing information flows.	• "Salespeople know individual client needs very well, but there is no way for marketing to systematically gather and analyze this information." (*Marketing leader, financial services*) • "Marketing rarely provides any competitive intelligence to the sales force." (*Sales leader, auto parts*)

Figure 19.7
Four Facilitators of Sales and Marketing Alignment

Sales-Marketing Alignment Facilitators

	Culture	People	Structure	Processes/Systems
Goals	• Customer focus • Trust, respect, and teamwork • Appreciation for diversity • "Oneness"	• Strong sales and/or marketing skills • Communication skills • Collaborative team players	• Organizational structures that define the right sales and marketing roles while facilitating needed collaboration and communication	• Processes and systems that encourage sales and marketing success while facilitating needed collaboration and communication
Representative Solutions	• Design *people, structure,* and *process/system* solutions to encourage the desired culture • Communicate the desired culture • Reward the desired behaviors • "Walk the talk"	• Recruit, train, and coach to create a team of people with strong skills and capabilities for sales, marketing, communication, and collaboration	• Establish sales and marketing teams of the appropriate size and degree of specialization • Have joint sales-marketing leadership • Utilize cross-functional task forces and integrating roles as needed to encourage collaboration and communication	• Define and document effective joint sales-marketing business processes • Use informal and formal communication channels • Provide effective information systems

four categories of facilitators that companies have used to create and sustain well-aligned sales and marketing organizations, along with the goals for each category and some solutions that companies have implemented to achieve these goals.

The most difficult sales and marketing alignment challenges require solutions from multiple facilitator categories. Several solutions are discussed here.

Creating a Customer-Focused, Team-Oriented Culture

Strong alignment of sales and marketing starts with the right culture. Companies where sales and marketing work effectively together describe their cultures using words such as "customer-focused," "trust," "respect," "teamwork," "oneness," and "appreciation for diversity." Company leaders help to foster consensus around and increase the intensity of this culture by demonstrating to the entire organization that they are committed to alignment. They use methods such as:

- *Communicating* the culture that the company prefers at every opportunity; celebrating sales and marketing heroes who consistently make appropriate customer-focused choices; and sharing stories that demonstrate how sellers and marketers have worked together to successfully address difficult challenges.
- *Rewarding* appropriate behaviors constantly and consistently. Because sales and marketing people typically have different pay structures and performance metrics, intrinsic rewards (such as appreciation and recognition) may be more effective than extrinsic rewards (such as bonuses or salary increases).
- *"Walking the talk"* by ensuring that company leaders' actions are compatible with their words.
- *Aligning* the other facilitators to support the culture by hiring and promoting the right *people* and implementing culture-compatible *structures, systems, and processes.*

Recruiting and Developing Team-Focused People Who Are Talented and Skilled at Sales or Marketing

Effective sales-marketing alignment requires having the right people in sales and marketing—people who are good at their jobs, but who are also open-minded team players who have communication skills to facilitate information flows and the collaboration skills to encourage effective joint decision making.

Effective recruiting and selection for the sales and marketing teams ensures that people with the right attitude and capabilities join the team. Once selected, development programs can help team members learn what they need to know to do their own jobs effectively and also broadly increase their skills and knowledge to work more effectively with one another. Development programs that can help sales and marketing people have greater empathy for one another's viewpoints include common sales and marketing training programs and job shadowing arrangements—for example, where marketing people visit customers with salespeople or where salespeople attend marketing meetings.

Companies have also had success using cross-functional job rotations and career paths to develop their people. For example, Intel (according to the company's web site, October 2009) has a sales and marketing rotation program for technical college graduates who seek careers in sales or marketing. Participants spend a year working in a technical marketing position, followed by a year focused on account responsibilities, enabling them to gain an understanding of Intel's products and services and business models from both a sales and marketing perspective. At the end of the program, participants are placed in a technical marketing or a technical sales position.

Establishing Organizational Structures that Encourage Alignment

In companies with strong sales and marketing organizations, both the sales team and the marketing team are sized and structured appropriately. Additionally, companies have implemented several structure solutions to encourage smooth information flows and cooperation between sales and marketing to accomplish joint activities.

Joint Sales and Marketing Leadership   When sales and marketing operate independently, each reporting to its own leader and coming together at the highest levels within the company (such as the division president, COO, or even the CEO level), silos can emerge that create a climate of tension and internal competitiveness. If the sales and marketing leaders report into a lower level, say a single vice president of sales and marketing, that individual can focus on making sure that sales and marketing are on the same page. When sales and marketing leadership are separate, a company can encourage alignment by selecting two leaders who have a cooperative working relationship. It can also use tactics such as locating the leaders' workspaces close to one another and using some common metrics to evaluate performance for both leaders.

Cross-Functional Task Forces   Temporary task forces composed of people from both sales and marketing can take responsibility for particular activities, such as the development of new sales collateral or the design of a computer tool to enhance salespeople's interactions with customers. By working together, sellers and marketers can create better outcomes by incorporating a wider range of views into the decision process. Task force members grow as they develop a more complete understanding of the entire sales and marketing organization. By making decisions jointly, team members feel a sense of ownership for their decisions and become stronger champions of those decisions.

Integrating Sales and Marketing Roles   New permanent sales and marketing roles can facilitate alignment. Companies can create an integrator role that gives a person or a team responsibility for improving the interaction between sales and marketing. Some integrators help to facilitate communications from salespeople to marketers and vice versa, but do not always have the authority to affect the way that work is done. Other integrators are given responsibility for specific joint sales-marketing projects, such as the development of sales forecasts or a pricing process.

Software company Siebel Systems Inc. (acquired by Oracle Corporation in 2005) had success using integrator roles to encourage sales and marketing alignment.[3] Siebel's marketing organization included corporate marketing and field marketing teams. Corporate marketing was responsible for areas such as product branding, trade shows, and public relations. Field marketing had people staffed in local sales offices to work directly with sales staff to design and implement demand generation programs that would help the sales force achieve its goals. Siebel also had a sales development organization that facilitated the successful transfer of leads from marketing to sales. This group qualified prospects, gathered and validated account and contact information, and created opportunities for the field sales organization, using both inbound responses generated by marketing campaigns and outbound reach efforts to targeted accounts. Success of the sales development group was enabled by detailed processes for generating leads and handing them off to sales, constant measurement against specific unified sales-marketing goals, and use of the company's own Customer Relationship Management (CRM) system to manage the lead-generation process.

Implementing Processes and Systems that Enable Alignment

Process/system solutions encourage cooperation and effective communication between sales and marketing by defining business *processes* for addressing specific

Figure 19.8
How United Airlines Revised Its Sales Strategy By Using a Structured Business Process That Was Enhanced By a Joint Effort Between Sales and Marketing

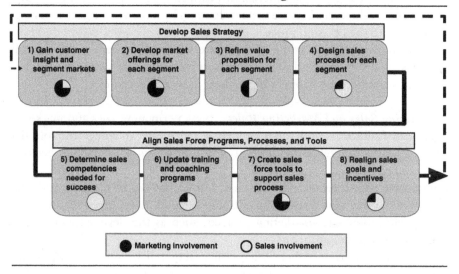

issues or opportunities. These processes specify goals, steps, and participants, clarify responsibilities, define terms (for example, what is a "lead" or what is "customer value"?), and specify the communication flows that need to occur between sales and marketing in order to make the best possible decisions. Often, these processes are supported by information *systems*, making them more efficient and effective.

Figure 19.8 shows the business process that United Airlines used to encourage strong alignment between sales and marketing as the company transformed its sales strategy for corporate and travel agent customers. With the industry facing significant financial challenges, United replaced the company's traditional sales approach (based on price and personal relationships) with a new value-based approach that encouraged salespeople to more deeply understand their customers' business needs, tailor customer-specific solutions, and continuously demonstrate the business value that solutions created beyond best-price alternatives.

The sales and marketing teams worked together to develop the new sales strategy and to implement it by aligning sales force programs, processes, and tools. Marketing took the lead role in some of the activities, while sales took the lead role in others. The cooperation of sales and marketing people, facilitated by the structured process, led to successful implementation of a new sales strategy that United company leaders felt made substantial performance contributions worldwide.

Processes that facilitate communication between sales and marketing can be both informal (such as town hall meetings or group outings) and formal (such as quarterly planning meetings or project reviews). Information systems that support sales and marketing processes encourage more effective communication while making the customer connection process more efficient and effective. Some examples of alignment-enabling systems are:

- *CRM systems* that manage customer databases and keep an integrated view of company-customer interactions, so that if multiple salespeople or marketers interact with the same customer, no one in the company is blindsided by what someone else has said, done, or promised.
- *Tools that strengthen the sales process* by assisting with selling tasks such as product configuration, customer solution development, and pricing.
- *Knowledge management systems* that facilitate sharing of insights across sales, marketing, and other company departments. For example, D. A. Stuart, a leading producer of lubricants for the metalworking industry, was a pioneer in giving salespeople access to the most recent marketing information via a company intranet. Marketing could post details about its latest activities—such as the updating of collateral, the mailing of promotional materials to specific customers or prospects, modifications to the firm's web site, and the uncovering of useful competitive information. Salespeople could access this information from anywhere at any time. Both marketing personnel and salespeople benefited from this process. Marketing saw its work communicated immediately to the sales force so that it could be put to use. Salespeople were never surprised by marketing activities and could leverage that work as appropriate.[4]

WHICH FACILITATORS TO USE TO ACCOMPLISH COMPANY GOALS

The facilitators can help companies increase the power of their sales and marketing teams both by improving the way that sales and marketing work together within a current organization, and by facilitating appropriate changes to the way that the sales and marketing effort is organized. The facilitators that companies should emphasize in different circumstances are described here.

Making a Current Sales-Marketing Organization Better

Once a company chooses the best way to organize its sales and marketing effort, it needs facilitators to ensure that all the organizations' components are working as effectively as possible. Recall that a successful sales and marketing organization requires four components to work successfully:

1. *Marketing activities* must be accomplished effectively.
2. *Sales activities* must be executed successfully.
3. Effective collaboration must occur to accomplish *joint activities*.
4. *Information flows* between marketing and sales must be strong.

Although the best way to facilitate the accomplishment of these objectives depends on the situation, we have observed that certain facilitators tend to be most effective for addressing specific issues or concerns (see Figure 19.9). Getting the right *people* in place is an important priority always, but it is especially critical when there is weakness in either the sales activities or the marketing activities. *Processes and systems* are critical for enabling effective collaboration around joint activities and encouraging strong information flows. *Structure* solutions can also be important for enabling the cooperation needed to accomplish joint activities, while *culture* is critical for enabling smooth information flows.

Changing the Way that Sales and Marketing Work Is Organized

Sometimes, companies discover that they can become more effective by changing the way that sales and marketing work together. There are many ways to

Figure 19.9
Facilitators that Address Different Sales-Marketing Concerns

Issue or Concern	Relative Importance of Facilitators for Addressing Issues			
	Culture	People	Structure	Processes/Systems
Sales is not doing its job well.	*	***	*	*
Marketing is not doing its job well.	*	***	*	*
Joint activities are not getting done well.	**	**	***	***
Information flows are not working well.	***	**	**	***

Figure 19.10
Two Common Ways that Companies Want to Change the Way that Sales and Marketing Work Together

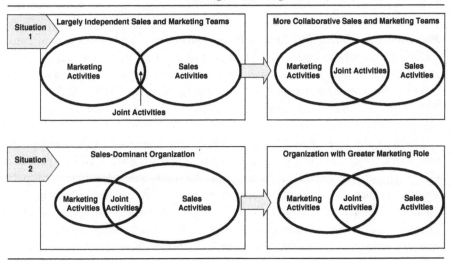

adapt the sales-marketing organization to enhance effectiveness in different circumstances, but here we focus on two situations that we observe frequently in business-to-business contexts and find most challenging (see Figure 19.10).

1. A company with largely independent sales and marketing teams wants to encourage greater sales-marketing collaboration.
2. A sales-dominated company wants to increase emphasis on marketing.

Facilitators for Increasing Sales–Marketing Collaboration   Often, companies want to increase sales and marketing power by encouraging greater collaboration around tasks that connect long-term strategies with day-to-day customer interactions—tasks such as market segmentation, lead generation, and pricing, for example. In the right circumstances, combined marketing and sales decision making about these issues leads to both better decisions and stronger commitment to those decisions. The right *culture* and *people* may be enough to allow marketing to simply "hand off" decisions to sales for execution; but successful collaboration and joint decision making around these issues typically requires *process/system* or *structure* facilitators, in addition to the right people and culture. United Airlines recognized this need when it adapted its sales strategy for increased effectiveness in a more challenging industry environment. Realizing that strong sales and marketing collaboration would allow development of the best possible strategy and enable more effective implementation, United used a defined business process (see Figure 19.8) to facilitate the sales-marketing collaboration needed to accomplish its goals.

Facilitators for Increasing Emphasis on Marketing   Sales-dominant organizations frequently discover that by devoting most of their resources to sales activities that address current issues for specific customers, they spend too little time thinking about the future and anticipating how the market might evolve. This can leave them vulnerable, particularly when customer needs and/or competitors change.

Building the role of marketing within a sales dominant organization starts with developing the right people and culture. This is illustrated in a plan that GE began to implement in 2006, as the formerly sales-dominant company sought to bolster its marketing capabilities to gain competitive advantage. GE established "Commercial Excellence" as one of six key components of its growth strategy (see Figure 19.11), with a goal of achieving greater organic revenue growth through increased emphasis on marketing activities (such as

Figure 19.11
GE's Commercial Excellence Commitment in Its Strategy for Driving Organic Revenue Growth

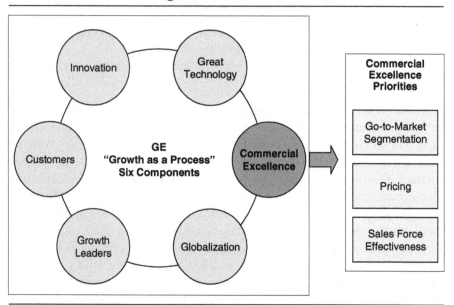

market segmentation and pricing) in addition to enhanced sales force effectiveness.

Establishing the right culture and getting the right people in place to lead this effort were key first steps in GE's Commercial Excellence plan. The GE chairman and CEO, Jeffrey Immelt, led the charge in getting the right culture to take root. He communicated his goals for company growth, his "growth as a process" plan, and his vision of Commercial Excellence at every opportunity. In early 2006, GE hired a chief marketing officer (CMO) to get the initiative up and running. One of the CMO's first tasks was to appoint global directors for each of the three Commercial Excellence priority areas—go-to-market segmentation, pricing, and sales force effectiveness. With the right culture and people in place, GE went on to create structures, systems, and processes that would strengthen its sales and marketing organization and help the company drive organic growth.

More information about the GE Commercial Excellence initiative is provided in our book *Building a Winning Sales Force*.[5]

SUMMARY

Although a strong sales–marketing alignment enhances the effectiveness of any customer-facing organization, it is particularly critical for companies that face uncertainty or significant competitive intensity, that have business concentrated among a few large customers, or that are launching new products and services. Effective use of the facilitators ensures that the different perspectives of people in sales and marketing are a source of strength for a company, rather than an impediment to sales and marketing effectiveness.

Andris A. Zoltners is the Nemmers Professor of Marketing at the Kellogg School of Management at Northwestern University. He is a founder and co-chairman of ZS Associates, a global business consulting firm with 1,500 people across 20 offices in North America, Europe, and Asia. He is the co-author of four books on sales force management including Building a Winning Sales Force (2009) and The Complete Guide to Accelerating Sales Force Performance (2001). He received his BS from the University of Miami, his MS from Purdue University, and his MSIA and PhD from Carnegie-Mellon University.

Prabhakant Sinha was a faculty member in the Marketing Department of the Kellogg School of Management from 1983 to 1987 and currently teaches in executive education programs on sales force effectiveness at the Kellogg School of Management and the Indian School of Business. He is a founder and co-chairman of ZS Associates, a global business consulting firm with 1,500 people across

20 offices in North America, Europe, and Asia. He is the co-author of four books on sales force management including Building a Winning Sales Force (2009) and The Complete Guide to Sales Force Incentive Compensation (2006). He received a bachelor degree of Technology from I.I.T. Kharagpur and his PhD from the University of Massachusetts.

Sally E. Lorimer is a consultant and business writer. She was previously a principal at ZS Associates, where she consulted with numerous companies on sales force effectiveness. She is the co-author of three books on sales force management including Building a Winning Sales Force (2009) and Sales Force Design for Strategic Advantage (2004). She received her BBA from the University of Michigan and her MBA from the Kellogg School of Management at Northwestern University.

Notes

1. Drucker, Peter F. (1973), *Management: Tasks, Responsibilities, and Practices*, New York: Harper & Row.
2. Zoltners, Andris A., Prabhakant Sinha, and Sally E. Lorimer (2009), *Building a Winning Sales Force: Powerful Strategies for Driving High Performance*, New York: Amacom.
3. Livneh, Eran (2003), "Marketing and Sales Alignment: How Siebel Does It," *WebProNews* (September 18), available at http://www.webpronews.com/topnews/2003/09/18/marketing-and-sales-alignment-how-siebel-does-it.
4. Cohen, Andy (1998), "Sales and Marketing: Separate but Equal?" *Sales and Marketing Management*, 150 (9), (September).
5. Zoltners, Sinha, and Lorimer (2009), see Note 2.

CHAPTER 20

CREATING SUPERIOR VALUE BY MANAGING THE MARKETING-OPERATIONS MANAGEMENT INTERFACE

ANNE T. COUGHLAN and JEFFREY D. SHULMAN

INTRODUCTION

Consider a house whose walls are each designed by a different architect, each with his or her different vision for the house. The consequences could be disastrous: the roofer may spend countless additional hours piecing together the different visions. The house may miss out on its true potential. Worse yet, the house may crumble.

Operations and marketing strategies and actions are like the walls of this house; both are crucial in building a strong foundation for market success. As an operations manager builds the house, his eye is on efficiency and cost-minimization.[1] As the marketing manager builds the house, his eye is on target customers and meeting their needs better than competitors. Left to their own devices, they can pull a company in different directions, causing it to miss out on the most profitable opportunities. However, if they work together or with aligned visions, managers can take advantage of the synergies between marketing and operations.

Indeed, actions taken on the marketing side of the business that ignore the operations side of the business (and vice versa) create profit leakages for the overall business. Successful companies recognize and manage positive and negative externalities between marketing and operations departments. This allows the go-to-market team to capitalize on synergies and/or avoid working at cross-purposes in order to improve profitability.

In this chapter, we first present four motivating examples that show the importance of the interaction between marketing and operational decisions. We then discuss how management of each of the marketing mix "four Ps" (price, product, promotion, place) can be enhanced by taking account of operations factors, and conversely, how operations decisions can be improved by recognizing the marketing factors in play in the form of the four Ps. We close with some recommendations about how to put into practice the ideas presented here.

OPERATIONS AND MARKETING: BOTH SIDES OF THE EQUATION

In many industries, viewing specific issues through both the marketing lens and the operations lens can often bring fresh management insights. Following are examples of issues that frequently confront companies and how they can be viewed from both sides of the equation.

Product Returns Management

It is estimated that 19 percent of all electronics purchases are returned even though they have no defects. It is also estimated to cost $13.8 billion to repackage, restock, and resell returned electronics products in the United States annually.[2] Similarly, catalog retailers' return rates are as high as 35 percent.[3] And across all industries, the annual value of returned goods is estimated to be $60 billion, with another $40 billion in costs of managing the associated reverse logistics processes.[4] It's clear that managing product returns is important to a company's bottom line.

However, consumer product returns are triggered for multiple reasons. One common cause is product malfunction (an operational issue). But even if the product is in perfect working condition, it may be returned because the buyer realizes only after purchase that the product does not fit his preferences (a marketing issue).

From a purely operational perspective, one way to improve profitability in the face of product returns is to take the return rate as a given and seek to minimize the cost of managing the returns process. This is an apparently sensible strategy if the previous $40 billion figure is even approximately correct. This approach leads manufacturers to think about how to handle the physical products being returned, whether to handle returns itself or force its retailer to handle them, and whether to charge consumers a restocking fee for returning products (which could lead to customer dissatisfaction with the company). Restocking fees vary across products but are commonly charged by many companies (e.g., the Apple Store charges a 10 percent restocking fee on opened products; Best Buy charges a 15 percent restocking fee on opened digital cameras; and the USA Wallpaper company charges a 30 percent restocking fee on returned wallpaper, even for unopened rolls).[5]

It has been shown that consumers will alter their initial purchase decisions depending on their perceived likelihood of having to return the product, the hassle cost of doing so, and the monetary loss of having to pay a restocking fee. Implementing a restocking fee might appear to lower the firm's costs of handling returns (because it both defrays the actual costs and because returns decrease). However, this approach ignores the possibility that some consumers never actually buy the firm's product because of the risk that they will want to return it and therefore incur the restocking fee cost.[6]

This example shows that an operations-focused product returns strategy would seek to minimize the cost of returns by minimizing returns themselves. But this lessens the ability of the marketing side of the business to attract customers who might in the end be profitable enough to merit the extra costs of running returns to begin with. Thus, a purely operational-efficiency approach ignores the marketing and consumer side of the process and the important demand-side questions regarding returns: *Why do consumers return no-defects products, and what are the effects on consumers of penalizing returns?*

For this reason, companies should consider a comprehensive, combined marketing and operational attack not only to manage the costs of returns, but also to manage consumers' incentives to return products in the first place.

Restaurant Dining

A restaurateur faces the operational challenge of ordering the right amount (and assortment) of food to feed diners each day. This would be a straight-forward problem if the restaurateur knew the number of diners in advance of the evening dinner period. Chez Panisse in Berkeley, California, has solved this problem by requiring reservations to eat in its main dining room and by offering a fixed menu each evening that does not allow diners to choose from an assortment of dishes.

Because of Chez Panisse's fame (and that of its founder, Alice Waters) and the strong positioning the restaurant enjoys in the "slow food, local food" movement, reservations fill up weeks in advance. In effect, the *operational challenge* (how much of what assortment of ingredients to have on hand each evening; how much wait staff to hire) is solved by restricting the variety of food offered and requiring reservations. However, this operationally efficient solution would not be possible if not for the restaurant's superb *marketing execution*. Chez Panisse has effectively created a brand position that enables the restaurant's reputation to ensure an almost-always-full restaurant.

Most restaurants do not enjoy the position of a Chez Panisse. Other restaurants may also offer reservations—for example, to appeal to a segment of consumers with high time costs and thus a high value for certainty in the timing of their dining experience—but they face periods of high and low demand nevertheless. Taking reservations also comes with its own costs: diners may not show up (leaving the restaurant with an unfilled table during peak dining hours), and personnel must be on hand to answer the phone throughout the day to take the reservations. Alternatively, the restaurant can fail to offer reservations, thus avoiding the cost of no-shows and of reservation personnel. But this strategy carries its own costs, both operational and marketing in nature.

On the operational side, a no-reservations policy increases the uncertainty in demand and thus the required levels of "safety stocks" of food to have on hand in case of a busy evening. The restaurateur may also have to juggle tables for large and small parties as they arrive (without prior notice) throughout the evening, creating inefficiencies in capacity management. On the marketing side, consumers with high time costs may not patronize a restaurant that does not offer reservations, because of the possibility of a long waiting time to be seated; this leads to lost sales opportunities.

All of these effects, meanwhile, are moderated by the overall attractiveness and popularity of the restaurant—in effect, how "hot" it is (which is a function of both marketing efforts and the operational quality of food and service).[7] The restaurant's operational decisions (restaurant capacity, staff on hand, amount and variety of food on hand, reservations policy) are thus closely interlinked with its marketing decisions. Focusing on one to the exclusion of the other would lead to suboptimal outcomes.

Online Grocery Shopping

Webvan, founded by Louis Borders (the former founder of Borders Bookstores), opened its doors in 1996, promising to provide time-efficient Internet shopping for groceries. The groceries would be delivered the same day to the shopper's home, within a 30-minute time window of the shopper's choosing (including late evening delivery).

Webvan planned to serve its consumers with a Web shopping interface, backed up by a hub-and-spoke delivery system. At each hub would be a 300,000- to 400,000-square-foot distribution center, holding up to 50,000 SKUs of grocery products (comparable to a large supermarket's selection), which could pick and pack consumers' orders in an automated way. The assembled orders would be delivered to a human packer in the distribution center, who would load each order into a truck for delivery to the appropriate spoke in the distribution network. A smaller truck would complete the delivery to the consumer's doorstep. At full capacity, a hub distribution center would fill 2.92 million orders per year (8,000 orders per day), with an average order value of $103, for an annual revenue throughput of $300 million through each hub.

Webvan's first launch was in the San Francisco Bay Area in June 1999, with a hub distribution center in Oakland, California. The hub's 8,000-orders-per-day capacity translated to more than 3 percent of the grocery business in the Bay Area. Webvan originally budgeted 3,300 orders per day to break even, but the average order size and average profit margin in the San Francisco market were higher than forecast (although it turned out that the *number of orders* was not); Webvan needed only 3,000 orders per day in order to break even over the 15-month planned horizon.

On the demand side, response was enthusiastic by Webvan adopters; on Epinions.com (an online ratings site), Webvan had an 89 percent approval rating from the 109 customers submitting reviews. The service was particularly attractive to segments like parents of small children, who were time-starved and who experienced above-average hassle levels in visiting a bricks-and-mortar grocery store.

However, not enough consumers bought—and repeat-purchased—from Webvan to bring the warehouse model to break-even levels. By September 1999, three months after launch in San Francisco, cumulative sales had reached only $4.2 million, with an average order size of only $71. There were about 60,000 orders over the three-month period, versus a break-even level of about 270,000 orders (3,000 orders per day for 90 days or three months). This represented less than a 20 percent capacity utilization rate of the warehouse system.

But this was, after all, the initial three months of operation; it was still possible that demand would build toward (and beyond) break-even over the ensuing months. However, by February 2001, Webvan had reached a sales level of only two-thirds that were necessary to break even. Although 6.5 percent of the Bay Area's households had ordered from Webvan, less than half repeat-purchased.

To increase revenue inflows, Webvan instituted a $4.95 delivery fee on orders of less than $75 and widened its delivery window to one hour. However, although these initiatives might have helped on the cost side, they could only hurt on the demand side, and customer volume never built to break-even levels. Webvan eventually declared bankruptcy in 2001 and dissolved its operations.

In this case, an overestimation of the ability of marketing to generate sales, combined with underperformance of marketing research activities, led to an overly optimistic forecast of market demand. This led the operations side of the business to invest in an unduly large scale of operations, which (along with overly aggressive market expansion) eventually killed the business. Note that the demise of Webvan was not due to obvious consumer dissatisfaction in the target market; rather, it was due to a lack of understanding of the nature and size of the true target market.[8]

The iPhone: Cool Technology, Bad Consumer Experience

When the Apple iPhone was released in 2007, Apple entered into an exclusive agreement with AT&T to market it by using the AT&T mobile network. AT&T in turn required subscribers to buy an unlimited data plan, at a uniform price per month, with a two-year time commitment. Subscribers' uses of AT&T's network bandwidth increased as the iPhone increased in popularity, partly because of the phone's many bandwidth-intensive applications and partly because the marginal price to the consumer of using the bandwidth was effectively zero (given the unlimited data plan pricing). The iPhone's data plan pricing thus gave no unilateral incentive for any individual subscriber to use less bandwidth.

By January 2009, bandwidth usage had increased so much (without commensurate investment by AT&T in bandwidth expansion) that AT&T's network was viewed by consumers as having the worst problems in speed and network availability among mobile network providers, as reported in a Gartner group study. The average iPhone subscriber was using 10 times the network capacity used by the average non–iPhone smartphone user, and the result was dropped calls, delayed delivery of voice and text messages, very slow download speeds, and angry customers.

AT&T's role as the exclusive carrier for the iPhone in the United States generated high revenues, with each iPhone subscriber paying AT&T $2,000 on average during his two-year contract (about twice as much as the average mobile phone user). But with such poor service, AT&T's $18 billion in network investment in 2009 was mostly targeted at upgrading the 3G network used by the iPhone. In December 2009, AT&T announced it was considering ways to urge subscribers to use "less wireless data." One industry analyst said that even with these moves on the consumer end, AT&T still needed to "improve things on the back end so they can deal with the issues of multiple users on the network at the same time."

AT&T's experience with the iPhone suggests that a "cool" technology, even when marketed well to consumers and supported by third-party applications that increase its attractiveness, is not enough for market success; the operational realities of providing the network backbone to literally produce the services subscribers want is also crucial. In effect, consumers do not want to consume the iPhone itself; they want timely access to the services (including completion of a simple phone call) that the iPhone provides. This timely access in turn is a function of the quality of management of the network's operations, and without high quality on this dimension, sales of the iPhone are less than they otherwise would be.[9] Both customer satisfaction and the AT&T/Apple relationship are threatened by these operational problems. This creates an opportunity for new competitive offerings, such as Google's Nexus One, which allows customers to purchase the phone in "unlocked" mode, allowing them to shop for the service provider of their choice.

THE VALUE OF INTEGRATING MARKETING AND OPERATIONS IN DECISION MAKING

As indicated earlier, ignoring the interaction between marketing and operations factors can lessen the effectiveness of a firm's overall strategy. Conversely, focusing on the marketing-operations interface can improve customer satisfaction and profitability. In fact, operations managers can benefit from marketers' demand-side insights that give guidance on issues such as how much to produce, how much safety stock to order, or how much capacity to provide. Meanwhile, marketing researchers benefit from understanding the operating constraints and costs facing the company. Without such knowledge, marketing researchers might otherwise mistakenly assume that product can be produced and supplied in the right quantity and at the right time, without undue production, storage, or shipping costs.

This highlights the central point of this chapter: *actions taken on the marketing side of the business, in ignorance of the operations side of the business (and vice versa), create profit leakages for the overall business. The failure to reach full profit potential can be either due to the failure to realize the full cost of an action (negative externalities) or due to unrealized synergies between business departments (positive externalities).*

A *negative externality* is a cost imposed by one entity (the "perpetrator") on another entity (the "victim"), rather than being borne by the perpetrator itself. The classic example of a negative externality arises from the operation of a polluting manufacturing facility. The manufacturer enjoys sales and profits from its production but does not bear the cost of the pollution it inflicts on neighbors in the process; thus, the cost is borne by an entity *external* to the process. Gains are enjoyed without bearing the concomitant costs. If incentives are not corrected, the perpetrator will persistently engage in *too much of the "bad" behavior* (e.g., polluting the environment), simply because it does not bear the full cost of its actions.

Conversely, a *positive externality* is a benefit enjoyed by a party who does not have to bear the full concomitant cost of creating that benefit. We often talk of "free riding" in this context: a free rider enjoys a positive externality without bearing its fair share of the cost of creating that benefit. Again, without appropriate adjustment of incentives, *too few positive externalities* will be created, and thus benefits that could have been enjoyed by the system are foregone.

In our context, actions taken on the operations side of a business affect the ability of marketers to optimize their market outcomes. Conversely, actions taken on the marketing side of the business affect the costs of running operations. Ignorance of these interactions can lead to lower profits or even business disaster, as our examples earlier illustrate:

- An operations-focused product returns strategy would seek to minimize the cost of returns by minimizing returns themselves; but this lessens the ability of the marketing side of the business to attract customers who might in the end be profitable enough to merit the extra costs of running returns to begin with.
- Controlling the costs of handling reservations can lead to lower-than-optimal revenue generation at a restaurant, because it fails to give diners the opportunity to lower their risk of a long wait at the restaurant by making a reservation for a specific dining time. It also leads to a higher need for food "safety stocks" and thus the possibility of greater food wastage and improper staffing levels.
- In the case of Webvan, overestimation of the ability of marketing to generate sales, and underperformance of marketing research activities, led to an overly optimistic forecast of market demand. This led the operations side of the business to invest in an unduly large scale of operations, which (along with overly aggressive market expansion) eventually killed the business. Note that the demise of Webvan was not due to obvious consumer dissatisfaction in the target market; rather, it was due to a lack of understanding of the nature and size of the true target market.
- The investments made by Apple in increasing the "cool factor" of the iPhone led to overuse of the network managed by Apple's partner, AT&T. This in turn led to negative brand equity for AT&T and the need for AT&T to incur high costs of investment in increased bandwidth (i.e., Apple's marketing investments generated negative externalities for AT&T). Conversely, the greater the investments AT&T makes in bandwidth, the more Apple benefits, as the "cool factor" of the iPhone is

dependent not only on the number and types of available applications for it, but also the reliable and quick execution of operations (i.e., AT&T's investments generate a positive externality for Apple).

Given the potential for both negative and positive externalities in the operations–marketing interface, it becomes important to contemplate how to *internalize these externalities*—that is, how to create the right incentives for each party to engage in behaviors that benefit the whole system (or company), not just itself. In this context, the benefit of thinking about marketing and operations decisions jointly is that the marketing researcher now views more elements as *choice variables* rather than as *parameters of the problem*. By simultaneously taking account of marketing and operations decisions, the appropriate incentives can be set for joint maximization in the system.

One important benefit of this approach is the avoidance of duplication in investment. For example, if the operations function is investing in optimizing reverse logistics by minimizing the cost of processing returns, while the marketing function is investing in reducing consumers' uncertainty prior to purchase—thus lowering the very incidence of returns—the two investments may be redundant and thus wasteful of resources inside the firm. Recognizing the substitutability of these investments can improve overall corporate profit by jointly managing the cost and the incidence of returns.

FOR MARKETERS: WEAVING OPERATIONS INTO YOUR DECISIONS

How can taking account of the marketing-operations interface concretely change the marketing decisions a firm makes? In this section, we consider each of the marketing mix elements—product, price, promotion, and place (or distribution)—in light of the examples developed above, in order to show how an awareness of operational considerations affects the marketing mix.

Product

Our example of *restaurant reservations* previously illustrates how operational decisions can augment (or fail to augment) a basic product or service sold to the consumer. Here, the basic "product" is a meal at the restaurant. However, the consumer is not buying simply a meal; rather, he is buying the meal at a certain time, with a particular level of predictability in timing and service.

Depending on the consumer's valuation for service predictability, providing reservations can increase the valuation the consumer places on this restaurant's offering, all other things being equal. The marketer who focuses solely on these consumer-level issues may choose to offer reservations to provide a better composite product to the consumer, but in doing so may ignore the operational costs of offering reservations: increased staff time to manage reservations, and the opportunity cost of no-show consumers on busy nights. Alexandrov and Lariviere highlight these tradeoffs and describe how firms can decide when it is (or is not) optimal to offer reservations: reservations can increase sales by shifting demand from the peak demand time to a less desirable off-peak time, and can be attractive in more competitive markets because they lower demand uncertainty for the restaurant.[10]

Our iPhone example also highlights how operational decisions (such as AT&T's decision about how aggressively to expand its network's bandwidth) change the "full product" offered to the consumer. Apple markets the iPhone 3G as offering a whole suite of functionality, including web browsing, video and music streaming downloads, and voice phone service and text messaging, among many other services. This suite of applications, along with the iPhone device itself, may be considered to be the "product" for sale. However, the consumer does not actually consume the iPhone or its applications; it consumes the value from having consistent and reliable access to them. When network capacity is insufficient, it is not particularly relevant how small and light the iPhone is, or how many applications it (supposedly) supports; what is salient to the consumer is how poor the service is. This apparently opaque investment decision, by a go-to-market partner of Apple's, has a profound effect on the perceived value of the iPhone and could affect Apple's decision about continued exclusivity with AT&T. Apple may choose to broaden the availability of the iPhone to multiple carriers as a result, when its exclusive contract with AT&T runs out—at least in part to solve the operational challenges to its overall marketing strategy.

These examples drive home the idea that operations activities help produce the "full product" consumed by the buyer. Ignoring the quality and efficiency of the operations side of the business can therefore imperil the overall product the manufacturer believes it is offering to the market; conversely, taking account of operational factors can not only safeguard overall product quality perceptions, but significantly enhance them.

Price

The research on optimal product returns policies highlighted above finds that the best product price to charge varies, depending on whether the marketer takes into account the effect of restocking fees and hassle costs on consumer behavior—including whether the consumer will buy the firm's product in the first place. In general, the higher the restocking fee, the lower the optimal product price (for example, deep-discount sale products are often offered with the caution that they cannot be returned for any refund, effectively charging a 100 percent restocking fee). This is because the "full cost" the consumer is willing to pay takes the expected value of both of these expenditures into account, and also because the probability of having to pay a restocking fee reduces overall willingness to pay for an initial purchase of a product of whose attractiveness the consumer is uncertain. Thus, both revenue per unit on initial purchase as well as the total number of units the firm can expect to sell are influenced by considering the jointly optimal product price and restocking fee to charge.

Further, in a channel context, choosing which channel member should handle returns influences not only the restocking fee charged, but both the retail and wholesale prices. Under many conditions, allocating the returns handling function (and the setting of the restocking fee) to the channel member who can handle returns most efficiently is optimal. However, there are situations where the manufacturer should handle returns, even when it is not as efficient at doing so as is the retailer. For example, PetSafe, a manufacturer of invisible dog fences, took returns from retailers and then shipped them to the third-party returns liquidator Channel Velocity to dispose of them. Presumably it would have been less costly to instruct the retailer to ship returns directly to Channel Velocity, yet PetSafe did not follow this path. One reason this product returns channel strategy could be sensible is that it gives the retailer the incentive to sell at a lower retail price, thus increasing market demand, which can more than compensate for the cost of handling product returns.

Our example of restaurant reservations illustrates the pricing implications of a joint focus on operations and marketing factors. The curious fact is that most restaurants offer reservations for free, rather than charging for this value-added service; thus, reservations are priced at zero. This generally causes consumers to overuse the reservation service, inflicting a negative externality on the restaurant system by generating no-shows that lower a popular restaurant's revenue on a busy night. The negative externality arises because consumers who would have liked to dine at that restaurant, but who called and could not get a reservation, proceed to make a reservation at a different restaurant; their dining revenue is lost to the restaurant that night. Meanwhile, someone who *did* make a reservation, but who does not show up, fails to pay the opportunity cost of that seating, leaving the restaurant with lower revenue for the evening, unless there is sufficient walk-in traffic at just that time slot to take up the unexpected slack capacity at the restaurant. This problem is costly enough to some very high-end restaurants (such as Tru in Chicago) that they charge for no-shows (Tru charges $75 per plate), in a bid to internalize the negative externality that no-shows create.[11]

The iPhone example provides a further insight into the interrelatedness of pricing and operational decisions. The required flat-rate, unlimited data plan pricing that AT&T used for the iPhone ignored the incentive it would create for subscribers to overuse the network's bandwidth. Although it might have seemed a lucrative way to garner high revenue per subscriber, as the example above documents, it also created an unfortunate incentive for subscribers to overburden the data network. Alternatively, viewing consumer behavior in response to the pricing incentive as normal and expected, the insight for the combined management of pricing and operations practice is that AT&T's flat-rate, unlimited data access pricing structure *should have been* accompanied by a much more aggressive investment in network capacity, in order to safeguard consumers' overall perceptions of the quality of the iPhone offering.

Promotion

The best illustration of the interaction of operational and promotion decisions comes from the product returns example. Recall that a consumer usually returns a well-working product because he realizes (after initial purchase of the product) that the product does not fit his preferences well enough to merit keeping it. Thus, consumer uncertainty at the point of initial purchase is a crucial input to the very phenomenon of returns. Recognizing this, some sellers engage in promotional activities that serve to increase the consumer's *a priori* knowledge about the fit between the product and the consumer's own preferences.

For example, some running shoe retailers allow customers not only to try on shoes, but also to wear them either on a treadmill or even outdoors for a run around the block, to make sure the shoe is right for them. Along with the "test run," the consumer gets advice from a trained salesperson in the store on the right running technique, foot position, and so forth, all offered in the spirit of excellent customer service—but with the ancillary benefit of reducing product returns after purchase. The operational benefit is fewer returns and thus a lower total cost of returns. Manufacturers that bear return costs and recognize this positive externality can create incentives for independent retailers to provide these "test run" services, in order to align the retailer's incentives with those of the manufacturer.

Place (Distribution)

In the product returns example, a purely operational point of view would suggest placing responsibility for product returns where it is most efficiently performed (i.e., in its lowest-cost position in the channel). In other words, if salvage value is maximized and/or reverse logistics costs are minimized by allocating product returns responsibility to the retailer, then that is where it should be allocated. However, this logic omits an important strategic factor. If instead the manufacturer takes responsibility for handling product returns, it can manipulate the retailer's incentives to set retail price and the retail-level restocking fee in order to increase initial quantity demanded for the product. When the profitability of this higher demand outweighs the incremental cost of taking on product returns processing, it is in the manufacturer's interest to move returns upstream. This strategic channel-management insight augments a purely operational point of view.

Similarly, in the iPhone example, the channel management problem appears to be that AT&T did not have the same incentive as Apple to invest aggressively in mobile network expansion, because it would cost too much (AT&T eventually spent $18 billion in 2009 to enhance its network for iPhone service provision). It is possible that the threat of losing its exclusivity could provide Apple with more leverage over AT&T, or conversely the promise of new access to iPhones will induce new providers to invest in network expansion. In either case, the distribution imperative is to offer the right rewards to the network partner to give them an incentive to invest heavily in bandwidth to enhance the usefulness of the iPhone's applications.

SUMMARY

These examples illustrate that taking account of operational factors, incentives, and costs can improve marketing decision-making across the entire marketing mix. Conversely, taking account of marketing realities can also improve operations decision-making. The two work synergistically.

Because the best way to take advantage of interactions between marketing and operations decision making is likely to be context-specific, it is difficult to offer a "one-size-fits-all" process to help companies recognize and benefit from these synergies. However, a three-step approach can help build a stronger foundation for profitability: (1) *gather relevant information;* (2) *choose the best alternative;* and (3) *implement the plan.*

The first job is to *gather all the relevant information* on both the operations management and the marketing sides of the business. On the *operations management side*, questions of interest include:

- What kinds of service augmentation takes place in your selling markets? What is the difference between the basic product you sell and the "full product" that is or can be made available to the consumer?
- How much does it really cost to provide various service options?
- Who performs the functions that generate service augmentation for the products you sell?
- Is that entity (department in your company, or channel partner) being compensated adequately for the performance of these functions? If not, they are generating a *positive externality* and likely do not have the incentive to perform it sufficiently intensively.

Similarly, *marketing managers* might consider the following:

- What value do consumers place on various feasible bundles of product-plus-service options?
- How does this value vary across consumer groups? This is a useful dimension for segmenting the market when seeking to jointly optimize marketing and operational investments.
- What is the opportunity cost, in terms of lost sales and/or worsened reputation, of failure to provide desired service that the operations side of the business produces?
- What is the effect on consumers' willingness to pay for your product of various levels of service that the operations side of the business produces?

Once operations and marketing information has been gathered, the data need to be evaluated to estimate the cost and revenue implications of different strategies. On the marketing side, standard research techniques like conjoint analysis can be used to quantitatively measure the incremental value consumers place on various service bundles. On the operations management side, the equivalent of an "activity-based costing" analysis may be necessary to measure the costs to various departments of the firm, or various channel members, of engaging in various combinations of marketing and operational investments (with an eye to minimizing redundancies, as discussed earlier).

Upon gathering all relevant information, the profitability of each possible "full product" can be ascertained, making it possible to undertake the second step: *choose the best alternative.* The highest revenue-generating option may require high costs. The cost-minimizing option may dampen revenue substantially. Due to positive and negative externalities between operations and marketing decisions, it may be necessary to forgo revenue or accept greater costs in order to achieve maximum profit.

Finally, with a desired strategy for the combined marketing/operations efforts behind the product, the third step—*implementation of the plan*-requires either a top-down, monitoring-focused process, or a bottom-up, incentives-focused process, to maximize the chances that the desired behaviors are in fact pursued by all parties.[12] Monitoring and incentives are substitutes for one another in influencing the behaviors of any agents, although the right balance between the two should recognize the value of direct observation and management (the monitoring option) when it is feasible and not overly expensive.

Once again, successful companies recognize and manage positive and negative externalities between marketing and operations departments in order to avoid working at cross-purposes and thereby improve profitability—a concrete result every company is looking for.

Anne T. Coughlan is the John L. & Helen Kellogg Professor of Marketing in the Marketing Department at the Kellogg School of Management. She is the academic director of the Distribution Channel Management: Bridging the Sales and Marketing Divide program at the James L. Allen Center, and the lead author of the leading textbook on distribution, Marketing Channels. She holds a BA and a PhD in Economics from Stanford University.

Jeffrey D. Shulman earned his PhD from the Kellogg School of Management, Northwestern University. He is currently an Assistant Professor in Marketing at the University of Washington's Michael G. Foster School of Business. In addition to his PhD, he received his BA and MS degrees from Northwestern University.

NOTES

1. The male pronoun is used throughout this chapter for ease of exposition only.
2. Lawton, C. (2008), "The War on Returns," *Wall Street Journal,* (May 8), D1.
3. Rogers, D. S., and R. S. Tibbens-Lembke (1998), *Going Backwards: Reverse Logistics Trends and Practices,* Reverse Logistics Executive Council.
4. Enright, Tony (2003), "Post-Holiday Logistics," *Traffic World* (January 6), 1.
5. Restocking fee information is taken from http://store.apple.com, www.bestbuy.com, and www.usawallpaper.com, all on October 12, 2009.
6. See Shulman, Jeffrey D., Anne T. Coughlan, and R. Canan Savaskan (2009), "Optimal Restocking Fees and Information Provision in an Integrated Demand-Supply Model of Product Returns," *Manufacturing & Service Operations Management,* 11 (4), (Fall), 577–594; Shulman, Jeffrey D., Anne T. Coughlan, and R. Canan Savaskan (2009), "Optimal Reverse Channel Structure for Consumer

Product Returns," Working Paper (December); and Shulman, Jeffrey D., Anne T. Coughlan, and R. Canan Savaskan (2009), "Managing Consumer Returns in a Competitive Environment," Working Paper (October) for investigations of the importance of information provision to consumers in the assessment of restocking fees in the returns process; the choice to allocate returns responsibilities to various channel members; and the effect of competition on restocking fees and returns management, respectively.

7. See Alexandrov, Alexei, and Martin A. Lariviere (2008), "Are Reservations Recommended?" Working Paper, Kellogg School of Management (July), for an interesting investigation of this problem.

8. This example builds on material in Bakshi, Kayla, and John Deighton (2000), *Webvan: Groceries on the Internet*, Harvard Business School case # 9-500-052 (May 5); Glasner, Joanna (2001), "Why Webvan Drove Off a Cliff," *Wired Magazine* (July 10), viewed online on January 3, 2010. www.wired.com/techbiz/media/news/2001/07/45098; and Hansell, Saul (2001), "Some Hard Lessons for Online Grocer," *New York Times on the Web* (February 19), viewed online on February 19, 2001. http://www.nytimes.com/2001/02/19/business/some-hard-lessons-for-online-grocer.html?scp=1&sq=Some%20Hard%20Lessons%20for%20Online%20Grocer&st=cse. Also see Chapter 2 in this volume, "Identifying Market Segments and Selecting Targets."

9. For background information on the iPhone and AT&T's network bandwidth problems see: Markoff, John (2009), "Chiefs Defend Slow Network for the iPhone," *New York Times* (June 29), online edition. http://www.nytimes.com/2007/06/29/technology/29phone.html?_r=1&scp=1&sq=Chiefs%20Defend%20Slow%20Network%20for%20the%20iPhone&st=Search. Richtel, Matt (2009), "3G Phones Exposing Networks' Last-Gen Technology," *New York Times* (March 14), online edition. http://www.nytimes.com/2009/03/14/technology/14phone.html?scp=1&sq=3G%20Phones%20Exposing%20Networks'%20Last-Gen%20Technology&st=Search. Wortham, Jenna (2009a), "Customers Angered as iPhones Overload AT&T," *New York Times* (September 3), online edition. http://www.nytimes.com/2009/09/03/technology/companies/03att.html?scp=1&sq=Customers%20Angered%20as%20iPhones%20Overload%20AT&T&st=Search. Wortham, Jenna (2009b), "AT&T to Urge Customers to Use Less Wireless Data," *New York Times* (December 10), online edition. http://www.nytimes.com/2009/12/10/technology/companies/10iphone.html?scp=1&sq=AT&T%20to%20Urge%20Customers%20to%20Use%20Less%20Wireless%20Data&st=Search.

10. See Alexandrov and Lariviere (2008), Note 7.

11. See Alexandrov and Lariviere (2008), Note 7.

12. See Jerath, Kinshuk, Serguei Netessine, and Z. John Zhang (2007), "Can We All Get Along? Incentive Contracts to Bridge the Marketing and Operations Divide," Working Paper, Wharton School, University of Pennsylvania (June) for an interesting discussion of incentive design to optimize cooperation between the marketing and operations functions.

INDEX